The D.A.

Also by Lawrence Taylor

To Honor and Obey

Trail of the Fox

A Trial of Generals

Born to Crime

The D.A.

Lawrence Taylor

William Morrow and Company, Inc.   New York

It is the policy of William Morrow and Company, Inc., and its imprints and affiliates, recognizing the importance of preserving what has been written, to print the books we publish on acid-free paper, and we exert our best efforts to that end.

Taylor, Lawrence, 1942–
    The D.A. / Lawrence Taylor.
      p.   cm.
    ISBN 0–688–11731–7
    1. Longo, Larry. 2. Public prosecutors—California—Los Angeles—Biography. 3. Prosecution—California—Los Angeles. I. Title.
KF373.L554T49 1996
345.794'01—dc20
[B]
[347.94051]
[B]   95–19075
                                              CIP

Printed in the United States of America

First Edition

1 2 3 4 5 6 7 8 9 10

BOOK DESIGN BY LEAH CARLSON

For Chris and Judy

Preface

I have spent much of my life in the courtrooms of Los Angeles. And I am weary of seeing the Hollywood version.

I approached my editor with the idea of a book chronicling one year in the life of a big-city prosecutor. I wanted to write about what it is *really* like to fight the daily wars of the criminal justice system. I wanted to show the chaos of morning calendar call, the long hours of preparation, the intense pressures of trial, the emotions, tactics, gambles, surprises, doubts, fatigue . . . the long sleepless nights and the sudden fateful decisions. I wanted a reader to follow a *real* trial lawyer, feel as he feels, react as he reacts, *experience* the intricate chessgame of trial, the complex psychology of cross-examination, the elation of a brilliant argument, the despair of sudden defeat.

I wanted the reader to *be* a trial lawyer for a few hours.

My editor was enthusiastic, but there were two questions. Which city? And who?

The answer to the first was obvious. Los Angeles, the so-called capital of the third world, was a city on the brink, a city of dramatic contrasts and sudden explosiveness. And the L.A. District Attorney's Office, with nearly a thousand deputies, was the largest prosecuting agency in the world.

The choice proved a stroke of luck. I could not know it at the time, but the year I picked to burrow into the Los Angeles D.A.'s Office would be the most eventful in the history of any prosecuting

agency: the Charles Keating savings and loan trial . . . the Rodney
King trial . . . the riots . . . Reginald Denny . . . the Menendez brothers . . . and, on the horizon, the O. J. Simpson case. Hanging over
all of this was a hotly contested political campaign for the office of
district attorney—a campaign that, as it turned out, directly affected
each of these cases.

Then . . . who?

The D.A.'s Office was packed with legal talent. Pamela Ferrero
had recently tried the McMartin preschool case. Dinko Bozanich convicted the Alphabet Bomber and headed the reinvestigation into the
Robert Kennedy assassination. Bill Hodgman, who was later named
to the O. J. Simpson team, had prosecuted *Different Strokes* actor Todd
Bridges. Marcia Clark was a rising star, fresh off a conviction in the
stalking murder of actress Rebecca Schaeffer. There were other skilled
prosecutors, the men and women who tried the Rodney King case,
the Hillside Strangler, Christian Brando, the *Cotton Club* murder, Roman Polanski, the Ellsberg "White House plumbers" break-in,
Charles Manson, the *Twilight Zone* case, the Menendez brothers. . . .

My choice was Larry Longo. He is not as well known as some
of the others. He is not a "top gun" in the D.A.'s elite Special Trials
unit, but a foot soldier in the front trenches of L.A.'s central courts.
He is not a hot new rising star in the office, but a gruff and scarred
veteran of over twenty years of trial warfare.

I chose Longo because he is the opposite of Hollywood's slick,
handsome, and cool young trial lawyer. He is short, stocky, and
middle-aged, with the pugnacious mannerisms of a New York cabbie.
He is a devoted family man, who still believes in things like honor,
loyalty, and justice. He is a simple man with simple values, and he
may be the last of a dying breed.

I also chose Longo because his daily experience in Department
127 of the Superior Court gives the reader a much more accurate
feeling for the D.A.'s world than would recounting a celebrity trial.
However, and perhaps ironically, a case arose during my year with
this prosecutor that provided the chance for an in-depth look into a
headline murder trial. It proved the perfect vehicle for experiencing
through Larry Longo's eyes the intricacies and drama of a high-profile
trial.

The D.A., then, is about deputy D.A. Larry Longo. But it is also about *being* a deputy D.A.; it is about nearly a thousand other prosecutors in the D.A.'s office. Thus, the reader will meet a wide range of prosecutors, from law clerks waiting to pass the bar exam to "frontline" trial lawyers to the "top-gun" deputies responsible for prosecuting the headline cases of the recent past. To maintain the dramatic focus on Longo's world, however, it should be noted that some of the cases and settings in which these real individuals are presented are composites of actual cases and settings; similarly, some of the defense attorneys and defendants are composites or have been given pseudonyms. These characters will be identified the first time they appear with an asterisk. Finally, some of the dialogue in the text has, of necessity, been reconstructed on the basis of the best sources available and does not necessarily represent verbatim conversation or testimony.

Acknowledgments

I would like to express my appreciation to the many members of the Los Angeles County District Attorney's Office who cooperated with me during my year of observing and interviewing in the Criminal Courts Building from mid-1991 to mid-1992. Specific thanks are owed to District Attorney Ira Reiner, Chief of Central Operations John Lynch, and Assistant Director Peter Bozanich, for permitting me to work within the office and for giving me access to personnel, facilities, and records.

I would also like to thank the many deputy D.A.s who found time in their busy trial calendars to provide me with fascinating insights into their professional and personal lives. Among them, particular thanks are owed to Craig Veals, Leonard Torrealba, Larry Boyle, Greg Dohi, Terry White, Marcia Clark, Katherine Mader, Sterling Norris, Dinko Bozanich, Phil Halpin, Pamela Ferrero, Lester Kuruyama, Stephen Kay, Steve Barshop, Roger Gunson, Dave Conn, Lea D'Agostino, Jeff Jonas, Bill Hodgman, Don Eastman, Richard Chrystie, Norm Shapiro, Richard Hecht, and Greg Thompson.

I am grateful to the staff of Los Angeles Superior Court's Department 127: Judge James Bascue, bailiff Tom Brooks, clerk Angelica Mares, and court reporter Cynthia Cartright. I am especially obligated to Judge Bascue for making his courtroom, chambers, and court files constantly available to me during that one-year period.

Thanks also to the following individuals for their helpful interviews: D.A.'s investigators Jimmy Sakoda and Cheman Park; Montebello police officer Monty Holden; D.A.'s media liaison Sandi Gibbons; D.A.'s political consultant Steve Teichner; defense attorneys Mike Yamaki, Phoebe Spence, Leslie Abramson, and Larry Rivets; deputy public defenders Karen Thompson and Nancy Richards; jurors Yolanda Jasmes, John Verdusco, Joseph Choate, and Bob Enrich; and judges John Ouderkirk and Jacqueline Bascue.

Of course, I owe more than I can say to the subject of this book, Deputy District Attorney Larry Longo, and to his wife, Aelina. For one year, Larry permitted me to "shadow" him for most of his waking hours. He opened his office to me and, characteristically, his home and family as well.

Finally, I would like to acknowledge the important contributions of my gifted editor at Morrow, Liza Dawson; assistant editor, Doris Cooper; my trusted agent, Reid Boates; and my friend and toughest critic, Judy Strother.

The D.A.s

Steve Barshop,
a blunt and outspoken "renegade" Texan, prosecuted Marlon
Brando's son for murdering the French lover of Brando's Tahitian
daughter.

James Bascue,
the presiding judge in Department 127, formerly was second in
command of the District Attorney's Office. He became chief counsel
for the state bar before his appointment to the bench.

Larry Boyle,
Longo's junior deputy in Department 127, is a gregarious,
wisecracking Irishman and former cop.

Dinko Bozanich,
one of the most respected prosecutors in the office, tried the
Alphabet Bomber and conducted the reinvestigation into the Robert
Kennedy assassination.

Peter Bozanich,
Dinko's younger brother, was head of the elite Special Trials unit
and assistant chief of Central Operations. He married Menendez
prosecutor Pamela Ferrero.

Richard Chrystie

is the quick-witted deputy in charge of training new prosecutors.

Marcia Clark,

a former cocktail waitress and dancer, conducted the "Russian Mafia" investigation and won a conviction in the stalking murder of actress Rebecca Schaeffer. She later gained worldwide fame as first chair in the O. J. Simpson trial.

Dave Conn,

an ex-Marine from the Bronx, prosecuted the *Cotton Club* murder case. He was later appointed lead counsel in the O. J. Simpson trial, then removed from the case after disagreements with District Attorney Ira Reiner and reassigned to the Menendez retrial.

Lea D'Agostino,

the Dragon Lady who tried the ill-fated *Twilight Zone* case, turned to law late in life, then sharpened her skills assisting Longo in the Beverly Hills prosecution of students rioting against the shah of Iran.

Greg Dohi,

a sensitive young Japanese-Spanish law clerk, became a deputy D.A. so he could help victims. A Harvard graduate, he was the most recent of Longo's "adoptions" and assisted him in the Yamaguchi trial.

Pamela Ferrero/Bozanich,

a debutante from Wellesley, prosecuted the second McMartin preschool trial, then was lead counsel in the trial of the Menendez brothers.

Roger Gunson,

head of the D.A.'s secretive Special Investigations Division (S.I.D.), previously prosecuted movie director Roman Polanski for drugging and raping a young girl at Jack Nicholson's estate. He also was in charge of the marathon first McMartin preschool trial.

Phil Halpin,
an embittered idealist, tried two of the longest criminal trials in history: the *Onion Field* case and the Hillside Strangler.

Richard Hecht,
the "godfather" of the D.A.'s Office, is head of operations outside central Los Angeles. He conducted the grand jury investigation into the burglary of the Beverly Hills office of Daniel Ellsberg's psychiatrist by Nixon's "White House plumbers."

Bill Hodgman,
Special Trials prosecutor who unsuccessfully tried *Different Strokes* actor Todd Bridges for attempted murder, then convicted savings and loan kingpin Charles Keating. Named second chair in the O. J. Simpson case, he developed heart problems early into the trial and was replaced.

Lance Ito,
the trial judge in the Keating and O. J. Simpson cases, was previously the deputy D.A. in charge of the office's "Hardcore" gang unit. He is Judge Bascue's closest friend.

Jeffrey Jonas
was Longo's immediate supervisor. The pressures of the tragic Morgan mother-and-son murder case and the danger to his own family from a Cuban assassin led to his own prosecution for shoplifting.

Stephen Kay
prosecuted Charles Manson with Vincent Bugliosi, followed by four later trials of Manson "family" members. He has been to forty-three parole hearings for Manson and his followers.

Lester Kuruyama,
one of the most popular prosecutors in the office and an avid surfer, served as second chair to Pamela Ferrero in the Menendez trial.

Katherine Mader,
the first prosecutor in the state to put a woman on death row, was previously a defense attorney for the Hillside Strangler.

Sterling "Ernie" Norris,
the top death penalty prosecutor in California, and a former
Wyoming cowboy and ex-Marine, got the death penalty for the
Freeway Strangler. The *Los Angeles Times*'s choice for district
attorney, he placed third in the elections.

John Ouderkirk,
formerly a D.A.'s investigator in the LaScala case, he passed the bar,
became a prosecutor in the office, and was the deputy D.A. in
charge at the Chinatown murder scene. Later he was appointed to
the bench, serving as trial judge in the Reginald Denny case.

Ira Reiner,
the district attorney of Los Angeles County, never personally
prosecuted a felony case. After the Rodney King acquittals, he was
defeated in his reelection bid by his former chief deputy, Gil
Garcetti.

Leonard Torrealba,
the easygoing heir to a Venezuelan cattle empire, is one of Longo's
deputies in Department 127.

Craig Veals,
Longo's smooth and articulate senior deputy in 127, and a product
of the ghetto, has never lost his sympathy for the oppressed. He was
appointed to the bench in 1995.

Stanley Weisberg,
a former deputy D.A. who prosecuted the murderer of
Bloomingdale mistress Vicky Morgan. After his appointment to the
bench he presided over three of the biggest trials of the decade: the
second McMartin preschool trial, the Rodney King case, and the
Menendez brothers case.

The D.A.

Chapter

1

"So then the cops, they take the money, an' they never give it back."

"They confiscated it?"

"Yeah, right, they confiscated it."

"The whole hundred and eight thousand dollars?"

"Yeah, right. They look in the briefcase, they see all that cash. . . . Man, I can see 'em thinkin' to theyselves, 'What's this nigger doin' with that kinda money?'"

Deputy District Attorney Larry Longo stepped back from the witness stand. He looked at each of the twelve faces in the jury box for a moment, then continued his questions as he walked toward the empty chair at the prosecution table.

"Awright," he said, "this was as you got off the plane at L.A. International?"

"Yeah, right."

"Lemme ask you this: Did you tell these DEA guys where the cash came from, that it wasn't dirty?"

"Sure." The witness shrugged. "I tell 'em same as I tell you, Mr. Longo." He drew a deep breath, then once again patiently recited the facts. "I'm a fight promoter from New York, I tell 'em. I'm here with cash to sign up some local fighters, a couple boys I wanna put on a card back at the Garden."

"Madison Square Garden."

"Yeah, right. So, 'course, I bring plenty of money. I mean, cash talks, y'know? You gotta show 'em you're for real."

"Uh-huh."

"An' you can see, man, these gentlemen, they ain't buyin' none of it."

"The cops didn't believe you."

"No, sir."

"They arrest you?"

"No, sir."

"Just took your money."

"An' the briefcase."

The prosecutor nodded slowly, then ran his fingers through the jet black hair that swept straight back toward his thick neck. He was a short, pugnacious-looking man, about fifty, with a compact, gristly barrel of a body, solidly muscled arms, and the powerful hands of a bricklayer. His large, round face was highlighted by a thick nose, intense dark eyes beneath bushy black eyebrows, and a broad mouth joining heavy jowls into a fixed scowl. To many, the face was vaguely familiar, for the man bore a slight resemblance to J. Edgar Hoover. The blue-collar coarseness of his features was in odd contrast to the impeccable double-breasted Armani suit, tailored white shirt, mauve silk scarf, brightly colored floral tie, and spotlessly shined Bruno Magli shoes. Deputy D.A. Longo seemed less a skilled trial lawyer than a grumpy old bulldog decked out in a thousand-dollar suit.

"You a drug dealer, Mr. Weston?"

The witness appeared startled, then grinned. "No, sir, Mr. Longo, you know I ain't."

"Yeah, see, but these folks don't," he said, sweeping his arm toward the jurors. "Awright, lemme ask you this: You were a fighter yourself at one time, right?"

"Yeah."

"You fought as a welterweight under the name Baby Harrold Weston?"

"Yeah, Baby Harrold," the man grinned. " 'Sweet as sugar.' "

"Sweet as sugar."

"That's what they called me, 'cause I reminded 'em of Sugar Ray, y'know?" He grinned again, then looked down and shrugged. He flicked at some imaginary dust on the silver-tipped toe of his black

Western boot, then leaned back in the witness chair. He was a small man in his forties, wearing a black three-piece suit that strained slightly to contain the body of an athlete turning slowly to fat. Light brown in complexion, Weston had thinning curly black hair heavily oiled and plastered to his scalp. His small, almost angelic face bore no marks of his years in the ring, save for a slight swelling around the eyes. In fact, the mischievous eyes and disarmingly open smile gave the appearance of a happy child. Weston seemed a little boy playing a grown-up game.

"Fact is," Longo continued, "you were pretty good, weren't you?"

Weston nodded reluctantly. "I did okay."

"You fought for the world welterweight championship in '79, that right?"

"In Puerto Rico," Weston said, his voice slightly lower now. "Wilfredo Benitez." He looked down briefly at his folded hands, then back up at the prosecutor. "Fifteen rounds. Lost a decision."

The D.A. nodded again. "A few months later, you fought Tommy Hearns, the number one contender?"

"They stopped it after six. I got a . . . whaddya call it . . . a detached retina. Couldn't see. So they stopped it."

"Way I recall, the judges had you ahead."

"Yeah."

"That was your last fight, wasn't it?"

"Yeah," the man said softly, looking back down at his hands.

"You had to turn down a fight with Sugar Ray Leonard?"

He nodded silently.

"So what did you do after that, Mr. Weston?"

The man shrugged. "Boxing's all I know. I mean, in Harlem you don't get no kind of education, 'cept how to fight. Boxing, that's all I know. An' I got my dad to take care of. So I got a job. At the Garden. They made me assistant, helpin' out with the matchmaker an' all."

"A matchmaker puts together fights, right?"

"Yeah."

"A couple years after that, though, you went out on your own, became an independent matchmaker?"

"Yeah, Ring Warrior Productions, I call it."

"Doesn't it take money to put together fights?"

"A lot of it, man," Weston said with a laugh. "I saved up my money, from the fights. My dad taught me to do that, save my money, don't go blowin' it all. All this time I'm fightin', man, I know it's goin' to be over someday. He taught me that. So I got this idea. I see the guys makin' the money, they ain't the guys fightin', y'know? They's the guys makin' the deals, who's makin' the money. So I tell myself, that's where I'm goin' to be someday. An' I save my money, don't spend nothin'. I keep it hidden, in cash. Don't trust them banks. My dad taught me that, too."

"Uh-huh."

"An' then, when it's over, I get a job at the Garden, learn the business. Don't spend none of that money."

"Yeah."

"An' then, with the money, I start puttin' together some fights."

"So now you got a couple fighters of your own?"

"Yeah, couple pretty good boys."

"Awright, let's get back to that hundred and eight thousand dollars."

"Yeah."

"Where'd that money come from?"

"That's what I saved up, y'know, from my fights. That's all of it, all the money I saved up."

Longo looked to his left, toward the defense table. Two black men sat next to each other, each a picture of studied indifference. The man closest to him was William McKinney, a tall, slender, and strikingly handsome lawyer in a dark brown pin-striped suit. McKinney had a quiet, confident air about him, the air of a gentleman. Longo knew McKinney to be a clever opponent and one of the most widely respected members of the defense bar.

Seated next to McKinney was Morris Thomas, another prominent member of L.A.'s defense bar. Thomas was an amiable-looking man in his early forties, with receding hair, kindly eyes, a small mustache, and an ever-present ingratiating smile. He had risen from poverty in Alabama to become a homicide detective on the Washington, D.C., police force in the sixties, later moving to California to attend law school at UCLA. He had been an attorney in Los Angeles for ten years now, had a beautiful wife and three kids, and had tried criminal cases against Longo on a number of occasions.

Today, however, Morris Thomas was sitting at the counsel table as the defendant.

"Mr. Weston," Longo said, pointing a stubby finger at Thomas, "you know this guy?"

"Yeah, I sure do."

"How do you know him?"

"That's the motherfucker stole my hundred and eight thousand dollars!"

"Objection," McKinney said with patient restraint, rising to his feet. "The fact of theft is a legal conclusion. There is absolutely no evidence that my client ever had the intent to permanently deprive this individual of any funds. What we have here is nothing more than a civil dispute."

"Sustained," Judge James Bascue said from the bench. "But let's save closing argument for the end of the trial, Mr. McKinney."

"My apologies, your honor," the lawyer said gravely as he sat down.

"Awright, lemme back up," Longo said. "How is it you met the defendant there?"

Weston snorted. "I hired the . . . I hired him to be my lawyer, to get my money back from the DEA."

"The agents took your money, confiscated it, because they figured that much cash had to be drug money."

"Yeah."

"And what was your deal with Thomas?"

"Deal?"

"Yeah, what was he gonna do for you?"

"The man says, he says to me, he's goin' to file some kinda papers with the federal court, y'know? Show that the money's clean, that the gov'ment don't got no evidence that it's from drugs. An' he has to get hisself an order or somethin' to make 'em give it back."

"And what were you gonna pay him?"

"He was goin' to keep twenty-five percent of the hundred and eight thousand dollars."

"That was the deal?"

"Yeah."

"Did you ever get any of that hundred and eight thousand dollars?"

"No, sir," Weston said in a low growl, staring darkly across the courtroom at Thomas. "I ain't seen nothin' to this day."

"What did the defendant tell you about the money?"

"He says, the defendant there, he says there's some problems, there's some problems, he can't get the money."

"He can't get the money."

"That's what he says to me. The gov'ment, they ain't goin' to give up the money, they goin' to keep it."

Longo glanced toward Thomas and McKinney seated to his left. The two men ignored him, both appearing to be faintly bored with the proceedings.

The prosecutor looked down at the table in front of him, began shuffling through the disorganized piles of documents, files, and scribbled notes spread across the table. He mumbled something to a neatly groomed young man sitting in the chair to his left. The man began searching through the stacks with him.

"Gimme a minute," Longo said to Weston, holding up his hand. "It was here a minute ago. Now what did I . . ."

The young man found a canceled check, handed it to the prosecutor.

"There it is," Longo said, holding it up toward the jury with a triumphant grin.

McKinney shook his head, faintly amused at the bumbling prosecutor's continuing ineptness.

"May this be marked People's exhibit number twenty-three, judge?" Longo asked as he walked toward the witness box.

Judge Bascue nodded. "It will be so marked."

Longo held the check up for the jurors to see as he passed by them. "Ever seen this before?" he asked, handing Weston the check.

The witness leaned forward and took the check. He studied it for a moment, then sat back and shook his head in disgust. "No, man, I never seen that, not till you showed me last week."

"That is a check from the U.S. government, made out for a hundred and eight thousand dollars, right?"

"That's what it look like, all right."

"And who is it made out *to*, Mr. Weston?"

The witness again leaned forward and glanced at the check. "Made out to me and Mr. Thomas over there."

"The check is made out jointly to you and your lawyer, the defendant," Longo said, "that right?"

"Yeah, jointly."

"And what is the date on that check?"

Weston glanced at the check. "November twelve."

"Over a month *before* he told you the government was going to keep your money."

Weston turned and glared across the courtroom at Thomas. "Yeah."

"So," Longo said, turning to look at the jurors, "when the defendant told you the government was going to keep the money, he had *already* got a check from the U.S. Attorney's Office for a hundred and eight thousand dollars." He turned back to Weston. "That about right?"

"Yeah," Weston said, nodding. "The motherfuck——the defendant, he had the money all the time, he was jackin' me 'roun'."

"Objection," McKinney said with an audible sigh. "This is mere speculation on the witness's part."

"Sustained."

Longo grabbed the check, turned it over. As he handed it back to Weston, it slipped from his grasp and floated down behind the witness box.

"Aw...Gimme a second, judge," Longo said as he looked behind the wooden railing. He got down on his knees and, reaching behind the box, retrieved the check. Then he stood up and handed it to Weston.

"That your signature?"

Weston studied it for a moment. "Uh-uh, no way. I never sign this." He looked up at the deputy D.A. "I'd remember signin' a check for a hundred and eight thousand dollars, Mr. Longo."

"You never endorsed this check from the U.S. government?"

"I never seen that check, ever."

"But you *did* sign some other things," Longo said, walking back to the table. "Right?"

"Yeah, right. Mr. Thomas, the defendant, he tol' me to sign

some papers, tol' me he needed 'em to deal with the gov'ment."

The young man handed a document to Longo. The prosecutor took it and held it up for the judge. "People's twenty-four?"

"So marked," the judge said.

The deputy D.A. continued to hold the paper up for the jurors as he again approached the witness. "Recognize this?"

Weston took the document, studied it. "Yeah, that's my signature. That's one of the things he tol' me to sign."

"It's a power of attorney."

"Yeah."

"Awright," Longo said, turning to glare at the two men seated across the courtroom, "lemme ask you this: Did the defendant over there ever tell you that with this paper he could endorse checks in your name?"

"No, sir."

Longo walked by the jurors, his eyes now locked on Thomas. Thomas seemed unconcerned, while McKinney continued to appear slightly amused at the crude mannerisms of this loutish prosecutor. "Did he tell you he could cash them without you knowing about it?" he asked as he rounded the prosecution table.

"No, sir."

Longo crossed to the defense table and stopped. He was now standing menacingly close to Thomas, who was ignoring him with a studied indifference.

"Did this man tell you that with this piece of paper, he could steal your life savings?"

"Objection, your honor," McKinney said patiently, again rising to his feet.

"Did he tell you he could destroy your dreams?" Longo snarled, taking a threatening step toward Thomas.

"Your honor!" McKinney repeated more insistently. "Mr. Longo is entirely out of line!"

Judge Bascue leaned forward. "Mr. Longo . . ."

"Withdraw the question, judge," Longo said, his eyes still on the seated figure. Then he turned and slowly walked toward the empty chair at the prosecution table. "Nothing further."

"Your witness," the judge said to McKinney.

The defense lawyer allowed himself a confident smile as he rose to cross-examine. He looked at the witness as he approached the jury box, eyeing him as a wolf would a lamb. "Now then, Mr. Weston," he said, "isn't it a fact that—"

"Oh," Longo said, standing back up. "One more question . . ."

McKinney stopped, glared at the deputy D.A. Then he looked up at the judge. "Your honor . . ."

Judge Bascue sighed with resignation. "Go ahead, Mr. Longo," he said. "*One* question."

Longo looked at the judge for a moment, then at McKinney. "Aw, never mind," he said with a wave to the lawyer. "Go ahead." Then he sat down.

McKinney looked at him as he would at a faintly annoying insect. Then he turned toward the jurors and gave them a long-suffering smile. Leaning confidently against the wooden jury railing, he once again addressed the witness.

"Mr. Weston, isn't it a fact that you were in Detroit before you left for—"

Longo turned to whisper to the young man seated to his left. As he did so, his arm brushed a file off the table, sending dozens of documents spilling across the floor in front of the jury box.

"Aw gee," Longo said loudly, throwing both arms up in exasperation. "Sorry, judge," he said toward Judge Bascue. He turned toward McKinney, shrugged helplessly. Then he got down on his hands and knees and began picking up the documents.

McKinney took a deep breath and shook his head slowly.

Chapter

2

The District Attorney's Office takes up the seventeenth and eighteenth floors of the Criminal Courts Building, buried deep in the heart of the city. From Longo's crowded little office, he had a view of L.A. in all its glory. Over the dingy Old Hall of Justice below are the red and yellow pagodas of Chinatown. To the left is the roar of the Pasadena Freeway, and in the hills above, Dodger Stadium and the police academy. To the right is the historic center of Old Los Angeles, the tourists' "authentic" slice of Mexico. But just beyond, on the other side of the barren L.A. River, is the real slice of Mexico—the sprawling barrios of east L.A.

On a clear day Longo had a breathtaking view of the majestic San Gabriel Mountains, Catalina Island, and the balmy beaches of Santa Monica. Spread out among lazy palm trees are Disneyland, the rolling hills of Hollywood, and the few remaining orange groves. After the hot dry Santa Ana winds have swept clean the city, the natural beauty of Los Angeles's setting can be stunning.

Today the view was of a hazy gray-brown muck.

Longo took a sip of cold black coffee as he looked out his window at the brightly colored signs of Chinatown below. More of them were now in the distinctive Vietnamese script. A couple of blocks to the west, the *hankul* symbols of Korean shop owners were popping up. To the east, next to Little Tokyo, the Mexicans were being pushed out by immigrants from El Salvador and Nicaragua.

Los Angeles was changing. Just beneath the blanket of smog, Longo knew, was a city evolving into one unlike any the world had ever seen.

Beyond the towering buildings of central L.A., the vertical world of government and business spread out into a vast horizontal one of ethnic chaos—Cuban, Laotian, Pakistani, Haitian, El Salvadoran, Mexican, Thai, Ethiopian, Filipino, Nigerian, Lebanese, Iranian, Jewish, Chinese, Nicaraguan, Hmong, Armenian, Samoan, Japanese ... over one hundred different national and ethnic groups. The city had more Koreans than any city but Seoul, more Mexicans than any city but Mexico City, more Salvadorans than any city but San Salvador, more Druze than anywhere outside of Lebanon, more Filipinos than anywhere but the Philippines.

Los Angeles was the promised land. For over a decade, immigrants had been pouring into the area. Now the stream was a flood. Over half the children under the age of eighteen had been born in another country. The overwhelmed public school system offered instruction in eighty-two languages. L.A. was becoming the capital of the third world. And what Los Angeles was today, Longo believed, America would become tomorrow.

The prosecutor's early-morning reverie was broken by the jarring ring of the telephone.

"Longo," he muttered. "Yeah ... yeah ... awright, read it to me."

He leaned back in his green vinyl chair, edging an eight-inch-thick murder file to the left with one brown wing tip shoe. Then he shoved a stack of unread memos to the right with the other; the memos spilled over onto a shorter pile of subpoenas and unanswered correspondence.

"Yeah ... what? ... Read that again ... yeah ... yeah ... aw, fer cryin' out loud ..."

He looked up as Greg Dohi walked into the tiny office. Longo waved him to a gray folding metal chair on the other side of the desk.

Dohi set his leather briefcase carefully across his lap. He was in his twenties and painfully thin; his narrowed, pitch-black eyes stared soulfully out from an olive-skinned Modigliani face. As usual, he appeared both perplexed and worried at the same time.

For the past three months Dohi had been anxiously awaiting

the results of the bar exam before receiving an appointment as a deputy D.A. Like the other interns, he spent most of his time reading manuals and doing boring research. So when Longo had asked for him as "second chair" in the Thomas trial, he had jumped at the chance. Few interns were permitted to serve as co-counsel in a major criminal case, much less to learn from a man with Longo's experience and reputation.

Longo was known to be a "loner" in trial, in contrast to the two-man-team approach to big cases gaining popularity in the office. But he also liked taking a promising rookie under his wing and teaching him the fine art of trial. As the senior deputy D.A. in Department 127, he was authorized to have three junior deputies permanently assigned to him. And he had carefully engineered the assignments of the three deputies now working in his courtroom. Each had exhibited personal qualities that Longo admired, and they had become part of his small "family"—or "my people," as he called them. Much as with sons learning the business, he had slowly groomed them in the trade of prosecuting and the art of trial, each according to his own unique abilities. And Longo took a very real fatherly pride in their growth and accomplishments. When he saw a prosecutor or a defense lawyer make a mistake in court, he would invariably say with satisfaction, "My people wouldn't have done that."

When Dohi was hired as an intern, he quickly caught Longo's attention. Something about him told the prosecutor that he had the rare makings of a courtroom artist. So he arranged to have the youngster assist him in the Thomas trial. Although Dohi could not actually take an active part in the proceedings until he passed the bar and was sworn in as a lawyer, he could help Longo investigate and prepare the Thomas case for trial. More important, he could sit at counsel table with the senior prosecutor and help with documents, motions, and evidence—and learn firsthand how a good prosecutor tried a case. And Longo never seemed to treat him as an inexperienced subordinate. In fact, he often asked Dohi for his opinion about a witness or a potential juror. And, to the young intern's amazement, the prosecutor often acted on these opinions.

In many ways, Greg Dohi was a symbol of the newly emerging Los Angeles. His father was a *nisei*, whose parents had come from Nagoya and Hiroshima; at the age of twelve his father had been incarcerated during World War II in a concentration camp in the high desert of California. His mother was a Spaniard, born in the province of Asturias. But if Dohi was a symbol, he was a reluctant one. "I'm not Japanese and I'm not Spanish," he would say, "I'm from the San Fernando Valley."

Dohi's sense of assimilation was not typical in the emerging ethnic mosaic of Los Angeles. In this new melting pot, very little was melting. Unlike the earlier immigrations from Europe, the new immigrants were simply not blending into the American culture. And this clashed with the two generally held views of Los Angeles's future.

The first was one expressed in a glowing Chamber of Commerce report: "Each of these groups makes its own special contribution to the rich mix that is creating a new heritage for the metropolitan area. Each brings its own ethos, arts, ideas and skills to a community that welcomes and encourages diversity and grows stronger by taking the best from it. They respect each other as mutual partners."

The second view was the oft-discussed *"Blade Runner* scenario," derived from Ridley Scott's dark film in which L.A. degenerates into a blended Asian-Hispanic urban jungle. This bleak vision suggested that any melting pot might just extract the worst rather than the best from each of its ethnic parts.

The emerging truth was to be found somewhere in between. The mosaic, it was turning out, was a brittle one: Los Angeles was evolving into a vast quilt of self-segregated enclaves. And as the dissimilar cultures inevitably came into conflict, the result was suspicion, anger, and, increasingly, violence.

Meanwhile, members of the indigenous black community viewed the new arrivals with resentment: Hispanics were taking away their jobs, Koreans seemed to own most of the neighborhood stores, and the success of other immigrant groups invited uncomfortable comparisons with the black experience. As for the Anglo population, they were fleeing to Washington State or retreating into their own steadily shrinking enclaves of west L.A. and the San Fernando Valley. These communities could readily be identified by their barred windows and signs prominently displayed on well-watered lawns reading ARMED

RESPONSE—WESTEC COMPANY. Ironically, Westec, the largest private security firm in L.A., was owned by a Japanese corporation.

It was clear that while the *Blade Runner* scenario had not yet arrived, neither had the vision of a happy world of "mutual partners." The melting pot was nearing the boiling point.

Longo dropped the phone loudly into its cradle, then looked across the cluttered desk at Dohi. "Nothing yet, Greg," he said. "That was Hernandez. They're still going through Thomas's house with a fine-tooth comb." He took another gulp of cold coffee.

Dohi looked at his watch. "Eight-fourteen."

Longo nodded. "Dahl called in at seven-thirty, outside Thomas's office. He was ready to serve the warrant at eight sharp. Should be taking the place apart about now." Then he grinned broadly. "I wish I could be there when McKinney hears about it! Search warrants in the middle of trial! He's gonna shit! He is just gonna sit down and shit!"

Dohi allowed himself a cautious smile before reverting to his usual worried look. "The state bar may not be too happy about this, Larry, going through a lawyer's files. . . . It's sort of a violation of client confidentiality, isn't it? I mean, whatever our investigators find, couldn't McKinney maybe get it suppressed?"

Longo winked at him. "I called the bar yesterday, Greg. Told them I was serving warrants on one of their illustrious members this morning, at his office and his home. I suggested they might like to come along to monitor the search. So they agreed to send a guy along with Hernandez. They're gonna make sure that only files on Weston and the mysterious Mr. Ali are seized. Those files, and anything about Thomas's finances."

Dohi nodded, looked nervously again at his watch. "Calendar call goes in fifteen minutes, doesn't it?"

"Yeah. Calendar at eight-thirty, about a dozen or so cases. Trial starts again at ten. By then, I figure McKinney and Thomas will have heard about the searches. They both got car phones. And they'll figure out that I timed it for when they'd be on their way to court." Longo's grin widened farther. "We're gonna have two very pissed-off lawyers screaming bloody murder in a few minutes, Greg. Pissed-off and maybe a little worried."

"When did the—"

Dohi was interrupted by the phone ringing.

With his feet still propped up, Longo reached for the phone. "Longo!" he barked into the receiver.

Dohi sat silently in the small, cluttered room, his eyes wandering around the familiar scene. He recalled the day when he had nervously reported to Longo's office—and had been stunned to see the cramped and chaotic conditions under which the near-legendary trial lawyer worked.

"Yes, ma'am," Longo said, his voice suddenly gentle. "Yes, ma'am, that's true, but—"

Measuring only about ten by twelve feet, the office was dominated by the government-issue metal desk set halfway back along the right wall and buried beneath paperwork. Dohi was beginning to suspect that the paperwork had been there for as long as the desk. A larger wooden chair of unknown origin was to his right, a stack of case files three feet high resting on it.

Close behind the chairs and flush against the near wall was an ancient wooden bookcase that rose almost to the ceiling, filled with old law books, outdated appellate case reports, three-ring vinyl binders, and thick D.A. manuals. The manuals bore titles like *Ballistics, Habeas Corpus,* and *Uniform Crime Charging Manual;* the binders had strange, hand-lettered names on the spines like "Thong Hung," "Jimmy Yee," and "Hac Qui." Perched high on top of the bookcase was a black antique Royal typewriter, rusted and unused for decades. Longo had once explained to Dohi that he just liked having "old things" around.

"No, ma'am," Longo said patiently into the receiver. "You don't have to come in until the deputy on the case calls you." He reached into a drawer, pulled out a hard-boiled egg, and sniffed at it; wedging the receiver between his head and shoulder, he began to peel the shell. "Yes, ma'am, I know the subpoena says that. But my preliminary hearing deputy put you on call. See, that way you don't have to wait around all day outside the courtroom. . . . Yes, ma'am, I know that's what it says. . . ." He looked up helplessly at Dohi, shrugged.

At the far end of the wall was a gray steel filing cabinet, three drawers high. Inside two of these drawers were files for the dozens of criminal cases calendared for Department 127 over the next two weeks; in the partially opened bottom drawer was a battered old pair of Nikes and a tangled pile of assorted sweat socks, gym shorts, and T-shirts.

"Yes, ma'am," Longo said. "I'm sure everything will be okay.... Yes, ma'am, you're very welcome.... Good-bye now." He hung up the receiver, then looked between his propped-up shoes at Dohi as he took a bite from the peeled egg. "Anyway, I got a hunch that when they search Thomas's office, they're gonna find—"

The phone rang.

"Longo!" the lawyer growled into the receiver again. "Hernandez? Yeah, whaddya got? . . . Yeah . . . yeah . . . The guy from the state bar there? . . . Yeah . . . In a pig's eye he does. . . . yeah . . ."

Longo put a hand over the phone, grinned at Dohi with unrestrained glee. "They found a letter from an offshore bank in the Caribbean," he said. "Our boy's got a secret account." Then, removing his hand, "Yeah . . . yeah . . ."

As Dohi looked around the tiny, claustrophobic office he once again felt that vague sense of discomfort. The sloppiness and complete lack of any organization unnerved him. How could anyone function under such chaotic conditions? How could anyone even *find* anything? Yet, how many times had he seen Longo looking for a letter or a document—and, digging halfway down one jumbled pile or another, magically pull it out?

"Take it all.... Yeah, just grab it and we can go over it later.... Well, you tell the office manager we'll take whatever we want. You explain to him, you tell him what a search warrant *is,* fer cryin' out loud. . . ."

Dohi smiled in disbelief as he continued to survey the confused scene. He let his gaze wander now to the beige walls in the hopes of finding some undiscovered clue to the enigma of Larry Longo. On the right wall nearest the tall bookcase was an old print of *Pinkie* set in a heavy antique frame; the painting seemed oddly out of place here in Longo's stark world of murder and mayhem.

Taped to the wall next to Longo's desk was a photo of a voluptuous woman about Longo's age, another photo of two muscular young men and a very pretty teenage girl, and a third photo of a 1962 Corvette sports car. From having been to dinner at the prosecutor's home in Malibu, Dohi knew the woman was Longo's wife, Aelina, and the three youngsters his kids. The Corvette was Longo's pride and joy—one of seven old cars that he kept in various states of disrepair, including the car he drove to work every day, a rusty Toyota van with 156,000 miles on it.

Across the room on the opposite wall, above the filing cabinet, was what appeared to be a wanted poster with an inscription beneath a man's photograph: "This drifter picked up two young female hitchhikers on Pacific Coast Highway and took them into Topanga Canyon where he injected them with heroin before raping them both, strangling one and leaving the other for dead. He should be considered armed and dangerous." The photo was of Longo in a tuxedo and silly grin, taken at a roast in his honor. Someone had carefully glued it over the original picture of the real fugitive.

Taped on the wall next to the poster was an official policy memorandum that Dohi had not seen before. He leaned forward and read the document.

SPECIAL DIRECTIVE 91–8

To: All Deputy District Attorneys
FROM: Ira Reiner, District Attorney
SUBJECT: State Bar Prohibition of Sex with Clients

As you may already know, the State Bar of California has recently promulgated ethical guidelines dealing with the thorny issue of attorneys engaging in sexual relations with their clients. Such relationships create an obvious appearance of impropriety and ought to be avoided in all situations. Because the Los Angeles County District Attorney's Office represents the people of the State of California, each and every citizen is our client. It is therefore the policy of this office that Deputy District Attorneys may not engage in sexual relationships with any resident of the State of California. You may engage in sexual relationships only with tourists and those persons who have been in the State of California for less than thirty days.

I am proud to say that the attorneys in this office have

always conformed to the highest level of professional and ethical behavior. I expect such conduct to continue.

Dohi was perplexed for a moment, then grinned and shook his head.
The "directive," supposedly from District Attorney Ira Reiner, was
one of many "renegade memos" that mysteriously appeared in the
mailboxes of deputies from time to time, the products of twisted legal
minds.

"Yeah . . . yeah . . . what? Aw, gimme a break. . . . Yeah . . . the
what? Well, I'll be. Yeah, read it to me. . . ." Longo listened for a
moment. "Yeah, good. Okay, gimme a call."

Longo hung up the phone, then returned to Dohi. "Dahl at
Thomas's office. A lot of computer stuff—everything's on computer
disks or something, I dunno. They gotta go over it later on a computer."

Dohi nodded.

"You get those cases?" Longo asked.

Dohi held up some papers in his lap. "It's pretty much like you
said, Larry. The cases say we can't offer evidence that Thomas committed other crimes to show he probably committed *this* one."

"Yeah, they call that 'propensity evidence.' "

"But . . . if there is a *similarity* between the crimes . . ."

"Same M.O."

"Yes. If they have a similar modus operandi to the charged
crime, we can offer evidence of the other crimes."

When the Thomas case had originally been filed, Judge Bascue
and Longo's deputies saw it as basically a civil dispute; the filing of
criminal charges against a prominent local attorney was seen as an
overreaction by a green filing deputy. The case was about to be plea-
bargained when Longo smelled something wrong. The prosecutor had
learned long ago to trust "sixth sense." And so he had dug a little
deeper. And, slowly, methodically, Longo had uncovered an amazing
story, one that went far beyond a simple embezzlement from a client.

Respected attorney Morris Thomas was allegedly involved in
some heavy international deals with a shadowy figure by the name of
"Sherif Ali." Through a series of cardboard corporations set up by
Thomas, the two men had allegedly posed as agents for oil interests
in Iran looking to invest millions of dollars in the United States. With

a failing economy and a reluctance by American banks to make loans, Thomas and Ali had no trouble finding desperate American businessmen willing to put up a hundred thousand dollars in "good faith deposit" money to get at millions in loans. Then, with the deposits safely tucked away in offshore accounts, Thomas would explain to the victim that the Iranian government had stepped in, killed the loan deal, and confiscated the good faith money.

The more Longo dug, the more victims around the country he uncovered. Unfortunately, Ali had heard that Longo was sniffing around and decided to take up residence in Switzerland. Then office politics reared its ugly head: The huge amounts involved in the thefts dictated that the case be handled by the D.A.'s Major Frauds unit, one of many specialized groups in the office. Longo had been forced to turn his evidence over to the unit and back off the investigation.

But that still left the Weston case sitting around in Longo's courtroom. Since it had nothing to do with the international loan scam, and appeared to be a "loser" in any event, Major Frauds was not interested. Longo knew that cases in Major Frauds could take months, even years, to investigate and bring to trial; there was also a good chance that because of jurisdictional problems they would never be able to put together a case against Thomas. But the Weston embezzlement had already been filed and was nearing its constitutional time limits; McKinney knew that the case was weak, that the signed power of attorney gave his client a way out, and he would be demanding a dismissal if something did not happen soon. The Weston embezzlement could be the only shot the D.A. had at the lawyer. And so Longo had announced ready for trial.

"Awright..." Longo leaned back as he looked across the desk at Dohi. "We got Thomas and his buddy Ali scamming loans from Iran. And we got Thomas getting a little side action ripping off a client here. Awright... so how do we tie them together? How do we let the jury know that this isn't just a civil dispute with a client? How do we let them know that Thomas is a big-time crook, that he's been swindling people all across the country?" He looked at Dohi. "Answer: We've got to get in evidence of the loan scams with Ali. And the only way to do that is..."

"Modus operandi evidence," Dohi said.

"Right." Longo nodded. "To get in evidence of uncharged thefts, we gotta convince Bascue that Thomas used a similar method. So . . . what's the Harvard man found in all that research?"

Dohi smiled. He had been an honors student at Harvard, later graduating from the University of California's prestigious law school, Boalt Hall; Longo had attended a small, unaccredited "blue-collar" law school at night while working during the day.

"Well," Dohi said with a shrug, "I think it's thin, but I've found this one case that deals with trust funds, same as Thomas. It seems to me that in both cases, Thomas takes the money and puts it in an attorney-client trust fund. That way, everything looks right. Then he writes checks on the fund and deposits them in phony—"

The phone rang.

"Longo!" Again, the gruff prosecutor's voice suddenly softened. "Sure, sweetie pie . . . don't worry about it. . . . No, everything's okay, I'll have Frankie take care of it. . . . No, sweetheart, don't worry . . ."

Dohi smiled. Sweetheart. Sweetie pie. He hadn't realized that there were people who still talked like that. But then the crusty prosecutor violated most of Dohi's long-held beliefs about attorneys. He had expected a successful trial lawyer to be smooth, sophisticated, articulate, and infinitely clever. But Longo had all the charm and poise of a New York taxi driver. Yet. . . . Yet it was a fact that the man had not given up an acquittal in eighteen years! Eighteen years! How was it possible?

According to everything he had learned in law school, Dohi believed Longo should never win a case. He had been watching him for over a month now, watching for some clue, some logical explanation for the man's phenomenal success with juries. There was none. Longo violated every rule in the trial lawyer's book. In fact, he conducted a trial more like a jackhammer operator than a lawyer. How could he keep getting convictions?

As always, Dohi felt a sense of frustration when he tried to understand Longo's success. Was it that instinct Longo seemed to have, that sense that something did not fit? Was it his unbending stubbornness? His rigid views of right and wrong? His obvious love of a good fight? Was it possible to win that many cases through sheer tenacity?

Dohi admired the way Longo had sensed something wrong in

the Thomas case, the way he had ignored the opinions of judges and superiors, had sunk his teeth into it and never let go. And that was his reputation—a stubborn prosecutor who did things his own way. There were those in the office who saw Longo as a relic of the past, a bumbling eccentric, and a loose cannon. Others saw him as a tough, clever, and totally dedicated prosecutor. But all agreed he was one of a kind. And that he did not lose.

The young intern repressed a wave of anger, a feeling he often experienced when things were not logical. Longo did everything Dohi had been taught *not* to do, yet he won. It did not make sense. He would learn though; eventually he would find the answer. For now, it was enough that this man accepted him as an equal, even treated him like a son. He knew that no other deputy in the office would have done that.

"I'll take care of it, sweetie pie," Longo said soothingly, nodding at his unseen wife. "I've got the number written down right here." Longo searched through the pockets of his coat. He pulled out a badly mangled piece of paper, looked at it. It was an L.A. County paycheck made out to him, issued three weeks earlier. He stuffed it back into the pocket, kept searching.

One of Longo's many idiosyncrasies, Dohi had learned, was that he hated to deal with money or banks. In his younger days he had always kept his money stuffed in socks hidden in his bedroom, and now he left all financial matters up to his wife. It was perhaps ironic that his godfather was L. M. Giannini, president of the Bank of America.

"Don't worry yourself about it, sweetie. It's all taken care of. Uh-huh, I'll see you tonight." He hung up the phone, then lifted his feet off the desk, spun around, and looked at Dohi. "Where were we?"

"The M.O. evidence."

"Oh yeah. Well, look, before McKinney puts on his next witness—"

The phone rang.

"Longo!"

Dohi smiled again. It was always like this. An unending string of phone calls and visits from frightened witnesses, frustrated cops, bureaucratic supervisors, harried junior deputies, pandering defense lawyers, angry judges, pushy newspaper reporters. . . . All in a tiny office that looked like someone had set off a hand grenade in a thrift shop. Crisis, confusion, chaos.

At 8:30, in less than ten minutes, Longo was due in Department 127 to supervise the day's calendar, disposing of ten or fifteen criminal cases with Judge Bascue and various defense lawyers, racing to meet the 10:00 deadline when the Thomas jury would return. And when he got back to the office at 12:00 for a quick sandwich, there would be a growing stack of telephone messages. All but the most urgent would be ignored, to be swallowed up somewhere in the paper jungle, as Longo scrambled to prepare for a cross-examination that would begin at 1:45. Yet, the man never got rattled, seemed even to thrive in the center of it all; the greater the pressure, the more ebullient he appeared.

Longo hung up from the call, then lifted his coffee mug and looked again at Dohi. "Anyway, what were you saying, Greg?"

"The only way we can get in the Ali evidence is if—"

"Shoot," Longo said, looking into the empty mug. "Gimme a second, Greg." He squeezed past the desk, sidestepped a stack of transcripts on the floor, and walked out of the room.

The young intern stepped to the window and looked out over the sprawling city below. Once again, he found himself pondering his future as a deputy D.A. Was this really the kind of life he wanted for himself and, someday, his family?

Every deputy in the office had his or her own reasons for passing up the big money and prestige of private practice to wage daily battle in the seedy world of thieves, murderers, and pushers. For the idealistic Dohi, it had been a deep, burning desire to be like his father and his mother—to use his life to serve humanity in some meaningful way as they had.

His parents had met after medical school, while pediatric interns at the Cystic Fibrosis Clinic of Children's Hospital in Los Angeles. They married soon thereafter. Dohi's father eventually became a pediatrician for the county health department, treating the children of the poor at Olive View Medical Center; his mother still worked with children at the Cystic Fibrosis Clinic.

The young intern had always admired his parents, had envied

the satisfaction they felt from their work. "My father can *see* the good he does," Dohi would say. "At the end of the day he can point to little kids and know their lives are better because of him. I want that."

Unlike many of his associates in the office, Dohi didn't have a "love of the law" or a need to punish wrongdoers; he didn't thrill to courtroom combat, lust for the power of the position, or feed off the excitement of trial. For Dohi, the D.A.'s office was simply a means for serving people, for protecting victims and giving them some justice.

How long would this view last in the disillusioning world of the criminal courts? Dohi could see the realities, understand the odds. He had seen the "burnout" rate among prosecutors. For now, though, it was enough to be able to point to someone at the end of the day and, like his father, know that person's life was a little better because of him.

The phone rang again as Longo walked back into the office, a fresh cup of coffee in his hand.

"Longo . . . yeah . . . just a second." Longo covered the phone with one hand and looked up at Dohi. "You seen Boyle or Torrealba this morning? They're screaming for a D.A. down in Division 38."

Dohi shook his head. Larry Boyle and Leonard Torrealba were two of the deputy D.A.s assigned to Longo in Department 127 of superior court. Division 38 was a municipal court that did preliminary hearings in felony cases before they were sent on to Superior Court for plea or trial. Longo's deputies were responsible for, among other things, conducting "prelims" in Division 38 on cases destined for Department 127.

"Well," Longo said, "the judge in 38's threatening to kick the case if we don't get a D.A. down there right now." He took his hand off the receiver. "Yeah," he said into the phone, "Boyle's on the way. He'll be there in a few minutes. . . . Just tell the judge he's on his way."

Longo hung up, then quickly redialed. "Leonard? Hey, you guys got a prelim down in 38, judge's screaming dismissal. Where's Boyle? . . . Uh-huh . . . get on down there and get that prelim rolling. . . . Yeah, I know . . . yeah, okay." He hung up, again looked up at Dohi. "Well, we better get down to court. We got a heavy calendar this morning. Bascue'll be pushing to get the trial started on time."

The phone rang.

"Longo!...Yeah...what!...Aw, fer cryin' out loud!... That's bullshit!...No, I'm not buying that...."

Longo looked up at Dohi. "State bar. They've changed their minds, they're not going to send that expert witness to testify. They say they can't get involved unless Thomas is suspended or disbarred."

Longo spoke back into the receiver. "Listen, you gutless bastards, what more do you want? I gave you the file. I gave you the evidence. The son of a bitch stole a hundred and eight thousand dollars from a client.... Look, all I want from you is an expert witness, someone who'll explain to the jury what an attorney-client trust fund is, what an attorney's duty is in handling a client's money...."

Dohi's worried look grew more worried.

"You gutless..." Longo slammed the phone down into its cradle. "Fer Chrissake," he mumbled to himself.

The temporary silence was interrupted by another visitor. A slender, immaculately dressed figure was suddenly standing in the doorway. He appeared to be in his early forties, a handsome man with angular Asian features, slightly marred by pockmarks on fine-boned cheeks. A vague smile stretched tightly across perfect teeth, a smile that clashed with cold, caculating eyes.

Dohi recognized the man as an attorney named Mike Yamaki. A politically powerful leader of L.A.'s Japanese-American community, he was a member of the Police Commission and a close ally of Mayor Tom Bradley. He was also one of the best criminal defense lawyers in the city.

The two men looked at each other silently, cautiously, Yamaki still standing in the doorway and wearing a fixed smile.

"Hi, Larry," Yamaki said softly. "Got a minute?"

Strangely, the prosecutor said nothing. Then he nodded slowly.

Chapter

3

"King."

"Huh?"

"King," the man said, leaning against the corridor wall. "I think they said the black guy's name was King."

"Yeah, well, I'll tellya, there's some cops going down on this one."

"I dunno."

"Whaddya mean?" the second man said, grimacing as he drank watery coffee from a white ceramic mug with the district attorney's emblem on it. "What I hear, it's a cold case. A dozen cops pounding on one guy."

"I heard different. High-speed chase. Guy's on parole for armed robbery. Bigger than your average gorilla and high on angel dust. Guy went crazy."

"What I hear, witnesses say he was down, and staying down. And he wasn't carrying."

"Hey, who's a jury gonna believe? A dozen LAPD or some doped-up parolee?"

"I hear there were witnesses."

The existence of one of the most famous videotapes in history would not be known for another day.

"What if there were? Hell, you know what it's like out there on the streets, Bill. There's a war going on. Far as the cops are concerned, it's the good guys and the bad guys. No middle ground. We come down hard on the cops, well, where does that put us? What kind of cooperation are we gonna get from them?"

Longo walked down the corridor toward the two deputy D.A.s. "Hey, Bill, Fred, you guys on hall patrol?"

"How's it going, Larry," Bill said. "You hear about that LAPD gangbang?"

"I heard."

"So whaddya think? Fred here figures we maybe don't file on the cops because we don't want to piss 'em off."

"Hey," Fred said, "I'm just saying Reiner's running for reelection, right? Does he want Chief Gates and half the cops in the state to come down on him right now?"

Ira Reiner, the incumbent district attorney of Los Angeles County, was in the middle of an uphill reelection campaign. At stake were the reins to the largest municipal prosecuting agency in the world; with nearly 1,000 prosecutors and a budget of $120 million, the office prosecuted over 225,000 criminal cases in 1992. More important, the position was a stepping-stone to higher political office.

"That's just it," Bill said. "Reiner's no prosecutor, he's a fucking politician. He knows where the votes are. The minorities control this county now, and that means he'd better come down hard on some white cops beating up on a black guy."

"He does, he loses half the Westside and the Valley." Fred turned to Longo. "Whaddya think, Larry?"

"I think if they committed a felony, they get filed on, same as anybody else."

"Yeah, but whaddya think Reiner's gonna do?"

Longo shrugged. Very few of the deputies in the office liked or respected Reiner. He was not one of them; he had never served as a deputy in the office. A former L.A. city controller and city attorney, he had not prosecuted a single felony case in his life. But he had defeated the incumbent law-and-order D.A. by appealing to the minorities' distrust of the police.

"If the evidence is there, he's gotta file against the cops," Longo said.

"Yeah? And what if the cops are acquitted?"

"Then he's got a problem."

"*Twilight Zone* all over again," Fred said.

"And McMartin," Bill added.

Since Reiner's election to the position of district attorney, the office had lost two headline trials. In what appeared to many to be a play for publicity, Reiner charged film director John Landis and others with negligent homicide in the deaths of actor Vic Morrow and two child actors during the making of *Twilight Zone: The Movie*. After a circus-like trial, all of the defendants were acquitted.

Another trial had started at about the same time: the infamous McMartin preschool child molestation case. After two and a half years of highly publicized testimony, the jury finally acquitted one defendant, deadlocking on the other. In a retrial of the remaining defendant, the jury again deadlocked; Reiner finally threw in the towel and dismissed charges.

Being the district attorney in L.A. was a lot like being an actor there: Two or three flops and you were out of work.

"Shit," Bill said, "he blows McMartin, then the *Twilight Zone* case . . . now this guy King. Reiner loses this one, three strikes, he's out."

"Hey," Fred said, "what about *our* cases?"

"Whaddya mean?"

"You know what our jury panels look like now. Not a whole lot of white faces, right? Well, how many of our trials depend on cops' testimony, huh? Defendant's word against the cop's?"

"Yeah," Bill said, thinking about this.

"Whaddya think's gonna happen to our conviction rate, with this King thing on every juror's mind?"

"Yeah . . ."

"Something else," Longo said.

The two men looked at him.

"Were you guys here for the Watts riots?"

Fred shook his head. "Hell, I was in Philadelphia, Larry, in high school."

"I was here," Bill said.

"It got started when some LAPD tangled with a black woman," Longo said.

Bill nodded slowly.

"Right," Longo said. "And would you say things are better out on the streets now than they were back then?"

The three men were silent.

"So who's gonna try the case?" Fred said.

It was a question that had been on each of their minds. When a big case broke, every ambitious prosecutor in the county waited and hoped for the phone call. "The big one" would make a deputy's career, possibly even open political avenues. But the action was downtown: Most of the top prosecutors were assigned to the Criminal Courts Building. And the selection would be made by "the front office," the corner of the eighteenth floor reserved for the D.A. and his chief deputy.

"Special Trials," Fred said. The Special Trials unit was home to the D.A.'s "top guns," ace prosecutors who were assigned to try headline cases like McMartin, the Keating savings and loan case, the Menendez brothers, and the O. J. Simpson circus.

"I heard S.I.D.'s got it," Bill said. "Maybe Gunson'll try it himself."

"Maybe," Longo said pensively.

The deputy was right: Unknown to the men, the case had already been assigned to S.I.D. The Special Investigations Division was a secretive unit of the D.A.'s Office housed behind locked doors on the seventeenth floor. Its purpose was to investigate and prosecute politically sensitive cases, commonly those involving politicians or police officers. Its chief was Roger Gunson, a tight-lipped, straight-shooting Mormon with a long career of colorful cases.

When the Rodney King case first broke, Gunson decided to send it to the state attorney general, feeling that decisions in the potentially explosive case might be influenced by the D.A.'s election. But this was immediately vetoed by Reiner; the King case could give him a chance to redeem himself after the McMartin and *Twilight Zone* fiascos.

The next question was how to conduct the investigation. Two detectives from LAPD's robbery and homicide division were building a criminal case against King to be presented to the D.A. At the same time, LAPD's Internal Affairs unit was conducting a secret investigation into the officers' conduct. Should S.I.D. cooperate with one of these inquiries, or continue with its own? Gunson conferred with Reiner and the decision was quickly made: The D.A.'s Office would continue with a separate and independent inquiry. Within twenty-four hours of the incident, Gunson assigned a "roll-out" team of D.A.

investigators who immediately began interviewing witnesses.

Longo checked his watch. "Jeez, I gotta get to court."

"Yeah, me too," Bill said.

"It's gonna hit the fan," Fred said. "You watch."

"Maybe," Longo said again. He walked past the men as they broke up, rounded a corner, and entered his office. Greg Dohi was sitting in the chair in front of the desk, waiting for him.

"Morning, Greg."

"Hi, Larry. You hear about those cops last night?"

"Yeah, I heard."

"Sounds pretty bad."

"Uh-huh."

"So who do you think is going to get the case?"

Longo shrugged. "Search me."

Not Gunson, Longo thought to himself. Good prosecutor. Solid, professional, experienced. His preparation in the Roman Polanski rape case had been brilliant. But . . .

Polanski, the gifted movie director who had recently finished *Rosemary's Baby,* had announced that he was looking for very young girls for parts in his future movies. One of the many "Hollywood mothers" who responded sent him photographs of her beautiful thirteen-year-old daughter. Polanski went to the woman's house, introduced himself, then explained to her that he wanted to shoot some pictures of her daughter. The mother consented, and Polanski drove the young girl to a secluded mansion located high in the hills above Hollywood. The mansion belonged to Jack Nicholson; the actor was living there with Anjelica Huston, but Polanski had been given use of the home while the two were gone.

Alone with the girl in the huge estate, Polanski fed her glasses of champagne secretly laced with Quaalude. Then he led the heavily drugged girl into an outdoor hot tub. She did not resist when he took her bathing suit off and began taking photographs of her in the nude. Then he took her back into the house, forced her to perform oral copulation, and finally had intercourse with her.

About this time, Anjelica Huston unexpectedly arrived home. The embarrassed Polanski hurriedly dressed the girl, put her in his car, and quickly drove away.

Gunson took the case to the grand jury and got multiple felony counts against the director, including rape with the use of drugs, forcible oral copulation, and statutory rape.

As part of his methodical preparation, the prosecutor read every book he could find about Polanski and watched every movie the director ever made. And he made a fascinating discovery.

In each of Polanski's movies there was a recurring theme, one the prosecutor characterized as "innocence meets corruption over water." In every movie there was a scene in which an innocent woman or young girl was somehow violated by an evil force, and always in the vicinity of a body of water. In *Rosemary's Baby,* for example, the devil had raped the young woman in the hold of a ship. And the woman's husband had served champagne to his wife beforehand, and had placed a drug in some chocolate mousse. The prosecutor recalled Polanski's use of the hot tub, the champagne, and the Quaalude.

Gunson found a copy of *Rosemary's Baby* and made plans to show the film to the jury.

Meantime, however, the girl's mother decided she did not want to have her daughter subjected to a trial. She hired a politically influential attorney who paid a visit to the district attorney. Shortly after this, Gunson received word from the "front office" to offer a plea bargain: Polanski pleads guilty to statutory rape, the heavier counts are dismissed, and the sentence is "open"—left to the judge to decide.

Reluctantly, Gunson followed orders. Polanski accepted the offer and pled guilty to felony statutory rape. On the day before sentencing, however, the movie director fled the country for France. He has never returned.

Yes, Longo thought, Gunson would be a good choice to prosecute the King case. Except there was no chance Reiner would give it to him. Roger Gunson had also been the prosecutor in the first McMartin preschool trial. And that was as good as branding a scarlet letter on his forehead.

The McMartin case had taken five years out of Gunson's life, five years of going to work at 5:00 in the morning and returning home late at night after his three boys were asleep. His youngest had been eight years old when Gunson had taken over the McMartin prosecution; by the end of the trial, the boy was in high school. His sons had grown up and he had missed it. Five years that he could not replace.

And Gunson had failed to win the McMartin trial. As far as trying high-publicity cases, his career was over.

No, it would not be Gunson. But who?

Longo leaned down and stacked three cardboard filing boxes on a luggage cart; one of the boxes contained files for cases on the court's morning calendar, the other two held notes and documents for the Thomas trial. He nodded at Dohi.

"Okay," Longo said. "Let's go to war, Greg."

Dohi grinned nervously as he rose to his feet. The two men walked out of the office and into the hallway, Longo towing the cart behind.

Someone from S.I.D.? Longo wondered. Or maybe one of the headline hunters in Special Trials. Bill Hodgman. No, he was already in trial on the Keating savings and loan case. Pam Ferrero and Lester Kuruyama were tied up with the Menendez brothers. Marcia Clark just got the Russian Mafia case. Ernie Norris, Longo thought. The top prosecutor in Special Trials, probably in the entire D.A.'s Office. Maybe in the state. He would be the perfect choice. Yes, Norris was the best man, Longo thought. And that was why Reiner would never appoint him.

Longo grinned as he thought of the stern, steely-eyed, silver-haired ex-Marine. The son of a Wyoming sheepherder, Sterling "Ernie" Norris had grown up on the back of a horse, then left home when he was old enough to join the Marines. And that experience defined him. Most of one entire wall of Norris's office was covered with a massive American flag that measured eight feet in length. Another wall was draped with a huge, bright scarlet Marine Corps flag; a bust of Chesty Puller, the legendary Marine war hero, rested on a bookcase underneath the flag like an icon at an altar.

It was Norris who had tried the "Freeway Strangler."

In 1980, Southern California was experiencing one of its periodic waves of terror caused by yet another serial killer. Over a period of months, the bodies of twenty teenage boys had been found dumped along the highways and freeways of Los Angeles, Orange, and Ventura counties. Each of the victims had been hog-tied, sodomized, and strangled. Norris was assigned to head a task force of police and sheriffs from the three counties in a search for the killer.

Eventually, the investigation focused on William Bonin, a small-time thief with an IQ of 139. Norris quickly had a surveillance team put on him. The tail worked: Bonin, driving a windowless van, picked up a teenage boy hitchhiking in Hollywood and drove him into the nearby hills. Within seconds after he had parked, detectives rushed the van and caught Bonin in the act.

Norris took the case to trial, winning convictions on ten of twelve first-degree-murder counts.

As the prosecutor turned his attention to the death penalty phase, Bonin's lawyer approached him with a proposal. There were accomplices to most of the murders, the lawyer said: If Norris would back off on the death penalty, Bonin would name them and testify in their trials.

The prosecutor was torn: He badly wanted to send Bonin to the gas chamber, but he knew he would never get the accomplices without the killer's help. Norris offered the lawyer a strange deal: He would meet with Bonin, listen to what he had to say. Then he would decide. If he turned down the proposal, anything Bonin said would not be used in court. The lawyer agreed.

Norris met privately with Bonin and the lawyer. For over eight hours Bonin described each of the torture-murders in grisly detail, naming who his accomplices were.

When it was over, Norris made a tough decision. He was convinced that Bonin was telling the truth. But he was also convinced that Bonin was the mastermind behind each of the murders.

He told the lawyer there was no deal.

When the jury returned after only four hours with a verdict of death, the mother of one of the slain boys rushed up to Norris and hugged him. "Thank you," she said, kissing him over and over, tears streaming down her cheeks. "Oh God, thank you, thank you."

Ernie Norris became head of the Special Trials unit and continued trying death penalty cases, eventually sending more killers to the gas chamber than any other prosecutor in California. But it was his continued success that proved his undoing. The prosecutor had become the media's darling; his exploits appeared regularly in the headlines. And that meant that he was a political threat.

Reiner removed Norris as head of Special Trials, relegating him to the position of an ordinary trial deputy in the unit. Although Norris was clearly the most experienced lawyer in the office, he was given only "second-tier" cases to try—cases that were of no interest to the media.

Ernie Norris's career as the top death penalty prosecutor in the state was over.

Longo walked out the security door and into the elevator lobby. He wheeled the cart over to one of the ten elevators and pressed the down button.

Dohi stood silently next to him, aware that something was bothering his mentor. He knew that Longo usually whistled cheerfully and loudly on his way to the courtroom when he was in trial; the sounds of the prosecutor's renditions of Italian opera echoing along the hallways were well known throughout the Criminal Courts Building. But on this morning he was strangely quiet.

Charlie Manson, Longo was thinking. Ernie Norris had been a victim of the "Bugliosi syndrome."

When the Tate-LaBianca slaughters had horrified the world, then–District Attorney Evelle Younger named the most experienced deputy in the office, Aaron Stovitz, to prosecute Manson and his "family" for the murders. A younger deputy by the name of Vincent Bugliosi was assigned to assist him.

The carnival-like atmosphere of the Manson trial quickly turned Stovitz into a media celebrity. The press seemed hypnotized by the charismatic Manson; stories of biblical prophecies, race wars, and sacrificial murders captured headlines for months. Younger, who was later to be elected attorney general of California and later still to lose in a bid for the governor's mansion, began to perceive his ace prosecutor as a political threat: Stovitz was seen as using his new fame to position himself for a run at Younger's job. In a pattern that was to become familiar in the office for many years to come, the D.A. removed Stovitz from the case, replacing him with Bugliosi.

Bugliosi, it turned out, was considerably more ambitious than Stovitz ever was. A younger deputy was assigned as "second chair" for the trial, but he was not to conduct any important cross-examination or present argument to the jury. The younger deputy sat silently at counsel table, content to research legal issues and organize witnesses, while Bugliosi performed daily before the world's press. Unknown to anyone at the time, Bugliosi had already arranged to write a book about the trial—with himself as the hero; his ghostwriter, Curt Gentry, was given a valued press pass and sat in the courtroom audience. The book, *Helter Skelter,* eventually became a bestseller. And, ironically, Bugliosi used his newfound fame to do exactly what Younger had feared of Stovitz—announce his candidacy for the office of District Attorney.

Reiner learned from Younger's experience. When the Roman emperors felt a general had become dangerously popular, he was banished to the command of a distant province. In the Los Angeles District Attorney's Office, a headline grabber was reassigned to an outlying branch office far removed from the media and the political power structure. Reiner knew that the keys to power were housed within one block of the Criminal Courts Building: City Hall, the County Hall of Administration, and the *Los Angeles Times* building.

One thing was probable, Longo thought as he absently stepped into the elevator. Whoever was named to prosecute the cops in the King trial would be a relative unknown; if you were seen as a possible threat to Reiner, you could not be given a chance for any more publicity. It was a Catch-22: If you proved you were good enough to win the big trials, you were too good to be assigned to them. That meant younger, less-experienced attorneys, like Pam Ferrero in the second McMartin trial, or Lea D'Agostino, the prosecutor in the *Twilight Zone* case.

Of course, Longo thought with a touch of anger, both of those trials were lost.

In any event, he knew *he* would not be chosen to try the case. He had long ago alienated the front office. Longo was blunt, completely lacking in tact, and saw things in black and white; when he disagreed with administration policy, he was not shy about letting it be known. This alone would have kept him off the list of favored deputies. But he was also deeply Sicilian in his attitude toward the world around him. You were either his friend or you were his enemy; there was no middle ground. And if you were his friend, he would defend you with his life. Because of his outspoken loyalty to banished friends, Longo had made plenty of enemies among Reiner's inner circle.

If this was not enough to keep Longo from being assigned to the King case, there was one further factor: He had been the deputy assigned to prosecute Leslie White. And the last thing Reiner wanted in this election year was any reminder of the Leslie White scandal.

The D.A.'s Office routinely used jailhouse informants, or "snitches," as witnesses to confessions made by other inmates awaiting trial. In exchange for special favors or reductions in their sentences, these snitches would testify to incriminating statements made to them in confidence by their cellmates. Defense attorneys had claimed for many years that the confessions were fabricated, but no one could ever prove it.

Then an inmate awaiting trial for purse snatching stunned the law enforcement community. White, who had been a jailhouse snitch for the D.A. repeatedly in the past, gave a simple demonstration from his jail cell of how he could fake the confession of an inmate he had never met. Using a phone available to the prisoners, he called law enforcement agencies and pretended to be a police officer seeking information about the inmate he was framing. Once he had the confidential information he needed to substantiate a "confession," he showed how to falsify records to indicate that he had once shared a cell with the inmate.

White then announced that he had committed perjury for the D.A.'s Office using this technique in at least twelve trials. The story was on the front page of the *Los Angeles Times* the next day. Shortly after this, White was featured on *60 Minutes*.

The D.A.'s Office immediately began reviewing over two hundred cases in which jailhouse informants had testified during the 1980s. At the same time, new policies were formulated concerning the use of snitches: A jailhouse confession could be used only if there was independent corroboration, and a central index of snitches and their reliability was created.

Meanwhile, White was awaiting trial on the purse-snatching charge. He was kept in Sirhan Sirhan's old high-security cell for his own protection; his sudden notoriety as a snitch had made him a target throughout the jail system. But White's lawyer was claiming that his client was being persecuted because he had embarrassed the district attorney. The front office had to find a deputy who was tough enough to deal with the inevitable media criticism and who was absolutely "clean." Ideally, it would be someone who had never used an informant, someone who did not even *believe* in using them. The choice was obvious: Larry Longo.

White's attorney immediately tried to have Longo removed from the case because of his association with deputies who did use informants. The trial judge refused. The attorney then tried to plea-bargain with the prosecutor. Longo refused. White finally pled guilty as charged and got the maximum sentence of six years in prison.

But the political damage had been done.

No, Longo thought, he would not be the deputy named to prosecute the King case. Reiner did not need the media being reminded daily of the "snitch scandal."

The elevator doors opened, then closed behind the two men as they walked down the crowded corridor in silence. Along the drab walls on both sides was the usual crowd of defendants, witnesses, and attorneys waiting out the slow grind of justice.

"Hey, whaddya want?" a puffy-eyed lawyer in an electric blue polyester suit was telling his client. "Time off for good behavior, you're out in three. But you go to trial..." He shrugged ominously.

"Sheeyit..." the client said. "You go tell that motherfuckin' D.A. I want a county lid."

"County lid?" The lawyer shook his head in amazement. "One year in jail for armed robbery? Hey, whaddya think, I'm Houdini?"

"Tell him, man."

Longo and Dohi walked farther on down the hallway. An old Hispanic woman was lying on the heavily waxed linoleum floor, asleep. Next to her, sitting on a wooden bench, were two black women, both staring vacantly into space. Across the hallway were three teenage boys in the uniform of the east L.A. gangs—"all cholo'd out," as the cops would say—white undershirts, oversized long-sleeved shirts buttoned only at the neck, and baggy black or tan cotton slacks worn high on the waist.

Farther down the hallway was a small group of young blacks, members of another gang. The blue items of baggy clothing, including bandannas, identified them as belonging to one of the dozens of Crips gangs franchised throughout the city. The boys glared menacingly at Longo and Dohi as they passed, daring them to lock eyes; the practice was known on the streets as "eye fucking."

The King case, Longo thought to himself. It was already beginning.

The two men ignored the gangbangers and continued down the corridor. Longo stopped outside of the men's room.

"Gimme a minute, Greg."

"Sure."

Longo opened the door, stepped inside. He walked over to two porcelain basins, one of them stopped up with paper towels and filled with water. Above them were two mirrors mounted on walls scrawled with gang graffiti.

He studied himself for a moment in one of the mirrors. He tightened the knot in his bright crimson tie and readjusted the matching silk scarf in his breast pocket. He tugged down on the lapels of the dark gray Italian double-breasted suit, smoothed them out, then took a step back. He studied his reflection for a moment, then turned sideways and noted the hang of the coat over his barrellike body.

The self-inspection was a ritual Longo always went through before trial. Like the athlete who carefully inspects his equipment before a game, or the soldier his rifle before a battle, Longo always checked his clothes before starting a new day in trial. Clothing, he believed, was a tool—a means for projecting an image of power, respect, success. In fact, he had sent many of his junior deputies in the past to see Umberto, his Italian tailor in Long Beach, to be fitted out for courtroom combat. "Dress well and look successful," he would tell his young charges, "and jurors will respect you."

The prosecutor had learned long ago that a trial was not a search for truth or justice. These were what a good deputy D.A. fought for. But a trial was ill suited to ferret out either; the archaic rules of evidence and procedure guaranteed that no juror would ever get a true picture of the facts in a case. A trial was simply a battleground, a place where two hired guns fought it out. Like any shoot-out, victory was not to the righteous but to the side that could hire the fastest gun. And having a faster gun meant the ability to persuade twelve people sitting in a box.

How did you convince twelve jurors that your cause was just?

To begin with, you had to capture and hold their attention. This meant that you had to entertain them. For a trial, Longo had come to realize, was nothing more than a staged show. The daily drama unfolded in a stagelike courtroom, complete with props such as podiums, witness stands, and exhibits. There was a script from which well-rehearsed witnesses could "testify" in reply to well-rehearsed questions. And there were clearly defined roles for the actors to play. One role was that of prosecutor, and Longo believed that a good suit was the costume essential for playing this role.

Satisfied, Longo stepped back into the corridor. He grinned at Dohi, then turned and walked the last fifty feet to the large double doors of the courtroom. The sign next to the doors read DEPARTMENT 127, HON. JAMES BASCUE. Dohi opened the door and the two men walked through.

Neither was prepared for what they encountered inside.

The courtroom was packed. Spectators were standing in the aisle and along the walls. And almost every one of the faces in the crowd was Japanese.

These spectators were not there for the Thomas trial.

Longo and Dohi squeezed their way through the mob, down the aisle and toward the swinging doors. The prosecutor recognized two reporters seated in the front row, one from the *Los Angeles Times,* the other from the local Japanese-American newspaper.

Longo nodded toward the bailiff. "Morning, Tom," he said as if nothing were unusual.

"Hi, Larry," the man replied amiably.

"Morning, Angie." Longo nodded toward the court clerk, a short, heavyset Latina looking harried at her desk next to the judge's bench. A telephone receiver was wedged between her ear and shoulder.

"Good morning, Larry," she called out, not looking up from a tall stack of files.

Longo and Dohi walked over to the prosecution table. One of his deputies, Craig Veals, was already seated at the table, ready to handle the calendar call with Longo. Veals looked at his boss, then back at the crowd.

"It's going to be an interesting morning," he said.

Longo shrugged with a nonchalant air as he went about unpacking the three cardboard boxes. But he knew why the mob was there. And he knew who was responsible.

For confirmation, he casually glanced behind him at the row of chairs reserved for defense counsel just inside the railing. Four of the chairs were occupied by attorneys, their leather briefcases resting neatly in their laps. But Yamaki was not among them.

Waiting to make the dramatic entrance, Longo thought to himself.

He checked his watch. Ten minutes late. Judge Bascue would be taking the bench any moment now that the senior prosecutor was here. Before the Thomas trial could reconvene they would have to dispose of a dozen criminal cases that had been set for arraignments, motions, probation violations, sentencing, and plea bargaining. If any case could not be resolved by the time the jury returned, the judge would have to continue it to another date.

Longo began arranging the contents of his boxes across the table . . . the canceled checks, already marked as exhibits . . . the statements from Thomas's Merrill Lynch client trust account . . . the "dailies" from yesterday's session of trial—transcripts of testimony typed up by the court reporter each night in important cases.

He was interrupted by a hand on his shoulder. He turned. A tall, muscular man in a powder blue blazer stood behind him, a police report in his hand. He was about thirty, had short blond hair, a thick blond mustache, and a broad smile.

"You the D.A.?" the man asked.

"Yeah."

"Craig T. Hannon,* LAPD narcotics. Checking in on the Castaneda case."

Longo turned to Veals. "Hannon's here on Castaneda."

"Castaneda," Veals repeated, searching through a stack of case files. He pulled one out. "Right . . . possession of coke, set down for a 1538." The term "1538" referred to a statute authorizing suppression of evidence: The defense attorney had demanded a hearing to suppress the cocaine on grounds that there was no probable cause to search his client. Veals found the officer's name on a list of witnesses, checked it off.

Longo grabbed the file, glanced at the fact sheet on the inside. "Any problems?" he asked the officer.

"Naw. Garden-variety. I see this low rider toolin' down Whittier in his piece-of-shit Chevy, one taillight out. Pull him over. Ask him for his registration, I see the coke layin' on the back seat, y'know? Plain view. I bust him, he cops out. Like I said, garden-variety."

"Guy says you searched his car," Longo said, looking up from the file. "Found the stuff in the glove compartment."

The officer winked at Longo. "Plain view," he said with a grin.

The prosecutor nodded slowly.

"Hey, it's the scumbag's word against mine, right? Who's gonna believe him? Got a rap sheet longer'n your arm."

"Yeah."

"Look, any chance for priority?" the cop asked. "Been up all night on a stakeout. Draggin' ass, y'know?"

"We'll see what we can do," Longo said.

"Appreciate it." He turned and walked back through the swinging gate.

Longo studied the officer as he found a space in the front row of the audience and sat down. Then the prosecutor returned to his box of documents and notes from the Thomas file. He unpacked the letters from Thomas to Weston, already marked as exhibits . . . a copy of the California Evidence Code . . . the scribbled notes for his direct examination of the next witness . . .

But Longo's mind was back in his office, back to Mike Yamaki sitting across the desk from him. The prosecutor did not usually let defense attorneys visit him in his office. He did not want them to see any confidential reports or memos that might be lying around, or to overhear any conversations in the hallways. And he wanted to avoid any later claims of misrepresentation or even bribery; limiting contact with defense lawyers to the courtroom was the safest course. But the most important reason for barring attorneys from his office was that Longo did not want his opponents to see his "inner sanctum," to see how he lived, how he operated—to get a feel for who he *was*.

Know thy enemy—and don't let him know you.

But there Yamaki had been, standing in the doorway. There was an armed guard at the entrance to the D.A.'s Office near the elevators. And the back door had a combination lock. How had he gotten in? Yamaki knew a lot of people, had a lot of influence, and that influence probably reached fairly high up in the office.

Longo had asked Greg Dohi to step outside for a few minutes. When the young intern was gone and the door closed, the two men had talked.

Know thy enemy . . .

Longo knew that Yamaki had been born and raised in the Japanese neighborhood in the southern part of the city. He had been in constant trouble as a boy, a gang member who was in and out of juvenile hall for everything from smoking marijuana to shaking down kids at school. After tests at Dorsey High School had shown him to be gifted, Yamaki was placed in special advanced classes. But the tough young gang leader was more interested in turf wars and stealing cars; his grades and attendance continued to be barely acceptable, and his probation officer continued to throw him back into juvenile hall on a regular basis.

Soon after graduating, Yamaki was arrested and sent to an adult jail. When his long-suffering mother came to visit, he saw for the first time the shame in her eyes. And it suddenly dawned on him that none of his gang had come to see him. He began to question the values he had held for so long, began to look at his life in a different light.

Yamaki enrolled at the local junior college. With top grades, he transferred to UCLA and, after graduation, was accepted at the University of California's law school. And promptly withdrew after the first year.

Frustrated, Yamaki enrolled in a small, locally accredited night law school in west Los Angeles. He financed his legal education by dealing blackjack in Las Vegas. When he finished his shift, he would hop on the casino's shuttle plane carrying busted gamblers back to L.A., arriving in time to attend the evening classes; when classes were over, he would catch the shuttle carrying fresh gamblers back to Vegas.

After four hard years, he got his law degree and passed the bar exam. And quickly built a reputation as a gifted trial lawyer and a politically astute leader of the Asian community. He had allied himself with the powerful mayor of Los Angeles, Tom Bradley; in return, he had been appointed to the Police Commission, a valuable position for a criminal lawyer. And he had married well: His wife was Tritia Toyota, the beautiful anchorwoman on Los Angeles's top-ranked network news show.

Yamaki was a smooth customer, Longo realized. Smooth and

clever. The man had a friendly, ingratiating way about him, an ability to manipulate, to wield power without offending. Somewhere along the line Yamaki had managed to shed the vestiges of his gangbanger past, had rounded the rough edges and developed the ways of a statesman. Yet, Longo knew that just beneath the surface lay a tough kid from the streets. Yamaki was smoother, more clever, but beneath it all there was still an infinitely more deadly street fighter.

Like a cobra, Longo had thought on more than one occasion.

The prosecutor tried to push Yamaki from his mind. He was in the middle of a knockdown, drag-out trial, he reminded himself; Yamaki's client was just another case, one of many routine arraignments on today's calendar. The Thomas trial would resume in an hour and a half. He had five witnesses lined up to testify, and had not even had time to interview them; he was stuck with "cold" testimony, always a dangerous thing. If he did not start concentrating on the trial, McKinney would have him for lunch. Concentrate, he told himself. Focus . . .

"Craig," Longo finally said to his deputy, "gimme the Yamaguchi file."

Veals scanned the row of legal-size manila files he had neatly lined up, pulled out a thick one, and handed it to the senior prosecutor.

Longo looked at it. On the cover was entered the procedural history of the case: Kazuhiko Yamaguchi . . . Municipal Court arraignment in Division 20, bail set at $500,000 . . . Preliminary hearing, Division 38, defendant held to answer for trial; Deputy D.A. Leonard Torrealba for the People, attorney Michael Yamaki for the defendant . . . Superior Court arraignment set for . . . today.

Longo opened the file. Attached inside and to the right were pleadings, motions, and court documents. On the top was the "information," a formal complaint charging the defendant with a felony; the purpose of today's proceeding was to formally serve him with a copy of the document, to enter his plea, and to set a date for trial. The information charged Yamaguchi with one count of violation of Penal Code section 187—murder. Date of incident, March 29, 1991. The victim was listed as Genji Kariya.

"All rise!"

Longo looked up from the report as the bailiff called out. The loud buzz of conversation in the courtroom subsided to a low din, then to a hush.

"Department 127 of the Superior Court of California, in and for the county of Los Angeles, is now in session, Honorable James Bascue, judge presiding."

Judge Bascue stepped quickly out into the courtroom, almost vaulted the three steps to the bench and sat down. A stack of files waited.

"Be seated," Tom, the bailiff, said loudly, continuing his litany. "Find a seat, or wait outside the courtroom. There will be no talking or reading while court is in session."

"Gentlemen," the judge nodded to the waiting lawyers. "Mr. Longo," he added, ominously, to the prosecutor. Judge Bascue was a stickler for punctuality and Longo had arrived ten minutes late; without a prosecutor, the judge could not proceed with any cases.

"Judge," Longo replied casually.

"Gentlemen," Judge Bascue repeated to the seated lawyers, "we have fourteen cases on calendar for this morning. And I will tell you right now that we are in trial, and that trial has precedence. The jury has been ordered back for ten o'clock." He looked up at the clock on the wall behind the audience. "It is now eight forty-one." He glared again at Longo, then looked back at the lawyers. "We will conclude the day's calendar at nine-fifty. Any cases not resolved by then will be continued to another date."

Longo's attention was focused on the Yamaguchi file. He looked at the documents attached to the left side of the folder, a series of police reports. He quickly scanned the first one.

Montebello Police Department . . . Officer M. D. Holden, serial no. 1232 . . . Shooting occurred between hours of 1:00 and 1:30 A.M. on March 29, 1991, outside of suspect's home, 836 N. Vail, Montebello . . . When officer arrived, observed suspect's wife, Mitsuru Yamaguchi, seated in passenger's seat of 1984 Nissan Maxima in front of above address . . . Victim Kariya was in driver's seat, slumped toward the right front passenger's seat, with head in suspect's wife's arms . . . Possible gunshot wound to head . . .

Longo flipped to the next page. His eye had become expert at cutting through the officious fluff and cop lingo of police reports and ferreting out the 10 percent that told what actually happened.

"People versus Jesus Miguel Castaneda," the judge called.

"In custody, your honor," Tom said.

"Bring him out," the judge said. "Tyrone Moore, too."

An older attorney rose slowly from one of the chairs as Tom unlocked a heavy metal door and stepped out of the courtroom and into the holding cell area.

"May it please the court, your honor," the lawyer said in a deep, rich baritone, "Edward Teacher* representing the defendant in this case, Mr. Jesus Miguel Castaneda.*" There was an almost British accent in the voice, but the Spanish pronunciation was perfect.

Longo recognized the voice and looked back.

The strong voice, articulate speech, and dignified bearing clashed violently with Teacher's appearance. His face was red, heavily veined from years of abusing alcohol, and his eyes were bloodshot with puffy bags sagging underneath. He was wearing a baggy green suit, badly wrinkled, and a white shirt frayed and browned at the collar. A thin red-and-black regimental tie with a large stain near the top clashed with the green suit.

At one time, Edward Teacher had been a prominent criminal lawyer, an eloquent advocate who had tried some of the biggest murder cases ever to hit the headlines. At one time, he had been one of the best trial lawyers in the city, had been able to perform magic with juries. But that was before it all fell apart. Before the drinking. And the cocaine.

Teacher now lived a dreary and humiliating existence taking handouts from the courts. Along with a dozen or so other broken-down "cop-out artists," he wandered the hallways of the Criminal Courts Building, asking the judges and clerks if they had any cases needing an appointed attorney. If the public defender was unable to represent a defendant for whatever reason, the judge appointed a private lawyer; there was usually an unspoken understanding that the lawyer would plead his client, rather than tie up the court with a time-consuming trial. In exchange for "copping" the client, the lawyer was paid a small amount by the state.

As always, Longo felt a sadness whenever he saw the man in court. And a faint specter of fear.

Longo returned to the Yamaguchi file.

The metal door opened and the bailiff came out with two men handcuffed together, each wearing an orange jumpsuit and floppy tennis shoes without strings. He sat them down at the end of the defense table, then pushed each of them as far as he could into the table. This made any sudden aggressive moves by either inmate more difficult.

"Your honor," Teacher said with an almost comically regal bearing, "may it please the court, the matter is here for a 1538.5 motion. My client is prepared to waive his rights under the Fifth Amendment to the United States Constitution and testify as to the circumstances of the vehicular search. The defense will—"

This was the case Hannon was on, Longo thought. The cop who was lying about the car search.

The prosecutor stood up. "The People are unable to proceed, judge."

"What?" Bascue said, perplexed.

"Unable to proceed," Longo repeated to the judge. He glanced back at the officer in the first row. "Witness problems."

Veals glanced at his boss. "Larry," he whispered, "our witness just checked in. Hannon. He's—"

"Are you asking for a continuance to locate your witness, Mr. Longo?" Bascue said.

"No."

Bascue considered this for a moment, then shrugged. "Very well," he said, shaking his head. "There being no opposition from the People, the defendant's motion is hereby granted. The evidence is ordered suppressed." He looked at the prosecutor. "Are you able to proceed without the evidence?"

"No," Longo said.

"Right," Bascue said. "Case dismissed."

The prosecutor looked back again as the officer stood and started to leave. He turned and glared angrily at Longo. Then he walked out.

Veals looked at Longo again, searching for some hint of what had just happened.

Longo winked at him, then sat down. He was not going to let the officer take the stand at a suppression hearing and lie about his search of the car.

Longo returned to the Yamaguchi file, fanning through more documents. He stopped at a California Highway Patrol report from an Officer P. G. Gruidl, serial no. 11965.

> On 03-29-91 at approx. 0117 hours I was obtaining a breath sample from an in-custody when I heard someone knocking on the front lobby door...Subject Yamaguchi stated, "Help me, please help me," and he held his arms out in front of him....He stated, "I just shot my best friend." He then reached into his coat right pocket and withdrew a blue steel model 60 revolver and placed it on the ground in front of me....He began to cry and stated, "I found my friend with my wife"...

Nothing unusual there, Longo thought to himself. A classic love triangle. Dime a dozen.

The loud clanging of the holding cell door jarred him, and he looked up from the report.

A young woman stepped out from the holding cell and into the courtroom. She was in her early thirties, plain-looking, and wearing an old cotton print dress and dull brown walking shoes that announced her indifference to appearance. She clutched a stack of half a dozen case files to her chest. The slump of her posture and the tired, cynical look in her eyes were clear signs of the criminal lawyer's occupational disease: burnout.

"Miss Thompson," Judge Bascue was saying, "are you ready on the Moore matter?"

"Yes, your honor," she said with a hint of irritation. She walked over to the defense table, dropped the stack of files loudly next to one of the handcuffed men, then looked combatively toward Craig Veals.

Karen Thompson was one of two deputy public defenders assigned to Department 127. At one time she had been, like so many others, an idealistic young lawyer ready to defend the oppressed and fight for justice. This enthusiasm had first been kindled while working for Larry Flint, the publisher of *Hustler* magazine, in his legal wars against evangelists Jimmy Swaggart and Jerry Falwell. Fascinated with the constitutional issues involved and eager to wage war in court against those who would deny them, Thompson found the transition to defending indigents an easy and natural one. And so she had fought, and fought hard, and long. But it had taken its toll.

Thompson was well on her way to becoming a bitter, disillusioned casualty of the system. She was losing that ability to divorce her personal feelings from the facts, and to know what a given case was worth. Like a punch-drunk fighter, she lashed out at everything, suspected every judge and prosecutor of conspiring against her, saw every case as yet another all-out war that must be won at any cost.

"Mr. Moore demands a jury trial," Thompson announced tersely, "and refuses to waive any time."

Judge Bascue looked at Veals. "Any way of working things out, Mr. Veals?"

"I don't believe there's any chance of a disposition, your honor," the deputy D.A. said. "We've offered Miss Thompson a plea to count one, kidnap, drop the remaining counts, but . . ." He shrugged.

The judge nodded, looked at Longo. "Mr. Longo . . ."

"Yeah, judge?" Longo said, looking up from the file.

"If you can find the time, would you and Miss Thompson care to approach the bench?"

The prosecutor stood and walked around the counsel table, joining the public defender in front of the judge's bench.

"What's the problem?" Judge Bascue said in a hushed voice. "We don't have time for this. I want this case dispo'd."

Thompson shrugged. "My client wants a trial, your honor," she said just above a whisper.

Bascue turned to the prosecutor. "Larry?"

"Gimme a second, judge," Longo said loudly, causing Bascue to grit his teeth. Bench conferences were not supposed to be overheard by the public, particularly not when they involved the undignified realities of plea bargaining.

The prosecutor continued scanning the notes in the file to refresh his memory. Thompson's client was charged with kidnapping and multiple counts of assault with a deadly weapon. Tyrone Moore was a member of the Rolling 60s, a Crips gang in south central Los Angeles, and a major crack dealer. He caught one of his street pushers holding back money and had him picked up and chained him to a bed in his crack house. There, Moore and other members of the gang beat him with clubs for two days, tore out chunks of flesh with a pair of pliers, and finally fed him to two pit bulls kept in the yard to discourage nosy narcs.

Amazingly, the man had lived—and fled to the police for protection. But how much longer he would live was another matter: The word on the street was that the Crips had a contract out on him.

Now Moore was instructing his public defender to demand an early trial. The usual strategy of the defense was to stall, hoping that witnesses would forget or tire of coming to court over and over. But this case was a fresh one. Moore obviously knew something.

Longo could guess what he knew, for the witness had recently disappeared; it was a safe bet he was now dead. But he also knew something that the crack dealer did not know. Longo, realizing that his witness might not live long enough to testify at trial, had weeks earlier ordered one of his deputies, Larry Boyle, to rush the case to preliminary hearing; under police escort, the man had testified in front of Moore and other gang members at the hearing. And Moore had been held to answer for trial.

Now Moore was confident that the D.A., unable to produce their only witness for a jury, would have to dismiss the case. What he did not know was that if the witness died, the transcript of the preliminary hearing was admissible: The man's earlier testimony could be read to the jury. Moore's victim would convict him from the grave.

"He's a bad actor, judge," Longo said. "Heavy dealer . . . rap sheet a couple feet long . . . kidnapped the victim, tortured him." He looked up. "I figure one count of kidnap is pretty damned generous."

"C'mon, Larry," Thompson snorted. "Kidnap with injury, and priors, he'll be getting Medicare before he gets out."

"Shoulda thought of that before he started confusing the victim with dog food."

A sudden murmur arose from the back of the crowded courtroom. Longo looked back. Mike Yamaki had just entered and was walking confidently down the aisle, his leather briefcase at his side. He smiled and waved to various members of the audience. Many in the crowd were nodding excitedly to each other and pointing at the handsome lawyer.

"Good morning, Mr. Yamaki," Judge Bascue said loudly.

"Good morning, your honor," Yamaki said with a broad smile as he walked through the swinging gate. He found a seat inside the railing and sat down. Then, casually, he looked at Longo, nodded. The prosecutor nodded back.

Once again Longo found himself wondering what Yamaki was up to. The lawyer had come to him in his office, offering a plea bargain on the Yamaguchi case. The defendant was a wealthy businessman in the Little Tokyo area of central Los Angeles and, like Yamaki, a leader of the Japanese-American community. No criminal record. He was charged with murder. And Yamaki wanted to plead him guilty to voluntary manslaughter.

The defense lawyer had said it was a typical triangle situation: Husband kills wife's lover. And the police reports seemed to verify that. A classic "heat of passion" killing. Garden-variety. In those cases the D.A.'s Office almost always accepted a plea to voluntary manslaughter. It seemed a fair plea bargain, even an obvious one. Yet...

Something wasn't right. It was that sixth sense again, that nagging feeling that the pieces did not fit. Why was Yamaki so anxious to plead his client to voluntary manslaughter? What was the hurry?

Longo knew that Mike Yamaki had not earned his reputation by pleading important clients to deals that any rookie public defender could get. This Yamaguchi was a big wheel in the community; Yamaki's reputation could be riding on the case. Something was wrong. Or *was* it? Was he just getting paranoid in his old age? he wondered.

"Like I said," Thompson continued, "Mr. Moore wants a trial." She looked at Longo. "Are the People ready?"

Longo was still lost in thought.

"Larry!" the judge hissed.

"Huh?"

"Miss Thompson wants to know if you're ready for trial."

Longo looked at the public defender, the facts of the case coming back to him. Tyrone Moore. Pit bulls. Dead witness... She *knows,* he suddenly realized. Thompson's client had told her the victim was dead. But she also must know that the preliminary hearing testimony was admissible. Yes, but she figured that a cold reading of the transcript wasn't quite the same thing as a live, bleeding witness. And she was right. But, if he could get in evidence of the witness's disappearance, and maybe something about the circumstances, then that "cold" reading could become pretty dramatic. The voice from the grave . . .

"Yeah, Karen, we're ready."

Thompson studied him in silence.

"Look!" Bascue whispered loudly. "The calendar's stacked up for the next month. I want this case dispo'd, you understand?"

"He's got a right to a trial, your honor," Thompson said, her eyes still locked on Longo.

"No deals," Longo said. "He pleads straight up."

Bascue snorted loudly, thought for a moment. "Very well," he said in a normal voice, looking at a calendar on the wall behind his clerk, "this case is set for jury trial on August twelfth." Then he shuffled through the stack of files in front of him until he found the one he was looking for. "People versus Kazuhiko Yamaguchi," he announced.

Yamaki stood up as Longo and Thompson walked back to their tables.

"Custody, your honor," the bailiff said.

"Bring him out."

Tom moved the two handcuffed men from their chairs, opened the metal door, and walked them back into the holding cells.

"For the record, your honor," Yamaki said, looking at the court reporter, "Michael Yamaki appearing on behalf of the defendant, Kazuhiko Yamaguchi."

Veals glanced at Longo.

Longo nodded at his deputy to proceed with the case, then wrote a single word on a legal pad lying on the table: "Discovery."

"Your honor," Veals said, "Craig Veals for the People. This is an arraignment, one count of 187."

Longo shoved the pad toward Veals. The deputy read it, nodded to his boss as he continued. "Will counsel waive a formal reading of the complaint and a statement of rights?"

"So waived," Yamaki said congenially.

Longo turned halfway around in his seat as his deputy continued with the formalities. As casually as he could, he looked out over the audience and began to scan the sea of Japanese faces that looked out at him. Most of them were women, in their fifties or older. Their small size, from a childhood diet of very little protein, told him they were from the old country. And, undoubtedly, Yamaki had organized this little show for Judge Bascue's benefit—a not-so-subtle demonstration of his client's position in the politically influential Japanese-American community.

But Longo was looking for one particular face. He did not know what the face would look like, but he had a feeling that he would recognize the woman if he saw her. He wondered if she would show up for the arraignment.

The metal door again clanged loudly. Every eye in the courtroom swung toward the holding cell.

A powerfully built Japanese man stepped out through the door, his wrists handcuffed in front of him, his head bowed deeply so that only his gray-black hair sweeping straight back was visible. He walked slowly into the courtroom, almost shuffling, his face still hidden from view. The floppy tennis shoes and the bright orange jumpsuit with "L.A. County Jail" stenciled across it seemed vaguely ludicrous on the man.

Suddenly he stopped, turned toward the audience and, for just a moment, glanced up. Piercing black eyes stared out from above the massive cheekbones of a face reflecting both power and dignity, eyes that seemed to be searching for something, someone. Then, quickly, he brought his feet together, pressed his cuffed hands straight down his thighs, and bowed very slowly and deeply to the crowd. He held the pose for a few long seconds.

Many in the audience returned the long bow.

The bailiff stepped toward the man and, grabbing his shoulder, gently nudged him toward the defense table. The man straightened up but kept his chin pressed down to his chest, eyes to the ground. He shuffled to the table and sat in the chair at the end, his head still bowed.

Yamaki pulled out a second chair. He set his burgundy leather briefcase on the table, opened it, then sat down.

A slightly built, middle-aged Japanese man wearing thick eyeglasses stepped forward from the front row of the audience. He bowed quickly toward the judge, then took a third seat at the table, slightly to the side and behind the man in the orange jumpsuit.

Judge Bascue studied the bowed figure, then turned to a file in front of him. "This is the time and place for the arraignment of Kazuhiko Yamaguchi." He turned again toward the seated figure. "Sir, is that your true and correct name?"

The man with the thick eyeglasses began speaking to the bowed figure, translating the judge's comments into Japanese.

There was a sharp nod from the bowed head.

"It is, your honor," the interpreter said.

Yamaki rose to his feet, looked across at Veals, then at Longo, and smiled. "Your honor," he said, "Mr. Yamaguchi requests that a plea of not guilty be entered."

"So entered," Bascue said. "Do we have a date for pretrial conference, gentlemen?"

Longo sat in silence next to Veals, casually studying his own fingernails.

"Your honor," Yamaki said, "I have reason to believe that we may be able to reach a disposition in this matter. May we put it over for, say, a month, to give us time to work something out?"

"Very well. I'll set it for pretrial hearing on . . ."

Longo coughed slightly.

"Ah, your honor," Veals said, "it's true there may be a plea bargain in this matter. In the meantime, however . . ."

Yamaki looked across at Veals, then at Longo.

". . . in the meantime, the People would demand full discovery in this case."

Veals was insisting that Yamaki turn over all documents, written statements, and physical evidence to the district attorney, as the D.A. was required to do for the defense.

"Well, your honor," Yamaki said, "I don't really think that's necessary. It's unlikely this case will go to trial."

"They have the right," Judge Bascue said. "I will order full discovery"—he looked down at Longo—"for *both* sides. Mr. Veals, you will turn over all discoverable material to Mr. Yamaki. Compliance to be shown at the pretrial hearing . . ."

Longo was no longer listening to the proceedings. He had grabbed a legal pad and was studiously reading his notes from the previous day of trial. He tried to concentrate on the words, tried to prepare himself mentally for the trial that would resume in an hour. He had a witness on the stand, a witness . . . Had he finished direct exam when court had adjourned yesterday? ... Yes, he remembered now, he had finished direct. But there were a couple of extra questions he had before McKinney took over, a couple of extra questions.... What were they again? Something about a phone call from Sherif Ali ...

But it was no use. They kept coming back to him, back from somewhere deep inside. The images that would not go away.... The body slumped on the floor, the still, silent body in the blood-soaked police uniform.... And then the second officer, lying on his back in the alley, dark scarlet liquid gurgling out through the jagged hole in his neck, fighting for air, drowning in his own blood....

And, looming over it all, the face of Yamaki's client, Hac Qui. Laughing at him.

Chapter 5

A blaring horn shattered Longo's thoughts.

He looked in the rearview mirror, saw the silver Porsche in the darkness behind him, then looked ahead and noticed that the traffic light had changed. He waved back at the driver and, with a loud clashing of gears, eased the rusty old Toyota van forward as the traffic surged past him along the moonlit coastline of Malibu. He glanced at the sleek and shiny BMWs, Mercedeses, and Jaguars as they raced by, elbowing and clawing their way along Pacific Coast Highway, rushing their suntanned owners from L.A.'s film lots and recording studios north to the exclusive beaches of "the colony."

A wave of fatigue suddenly swept over Longo. It had been another long, grueling day of combat. The kind of day that ground away at you and finally forced you to confront the hard truth that every prosecutor came to know: Trial was a young man's game.

As a star running back on the Loyola High School football team in central Los Angeles, Longo had practiced for hours every day knocking bigger men to the ground. During the scorching summers, he had worked at the backbreaking job of hauling crates in the grape fields of the San Joaquin Valley. But he had never found anything as physically exhausting as trying criminal cases. Trial work demanded mental agility and emotional toughness—but neither was possible without physical endurance.

There were, Longo believed, two basic secrets to success in trial.

The first was endurance. Trial went on day after day, week after week, with never a moment to rest or let down your guard. Longo knew that this required mental toughness and physical conditioning. Fatigue was deadly; a tired body meant a tired mind, and that meant slowed mental reflexes and critical errors in trial. Stamina would win over cleverness; the rabbit usually lost to the turtle.

And so, at age fifty-two, Longo squeezed in a workout every day at the downtown YMCA. During the lunch hour he would lift weights, ride the bicycle machines, work on the stair climbers, develop strength on the Nautilus equipment. Afterward, he allowed himself the reward of a soothing steam bath.

His second secret to winning was a simple one: It was absolutely necessary that you believe in your cause. If you did not believe in the depths of your heart that the defendant was guilty as hell, then you would lose. "If I can get a jury to understand that *I* believe in the case," Longo was fond of saying, "then *they* will." Jurors were not always terribly bright, but Longo knew they were very good at detecting whether a lawyer was sincere. "The problem with D.A.s today is they don't believe," he would lecture his junior deputies. "They only want to win."

Endure and believe.

Today, however, Longo had missed his workout. In fact, he had missed it all week long. The Thomas trial kept him from going to the Y during the noon recess; he needed that time to prepare for the afternoon session. And there was no time at the end of the day; as usual, he had stopped on the way home to spend time with his invalid mother.

Audrey Longo was seventy-nine years old. She had been a beautiful woman in her time, a Texan who traced her Irish and Scottish heritage back to the *Mayflower*. One of a family of six, she had left Texas as soon as she had been old enough for the bright lights of Hollywood. Following a script that had been acted out by many before her, she became a promising young starlet and had what appeared to be a bright future—when she met a young man.

Frank Joseph Longo was one of eleven children born to parents who had immigrated to Los Angeles from Calabria, Italy. He grew up in central Los Angeles—only a few blocks from the Criminal Courts Building. He dropped out of school in the fourth grade to go to work and labored at odd jobs throughout his childhood. At one point his talent in fistfights launched a career as a prizefighter, a career that was cut short after he was badly beaten in the ring. Finally he went to work for the Bank of Italy, later to become the Bank of America, and quickly rose in the ranks. He soon attracted the attention of the bank's founder, A. P. Giannini. With Giannini's guidance, Frank Longo began investing his money in business ventures and quickly discovered he had a golden touch. By the time he was fifty, he had extensive real estate holdings and owned a number of restaurants and other businesses—including an interest in the Stardust Casino in Las Vegas.

Longo's father died at the age of eighty-seven. He left Larry's mother financially well off, in a large home in the "old money" neighborhood of Hancock Park. Larry constantly worried about her being alone in the huge house, but the tough old woman refused to move into his home and would not let him hire "some stranger" to care for her. And so he had made it a habit to stop off on the drive home every day to see his mother. In fact, he had twice turned down offers of a transfer to the D.A.'s Santa Monica office; although the drive home from the Criminal Courts Building in central Los Angeles was far longer, it took him by Hancock Park.

Longo eased the Toyota van to a stop behind a long line of cars at a red light. To his left, the Malibu pier was barely illuminated as it stuck out into the blackness of the Pacific. How many times had he seen that pier in movies? he wondered absently.

It was almost eight o'clock. A long day. And tomorrow, a full court calendar at eight-thirty. Then, at ten, McKinney would be waiting for him.

Again he felt the overwhelming fatigue.

He let out the clutch and lurched forward as traffic around him began to move again.

How much longer? Longo wondered. How many more years do I have?

As he had so often lately, he called forth the old, familiar faces. Warriors from the past, comrades in arms, tough old prosecutors who could drink all night and the next morning stumble into court, grab a case file sight unseen, and start picking a jury. But they were almost all gone now. Kicked upstairs. Turned into desk commandos.

Hired away by the downtown firms. Appointed to the bench. Retired. Dead of heart attacks, strokes, cirrhosis of the liver . . .

Who was left?

He drifted once again back to his early days, back to the last of the old-time, whiskey-drinking D.A.s, Joe Busch. Back to when the office was small, where everyone knew one another and you got together after work to trade war stories over a pitcher of beer. Back to when lawyers were professionals, and giving your word meant something, and there was honor in it all. To when you shot from the hip and common sense counted for something. Before it all changed, before the office turned into a collection of ambitious little bureaucrats, bright and clever young survivors of the best law schools. Each of them with the soul of a CPA, totally lacking in . . . what was the word he was looking for?

Passion.

He turned left off Pacific Coast Highway and onto Point Dume, a hilly peninsula that jutted out into the Pacific, separating the parade of seaside homes in Malibu to the south from the rugged green hills of Zuma Beach and Ventura County to the north. He drove by the gas station and the supermarket and turned left again, onto a street of older ranch-style homes. Corrals spread out from some of the homes, with well-groomed horses standing peacefully in the darkness.

There *was* something missing in the "new breed" of prosecutors, he thought. True, the younger deputies were smarter, harder-working, more aggressive than ever before. But they lacked an instinct, a feeling for people. A trial lawyer was an artist, but the new generation of prosecutors were . . . technicians.

No, not all of them, Longo realized. There were still young men like Greg Dohi—and women—who had the right kind of heart, who just needed a little guidance to achieve greatness in the courtroom.

If only there had been someone to point the way for *him* when he had first walked into a courtroom so many years ago, Longo thought. But there had been no one. It had been a stumbling parade of errors, one painful mistake after another.

Another face from the past drifted by, and with it a memory. Longo found himself escaping into the warm familiarity of the past.

The face belonged to cantankerous old Judge Leo Freund. And the memory, to one of the first preliminary hearings Longo had ever done.

Judge Freund was the gruff, foul-mouthed, and short-tempered old tyrant of the west L.A. Municipal Courts, a man who hated defendants, cops, defense lawyers, prosecutors, witnesses, victims, and people in general. Above all things, though, he hated young lawyers who made mistakes in his courtroom, particularly young prosecutors. Freund enjoyed nothing more than chewing on brand-new deputy D.A.s and humiliating them in public. Of course, supervisors in the D.A.'s Office were aware of this—and found it hugely funny to assign "virgins" to Freund's courtroom for their baptism of fire.

So it was that Longo found himself as a new deputy in Freund's court, all alone and responsible for putting on preliminary hearings. One of the first of these involved a wife who had walked into her bedroom one day and discovered her husband *in flagrante delicto*.

Longo quickly reviewed the file, then immediately called his first witness, the wife. The heavyset Hispanic woman took the stand and testified that she had come home earlier than usual one day. As she walked into the kitchen, she heard strange, animal-like shrieks coming from the bedroom. She walked down the hall and opened the door. There she found her husband lying naked on the bed. He was flat on his back, frantically holding on to a chicken which was flapping wildly and squawking at the top of its lungs, feathers flying everywhere. The chicken was firmly impaled on his penis.

The woman stared wide-eyed for a moment, then started screaming. The startled husband quickly yanked the chicken off. The poor animal fell off the bed and began flopping around on the floor, squawking and bleeding all over the carpet.

As the woman came to the end of her testimony, Longo's investigating officer came into the courtroom and handed him a large brown cloth bag. The bag was sealed with an L.A. Police Department evidence tag, and there was a terrible smell coming from it. The smell quickly permeated the hot, stuffy courtroom, the air-conditioning having once again failed in the midst of the latest heat wave.

"Your honor," Longo said to Judge Freund, "may the record reflect that I have a . . . bag, sealed with an LAPD evidence tag. May this be marked People's exhibit number one?"

"Get on with it, junior," Freund snarled. Then he sniffed, narrowed his eyes. "What the hell stinks in here?"

"Uh . . ." Longo looked uncertainly at the bag. "May the record reflect that I am now breaking the seal, and opening People's one . . ."

"What the hell is that smell?"

"Your honor . . ." Longo reached in and pulled out the dead chicken, held it up by the legs and as far away as possible. "It's the, uh, the evidence . . . the chicken . . . your honor."

"Jesus H. Christ," Freund roared. "You fucking idiot . . ."

The chicken had succumbed to internal hemorrhaging soon after the wife had run screaming out of the bedroom. The woman had gone to the police, insisted on pressing charges for bestiality, then returned with an officer to the scene of the crime. The husband was gone, but the chicken was found dead in the bedroom, its corpse surrounded by splattered blood and feathers. The officer dutifully collected the evidence and stored it in a refrigerator at the police station.

The investigating officer had retrieved the chicken and brought it to court three days earlier. Unfortunately, the preliminary hearing had been delayed, and the evidence sat in the trunk of the officer's squad car to bake in the Southern California heat.

"It's evidence, your honor," Longo repeated uncertainly. "She . . . the witness . . . she's gotta ID it."

"You idiot," Freund said between gritted teeth. "This better be the fastest prelim on record, got me? Or so help me God, you'll be eating alphabet soup back there with the other scum."

"Yessir." Longo walked past the seated defendant, a pathetic, skinny little man trying hard to melt into his chair, and held the chicken out to the stocky woman in the witness box. "Uh, ma'am, do you recognize People's exhibit number one?"

The woman recoiled slightly, turned her head away in disgust. "That's it, that's it."

"Objection, your honor," the deputy public defender said, rising to his feet. "This witness can't ID this chicken from any other." He paused. "Maybe we need a lineup."

"Shut up and sit down," Freund said.

The P.D. sat down, a slight smirk on his face.

"Your honor," Longo said, turning to Freund and holding the

rotting chicken up toward him, "may People's one be received into evidence?"

"*What!*" Freund yelled, a handkerchief now held over his nose. "You want that . . . that . . . that stinking piece of shit in my . . . in my . . ." His face was beginning to turn red.

"It's . . . *evidence,* your honor." Longo shrugged. "I mean, she ID'd it."

"You fucking idiot!"

"It's—"

"You fucking idiot!" Freund screamed, his face bright red behind the white handkerchief.

Longo grinned widely as he recalled the incident. It had been one of the first preliminary hearings he had ever done; it had certainly been the fastest. Old Judge Freund was long dead now, and, strangely, Longo missed the cranky old bastard; he had been one of a kind. But he often wondered what ever happened to the chicken. By law, exhibits received into evidence had to be kept in court files for a few years after the case was completed. He had heard a rumor once that they had kept the chicken in the morgue because of the refrigeration. Longo smiled again at the image of the scrawny little chicken laid out on a cold stainless-steel slab, one in a row of slabs with human stiffs awaiting autopsy.

Ahead of him the street dead-ended at a winding road running along a cliff overlooking the ocean. He turned left, then after a hundred yards turned left again and climbed up a steep driveway. An older two-story brick and wood house was set into the side of the hill, nestled in among trees and shrubs. To the right was a deep ravine, covered with thick brush and poison oak, and crawling with rattlesnakes. To the left, hidden behind the vegetation, was the home of his neighbor, the singer Bob Dylan.

Longo pulled the old van up to the garage, in between a 1985 Cadillac convertible and a 1984 Toyota Corolla. Three other cars stood in the driveway, including a 1978 Cadillac Fleetwood that he was restoring. And inside the garage was his pride: the 1962 Corvette Stingray. In all, Longo owned seven cars, none of them new. The motley collection was considered an eyesore by some of his Lexus-owning neighbors.

As Longo wearily stepped out of the van, he was greeted by a pack of five dogs loudly charging down the hill. Two were vicious-looking pit bulls; the other three were of unknown origin. Longo smiled as they reached him and began running around in circles and jumping up on him. He petted one of the dogs, then another, as they fought for his attention. There were a total of six dogs in the Longo household; a smaller dog and two cats stayed inside the house because of marauding coyotes in the ravine.

He tried to brush some of the dog hair off his suit as he walked toward the front door, the dogs happily following. He opened the door and stepped into chaos.

In the kitchen to his left, Frankie, Longo's twenty-two-year-old son, was in a shouting match with his fourteen-year-old daughter, Gina. Aelina, Longo's statuesque wife, was talking on a phone cradled on her shoulder while stirring something in a large pot on the stove; she was the ebullient and fiercely protective mother in every Italian movie. The television was blaring loudly from the family room next to the kitchen; standing in front of the television, slowly pumping a large black dumbbell and oblivious to the fight in the kitchen, was his nineteen-year-old son, Marco. The pounding drums of a rock band could be heard from somewhere in the house. Three of the dogs had come in through the door with Longo, and they instantly took off barking after the two cats.

Longo surveyed the typically riotous scene. "Hey!" he yelled out, "gimme a break!"

Marco looked up from the television. "Hey, Dad," he called out above the din.

Aelina looked toward him, smiled and waved, then returned to her phone conversation. She was still a fine figure of a woman, he thought. She had been a professional nightclub singer when he had first seen—and fallen heavily for—her.

"Daddy," Gina screamed, "Frankie's doing it again! He promised, and he's doing it again!"

Longo laughed, then walked into the kitchen and grabbed Aelina from behind, squeezing her and kissing her on the back of the neck. She swatted him away as Frankie and Gina resumed their argument.

Longo was proud of them all. Marco was a star football player and a serious bodybuilder, with plans to become a fitness trainer. Frankie, also a gifted athlete, was attending law school and planning to follow in his father's footsteps. And his beautiful daughter was, like her mother, a talented singer; at fourteen, Gina had already been signed by an agent.

Longo opened the refrigerator, grabbed a small bottle of sparkling water, and sat in a chair in the corner of the crowded kitchen. To the loud accompaniment of a TV sitcom and pounding rock music, he watched his family.

He felt supremely happy.

Longo lay in the dark, staring at the ceiling. He could hear Aelina's regular breathing next to him, feel the warmth from her body. In the distance, he heard the low, calming roar of the surf.

As he did every night when he was in trial, he replayed the events of the day. He had scored big against McKinney, he thought. He had caught the lawyer unprepared, hurt him badly with Tarnitzer's surprise testimony. The witness described for the jury how Thomas and Sherif Ali had arranged a $30 million business loan for him from shadowy sources in Iran—a loan that suddenly disappeared along with his $250,000 "front money." McKinney had been prepared for this; Judge Bascue had ruled that the similarities in the use of trust accounts made it admissible "M.O." evidence, and McKinney was ready to make it look like a simple civil dispute. But he had not been prepared for "the bomb."

Just before taking the stand, Tarnitzer told Longo that he had received a long-distance phone call from Switzerland at 8:30 the previous evening. The caller was Sherif Ali. In carefully veiled language, Ali offered to return the $250,000—if Tarnitzer would agree not to testify against Thomas. Tarnitzer said he would think it over.

The witness's account of the attempted bribe just hours before his testimony was devastating.

One for the good guys, Longo thought in the quiet darkness. A lucky break. But he knew the trial was not over. McKinney still had plenty of bullets of his own. Longo had to be careful. Most of all, he had to stay focused. He could not afford to let another case interfere with his concentration, or McKinney would cut him off at the knees.

Yet, two or three times that day his mind had drifted. . . .

Longo had sent a D.A.'s investigator out to look into the Ya-maguchi case. The investigator, Jimmy Sakoda, spoke Japanese and was familiar with Little Tokyo, or J-Town as it was known to the cops. He had done a little digging and had reported back. No one in J-Town was talking to authorities about the killing. But Sakoda had heard one interesting rumor. The murder, according to the rumor, was tied to the Yakuza—the secretive Japanese version of the Mafia. Yamaguchi had been under orders to "hit" Kariya and to make it look like a heat of passion killing.

Rumors meant little to Longo. Of course, that might explain why Mike Yamaki was so anxious to get a voluntary manslaughter deal.

Yamaki. Yakuza. It was uncomfortably familiar.

Yamaki. Wah Ching. Chinatown . . .

Longo tried to force the images from his mind, tried to bring his thoughts back to the Thomas trial. But they came anyway. The laughing faces. And then it started all over again.

The body in the blood-soaked police uniform, lying still on the floor of the small jewelry store. And another cop, lying in the alley, lying there in the rain and the mud, fighting for air through the blood gurgling out of the gaping hole in his neck.

Peter Chan . . . Hac Qui . . . Mike Yamaki . . .

The faces once again floated before Longo's eyes. Peter Chan, the ringleader, the brains from the infamous Wah Ching gang in New York. Grinning at Longo as he lay there in bed. Hac Qui, the Viet-namese hit man with the Uzi submachine gun. And the three Chinese gunmen. They were all laughing at him.

It was December 19, 1984. The week before Christmas and a black and rainy day in Chinatown. Five men were driving in Chan's white Pontiac Trans Am along Broadway, the main artery leading north from the Criminal Courts Building into Chinatown. Two of the gunmen in the back of the car wore almost identical dark business suits; they were carefully scouting the area. The third was reloading his Titan .25 automatic for the second time. In the front passenger seat, Hac Qui was again checking the action of the Uzi.

The alley dead-ended one block ahead, at Hill Street. Chan drove slowly down the alley until he came to a small, run-down white duplex on his left. On the front of the building was the number 412 and a small sign that read JIN HING—BY APPOINTMENT ONLY. Despite its small size and seedy location, Jin Hing was a jewelry store that was known in Chinese communities across the country; huge amounts of money were discreetly spent here by knowledgeable buyers of diamonds and precious stones imported from Asia.

The owner of the Jin Hing jewelry store was standing behind the counter when he heard the buzzer. His son walked to the door and looked outside. Two Asian men in dark suits stood under umbrellas in the rain. Satisfied that they were customers, the son unlocked the door and let the men in.

An employee was standing at the counter with the owner as the men approached. One said he wanted to see an Indian head ten-dollar coin. The owner disappeared into the back room to get the coin out of a safe. As he finished opening the safe, the man walked into the room with his automatic drawn. "This is a hold-up," he said. He began clearing out the safe, not noticing as the owner leaned against a desk and pressed a silent alarm button.

The gunman at the counter pulled out his revolver and pointed it at the son and the employee. He pushed both of them into the back room, then returned to the store front and started ransacking the jewelry in the display counters.

The sound of knocking came from the front of the store. The man at the counters looked up, then went to the door and looked out into the rain. Two of the gang stood at the door, one of them Peter Chan. The man let them in.

Chan looked around the store, then silently walked into the back office. He glanced at the gunman cleaning out the safe, then at the three hostages.

"Kill them if they move," Chan said.

The man nodded.

A knocking came from the front door once again.

One of the men in the front of the store looked up and saw two more figures at the door. As he stepped toward the door, he realized that they were police officers.

He quickly retreated to the back room. "Cops," he hissed at Chan. The room turned dead silent.

"Let them in," Chan said finally. He pulled out his .357 Colt

Python, then told the first gunman to keep the hostages covered. He peered around the corner into the storefront as one of the other gunmen walked to the door and unlocked it.

A tall blond police officer stepped inside, shaking rain from his yellow slicker. "Your alarm went off," Duane Johnson said as he started walking toward the rear of the store. "Is everything okay?"

"Yeah," the gunman said, following the officer.

Archie Nagao, a Japanese-American rookie officer, stepped in from the rain and started to follow the two men. In the back of the store he noticed another man in a blue suit step out from behind a wall. The man was pointing something at his partner.

Suddenly the man next to Johnson spun around, pulling a gun from his waistband. Nagao heard a deafening explosion from the back of the store, then another. His partner was down. The man in front of him quickly raised the gun and pointed it directly at Nagao's head.

The rookie desperately grabbed for his own gun, drew it from the black leather holster as he heard another explosion. He felt a burning sensation in his neck as he fired back at the man pointing the gun at him.

Nagao staggered backward and kept firing, the explosions now coming from everywhere, one on top of another, deafening him. He fell into the alley and lay there, the heavy rain pounding on him as he sucked for air through the hole in his blood-clogged throat.

By the time help arrived, Johnson was dead. Nagao was rushed to the hospital. Two of the gunmen had been killed in the gunfight. Following the largest manhunt in L.A. history, Chan and the remaining two accomplices were arrested and charged with murder.

After intense questioning, Hac Qui finally confessed to police interrogators, implicating Chan as the mastermind of the robbery. Because of a Supreme Court decision, however, the confession could not be used against Chan and the other henchman: Qui had to be tried separately.

Qui's lawyer was Mike Yamaki.

Deputy D.A. Bob Morrell was assigned to prosecute the three men, Qui first. After a hard-fought trial, the jury returned with the verdict: Hac Qui was not guilty. Incredibly, Yamaki had "walked" his client.

The acquittal caused a furor in the D.A.'s Office and in the rank and file of LAPD. The district attorney quickly pulled Morrell off the case and appointed a new deputy to prosecute Chan and his accomplice: Larry Longo.

Longo knew the second trial would be a tough one. Leslie Abramson, one of the best defense attorneys in the city, was representing Peter Chan. The tiny, frizzy-haired Abramson later gained greater fame in the Menendez trial, fascinating the nation's television audience with her courtroom persona of a cornered wildcat high on "speed."

The trial date was nearing and Longo was scrambling to put together a case. The eyewitnesses had made contradictory identifications of the robbers. And the ballistics evidence was a nightmare: With seven or eight guns involved and dozens of shots fired, the experts could not tell who had fired the bullets that wounded Nagao and killed Johnson.

Meanwhile, Longo got a phone call from LAPD officer J. R. Kwok. Hac Qui had approached him, the investigator said, and asked if he could get immunity for testifying against Chan. Longo told Kwok to contact Yamaki. Within days, Longo and Kwok were sitting in Yamaki's office.

Hac Qui, Yamaki said, was willing to testify against Chan.

Yamaki explained to Longo that his client was frightened of Peter Chan. Qui had heard from a source in the Wah Ching gang that there was a contract out on his life because he had confessed to the police.

His client would "turn state's evidence," Yamaki explained, in exchange for immunity and protection.

Longo was suspicious. Why would Qui want immunity? He had already been acquitted of the robbery-murder; he was protected by double jeopardy from ever being prosecuted for the same offense again.

Yamaki explained that there were other robberies that Qui had been involved in with Chan, robberies for which he could still be arrested and charged.

Longo still had an uncomfortable feeling. He was unaware of any other robberies. And he doubted that Qui, after being involved in a cop killing, would have faith in the police to protect him from anyone.

But if Hac Qui *did* testify, if he took the stand and pointed to Chan and the fifth gunman . . .

In the end, Longo agreed to the deal. He would give Hac Qui immunity and police protection, he told Yamaki, in exchange for his testimony at the trial.

The long process of jury selection began. Longo and the defense lawyers questioned and excused over a thousand men and women, taking over two months before finally agreeing on two separate juries. It would be another year and four months before those juries would return verdicts.

Leslie Abramson's defense for Chan became clear as the trial wore on. Her client was not the clever mastermind and vicious gang leader painted by the prosecution. He was the helpless pawn of the true leader and real culprit: Hac Qui.

As the trial wound its way toward the end, Longo realized that putting Hac Qui on the stand had played right into the defense lawyer's hands. He knew she could have called Hac Qui on her own. But he also knew that a witness given immunity for other robberies made a much more believable "heavy." Hac Qui had been a Trojan horse, Longo realized. And he had fallen for it.

When the verdicts were finally returned, the courtroom was packed with reporters and police officers. The first jury returned its verdict: The gunman was guilty of first-degree murder.

A wave of relief swept through the audience.

Then it was time for the second jury's verdict. The clerk read the form that was handed to her. Peter Chan, she read, was guilty of . . . *second*-degree murder.

The courtroom was dead silent at first, stunned by the verdict. Then there were loud murmurings in the audience. Chan had gotten away with it. He had avoided the gas chamber. The Wah Ching gang leader and cop killer would be back out on the streets in a few short years.

Longo knew he had blown it.

"My God, did you see it?"

"Yeah, Manny." Longo scowled as he shuffled through the row of case files spread out across the counsel table. "I saw it."

"A fuckin' *videotape,* for God's sake." The defense lawyer* shook his head in amazement. "The whole thing's on a fuckin' videotape. Half of LAPD just beating the shit out of that guy on the ground. Right there on TV."

"Yeah," Longo said, turning to check the clock in the back of the courtroom. Judge Bascue would be taking the bench any minute now. "What did you say your client's name was again?"

"Kwan," Manny said. "Tommy Kwan."

"Kwan, right, a 211, armed allegation. What do you want to do?"

"Look, it's his first robbery, he was a lookout is all."

Longo nodded. "He pleads straight up, but I'll drop the armed allegation. It'll shave a couple years off."

"I'll talk to him," the attorney said with a shrug. Then he shook his head. "A fuckin' videotape . . . So who's getting the case, Larry?"

"Terry White."

"Terry *who?*"

"White."

"Terry White," the lawyer repeated with a frown. "Never heard of him."

"New guy in S.I.D."

The videotape had hit the D.A.'s Office like an earthquake.

News of a tape had surfaced the day after Rodney King was beaten and arrested. Before anyone from either LAPD or the D.A.'s Office could track it down, however, the tape was purchased and quickly aired by a local television station.

Reiner was now confronted with a case that could possibly pave his way to the governor's mansion—or destroy his political career forever. After the McMartin, *Twilight Zone,* and Leslie White cases, he found himself locked in a close reelection campaign with his former chief deputy.

Reiner knew that a conviction in the Rodney King trial would save him. The simple fact was that the district attorney of Los Angeles County lived or died by the headlines. It did not matter that a 1992 grand jury report showed the office had a 94 percent conviction rate in felony cases, 99 percent in misdemeanors. Nor did it matter that this was accomplished with one fourth as many prosecutors per capita as in New York. Public perception was shaped by the headlines. The reality of political life in L.A. was that a D.A.'s reelection hinged on winning "the big ones."

The selection of a prosecutor to investigate and try the King case was critical.

Reiner had shown particular interest in a deputy who had just been assigned to Gunson's S.I.D. unit six weeks earlier, Terry White. The front office knew that White was a relatively inexperienced prosecutor; he had tried only a few felony cases. But he had a very important qualification: He was black. There was some feeling that a black prosecutor might be more effective with a jury in the King case. More important, however, Reiner was aware that there was a strong political advantage to appointing a black man to prosecute the white officers in a minority-dominated city that would be screaming for blood. And, whether or not he was inexperienced, there were no better qualified black lawyers in the office.

But Terry White was attractive to the district attorney for a second reason. Reiner had a history of managing high-publicity cases behind the scenes. Talented, experienced prosecutors did not take to being puppets. The role called for a young, relatively inexperienced deputy who would follow orders.

In taking control of high-publicity cases, Reiner was ignoring a basic axiom of the courtroom. As one veteran prosecutor put it, "A trial is almost a living thing; the chemistry changes between lawyers and jury. Sometimes only the people in the courtroom can feel that chemistry and understand what needs to be done." And there is the critical question of self-confidence. "When you start second-guessing trial lawyers," another top deputy D.A. observed, "it causes them to second-guess themselves. The one thing you never do is tell trial lawyers to signal before they turn left."

Reiner would end up making many of the strategic and tactical decisions in the King case. He had, apparently, not learned his lesson from the *Twilight Zone* trial.

On July 23, 1982, Hollywood director John Landis was filming a scene for his new film, *Twilight Zone: The Movie.* In the scene, actor Vic Morrow was trying to rescue two Vietnamese children during a Vietcong attack; the two child actors, ages six and eight, were on the set with their mothers. A combat helicopter was hovering twenty-four feet directly above Morrow and the children, and explosive charges were set off to simulate mortar explosions. Suddenly, one of the explosions misfired, damaging the helicopter's rotors. The aircraft began spinning out of control, its long rotors slicing wildly through the air. Morrow and the two children were decapitated as the mothers watched in horror.

Reiner ordered manslaughter charges filed against Landis, as well as four other members of the film crew. Deputy D.A. Gary Kesselman was appointed to prosecute the highly publicized case. But after two years of pretrial procedures, he and Ira Reiner had a violent argument over whether to accept a plea-bargain offer from the defense. Reiner, Kesselman claimed, was refusing to accept justifiable pleas simply because he craved the publicity of an unnecessary trial.

In September 1985, Kesselman was removed from the case. Reiner then looked for a more compliant prosecutor.

Lea D'Agostino, born Lea Sheinbein in Israel, was already in her forties when she had decided to become a lawyer. She had spent her first years in the D.A.'s S.A.P. unit, the Sexual Assault Program. Her success there with abused children and rape victims attracted Reiner's attention.

Reiner made it clear to her that the *Twilight Zone* case was to be tried to a jury, not plea-bargained. In the months that followed, and during the trial itself, D'Agostino would periodically report to Reiner and receive instructions on strategy and tactics.

When the trial finally began, D'Agostino put on her first witness, Landis's production secretary. The secretary testified that just before the accident she overheard Landis tell his associate producer, "We're all going to jail" for illegally hiring the two child actors. The associate producer replied that state officials would "put my butt in jail too" if they knew explosions were going to be used on the set. Under cross-examination, however, the woman dropped a bombshell: The former prosecutor in the case, Gary Kesselman, had told her he would keep this information from the defense until trial—a clear violation of a court order to turn over all relevant evidence to the defense.

Kesselman denied making the statement and called the woman a liar. This, of course, placed D'Agostino in an awkward position; a fellow deputy D.A. was attacking the credibility of her key witness. She immediately reacted by telling the press that she stood behind the woman. Kesselman was furious.

When D'Agostino finally rested her case, the defense called a surprise witness: Gary Kesselman. And the deputy D.A. had some startling testimony. D'Agostino, he said, had tried to pressure him into testifying that the secretary's testimony was true. The witness's credibility was critical, she had told him; the trial was more important than either of them.

D'Agostino angrily denied the accusation in front of the jury, accusing Kesselman of trying to get back at the D.A.'s Office for removing him from the case. Kesselman replied by testifying that he had begged to be taken off of the case, implying to the jury that he believed the defendants were not guilty.

The media had a field day. And the jury was treated to the unusual spectacle of two prosecutors attacking one another while the defense gleefully sat back and watched.

In the end it was the testimony of Kesselman that proved decisive, and the jury returned with verdicts of not guilty as to all defendants. One juror said afterward, "Somebody ought to go through that D.A.'s Office with a bottle of castor oil."

D'Agostino was abandoned to the Van Nuys office, never again to try an important case. And a new regulation was adopted in the D.A.'s Office, the so-called second chair policy: In any high-publicity case, there would always be at least two prosecutors assigned.

The trial proved devastating to the office. Morale plummeted as a result of the highly publicized defeat and the public airing of dirty laundry. And Reiner's political future suddenly looked considerably darker.

Now the Rodney King case was squarely in the district attorney's lap.

Reiner finally chose Terry White to try the case. Then he assigned a more experienced prosecutor, Alan Yochelson, to sit as second chair.

Terry White was a quiet, soft-spoken man, almost shy in his manner. The impression was reinforced by his bookish appearance of tortoiseshell eyeglasses, a receding hairline, a small, neat mustache, and staid three-piece suits.

White had joined the D.A.'s Office seven years earlier—one day before his twin brother, Kerry. He had been working for a conservative public interest firm in Sacramento, writing opposing briefs in cases brought by liberal groups like the ACLU. White enjoyed writing and appellate argument, but he had visions of becoming a partner in a prestigious law firm. After he and his brother talked it over, they decided to get some trial experience as prosecutors and then go on to a big civil firm.

Soon after joining the office, White was assigned to Central Trials, the unit responsible for staffing all felony courts in the Criminal Courts Building; Longo was in Central Trials. Two years later White was sent to the Organized Crime and Anti-Terrorist unit. Then, in 1991, he was transferred to Gunson's secretive S.I.D. Six weeks later, Gunson called him into his office and handed the inexperienced prosecutor what was to become perhaps the most important trial of the decade.

That night White interviewed his first witnesses in the case, two husband-and-wife Highway Patrol officers. The officers gave a damning account of how, after a wild car chase, city cops had repeatedly kicked and struck the prone suspect with their batons while others, including a supervising sergeant, stood around and watched. It was not until the next day that White learned there was a videotape of the incident.

White finally presented the case to the grand jury, asking for the indictment of four officers. The four were invited to testify, but declined. White subpoenaed the tape from the television station, managing to seize it one hour before the FBI arrived to confiscate it. After seeing the tapes, the grand jury returned the indictments.

"All rise!"

Longo looked up as Judge Bascue walked out and took the bench.

"People versus Typhus Henderson,*" Judge Bascue called out.

"In custody, your honor," the bailiff said.

"Bring him out." The judge looked at the next file in the stack in front of him. "And bring out Ramirez too."

"Yes, sir." The bailiff disappeared into the holding cell area, the steel door clanging behind him.

"Gentlemen?" the judge asked, looking at Longo and Craig Veals seated at the prosecution table.

Veals stood, clearing his throat. He opened a manila file and began reading from it. "Typhus Henderson, aka Tyree Hanson, aka Tomcat . . . Kidnap, six counts of rape, five of oral cop . . . two counts sodomy . . . one count extortion . . . We're alleging two prior convictions, your honor, armed robbery and ADW."

"I can read, Mr. Veals. But refresh my memory. What's the case about?"

"Yes, your honor." The young deputy D.A. continued without looking up from the file. "The victim in this case is a young woman, a schoolteacher. Her car broke down in the Marina del Rey area. The defendant was apparently driving by and stopped. He offered to help her, to take her to get a tow truck."

"Cut to the chase, Mr. Veals. We've got a heavy calendar this morning."

"Yes, your honor," Veals said patiently. "The victim accepted the defendant's offer of a ride. But rather than take her to a mechanic, he took her to his house in the Watts area." He looked up at the judge. "The victim is white." Then he looked back at the file. "When she resisted, he threatened her with a knife. He kept her tied up in the house for three days. During that period of time, she was forced to engage in various sexual acts with approximately twelve men. The victim is not sure of the exact number." He looked up again. "She has been unable to ID any of the other perpetrators."

"So where's the extortion?"

Veals returned to the file, read in silence for a moment. Then he looked up. "Apparently, when the defendant tired of this, he called the victim's sister on the telephone. Her sister lives in the Valley. He told the sister that he had the victim and that she was . . . being used. He put the victim on the phone to verify this. Then he told the sister that he would sell her back for five hundred dollars."

"Sell her."

"Yes, your honor."

Judge Bascue shifted his gaze to Karen Thompson. The deputy public defender rose to her feet.

"This is all a fantasy, your honor," she said, a hint of fatigue in her voice. "There was sex, but it was purely consensual. My client advises me that the woman approached him at a theater in Marina del Rey and . . ."

Longo grabbed the file Veals had laid on the desk in front of him, quickly scanned the fact sheet on the inside cover. Satisfied, he replaced it in front of his junior deputy, leaned back, and watched him continue with the morning calendar call.

Craig Veals was the most experienced of his junior deputies and Longo had confidence in his maturity and judgment. He was a tall, slender, thirty-five-year-old, strikingly handsome black man, with a calm, dignified, relaxed manner and a ready smile. Like Longo, he was always dressed impeccably, but in suits cut along more traditional lines. With his male model looks and his sartorial splendor, Veals appeared more at home on the cover of *GQ* than in a criminal court.

Buried not so far beneath this polished appearance, however, was a boy who had survived the black ghettos of Los Angeles. Veals's mother had died of cancer when he was seven; his father had been killed in a car accident two years later. The youngest of seven children, he was raised by his oldest brother. Because his brother's wife resented him, he spent many nights sleeping in neighborhood parks. He would often go for two or three days without eating.

Veals liked being a deputy D.A. It gave him the power to accomplish justice in a way that a defense attorney could not. Although he hated the violence of the streets and felt deep sympathy for the victims, he had compassion for the accused as well. "People make mistakes," he would say. "Sometimes it's best to show mercy." But he found that this concern for justice—for both victims and defendants—often clashed with office policies. It seemed to him that administrators were more concerned with high conviction rates than with what was right. And on more than one occasion he had been criticized for going easy on a defendant.

Veals was a good prosecutor, one who was interested in more than just winning. But Longo realized that it was this sensitivity and caring that would someday end his deputy's career. The criminal justice system wore down men like Craig Veals. Without a change, he was doomed to burn out before many more years passed. That change would come two years later, with his appointment to the municipal court bench.

Longo listened as Veals discussed the Henderson case with Judge Bascue. He had placed Veals in charge of calendar call for the week. But, unlike many other senior deputies in the courthouse, Longo made it a point to rotate the assignments among his three junior deputies so that each gained the widest range of experience.

Most trial courts had only three prosecutors: the supervising deputy and two junior deputies, usually a "grade three" and a "grade two." Veals was the grade three and Torrealba the two, both handpicked by Longo. But in Larry Boyle he had seen the raw makings of another top prosecutor. So within days he had finagled authorization for a second grade two and Boyle joined the team in 127.

Greg Dohi was the most recent addition to Longo's growing staff. Yesterday, Longo had stunned the young law clerk by handing him a burglary case to try before a jury in two weeks. Dohi was not yet admitted to practice, but bar rules permitted law students to make appearances in court if accompanied by a licensed attorney; Longo would sit at his side during the trial. Dohi was terrified. Longo knew he would be nervous, would make mistakes, might even lose the trial. But he would learn.

Dohi . . . Veals . . . Boyle . . . Torrealba. They were Longo's "family." Fine young lawyers, he thought, and he was proud of how they were developing. Each had his own strengths, his own unique style. They would all make good prosecutors.

The steel door suddenly swung open and the bailiff brought out two men in orange jumpsuits handcuffed to one another. One was a tall, powerfully built black man with strangely pale blue eyes. The other was a small, wiry Hispanic with an overpowering Pancho Villa mustache. The bailiff pulled out two chairs and sat the two men down, then pushed the chairs as far into the defense table as he could.

"As I was saying," Karen Thompson continued, "Mr. Henderson here absolutely denies this woman's story." She paused, then looked across at Veals defiantly. "He is prepared to go to trial."

Judge Bascue looked at the young prosecutor. "Good IDs?"

Veals nodded. "She six-packed him. But . . ."

"But she blew the Evans," Thompson said.

"She made him at the prelim, your honor."

The victim had correctly picked Henderson from a display of six photographs, or mug shots, shown to her by the investigating officer. But the Evans decision by the California Supreme Court gave the defense the right to have a live lineup at a later stage of the proceedings. The public defender had demanded such a lineup, and the woman had been unable—or unwilling—to identify him from five other tall black men. At the preliminary hearing, however, she had pointed to Henderson as the man who had abducted her.

"Well, boys and girls?" Bascue said with a sigh.

Veals looked down at Longo. The senior prosecutor nodded. Veals looked across at Thompson. "Plead to the kidnap and one count rape, admit the priors, we drop the rest."

Thompson leaned down and whispered to her client. He listened, then mumbled something back. She looked up at Judge Bascue. "No deal," she said. "He says he didn't do it."

Bascue shook his head in frustration, looked at the clock on the back wall. Then he signaled the two attorneys to approach the bench.

As Veals and Thompson walked toward the bench with their files, Longo leaned back and looked to the right of the courtroom, past the empty jury box, to the door at the far corner that led into "the room." The room where twelve jurors were at this very moment deciding on a verdict in the Thomas trial.

He felt the emptiness in his stomach again, the same cold, aching emptiness he always felt when he had a jury out. He had felt something like this at the hospital when each of the kids had been born. Waiting. Not knowing. Helpless. His fate in the hands of others.

As every trial lawyer does, Longo kept trying to imagine what was going on in the jury deliberation room. How had the last vote gone? What were the jurors arguing about? Who were the leaders? Was there a holdout? Were they deadlocked?

And, as every lawyer does, Longo replayed the trial in his mind. Each time, looking for something that would give him a clue as to what was happening behind that door.

Weston's testimony had gone well, he thought, and the former boxer had made a good impression. Or were the jurors buying McKinney's smoke screen about Weston being a drug dealer?

And what about all the technical stuff? Did they understand about attorney-client trust accounts? Longo had subpoenaed the checks and statements from Thomas's account at Merrill Lynch, had even brought in his account executive to testify. Did the jurors understand? Could they follow the paper trail? Were they confused by all the numbers and documents?

Longo had the most important checks and statements blown up to poster size so the jurors could see them during testimony. And he had subpoenaed the assistant U.S. attorney who had authorized the release of $108,000 to Thomas. But McKinney kept waving that damned power of attorney at the jury. Did they understand that the document Weston signed was only a defense to forgery, not to embezzlement?

And then there was Thomas's testimony. A charming guy on the stand, and a clever lawyer. He explained that he had not paid the money to Weston because there had been a disagreement over the amount of his contingency fee. He was simply holding back distribution of the funds until he and his client agreed on what percentage should be kept by Thomas.

On cross-examination, Longo had torn into him. He had shoved a copy of the contingency agreement in his face. He had thrown canceled checks in his lap, demanding to know why he had taken money from the trust account for his own personal expenses. He had angrily confronted him with the secret offshore bank account, waving the letter that had been found in the search. But Thomas had remained calm, spoken in a gentlemanly, even amiable manner. For everything he had had a reasonable explanation.

It was not until the third or fourth hour of Longo's grilling that Thomas had begun to lose his temper, begun to react without thinking. Begun to make small mistakes.

Longo went back over his closing argument, trying to gauge its effect on the jurors. He had been his usual self, pacing around the courtroom, pounding on the jury railing, pointing accusingly at the defendant, taking the witness stand and dramatically reenacting key testimony.

But McKinney had been good. His argument had been smooth, cool, articulate, and reeking with utter confidence. The power of attorney clearly gave Thomas the right to sign his client's name to the government check. And he was simply holding distribution of Weston's share until their disagreement over the attorney's fee was resolved. Nothing more than a civil dispute: Why had the D.A. blown it out of proportion? Was it perhaps because Mr. Thomas was a lawyer? McKinney had asked with a raised eyebrow. A criminal defense lawyer? A *black* criminal defense lawyer?

There it was again. The Rodney King incident.

Longo knew the jury could go either way, could even hang. The informal vote of the courtroom staff—bailiff, clerk, and reporter—was 3–0, not guilty. Not a good sign.

Veals and Thompson were stepping back from the judge's bench, returning to their counsel tables. As the public defender held a whispered meeting with her client, Veals sat down next to Longo.

"Tomcat over there wants his day in court," Veals said with a shrug. "So Bascue suggested an S.O.T. plus."

"Bottom line?" Longo asked.

"The kidnap count and the priors."

Longo thought about this for a moment. Many defendants refuse to plead guilty simply because they do not want to publicly admit what they have done. Others refuse because they see this as quitting; they have to do the macho thing and go down swinging. For these individuals, the S.O.T. plus often saved the time and effort of a full-blown trial. If the defendant agreed, his attorney would S.O.T. the case—submit it on the transcript. The judge would first read the transcript from the preliminary hearing. The "plus" was the live testimony of the defendant himself: He would take the stand and testify, be cross-examined, and then have this considered along with the testimony in the transcript. The judge then rendered a verdict of guilt or innocence. The S.O.T. plus saved time and gave the defendant the feeling that he had gotten to tell his side of the story.

In most cases, it was understood by both attorneys that the judge would reach a certain decision. After reading the transcript and listening to Henderson testify, for example, he might find him guilty of the most serious offense, kidnapping, and not guilty of the remaining counts. And everyone would be happy: The defendant would feel he got his day in court, Thompson would avoid a no-win trial on all of the counts, Bascue would keep his crowded calendar moving, and the prosecution would watch Mr. Henderson go off to San Quentin for a long stay.

Longo studied the judge as the public defender played out her role, putting her client on the stand. He recalled a bit of information that Angie had given him yesterday. It seemed Bascue had suddenly received a flood of letters from various influential members of the Japanese-American community, each of them praising Kazuhiko Yamaguchi as a man of impeccable character. One of the envelopes, however, also contained a very interesting document. From a public relations firm in Century City, it had apparently been accidentally included with the character letter. It was a set of instructions, explaining how to send letters to Judge Bascue praising Yamaguchi, including suggestions that they point out what an important leader of the community he was, what pressures had been on him that led to the "unfortunate" shooting, how the "incident" had affected his family, and why leniency was called for.

Longo had seen thousands of character letters sent to judges on behalf of defendants, but not usually until *after* there had been a guilty plea in the case and the judge was about to sentence him. And he had sure never seen a public relations firm used before.

He was beginning to get an uneasy feeling about Bascue and the Yamaguchi case. The judge had made some comments to him indicating that it was an "obvious" voluntary manslaughter. Why was he taking such an interest in the case?

Longo knew that Bascue's wife, Jackie Connors, was a Superior Court judge on another floor in the same building; like Bascue, she had been a deputy D.A. before being appointed to the bench. More important, she had been raised in Japan—in fact, although she was an American citizen, she had never seen the United States until she attended college at USC. She spoke perfect Japanese, was an admirer of Japanese culture, and had many Japanese friends. Further, their best friend was Lance Ito, a Japanese-American judge and former deputy D.A. Ito, whose parents met in a Wyoming internment camp during World War II, later gained fame as the trial judge in the O. J. Simpson case. He introduced Bascue to Jackie Connors, served as best man at the wedding, and was the trustee for their children.

Could there be a personal connection between Bascue and Yamaki? Or was it Yamaki's political power?

My God, Longo suddenly thought, I'm becoming paranoid. Yamaki was just doing his job in getting character letters. And Bascue was right: The Yamaguchi case *did* look like a typical heat of passion killing.

The old joke flashed across his mind: "Just because I'm paranoid doesn't mean someone isn't following me!"

Longo had known of Bascue years earlier, when they had both been junior-level deputies in the office. He grinned as he thought of the hard-drinking, hell-raising reputation Jim Bascue had earned in the office. Even today, the man drove a black 3.8-liter "Grand National" Buick—a rumbling, turbocharged hot rod that seemed way out of place among the stately Lincolns and Mercedeses in the judges' parking lot.

Jim Bascue had been born dirt-poor. His father was a small farmer and sharecropper in Arkansas who lost their farm to the bank during the Depression. He packed the family in their broken-down car and joined the ragged procession of Oakies on their way out to the promised land of California. When they arrived, of course, the reality was long, backbreaking days of picking fruit in the orchards. By the time Bascue was six years old, he had joined his family as a laborer in the fruit orchards.

As a junior deputy, Bascue was assigned to the Santa Monica branch, where he met and became close friends with a small group of deputy D.A.s who later distinguished themselves. Bob Philibosian served as district attorney of Los Angeles. Stanley Weisburg became a judge, presiding at the McMartin, Rodney King, and Menendez trials. John Ouderkirk, one of Bascue's hell-raising sidekicks, also became a judge; he later presided over the Reginald Denny case. Roger Gunson was now the chief of S.I.D. And Harlan Braun helped prosecute the Manson case, then went into private practice; he was defense counsel in the *Twilight Zone* trial and was now representing one of the officers in the Rodney King case.

Bascue quickly gained a reputation as a tough, no-nonsense prosecutor. When the attorney general of Montana called District Attorney Joe Busch for help in combating corruption at the highest levels of state government, Bascue was one of three deputies who were sent to Helena for one year as independent special prosecutors. He conducted grand jury investigations of the governor and other politicians, secured indictments, and even thwarted a conspiracy to assassinate the attorney general.

Soon after his return to the D.A.'s Office, Bascue was put in charge of the "Hardcore" unit, assigned to prosecuting murders committed by leading members of L.A.'s juvenile gangs. His assistant was Lance Ito.

Bascue eventually rose to become chief deputy under District Attorney Bob Philibosian—second in command of the largest municipal prosecuting agency in the world.

When Ira Reiner defeated Philibosian in the next election, however, Bascue was demoted and banished to the Santa Monica office from where he had originally come. Seeing the writing on the wall, he turned in his resignation and accepted a position as chief counsel for the state bar. For the next few years he was responsible for prosecuting lawyers for unethical conduct.

Then Bascue received a phone call from his old friend. Phili-

bosian was now the chief assistant to Governor George "Duke" Deuk-
mejian, and he had not forgotten his former chief deputy. Was he
interested in an appointment to the bench?

Judge Bascue looked at the next file in front of him. "Ramirez?
Johnny Mack Ramirez*?"

Thompson also grabbed a new file from the stack in front of
her. "Your honor," she said resignedly, "Mr. Ramirez wishes to make
a *Faretta* motion."

"Aw fer cryin' out loud," Longo muttered to Veals. "Gimme a
break."

A *Faretta* motion was the bane of prosecutors, and a particular
irritant to Longo. The motion was named after a Supreme Court case
that said a defendant was constitutionally entitled to represent himself
in court; a lawyer could not be forced upon him. But this meant the
trial judge had to walk a fine line, trying to balance this right with
the constitutional requirement of a fair trial—and pitting an unedu-
cated defendant against an experienced prosecutor did not often result
in a fair trial. The judge was required to question the defendant to
make sure that he had a minimal education and understood at least
the basics of what a trial was all about. Even then, it was difficult to
deny him the right to proceed *in propria persona,* as self-representation
was called.

Longo detested *pro per* trials and assigned them to his most
junior deputies. There was no satisfaction in courtroom combat with
defendants; it was like shooting fish in a barrel. In fact, jurors often
sympathized with the defendant simply because he was so clearly overmatched. And *pro per* trials usually took twice as long because everything had to be constantly explained to the defendant.

More important, however, the appellate courts were very sensitive on the subject. Many *pro per* convictions were reversed because
the defendant was so overmatched in trial. But if the judge refused
to let a defendant represent himself, the conviction was overturned on
appeal for denying him this right. It was often a no-win situation.
The "jailhouse lawyers" knew this and they had spread the word.

"Interpreter?" Bascue asked of Thompson.

"He speaks English, your honor."

"Mr. Ramirez?"

The small man stood, his right hand handcuffed to the left hand of Henderson seated next to him. "Yes, sir."

"Mr. Ramirez, I understand you want your counsel here, the public defender, excused from the case. Is that correct?"

"I wan' to fire her."

"Uh-huh. And you have filed a motion to substitute yourself as counsel?"

"I wan' a *real* lawyer."

"Well, you understand that Ms. Thompson *is* a real lawyer, don't you?"

"No, man, she's a public defender."

"Yes, but she *is* a lawyer."

"If she's a lawyer, how come she don' go out an' make a lotta money, huh?"

Bascue shook his head. "I'm sure she gets paid quite well in her present position."

Ramirez just snorted, looked away.

"Mr. Ramirez?"

"Hey, your honor, she work for the government, right? Same as those guys over there." He pointed to Longo and Veals. "They all gettin' paid by the government, right?"

"Well, technically, yes, Mr. Ramirez, but I assure you—"

"The government, they gon' to pay those guys over there to fry my ass, and same time they gon' to pay this lady to get me cut loose?" He snorted again loudly. "No, man, I don' think so."

"I see that you have filed a *Faretta* motion with the court."

"Yeah, your honor, I wan' to go *pro per,* you know?"

"You are asking to represent yourself. Is that still what you want?"

"Yeah, I can' have a real lawyer, I wan' to do it myself."

"Mr. Ramirez," Bascue said with a deep sigh, "I strongly advise you against this course of action. A trial is a very complicated thing. And Mr. Longo over there, he's a very experienced, very capable prosecutor."

Ramirez looked across at Longo, stared malevolently at him. Longo glanced back, then looked away, bored with the pathetic attempt at eye fucking. He decided to assign this case to Greg Dohi.

"And I will tell you," Bascue went on, "you will receive no

special favors in this court. I will not tell you when to object, or what the grounds are, or what motions to make ..."

But Longo knew this was absolutely untrue. The fact was that every judge was frightened to death of being reversed on appeal. And so *pro per*s were given every advantage possible. Defendants representing themselves while in custody were given access to a law library in the jail for two hours every day, were provided with appropriate legal forms, and were allowed unlimited phone calls during the two-hour period. If needed, a private investigator was appointed at county expense, along with a "legal runner" to deliver motions to the courts or serve subpoenas on witnesses; the defendant was guaranteed access to these two individuals for thirty minutes each day. And during trial, the judge would bend over backward to help the defendant, often to the point of making objections and motions on the defendant's behalf—and then ruling on them.

"... you will be entirely on your own, Mr. Ramirez, and I assure you that Mr. Longo will have no sympathy for you. He will show you no quarter."

"I ain' afraid of him," Ramirez said.

"Mr. Ramirez, I'm required to ask you a number of questions about your understanding of the legal system."

"Yeah, I understan' it."

"Do you know how many challenges you have during jury selection, Mr. Ramirez?"

"Challenges ..."

"Let me back up. Do you know what a jury *is?*"

"A jury ... yeah, sure, I understan'."

"How many people are on a jury, Mr. Ramirez?"

"Ah, a jury, they got, ah—"

A loud buzzer suddenly rang out, startling the wiry little man. Then, immediately, a second loud buzzing sound.

Longo's heart skipped a beat, began pounding harder. His stomach felt very cold. Twenty-three years, he thought to himself, and it never got any easier.

The buzzer was a signal from the jury deliberating in the Thomas case. One buzz meant they had a question.

Two meant they had a verdict.

"I got to the scene at oh-one-thirty," Detective Monty Holden said.

"Victim's body still there?"

"Yeah, lying on the ground next to the car. Paramedics pulled him out."

Longo leaned back in his chair, propped his feet between piles of papers on his desk, and continued to review the two-inch-thick homicide report from the Montebello Police Department. It had been only a few hours since the jury had slowly filed into the box for the last time. Morris Thomas and William McKinney had stood in stunned disbelief as the guilty verdicts were read in open court. Afterward, Longo had allowed himself the luxury of a workout and an extra-long steam bath at the Y. Back at the office, a phone call to Harrold Weston in Detroit and the deep satisfaction of telling him that justice had been done. Then it was on to the next trial.

Yamaguchi.

"When did you interview Yamaguchi's son ... What's his name?"

"Ken," Holden said. "Kenneth Yamaguchi. Twenty-two years old, lives at the home. I talked with him at oh-three-ten hours, back at the Detective Bureau."

"Run it by me again, okay?"

"Sure. Says his dad comes home about oh-one-hundred hours. Comes in and says, 'Oh, your mom's not home yet?' And the son, Ken, he says no. And then the dad, he calls his brother-in-law, the wife's brother . . ." The stocky detective glanced at his own copy of the reports. "Ma-mo-ru Ha-ne-mu-re." He looked back up. "Christ, these names . . ."

"Yeah."

"So anyway, his dad and this Hanemure guy talk on the phone for a little while, but the son can't quite hear what they're saying. So then the dad hangs up and walks out of the house."

"Uh-huh."

"So then, about forty minutes goes by. And then the kid's mother starts pounding on the front door. And she's yelling, 'Call nine-one-one, call nine-one-one, Mr. Kariya was shot, your dad shot him.' "

"Yeah."

"So the kid goes outside and sees the guy lying in the driver's seat. And he goes back in and calls nine-one-one."

"Does the son know the victim in this case? What's his name again?"

"Kariya," Holden said, glancing again at the report. "Guy's name is Genji Kariya. Says the guy worked at the restaurant his parents both owned, down in J-Town. Guy was a handyman there for two, three years."

"He know of any marital problems his folks were having?"

"Says he thinks they were having some problems, but he doesn't know if they involved this Kariya guy."

"Anything else?"

"Naw. The kid didn't have much to say."

"Okay." Longo flipped a page of the report. "What about this brother-in-law? You interviewed him a couple hours after the shooting, right?"

"Yeah. Hanemure. A very cool customer, y'know? Close to the vest."

"Uh-huh."

"Anyway, I talked with him at the bureau right after the kid. I ask him if he got a phone call that night from Yamaguchi. Guy says yeah, about a half hour after midnight. Yamaguchi tells him, 'The same thing is happening. It's going to continue. Please take care of things.' "

"Please take care of things."

"Yeah, that's what he said. I asked him what he thought Yamaguchi meant by that. Guy says Yamaguchi suspected his wife, the guy's sister, was having an affair with an employee at the restaurant, suspected it for a month or so. Guy says he's been counseling Yamaguchi for the past three weeks about it, telling him not to do anything foolish. Says Yamaguchi had a gun, shot it at his wife three weeks ago."

"Yamaguchi shot a gun at his wife?"

"That's what this guy says. Carried it in a brown bag, and he pulled it out when they were at their home and fired it at her. Didn't hit her. Just trying to scare her, he thinks."

"Uh-huh."

"So anyway, I ask him when the last time he saw any of them was. And I guess earlier that night, there's some kind of a shindig at the restaurant Yamaguchi and his wife own. Well, this guy Hanemure also owns a restaurant in J-Town, right nearby. And about twenty-two-fifteen hours, the victim, Kariya, he's in Hanemure's restaurant. About that time Yamaguchi's wife walks in, and the two of them, her and Kariya, they go off in a corner by themselves. After a while, Hanemure leaves and he doesn't come back until they're gone. Then he gets the call from Yamaguchi, about half hour after midnight, like I said."

"Okay." Longo continued scanning the homicide report. "What about the wife?"

Holden glanced again at the reports. "Mi-tsu-ru," he said slowly. "I talked to her right after the kid and the Hanemure guy. At the bureau. I had to wait for an interpreter."

"Yamaguchi's wife doesn't speak English?"

"I guess not. Anyway, she confirms she met with Kariya at her brother's restaurant that night. Then they go to a Denny's restaurant. About twenty-three-hundred hours, she calls her husband back at their own restaurant. She tells him she's going to be home late, and he asks her who she's with, and she says she's with this Kariya."

Holden was interrupted by a middle-aged man in a dark gray pin-striped suit standing in the doorway. He had curly gray hair, thick black eyebrows, and an intense look in his dark eyes. It was Ira Reiner, the district attorney of Los Angeles County.

"Larry . . ." Reiner said.

Longo looked up.

"Congratulations on the Thomas verdict," Reiner said. "Nice job."

"Thanks."

Reiner disappeared down the hall, on his way back to the front office. Longo was mildly surprised at the visit. The guilty verdict in the Thomas case had been a big win for the office, but it had been overshadowed by an even bigger one the very next day. After months of a highly publicized trial presided over by Lance Ito, Bill Hodgman had finally convicted Charles Keating. Neither verdict had hurt Reiner's reelection campaign.

Hodgman had gotten a forty-two-count indictment against Keating and three of his associates for committing fraud in their manipulation of Lincoln Savings and Loan. Thousands of bondholders were wiped out in what was the largest S & L failure in U.S. history, many of them elderly people whose entire life savings had simply disappeared. The D.A.'s Office decided not to wait for the slow-moving Feds. The case represented the first major attempt by a local prosecuting agency to demand a higher level of integrity from corporate officers in dealing with the public.

Reiner had been criticized for interfering in what appeared to be a federal matter; it was seen as yet another attempt by him to grab headlines. He was also criticized for selecting Hodgman to take on the complex case. As Reiner's critics were quick to point out, Hodgman had absolutely no experience in white-collar crime. In fact, the deputy's only claim to fame was that he was the prosecutor who lost the Todd Bridges case. Bridges was the former child actor in the hit television series *Different Strokes;* he was also a heavy rock cocaine user who shot a drug dealer's enforcer, almost killing him.

Longo looked back at the Montebello detective. "Yeah?"

"So, anyway, the wife and Kariya talk at Denny's until about oh-one-hundred hours, at which time he drives her home, to Montebello. They're pulling up, Yamaguchi runs to the driver's door and puts one through Kariya's head. Then he leaves. Never said a word, just leaves."

"Okay. What about the eyewitness?"

"Nicholas Carmona. Positive ID, six-packed him. Kid was in a car across the street from where Kariya's car pulled up. He was in there with a girlfriend." He smiled. "Seems he was getting married to some other woman, and he was saying his good-byes."

"Uh-huh."

"Nighttime, of course, but he had a real clear view. Anyway, he sees this car pull up, and Yamaguchi runs up and leans down. And then there's a shot, then another one. And then he says Yamaguchi just stands there for about half a minute."

"Just stands there?"

"Yeah, like he's talking with his wife. But he can't hear anything from where he's sitting, you know?"

Longo pondered this for a moment. Yamaguchi's wife had said he left immediately, without saying a word.

"How soon after the shooting did Yamaguchi get to the CHP station?"

Detective Holden scanned a few pages from the report for a moment, then looked up.

"Estimate the shooting about oh-one-fifteen hours. He got to the station at oh-one-seventeen hours." He read some more, looked back up. "One of our detectives, Govan Yee, he drove the distance between the house and the station. Normal speed. It's six tenths of a mile. Did it in one minute, forty-four seconds."

"Okay, so Yamaguchi drove straight to the CHP station after the shooting."

"Looks like it."

"Like maybe he had already planned to turn himself in, before he shot Kariya."

Holden shrugged.

Longo pondered this. "When you talked to him a couple of hours later, Yamaguchi clammed up, right?"

"Yeah. I Mirandized him, and he said he wanted a lawyer."

"But he confessed to the CHP when he turned himself in."

Holden thumbed through his report. "Gruidl. He was on duty

at the CHP office in Montebello. At oh-one-seventeen hours, Yamaguchi pounds on the door, yells, 'Help me, I just shot my friend.' Then he pulls out the gun." He grinned. "Really freaked out the Chippy. Pulls out his own gun, and I guess it was tense there for a minute."

"Uh-huh."

"Anyway, he tells Yamaguchi to lay the gun down real slow, and he does. And after the Chippy gets him handcuffed, he asks him where this all happened. Yamaguchi says back at his house and gives the address. Then he says, 'I found my friend with my wife.' And that was it, that was all he said."

"Wait a minute," Longo said. "You said you Mirandized Yamaguchi, and he said he wanted a lawyer?"

"Yeah?"

"He *understood* what you said?"

"Sure."

Yamaguchi understood English, Longo realized. But at the arraignment he had needed an interpreter.

"And the Chippy, Gruidl, he says Yamaguchi was talking to him in English?"

Holden shrugged. "Yeah."

Yamaki. Yamaki had demanded an interpreter for Hac Qui, too. The son of a bitch was using an interpreter to shield his client, to give him time to think before answering. And he could always blame faulty interpretation if the client was caught later in an inconsistency. A very effective barrier to police interrogation. Or cross-examination in trial.

Yamaguchi's wife had asked for an interpreter at the police station. Had she called Yamaki after getting a phone call from Holden to come down to the station?

"What about the gun?"

Holden looked back at his report. "Smith and Wesson .38 Special, double action. Five chambers, three live rounds, two spent."

"You recovered the spent bullets?"

"Yeah. One entered Kariya's head. The other went into the roof just above the passenger's headrest."

Longo looked up from his copy of the report. "The second bullet hit near the *wife's* head?"

"Yeah." The detective shrugged. "I guess one of his shots missed Kariya and hit the other side of the car."

"From one foot away?"

"First shot could have jerked Kariya's head back, throwing off his second shot."

Or was Yamaguchi shooting at his wife? Longo wondered. But there were three more bullets in the gun. If he had been shooting at his wife, and missed, why hadn't he fired again? Had he been trying to scare her? Or had he felt a change of heart? Or, like Holden said, had he just missed a second shot at Kariya?

"Ballistics?" Longo asked.

"Test-fired two of the live rounds. They matched both recovered bullets."

"Prints?"

Holden shook his head. "Negative. But they found a white athletic sock in his pocket, one of those tube socks, you know?"

"A sock."

"Yeah. And the eyewitness, Carmona, he thought he saw the guy with something white on his arm. Guy probably had the sock on his hand to keep from leaving prints on the gun."

"But Yamaguchi turned himself in at the CHP station a few minutes after the murder, right?"

Holden nodded. "I dunno, it doesn't make sense, does it. And another thing . . ."

"Yeah?"

"The CHP, they found something else in his pockets. A speedy loader."

"Yamaguchi had a speedy loader on him?"

"Yeah, and there weren't any bullets in it."

A "speedy loader" was a second set of revolving cylinders that was used by some police officers for quick reloading in a gunfight. By removing the original cylinders after all the bullets had been fired and replacing it with a previously loaded second set, the officer saved critical time.

But what was Yamaguchi doing with a speedy loader? And why was it empty?

"Pretty strange, huh?"

"Yeah," Longo said. "Pretty strange." And it was beginning to feel uncomfortably familiar. A simple case on the surface. But just underneath it, unanswered questions. Beneath that, the beginning of a maze of confusion and contradictions. And the deeper you dug, the more hopelessly lost you became.

"Okay," Longo said. "You take a GSR?"

The prosecutor was asking if the Montebello police had taken any swabs from Yamaguchi's hands for a gunshot residue test. If antimony or barium were found, it would indicate the presence of residue from the explosion of the primer in the cartridge, confirming that he had recently fired a gun.

"Yeah. Got swabs from right and left palms, and backs of his hands. Sheriff's lab's still got them."

"Uh-huh." He scanned the report again. "When you picked up the gun from the Chippy, did you—"

Longo was interrupted by a small woman standing in his open door.

"Larry, darling!"

"Lea! How the heck are you?" Longo jumped to his feet, quickly squeezed between the desk and the bookcase, and grabbed the woman in a bear hug.

The woman laughed in delight. She was maybe fifty, very slender and fine-boned, almost emaciated in appearance. Her skin was pale, nearly translucent, made even more so by jet black eyes, heavily mascaraed eyebrows, blood red lipstick, long, brightly painted fingernails, and thick raven hair swept back dramatically. Despite the frail appearance, she radiated a dynamic energy, every movement with a dramatic flourish. The woman dressed like a wealthy socialite, complete with array of jewelry, and carried herself like a grande dame. She was Gloria Swanson in *Sunset Boulevard*.

"Son of a gun, Lea," Longo said, stepping back to look at her, "you look great!"

But both knew the truth. Lea D'Agostino was not the same woman who had tried the *Twilight Zone* case.

D'Agostino laughed again, shaking her head in mock disgust. "Such a liar you are, Larry!"

"No, I mean it! I—oh, sorry." He waved toward Holden. "Lea,

this is Monty Holden. Detective with Montebello P.D." He looked back at the woman. "Monty, meet Lea D'Agostino, a deputy out in the Van Nuys office."

"Detective," D'Agostino said demurely, holding her pale hand out, palm down in the grand fashion.

Holden took it awkwardly, shook it. "Glad to meet you, ma'am."

"The Dragon Lady," Longo said, grinning. "I taught her everything she knows."

D'Agostino laughed. "Those were good times, weren't they?"

Years earlier, when she had been waiting for the results of the bar examination, D'Agostino was assigned as a law clerk to a top prosecutor trying a big case in Beverly Hills. The prosecutor's name was Larry Longo, she was told, and she could learn a lot about trial work from him. And the case was a political hot potato: Longo was prosecuting Iranian students for rioting and assaulting police during a visit by the shah of Iran.

The courtroom was a circus, packed with Iranians loudly supporting the defendants. Unfortunately, D'Agostino bore a striking resemblance to the shah's sister. Word soon spread that the striking woman who sat with the prosecutor in trial was the princess of Iran. She soon began receiving death threats. And outside of the courtroom, students chanted, "You will die, Princess."

When she reported to Longo that she had been followed home, he insisted on driving her home himself. It was during one of these late-evening drives after a hard day in trial that he noticed a black car following them.

He turned off onto a side street—and the car followed. He turned again, and the car stayed with them, closer. He accelerated, but the car kept closing. He could see five men in the black car.

Longo turned again, heading for the Beverly Hills police station, and floored the accelerator. Within seconds, he and a terrified D'Agostino were flying through Beverly Hills at one hundred miles per hour, tires screaming, the black car in hot pursuit.

The five men had closed to within fifty feet when Longo made the final screeching turn and slammed on the brakes in front of the station. The black car veered off as Longo and D'Agostino jumped out and ran toward the station, then sped off into the darkness.

After that, the Beverly Hills police department began checking her car twice a day for explosive devices. They inspected the women's rest room in the courthouse each morning and posted a guard at her home.

"Good times," Longo said.

"By the way, did you get Ernie's memo?"

Longo nodded. "Yeah, I saw it."

Everyone in the D.A.'s Office had received a copy of a confidential memo from Ernie Norris. He had decided to throw his hat in the ring, the memo read; he was running against Reiner in the coming elections. The message went on to request campaign contributions. Any responses would be kept secret, Norris promised in the memo; Reiner would never find out which of his deputies was contributing money to his opponent.

"He's got my money," D'Agostino said.

"Mine, too."

"Too bad he doesn't have a chance."

Longo nodded silently. The ironies of power, he mused. Reiner had demoted Norris to remove him as a political threat. But Norris was a professional; all he wanted to do was try cases and put "bad actors" away. He had no serious interest in politics. Removing him as head of Special Trials and keeping him from trying important cases had deeply angered the prosecutor. And the anger became bitterness, until finally he lashed out and did the very thing that Reiner feared.

Norris was clearly the best candidate, Longo thought. But as a law-and-order Republican, his chances in today's Los Angeles were almost nonexistent.

"Well, I just drove in for a meeting, darling," D'Agostino said. "And I've got to run. I'm late."

Longo grinned. "Same old Lea."

"Of course."

Longo paused, serious now. "Everything okay?"

"Fine." She looked at him for a moment, a trace of pain now in her eyes. "Just fine."

Longo nodded slowly.

"Well . . ." She looked at Holden. "It was nice to meet you, Detective."

"Same here," he said.

"Larry," she said to the prosecutor, "if you're ever out in the Valley . . ."

"I'll do that, Lea."

D'Agostino smiled, then turned and quickly walked out the door.

Longo walked back to his seat and sat down. He was silent for a moment. Then he looked at Holden. "Yeah, where were we?"

"Uh, lemme see . . . the gun."

"Right."

Once again Longo went over his notes on the Yamaguchi case. What was Yamaki up to? he asked himself. Why had Yamaguchi worn a sock, yet immediately turned himself in? Why the speedy loader? Why did the wife lie about Yamaguchi saying nothing? Why . . .

The prosecutor looked out the window and was surprised to see that it was dark outside. He checked his watch: 7:40. He sighed, then stood up and grabbed his coat and briefcase. He looked out the window again, this time past the old Hall of Justice to the bright neon lights of Chinatown.

He could just see the Phoenix Bakery. And next to it, the entrance to the alley called Bamboo Lane.

Chapter

8

The Rodney King incident had turned Los Angeles into a powder keg of racial tensions. Now, the Latasha Harlans case seemed to
be the closest lit match.

Longo sat in the courtroom audience, waiting for McKinney to
arrive for Morris Thomas's sentencing hearing. It had been four weeks
since the lawyer had been found guilty of embezzling from his client
Baby Harrold Weston. The probation officer's report was finished and
in a few minutes it would be time for Judge Bascue to decide on a
sentence.

Longo watched from the audience as his junior deputy Larry
Boyle paced in front of a jury while questioning a Highway Patrol
officer on the stand.

Longo wondered what kind of pressures the Harlans case had
put on Judge Bascue.

A teenaged black girl, Latasha Harlans, had tried to steal a
bottle of orange juice from a small grocery store in the ghetto of south
central L.A. The fifty-one-year-old Korean woman who owned the
store, Soon Ja Du, caught the girl and wrestled with her for the bottle.
Harlans punched the older woman in the face, then turned to leave.
Du pulled out a gun and shot her in the back of the head.

The woman was charged with second-degree murder. And as
in the King case, there was a videotape; a security camera had recorded the entire incident. After viewing the tape, a jury found Du

guilty of only involuntary manslaughter. Judge Joyce Karlin considered the favorable probation reports, then had granted Du probation for five years and ordered her to perform four hundred hours of community service.

The black community exploded in rage at the lenient sentence. A mob of 350 surged past guards and into the courthouse, chanting "Karlin must go." Demonstrators paraded outside of the judge's home. Local black leaders held endless press conferences; some vowed to "make Karlin's life as uncomfortable as possible."

The politicians, of course, had moved quickly to take advantage of the Harlans case. Reiner, with the elections not far off, held his own press conference and called the sentence "a stunning miscarriage of justice." Declaring that "there is no way I can send deputy district attorneys into her courtroom," he ordered all deputies to refuse to handle criminal cases in Judge Karlin's court. Presiding Judge Ricardo Torres, a former deputy D.A. himself, lashed back with a press release that accused Reiner of "usurping the independence of the judiciary" and promised that "the Los Angeles Superior Court will not be intimidated by Mr. Reiner's shrill antics."

The whole thing reminded Longo of a book he had recently read, Tom Wolfe's *Bonfire of the Vanities*.

But the incident had escalated the steadily building racial tensions between the black community and the dozens of Korean merchants in the area. Those tensions would finally be ignited a few months later with the Rodney King verdict; despite the seeming random nature of the ensuing riots, it was clear that the Korean-owned businesses were specifically targeted for looting and burning.

Longo glanced at the clock on the back wall, then directed his attention again to Boyle's direct examination.

"Officer Crepin," Boyle said, "would you please estimate the speed of the defendant."

"Yes, sir. Mr. Contreras was going approximately ninety miles per hour."

"Ninety."

"Yes, sir."

"In a tow truck."

"Yes, sir."

Longo thought back to the day Boyle had brought the case to

him. It had not been a particularly unusual case. A "bandit" tow truck driver had been racing another tow truck, side by side at eighty miles an hour through a residential area of west Los Angeles, each trying to be the first to an accident scene. A young woman and her thirteen-year-old boy were stopped at a traffic light. The driver of one of the trucks could not stop in time and slammed into the rear of the car, injuring the woman and killing the boy. It was a garden-variety vehicular manslaughter case.

But Boyle was enraged when he had gone over the file. The driver had already received twelve citations in the previous year and a half for speeding, reckless driving, and running red lights; he had been given a ticket just three days earlier and was driving on a suspended license when he killed the boy. And Boyle discovered that when the driver had heard the accident report on his radio that day, he had been at the garage waiting for a brake job; he had grabbed his truck and taken off at high speed with defective brakes. This was more than just manslaughter, Boyle felt; this was murder.

Boyle argued to Longo that the case was more than just a grossly negligent homicide. If he could prove that the tow truck driver *knew* his driving was likely to kill someone, he might be able to prove malice—and get a murder conviction.

Longo was skeptical. He knew that it would be extremely difficult to prove that kind of knowledge. It had never been done before in California; a conviction would make legal history. But at least in theory Boyle was right. Contreras deserved to go to prison, and this would send a chilling message to the tow truck drivers. It was a gamble; if they went for broke and lost, the defendant would walk out of the courtroom a free man.

Longo told his junior deputy to go ahead and amend the complaint to second-degree murder.

"And why was this, Officer?" Boyle continued. "Why was it important to be the first on the scene of an accident?"

"Well, sir, the first tow truck there gets the job."

"You mean, the police at the scene award the towing job to the first truck to arrive?"

"Yes, sir, generally."

Boyle walked toward the jury box, looked each of the twelve jurors in the face, one at a time.

Longo felt a twinge of pride. The ex-cop was turning into a top-notch prosecutor and a gifted trial lawyer.

Although he was the least experienced of Longo's deputies, Boyle was no kid. He was forty-four years old with a middle-aged paunch and a full, pleasant face accented by thick black hair, a bushy mustache, and heavy dark eyebrows. It was the face of the neighborhood butcher. And behind it was a fun-loving, fast-talking Irishman with a quick wit and a bawdy sense of humor.

Boyle had been an officer with the Long Beach Police Department for eight years when a drunk driver rammed into his patrol car, putting him in the hospital and ending his career. But he had earned a law degree years earlier.

As a new deputy D.A., Boyle quickly found that trying cases gave him a high. But he also learned that trial work took a tremendous physical toll; he was not a young man anymore. Yet, he began to put together a string of misdemeanor trial victories and soon attracted Longo's interest.

Longo knew that there was no "mold" for a good trial lawyer; as with any artist, each had his or her own unique characteristics. Boyle had the benefit of life experience and common sense, an ability to understand human nature that many younger deputies lacked. But perhaps his chief strength lay in his "command presence," an ability to instill in the jury the feeling that he was utterly confident and completely in control.

When Longo had asked him about this, Boyle explained that he had learned it in the police academy and, later, had refined the technique as a cop on the beat. When you dealt with potentially dangerous situations, it was critical to give the appearance of being in control; if others sensed that you were hesitant or unsure of yourself, you were dead. If you *acted* as if you were in charge, you *were* in charge. This approach worked on the beat and, he discovered, it worked just as well in the courtroom.

In many ways, the easygoing, wisecracking Irishman was the exact opposite of the restrained, sensitive Craig Veals. And, in fact, Longo's two deputies had little use for each other. Boyle felt Veals was a bleeding heart; worse, he was a loner rather than a team player. Veals, on the other hand, thought the ex-cop was too ambitious, more concerned with winning cases than achieving justice. On many occasions, Longo had found it necessary to call a meeting of his family to calm tempers and air out real and imagined grievances.

Longo checked his watch, then looked back at the entrance to the courtroom. He expected McKinney to walk in any minute for the sentencing hearing on Thomas. And Yamaki had called, had left a message that he wanted to meet this morning in court to talk about something.

Longo wondered how his other charges were doing. Torrealba was tied up all day in Division 38, putting on four preliminary hearings. Dohi was out interviewing witnesses on the Yamaguchi case. And Veals was at L.A. County General Hospital, doing an attempted murder "prelim" in the burn ward.

A sixty-six-year-old wino living in a flophouse off skid row had suspected his sixty-two-year-old male lover of being unfaithful. He had waited until the man was asleep, then soaked him with lighter fluid and set him afire. The man was now wrapped in bandages from head to toe, unable to be moved and barely able to speak. He was not expected to live. But he was the only witness; Longo needed his testimony recorded before he died. And so the preliminary hearing was moved to the hospital. When he did finally die, the attempted-murder charges would be amended to first-degree murder. The old wino made a pathetic defendant and probably would not live much longer himself. But murder was murder.

McKinney entered the courtroom. He walked down the aisle and sat down in a pew across from Longo. He looked at the prosecutor and nodded solemnly.

Judge Bascue spotted him too. He looked at the clock on the back wall.

"Mr. Boyle," he said, "I think this would be a good time to break for lunch. I have a matter left over from this morning's calendar, and I see that counsel are here on that now."

Bascue gave the jurors the standard instruction not to discuss the case among themselves or with anyone else during the break and to return at 1:30. As they filed out of the courtroom, he called the Thomas case. Then he told the bailiff to bring the defendant out from "lockup."

McKinney approached the counsel table, began pulling papers out of his burgundy leather briefcase.

Longo walked up to Boyle. "If I didn't know better," he said to his junior deputy, "I'd think you were enjoying all this."

Boyle grinned. "Better than sex."

Longo shook his head. "The Irish are a strange race."

Boyle laughed as he finished gathering his documents into his briefcase.

The metal door swung open and the bailiff escorted Morris Thomas out into the courtroom. He was wearing an orange jail uniform and his wrists were handcuffed in front of him. He seemed confused, disoriented as he took a seat at counsel table next to McKinney.

Boyle looked at Thomas, then back to Longo. "Good luck," he said. Then he walked out of the courtroom.

"The case of the People versus Morris Thomas," Judge Bascue announced, shuffling some files in front of him. "Mr. McKinney, I have read the letters forwarded on behalf of your client. And I have reviewed the probation report. You may proceed."

"Thank you, your honor," the lawyer said. "I promise to be brief."

Longo glanced at his copy of the probation report. Deputy Probation Officer Kenneth Huggler had done a pretty good job of checking Thomas out this time. But the same Deputy P.O. Huggler had also done an earlier report, with a very different result.

In most criminal cases that were sent to Superior Court, the judge ordered a "preconviction" probation report. The probation department was ordered to investigate the defendant's background, interview the victim and witnesses, check for a criminal record, and, if the defendant waived his right to remain silent, talk with him about the crime. This was done so that the judge would have background information when he discussed possible sentences in plea-bargain sessions.

Huggler had checked out Thomas and the Weston case, but he had not bothered to question Longo. His recommendation to the court had been simple: Thomas should be given probation on the condition that he pay back the money to Weston.

When Thomas had been convicted by the jury, a new probation investigation was ordered. Huggler again looked into Thomas's past, but this time armed with the facts Longo had brought out in trial.

His supplemental report concluded that "what initially appeared to be an isolated incident, the Weston case, now appears to be part of an ongoing pattern of misappropriation, diversion, and theft . . . During the trial it came to light that the defendant was involved with another individual in a preloan fee scam leaving a trail of victims across the United States. In light of the new allegations of misconduct, it is believed that a change in the probation officer's recommendation is appropriate." His new recommendation: state prison.

But Longo knew that the judge was free to ignore the report and its recommendation. Thomas could still walk away from this and, with his secret bank accounts, live like a king in the Caribbean for the rest of his life.

"Unfortunately, your honor," McKinney said, "the supplemental report does not address the issue in this case, and that is the Weston incident. Rather, the report addresses matters that are pure speculation, allegations by the district attorney that have not been proven."

He turned to look at Longo.

"Mr. Thomas is presumed innocent of these accusations, and he *is* innocent. And it would be manifestly unfair to send him to prison based upon such false, unproven charges."

McKinney looked back to Judge Bascue.

"I believe that the original report does an excellent job of detailing the outstanding, even inspirational, background of my client. The son of poor sharecroppers in Alabama, he pulled himself up by his bootstraps, pulled himself out of that hopeless world, to become a member of the Washington, D.C., police department, a respected detective of homicide. Then . . ."

The prosecutor looked down the table at Thomas seated next to his attorney. He looked worried, even frightened, a very different man from the successful, confident lawyer. But, then, wearing an orange jumpsuit and tennis shoes without laces could do that to a person.

When the verdict of guilty had been announced, Longo had quickly asked Judge Bascue to revoke Thomas's bail and take him into custody until the sentencing hearing. McKinney was outraged, pointing out that Thomas was a member of the bar with a home and family in Los Angeles, and was therefore unlikely to flee the jurisdiction before sentencing. He accused Longo of seeking vengeance against his client, of trying to humiliate him. In any event, McKinney argued, it was probable that Thomas would be given probation; the first probation report had recommended it, he had no criminal record, and he would clearly make restitution of the full $108,000 to Weston. There was certainly no reason why his client should be deprived of his liberty now.

Longo then pointed out an interesting fact: All the wealthy lawyer's "property" in California was rented or leased—his expensive home, his law offices, his new Lincoln, everything. He could no longer practice law in the state, as Bascue had ordered him to cease practicing and the state bar would now finally move to have him disbarred. And he reminded the judge of the letter that had been found during the surprise search of his office: Thomas had huge amounts of money secretly socked away in Caribbean and Swiss bank accounts. The simple fact was that there was little left to keep him in this country, and everything to be gained by leaving. Had not his partner in crime, Sherif Ali, fled to Switzerland when Longo started breathing down his neck?

Thomas's bail was revoked, and the bailiff unceremoniously slapped handcuffs on the stunned lawyer and took him into custody.

"Furthermore, your honor, Mr. Thomas is a respected deacon and an elder in his church." McKinney pointed back at the audience. "In fact, there are over twenty members of his church seated in the courtroom at this very moment, prepared to testify on his behalf."

Three rows of wooden pews were filled with men and women dressed in conservative suits and dresses and nodding their heads solemnly in agreement.

"Mr. McKinney," Judge Bascue said, "if you wish to call them, that is your privilege. But I have already received approximately thirty letters on your client's behalf. I think anything further along those lines might prove cumulative and redundant."

"As you wish, your honor. I only want to point out that the very presence of these distinguished members of the community is an indication of the esteem in which my client..."

Longo turned around in his seat and looked at the audience. He wondered how many of them knew what their respected deacon was doing with piles of money stashed away in offshore bank accounts.

"...and he is not a danger to the community, your honor," McKinney continued. "To the contrary, he is an asset, a valuable asset.

I suggest that much more can be gained by taking advantage of this man's education and experience, by ordering him to perform community service in an appropriate manner. Why, it would be a waste to send him to prison...a *waste,* your honor!"

"Gimme a break," Longo muttered.

Bascue glanced disapprovingly at the prosecutor, then looked back patiently at McKinney.

The defense lawyer paused dramatically. "I find it of more than passing interest that only a few days ago, your honor, a member of the bench in this very city...a fellow judge, a *white* judge..."

For cryin' out loud, Longo thought. Here it comes.

"...chose to give probation to a defendant who shot and killed a poor black girl."

Longo sighed, shook his head in disgust.

"In closing, your honor, I would ask the court to consider Mr. Thomas's family..." McKinney turned toward the audience. "His lovely wife, and his young children, seated behind me. For it is this poor woman who will suffer if she loses her husband, these young children who will suffer if their father is taken from them and sent off to prison."

"Are you finished, Mr. McKinney?"

"I would only add that Mr. Thomas has already been punished, your honor. The greatest punishment he could suffer: the loss of respect and standing in the community..."

Bored now with the defense lawyer's rambling oratory, Longo gazed around the courtroom. He looked at the large replica of the state seal mounted on the wall behind Judge Bascue. "The Great Seal of the State of California" it read. It appeared to be made out of bronze, but Longo realized that it was only a plastic imitation. He looked at the witness stand, the judge's bench, the jury box. All appeared to be made of walnut, but were really a cheap composite. The chair he sat on had the same look of rich walnut, but it was plastic. Even the linoleum floors in the audience area had a phony marble look to them.

Nothing is ever as it appears in the criminal justice system, Longo thought.

It suddenly struck him that this was only a *replica* of a courtroom. Like so much in Southern California, it was an imitation of reality, a movie set carefully designed to give the illusion of a court-room. Plastic, fake, sterile. A careful copy of the real thing, like the stucco architecture of Spanish villas, Chinese pagodas, and Tudor mansions that grew around Los Angeles like weeds . . .

"Mr. Longo?"

"Huh?"

"Would you like to be heard?" Judge Bascue asked.

"Oh yeah, thanks, judge." Longo rose to his feet. "Well, that first report, the P.O. didn't know what he was talking about . . ."

Judge Bascue sighed, then leaned back in his chair.

"There was nothing in there about the millions of dollars this guy's ripped off from people all across the country. There was nothing in there about the offshore bank accounts where he's got all that money stashed away. There was nothing in there about the Major Frauds investigation going on—"

"Objection," McKinney said, rising to his feet. "Mr. Thomas is being sentenced for the Weston incident. The rest of this is sheer speculation."

"The court can consider matters other than the conviction itself in passing sentence, judge."

"I am aware of that," Bascue said. "Please continue."

Longo sensed something behind him, turned slightly and glanced back toward the audience.

Mike Yamaki was walking through the doors. He smiled at the prosecutor.

Longo turned back to the judge.

"I won't take up your time going over all those thefts, judge. I filed the papers and I guess you've read them."

"I have."

"The thing is, the P.O. didn't know about all these other rip-offs. And Thomas over there, he just snowed the guy with all this stuff about being a deacon and an elder and all. The guy's a *thief*!"

Judge Bascue slowly massaged the bridge of his nose.

"I mean, I'm sitting here listening to McKinney go on about what a great guy Thomas is, how he was a cop, and a lawyer, and a leader of the community and all."

Longo stepped back from the table, began to walk toward the defendant and his lawyer.

"Well, seems to me that this guy's had all the breaks, you know? He's got an education, he's got a career, he's got lots of money. He's not like some poor clown who never had a chance, who doesn't know any better. This isn't some guy who was beat on the head every day as a kid, and got in with the wrong crowd, and had to fight and steal to survive. This isn't some guy who doesn't know any better."

As Longo approached the two seated men threateningly, McKinney began to stand.

"Your honor ..." the defense lawyer protested.

Longo stopped, stared at Thomas. "This guy's a lawyer. He *knew* better. He knew what was right and what was wrong. He had it all, he didn't *need* to steal. But he stole anyway."

The prosecutor turned, walked back toward his seat. "This man stole for one reason: greed. He stole Harrold Weston's life savings. He stole everything that man had fought for—and I mean *fought* for, spilled blood for. He stole that man's dreams, his life."

Longo paused for a moment, looked back at Thomas.

"This guy had all the breaks. And he chose to be what he is, a thief."

Then he sat down.

Judge Bascue said nothing at first, his head bowed in thought. Then he looked up and took a deep breath.

"I get no satisfaction out of this," the judge said. "It is a source of great disappointment. Morris Thomas has long been a respected member of the legal community." He looked at the defendant. "I must admit that when I first saw this case, I thought it was just a fee dispute, at most a state bar matter. I thought the district attorney had overfiled the case."

Longo turned slightly, glanced back at the audience. Yamaki was sitting in the back row.

"But this was no fee dispute," the judge continued. "The defendant stole money. He took advantage of his position of trust and stole money from a client. Then he took the stand and committed perjury. And he has shown no remorse."

Bascue looked down at Thomas. "Are you ready for sentencing?"

Thomas rose to his feet unsteadily. McKinney stood up with him.

"I hereby sentence you to serve three years in state prison, and I further ..."

Yes! Longo thought to himself, clenching a fist triumphantly. Got you, you son of a bitch!

When Judge Bascue had finished sentencing Thomas and adjourned for the noon recess, Yamaki walked up to Longo at the counsel table.

"Congratulations, Larry."

"Thanks, Mike."

"That was a nice win. There wasn't a lot of money on you pulling it off."

"Yeah." Longo looked at him expectantly.

"Can we talk?"

"Sure."

"Look, Larry, I've spoken with Mr. Yamaguchi ..."

"Uh-huh."

"The thing is, he's prepared to enter a plea to voluntary manslaughter."

"So what's new."

"We'll agree to him doing some time, say a year in county jail."

Longo had thought about this, had even expected it. Bascue had been pushing him to work a deal on the case: It looked to be a typical heat of passion killing, an obvious voluntary manslaughter. Why take the court's time with a trial?

But the prosecutor still smelled something. He was convinced there was more to it than a jealous husband killing his wife's lover in an uncontrollable rage. He smelled a cold-blooded murder.

Or was it because of Yamaki? Was it the haunting memory of Chinatown that was blinding Longo? Was this his professional judgment—or was it personal?

Yamaki was now sweetening the deal, agreeing to go along with a short jail sentence. And, given the facts so far, it seemed a fair disposition of the case.

"No deal," Longo said.

"Larry ..."

"He's charged with first-degree. I'll take a plea to second."

"Second-degree murder."

"Yeah."

Yamaki looked down at the floor, shook his head slowly. Then he looked up.

"Larry, there's more to this case than you know." He paused. "If we go to trial ..."

"*When* we go to trial," Longo said.

"... I won't be going for voluntary manslaughter."

"Uh-huh."

"I'll be going for a complete acquittal."

"I'll be going for first-degree murder."

"Larry," the lawyer said quietly, "believe me, you don't have a case."

"That's what McKinney said."

Yamaki smiled, shook his head almost sadly. Then he looked the prosecutor directly in the eye, his smile suddenly gone.

"You won't win this one," he said. Then he turned and walked out of the courtroom.

Chapter 9

Longo stepped out of the Criminal Courts Building and onto Temple Street, a ham and cheese sandwich in his hand. He turned right, D.A. investigator Jimmy Sakoda following along beside him.

"His name is Takeshi Uchida," Sakoda said.

"Uh-huh."

"He's a close friend of the victim, Kariya. Known him for about thirteen years."

Longo nodded, then took another bite out of his sandwich.

"Uchida owns a nightclub in J-Town," Sakoda said. "A place called the Albatross."

The investigator continued, "Uchida knows Yamaguchi too. They're business neighbors. Yamaguchi and his wife own the Mitsuru Cafe, named after the wife. It's over in J-Town too."

"This guy we're going to interview, Yamaguchi's brother-in-law . . . what's his name? Hanemure?"

"Mamoru Hanemure."

"Yeah. He owns a restaurant there too, doesn't he?"

"Yep, not far from Yamaguchi's."

"How long have Yamaguchi and Hanemure known each other?"

"Since Hanemure was a teenager. They're all from the old country, from the same province. Yamaguchi was a cop there and Hanemure was—"

"Yamaguchi was a cop in Japan?"

"Yep, a long time ago."

Longo pondered this for a moment as he came to a stop at an intersection. He took another bite of his sandwich.

"So he's pretty good with a gun," Longo said, the words muffled by ham and cheese.

"I guess so. Anyway, Yamaguchi met Hanemure's sister, Mitsuru, over there, and they got married and came to the U.S. After they'd been here for a while, Hanemure came over. By that time, Yamaguchi owned a lot of real estate and businesses around L.A., and he gave one of his restaurants to his brother-in-law."

"Just gave it to him?"

"Well, not exactly. It was one of those sweetheart deals. No money down, low payments when he could afford it . . ."

The light changed and Longo stepped out across Spring Street, then turned right

"Go on, Jimmy."

"Well, Uchida tells me that one of Mitsuru's little sidelines is running the Mitsuru Kayogakuin. . . ."

"The what?"

"It's a school in J-Town, a music school on the floor above the Mitsuru Cafe. They teach popular Japanese songs."

"Uh-huh."

"So one of the students in the school was this guy Kariya. And I guess Mitsuru took a liking to him. She hired him to help out at the restaurant, do odd jobs around the place."

"Okay."

"Kariya did some painting and stuff like that. But then he started taking on more and more responsibility, in the restaurant and in other businesses the Yamaguchis owned. And there was this entertainment business . . ."

The two men walked past the old City Hall, once the tallest building in Los Angeles and still one of the most recognizable landmarks of the city. At First Street they turned right, past a small food stand with a large sign reading KOSHER BURRITOS.

". . . The Yamaguchis put on these shows for the locals, sort of variety shows from the old country. They'd book entertainers from Japan to come over and perform."

"Okay."

"Well, by this time Kariya had pretty well worked himself into Mitsuru's confidence. And he was doing a lot of the work on these shows, going over to Japan and booking the groups, doing the promotion, building the sets and so on."

"He and the wife, Mitsuru, they having an affair?"

"Uchida thinks so."

"Go on."

"Well, they put on this show, the first one Kariya's done all the work for. And it's a big hit, makes a lot of money. And I guess the one before that, one Yamaguchi himself put together, it was a flop. They lost a bundle."

Longo nodded.

"So, about a week before the shooting, they're having this big dinner party over at the Mitsuru Cafe, just before the next show. The Yamaguchis and some of their friends and business contacts, including Uchida. And Kariya's there. And Uchida says that all of a sudden, Mitsuru raised her voice and started chewing out Yamaguchi. Criticized him for screwing up on booking the singers from Japan or something. And she's doing this in front of everyone. Big loss of face, right?"

"I guess so."

"Believe me. And then Kariya jumps in, and he starts criticizing Yamaguchi too, saying that he really screwed up, and that he screwed up in the show before that too, and lost a lot of money. And this is Yamaguchi's employee, right in front of everybody."

"Yeah."

"Well, Uchida says Yamaguchi didn't say much, just kept quiet. But his face got real flushed, and it looked like he was trying real hard not to lose his temper."

"Uh-huh," Longo said. "Still, not exactly a motive for murder."

"There's more."

The two men crossed Los Angeles Street, entering the area of the city known as Little Tokyo. To their right was the fifteen-story New Otani Hotel and Garden, one of the most modern and beautiful structures in the Civic Center area. Although most of its guests were businessmen from Japan, its fine restaurants had become an immediate hit among lawyers and politicians; Judge Bascue was one of the many lunchtime regulars. Just past the New Otani, on a walkway with a statue of the first Japanese-American astronaut, was the Sumitomo Bank Building. Beyond that were the Mitsubishi Bank and the Bank of California, now a subsidiary of a Japanese corporation. Tucked in behind these massive office buildings, almost surrealistic in the shadows of their modern steel and glass, were the Jodoshu Buddhist Temple and the Higashi Hongwanja Buddhist Temple.

Longo ate the last of the sandwich, then threw the cellophane wrapper in a trash can.

"Right after that," Sakoda said, "three days before the shooting, Kariya came to the Albatross nightclub to see Uchida. Kariya was real mad. He said Yamaguchi threatened to fire him, and they got into a shouting match. Kariya called Yamaguchi incompetent, and reminded him of how his show had failed and how the one he'd done, Kariya, had been a big hit. Anyway, I guess it got pretty hot."

Longo glanced at Sakoda as they continued walking and going over his interview with Uchida. Sakoda was tall for a *nisei*, trim and athletic, with short, neatly trimmed hair and a slender, youthful face. At fifty-six, he looked like a man twenty years younger. Only a quiet, dignified manner and a gentle sense of humor reflected his true age.

Longo knew the man had been an L.A. cop for twenty-six years before joining the D.A.'s Bureau of Investigations. He also knew that Sakoda had spent four long years in a relocation camp in the desolate wastes of Gila Bend, Arizona; the Japanese bombed Pearl Harbor when he was seven years old.

He noticed that the investigator wore the uniform of all cops and D.A.'s men, a traditional sports coat and conservative tie; suits were strictly for the lawyers.

Sakoda was one of the best in the office, and Longo knew he had been lucky to get him on such short notice. It had been Sakoda to whom Longo had turned for help in the Chinatown case.

When Sakoda first joined the Los Angeles Police Department, he was immediately assigned to walking a beat in Little Tokyo. During the next twenty-six years with LAPD, he served with narcotics, vice, juvenile, burglary, robbery, and homicide. But his work in the Asian areas of Los Angeles—Chinatown, Little Tokyo, Koreatown, and the exploding Vietnamese community—made him realize that there was a need for a special group of officers with Asian backgrounds and expertise in the ways of the Asian-American communities. The language problem alone was formidable: There were over ninety languages and dialects spoken in the Asian communities of the city. The simple fact was that Anglo cops were foreigners in these neighborhoods; they did not speak the language, did not understand the culture, and the local residents did not trust them.

The problems in the Asian enclaves of L.A. were very different from those encountered in other areas by white patrolmen and detectives. Chinatown was run by gangs associated with the ancient tongs of Hong Kong—the "heroin highway" ran all the way to the opium fields of the Chinese warlords in the Golden Triangle, high in the mountains of Southeast Asia. In Little Tokyo, the Yakuza of Tokyo and Osaka had their fingers in the Japanese-American community, running businesses, smuggling guns, and laundering syndicate money from Japan. A flood of refugees from Vietnam had brought with them their own criminal element, many of them corrupt politicians and battle-hardened soldiers; the Chinese commonly used thugs from L.A. or Little Saigon in nearby Orange County as their "muscle." The Korean population had its own street gangs and secret societies with roots in the motherland. And then there were the Thais, and the Filipinos, the Taiwanese, the Cambodians . . .

Sakoda was finally given permission to organize an Asian task force within the Los Angeles Police Department, made up of officers of Asian heritage. The special unit would coordinate its activities with the FBI, the DEA, Interpol, and other agencies in attacking international criminal activities operating within the Asian communities of Los Angeles. Sakoda recruited more than a dozen cops—Korean, Chinese, Japanese, Filipino, and Thai—from within the department.

The task force proved a huge success. But Sakoda soon became disillusioned with the way his unit was being treated by LAPD's administration. It was clear to him that Chief Darryl Gates was refusing to promote the men in the task force, a refusal that Sakoda saw as discrimination against minorities. When disillusionment finally turned to anger, he submitted his resignation.

When officials in the District Attorney's Office heard about Sakoda's departure, they contacted the ex-cop and asked him to start a smaller version of the Asian task force within the D.A.'s own Bureau of Investigations. The bureau's job was to assist prosecutors in investigating and preparing special cases for trial. Although they had the same powers as the police, investigators in the bureau were not limited by any city or county jurisdictional lines; they were free to go anywhere. Nor were they limited to investigating only certain kinds of cases, such as homicides or narcotics; the bureau worked on any kind of case that required "special attention." This often meant cases involving organized crime, politically sensitive cases, or cases where there was possible police misconduct.

Sakoda agreed to join the bureau. He quickly recruited three men for the new group, now called the Asian Criminal Investigation Unit.

When Longo had been given the Chinatown case years earlier, he had not trusted the LAPD homicide cop who had been assigned to the investigation and had gone to the chief of the bureau's Asian task force instead. Sakoda gave him one of his best men, Benny Lee, who knew the underground of Chinatown and was trusted in the community. And Lee produced results.

Now it was Sakoda to whom Longo had once again turned for help.

"So the next morning after the shooting," Sakoda said, "Uchida says he got a phone call from Yamaguchi's wife. She asked him to come to the restaurant that evening. Didn't mention the shooting, just asked him to come. I guess she wanted to make an announcement, and plan Kariya's funeral."

"Uh-huh."

"Well, Uchida went to the gathering about nine forty-five that night. And he ran into this friend of the family, Matsumoto."

"Matsumoto."

"Yep, Kohei Matsumoto. So the two of them go outside and start talking. And Matsumoto tells Uchida about Yamaguchi shooting Kariya the night before. And then he says Yamaguchi told him a few days before that he was going to finish Kariya. He had hired a P.I. to follow his—"

Longo stopped, looked at Sakoda. "Yamaguchi told this guy he was going to *finish* Kariya?"

"Yep. And he had a P.I. following his wife."

"Yeah?"

"Well, about this time, Yamaguchi's brother-in-law, Hanemure, joined the conversation . . ."

"The guy we're going to see now."

"Yep. So Hanemure said to the other two, he said Yamaguchi told him he caught Kariya and his wife together a couple of nights before. They were in a house the Yamaguchis owned in Boyle Heights, one they were fixing up to sell. And he caught the two of them upstairs. Kariya was just taking his shirt off."

"Uh-huh."

"Yamaguchi called Hanemure on the phone and told him that he had been patient long enough, he was going to take care of the matter himself."

"Take care of the matter."

"Yep. So Hanemure said he told Yamaguchi to calm down, he would talk with his sister."

"Uh-huh."

"So then the next night, the night he killed Kariya, Yamaguchi called Hanemure again. He said the same thing was happening, they were doing it again. He said he was going to finish Kariya. And then he said—"

"Finish him . . ."

"Yep, same thing he said to Matsumoto. He said, 'I'm not going to be patient anymore, I'm going to finish him.' "

Longo nodded slowly.

"And then he said Yamaguchi asked him, Hanemure, to take care of things after he finished Kariya."

"Take care of things?"

"I guess he meant get a lawyer, a bail bondsman, I don't know. Maybe take care of his businesses after he was arrested, or after he skipped."

Longo realized that this was critical testimony. Yamaki would present evidence that this was a killing that resulted from a sudden "heat of passion." Because of the lack of clear thinking or planning, the homicide would not be considered murder; it would only be voluntary manslaughter. With a clean record, Yamaguchi would probably walk out of the courtroom on probation. But his statements to Matsumoto and Hanemure indicated cold-blooded premeditation. And that was murder.

"The I.O. on the case," Longo said, referring to the investigating officer, "Holden, he interviewed Hanemure a couple hours after the shooting."

"I read the reports."

"Hanemure never said anything about Yamaguchi telling him he was going to kill Kariya."

Sakoda shrugged.

The two men continued along First Street. Along the left side of the street were small redbrick storefronts that appeared old and run-down, with cracked and faded signs in English and Japanese hanging over the doors. From there they turned into a redbrick walkway that led into an area called the Japanese Village Plaza. It was lined with attractive restaurants and stores, festively decorated with large red paper lanterns, streaming banners, and pink plastic *sakura,* or cherry blossoms. Most of the signs were written in black *kanji,* the picture language borrowed by the Japanese from China. Small, carefully manicured trees dotted the walkway. Long felt as if he had wandered into a corner of some Asian version of Disneyland.

"What else did this guy Uchida tell you?"

"Well, he said Kariya is kind of a big mouth, a braggart, you know? I mean, he's Kariya's friend, but he said the guy's got a big mouth. And Yamaguchi, he's just the opposite. Real quiet, keeps things to himself. But when he finally blows, he really blows."

"Whaddya mean?"

"One time, Uchida saw Yamaguchi chasing a guy out of the restaurant a few years ago with a knife in his hand. Doesn't know why."

"Yeah?"

"Yamaguchi was yelling, 'I'll kill you.' "

Longo was digesting all of this information, analyzing it in terms of what was admissible and what was not. The incident with the knife was out, since past acts of violence were not permitted for the purpose of showing that he committed the crime with which he was charged—unless the defendant raised the issue himself by offering evidence that he was *not* a violent person. As for the statements about "finishing" Kariya, that was hearsay. But there were exceptions to the hearsay rule, and Longo thought he could get it into evidence.

"Jimmy, you talking to this guy in English or Japanese?"

"Mostly Japanese."

"Okay."

"Another thing . . . The night before the shooting, Kariya asked Mrs. Yamaguchi to marry him."

Longo looked at the investigator.

"Uchida says she told him she had to think about it. Said she had to think of the kids, and the businesses."

"Where'd this guy Uchida hear that?"

"It was either Hanemure or Matsumoto, he couldn't recall which."

This was sounding less like a Yakuza hit, Longo thought, and more like a garden-variety triangle. But this was not a heat of passion killing, a case where the jilted husband walks in on his wife in bed with the other man. Yamaguchi had carefully planned out the murder. And he might have done it for reasons that had nothing to do with passion. Reasons like loss of face. Defending your territory. And money: If Yamaguchi's wife divorced him for Kariya, he would probably lose half of all his holdings.

"Anything else?"

"Not from Uchida. I tried to get ahold of this Matsumoto. Lives by himself, out by you, Larry, up in Malibu."

"Yeah?"

"He's been buddies with Yamaguchi for about fifteen years, eats at the restaurant maybe five times a week. Anyway, I think he's lying low, avoiding me. Every time I call, he's busy. I go out there, he's on his way out."

"Keep trying."

"Sure. So then I made an appointment to talk with Mrs. Ya-maguchi."

"Uh-huh."

"We set up a time, at her restaurant. So I went over there and she took me upstairs, above the restaurant."

"What'd she say?"

"Well, just before we got started, she left the room. When she came back, her kid was with her, Ken Yamaguchi."

"Uh-huh."

"And the kid told me that she didn't have to talk with us. I told him that was true, she didn't have to, but she agreed to over the phone. And that's why I was there."

"Yeah?"

"And the kid told me that he talked with their lawyer, and their lawyer said she didn't have to talk with me."

"Their lawyer . . ."

"Yep. Mike Yamaki."

Yamaki, Longo repeated silently to himself. What was he doing representing the wife—when he already represented the husband for killing her lover?

"Okay," Longo said. "So she clammed up?"

"Yep. Wouldn't say a word."

Longo walked in silence for a moment.

"This is it," Sakoda said, pointing to a small storefront.

The restaurant had a new blue-and-white sign that read MI-TSURU CAFE. Plastic *sakuras* hung above the door, and a tray of what appeared to be small pancake sandwiches was displayed in the window. A sign explained that these were called *imagawa yaki,* a specialty of the house made from mashed red beans and resurrected from a 150-year-old Tokyo recipe.

"Jimmy, this guy we're going to see, Hanemure . . ."

"Mamoru Hanemure."

"He said he was willing to talk?"

"That's what he said. Three-fifteen at the Mitsuru restaurant, he'd tell us anything we wanted to know."

Longo nodded as the two men entered the restaurant. Although small in front, the restaurant seemed much larger inside. The room was two stories tall and narrow but deep. A long serving counter with chairs ran along the left, and a series of tables were set up along the right. At the back of the restaurant was a flight of stairs leading up to a loft overlooking the dining area.

Sakoda pointed to their right at a man seated at a table.

"Hanemure," he said quietly.

Mamoru Hanemure was about forty, with a powerful build, a square jaw, brooding eyes, and long black hair slicked straight back. With his black silk shirt, white tie, and double-breasted gray sports coat, he looked like a Japanese version of a thirties gangster.

The word "Yakuza" again flashed through Longo's mind.

Seated across the table from Hanemure was Mike Yamaki.

Longo and Sakoda walked over to the table.

"Hello, Larry," Yamaki said with an ingratiating smile as he stood up.

"Mike," Longo said. He looked at Sakoda. "Jimmy, you know Mike Yamaki?"

Sakoda nodded.

"I don't believe you two gentlemen have met Mr. Hanemure," Yamaki said, indicating the man still seated at the table.

"Mr. Hanemure." Longo nodded at the seated man.

Without getting up, Hanemure nodded very slightly in return.

"Have a seat, Larry," Yamaki said pleasantly.

Longo sat down across the table from Hanemure. Yamaki regained his seat next to the man. Sakoda walked over to the next table and sat down, facing the three men.

"I understand you have some questions for Mr. Hanemure," Yamaki said.

Longo turned to Yamaguchi's brother-in-law. "Mr. Hanemure, I understand you're Mitsuru Yamaguchi's brother, that right?"

Hanemure nodded.

"Okay. On the night Kariya was killed, there was a dinner party here at this restaurant, right?"

Hanemure nodded.

"Some time later that night, Kariya and your sister met at your own restaurant?"

Hanemure nodded.

"Were they having an affair?"

Hanemure looked at Yamaki, then back at Longo. "I believe my brother-in-law thought so."

"Did he ever tell you that?"

"I believe he talked with me about it, possibly a month before . . . before the shooting. I told him that everything would be all right, that I would talk with Mitsuru, with Mrs. Yamaguchi."

"Uh-huh. And did you?"

"Yes. I reported back to him that everything was all right."

"But the night of the shooting, they met at your restaurant, your sister and Mr. Kariya."

Hanemure nodded.

"What time did you first see them that night?"

"Mr. Kariya was with me at my restaurant, and I received a call from Mr. Yamaguchi at about nine. He asked me to come to his restaurant."

"And then?"

"I came here. They were both here, Mr. Yamaguchi and my sister."

"And when did they leave?"

"I believe my sister left about ten or fifteen minutes after I arrived."

"Did you talk with Mr. Yamaguchi?"

Hanemure glanced at Yamaki, then back at Longo. "I believe so."

"And?"

"Mr. Yamaguchi asked me if Mr. Kariya was at my restaurant, and I told him he was."

"Did Mr. Yamaguchi say anything else?"

"I believe he said that he suspected my sister went to see him."

"*Did* Mrs. Yamaguchi leave to go see Mr. Kariya?"

Hanemure again looked toward Yamaki. "I believe so."

"Well, did you *see* the two of them together?"

"Yes."

"Was this at your restaurant?"

"Yes."

"Were they together?"

"I believe they were sitting at a table, in the back of the restaurant."

"Uh-huh. And what did you say to Mr. Yamaguchi when he said he suspected his wife had gone to your place to see Kariya?"

"I believe I told him not to worry, that I would go back and keep an eye on them."

"And so you went back, and saw them."

Hanemure nodded.

"When did they leave your restaurant?"

"When I closed, about ten."

"They were still together?"

"I believe—"

"You believe so."

Hanemure nodded again.

Longo looked at Yamaki, then back at Hanemure. "Did you see either of them again that night?"

Hanemure shook his head slowly.

"But you got a phone call from Yamaguchi."

Hanemure nodded.

"What time was this?"

"I believe it was about a half an hour after midnight."

"Want to tell me what he said?"

"Mr. Yamaguchi said that my sister called him and told him she would be home late. She said Mr. Kariya would give her a ride home. And she asked him to buy some cold drinks for their daughter."

"She didn't hide the fact she was with Kariya?"

Hanemure shook his head.

"What else did Mr. Yamaguchi tell you?"

"He said, 'The same thing is happening, it's going to continue.'"

"Go on."

"He said, 'Please take care of things.'"

"And what did you understand him to mean by that?"

"My brother-in-law was going to commit suicide."

Longo grinned, shook his head. "Do you know a guy named Uchida?"

Hanemure looked quickly at Yamaki, then back at Longo. "I don't . . . I may have met him, I'm not sure."

"Did you meet this guy here the night after the shooting?"

"I may have."

"Didn't you tell him that Yamaguchi said he was going to *finish* Kariya?"

Hanemure shook his head. "No, I never said that."

Yamaki continued to sit in silence, studying Longo.

"Didn't you tell him," Longo said, "that Yamaguchi shot a pistol at his wife maybe three weeks earlier?"

Again Hanemure shook his head. "No," he said, glancing at Yamaki.

"I see." Longo tilted back in the chair. "So this midnight phone call from Mr. Yamaguchi, what did *you* say?"

"I told him not to do anything foolish."

"Meaning?"

"Not to commit suicide."

"So you're saying Yamaguchi was going to take care of the problem by killing himself."

Hanemure said nothing.

"Do you remember talking with a Detective Holden a couple hours after the shooting?" Longo asked. "At the Montebello police station?"

"I believe so," again glancing at Yamaki.

"Didn't you tell him that Yamaguchi shot at your sister with a pistol three weeks before he killed Kariya?"

Hanemure shook his head. "I never said that."

"Uh-huh." Longo looked at Yamaki.

The lawyer smiled back.

"Well, maybe you can tell me just what you *did* say to Detective Holden."

"I answered his questions. I cannot recall now exactly..."

Longo studied Hanemure as he talked, watching his mannerisms, assessing the impressions he would make on a jury, searching for weaknesses that he might be able to exploit on the witness stand. The man would be subpoenaed by the prosecution, but Longo was sure he could qualify him as an "adverse witness"; under the Evidence Code, he could then treat Hanemure as if he were a defense witness, permitting him to ask leading questions and attack his own witness's credibility.

The case still looked like murder one to Longo. The kid in the car would testify that Yamaguchi was sitting in his Mercedes for half an hour that night, lying in wait for Kariya. That was plenty of time for premeditation right there. And he had the statement from Hanemure that Yamaguchi had lost his patience and was going to "finish" Kariya—clear evidence of premeditated intent to kill.

Of course, Hanemure would testify that Yamaguchi never said that, but Longo could then put Uchida on the stand to tell what Hanemure had told him at the restaurant.

Would the wife testify to the killing? Longo knew that he could not force her to testify: California law recognized the marital privilege, the right of a witness to refuse to testify against her husband. Would she take the privilege? Or would she want justice for her slain lover and take the stand?

Then he had the cop-out from Yamaguchi to the highway patrolman, a full confession to the killing. And the gun, with matching bullets. And there was the sock and the speedy loader—more evidence of planning and premeditation. He might even be able to get in Hanemure's statement to Detective Holden about Yamaguchi taking a shot at his wife three weeks earlier.

It was murder one. If the jury went for an argument that Yamaguchi was too upset to meaningfully premeditate, it was still murder two. Hell, he thought, even if the whole case fell apart, the jury would at least convict on voluntary manslaughter; there was no question that Yamaguchi had shot Kariya.

So why was Yamaki so damned confident of an *acquittal*? The only complete defenses that Longo could think of were insanity and self-defense. But there was nothing to indicate either.

What had Yamaki meant, "There's more to this case than you know"?

Chapter 10

Longo turned slightly in his seat, looked back at the audience.

A darkly beautiful Asian woman of about forty sat in the last row of the audience, regally erect with her strong chin held high. She was returning his glance with a heavy-lidded air of vague interest, as if studying a small insect. Longo knew this could only be Mitsuru Yamaguchi.

Sitting next to her was a small, wiry woman with long, bleached blond hair, the trademark briefcase resting on her knees. The eyes of Mrs. Yamaguchi's lawyer were cold, calculating, hungry. A Japanese version of Leslie Abramson.

Mike Yamaki sat a discreet distance from the two women.

The prosecutor turned back in his chair. His youngest deputy, Leonard Torrealba, stood next to him, waiting for Judge Bascue to finish his silent reading of a letter Torrealba had just handed him: "I'm gonna buy a big, thick, leather strap, a nice fat, heavy leather strap to beat you with until you come in your panties over & over until my BABY is sopping wet. I loves you, Ram Bam. I'm gonna wiggle my tongue up your butthole & I'm gonna French your asshole before I slides my cock up inside your cute little butt. You're gonna love it so much you'd kill for it . . ."

Judge Bascue looked up from the letter. "As I understand it," he said to the young prosecutor, "Mr. Freshour was in custody at the time?"

"Yes, your honor," Torrealba said. "The defendant was serving a short sentence for assault at Men's Central Jail."

"And the victim, the woman to whom he sent this letter, she's a police officer?"

"Deputy Sheriff Miriam Ramirez. She's assigned to Men's Central. It seems Mr. Freshour fell in love with one of his jailers."

"I see."

"Shortly after sending that letter to Deputy Ramirez, the defendant sent a second letter from his cell." Torrealba handed a sheet of paper to the bailiff who carried it up to the judge.

Judge Bascue began reading the second letter. "Ram Bam, there's a Hulk Monster deep inside of me, there always has been. If you don't surrender yourself to me you're going to suffer consequences far greater than anything you can imagine in your darkest deepest nightmares..." The judge glanced down at Bobby Freshour, seated next to the newly assigned public defender. The short, muscular man continued to sit rigidly in his chair, staring darkly straight ahead, oblivious to his surroundings. Bascue resumed reading to himself.

"The defendant," Torrealba said, "sent a total of eighteen letters to Deputy Ramirez. The first fifteen were sent while he was an inmate, deposited in the 'inmate complaint box.' The last three were mailed to her at the jail after he was released."

"I see."

The judge looked down at the new public defender who had just been assigned to Department 127. "Ms. Richards?"

Nancy Richards rose to her feet.

Karen Thompson had been "rotated out" of Department 127 two days earlier. As happened so often with public defenders, she had finally reached the point where the accumulation of defeats and perceived injustices interfered with her effectiveness in negotiating plea bargains and handling her caseload. Karen Thompson was sent by her superiors to the court of another judge and another set of prosecutors for a fresh start.

From his seat next to Torrealba, Longo watched as Thompson's replacement quickly scanned her client's file.

Deputy Public Defender Nancy Richards was a tall, shapely woman of about thirty, with milk-white skin, blue eyes surrounded by heavily mascaraed lashes, and long blond hair that fell in wild curls past her shoulders. She was wearing a loose-fitting silk print dress that looked vaguely bohemian yet clung to her body like a wet Kleenex. Nancy Richards was a stunningly beautiful woman. The effect, unfortunately, was destroyed by her habit of constantly chewing gum.

"Mr. Torrealba failed to mention that my client mailed two packages to Deputy Ramirez," Richards said. "A box of chocolates . . . and a wedding ring."

"A wedding ring," Judge Bascue repeated.

"The fact is, your honor, this case does not belong in this court."

"Perhaps you can explain that to me, Ms. Richards."

"Of course." She picked up a document, handed it to Torrealba. "I'm giving the district attorney a copy of a psychiatric evaluation, your honor."

Torrealba began reading the report to himself.

"After he was released," Richards continued, "he wandered around the city for three days, sleeping in public parks. He had no shoes and developed blisters. Because he was hungry and the blisters were bleeding badly, he went to the V.A. Hospital in west L.A. for food and treatment. I should perhaps mention that Mr. Freshour is a former member of the Marine Corps and saw extensive combat in Vietnam."

"I see."

"Because of what appeared to be irrational conduct during this visit to the V.A., he was sent to the psychiatric unit and held for observation."

Longo glanced down the table at the defendant. Bobby Freshour continued to stare rigidly ahead.

The prosecutor looked at his watch, then back at the stack of files on the table in front of him. It had been a long calendar call. Two files left. The Rivera case, on calendar for a motion. And Yamaguchi.

"He was very hostile, irritable, and threatening. While on the ward, he threatened to stamp another patient's head in with his foot. He continued to make threatening phone calls to the UCLA chancellor, including death threats . . ."

Longo looked at Freshour again, then at Nancy Richards. He

studied the woman as she continued reading from the psychiatric evaluation. He had already checked her out with some old friends in the P.D.'s office.

Richards had been born and raised a Quaker, first in Pennsylvania, later in Nebraska. Her parents had been active in the antiwar movement as well as in other moral causes, and had long records of arrests for acts of passive civil disobedience. She had grown used to seeing her father and mother being hauled away by police when standing up for what they believed in. From an early age she learned the sanctity of nonviolence, the importance of the individual, and the existence of a higher law than that of man. She was, some would say, born to be a public defender.

Soon, though, she learned the frustrating realities of her profession. The judicial system was basically designed to warehouse the accused; defendants were processed through the system like cattle, police officers routinely lied on the stand, and justice was little more than an abstract concept. And her clients were usually members of minority groups who viewed a white government-paid lawyer as the enemy. She also discovered that being a defense lawyer meant confrontation and conflict—things that ran against her grain as a Quaker pacifist. But she found that combat was not the only way to help her clients: Dealt losing hands, she came to realize that tact usually accomplished more than trial.

Richards was no less dedicated than Karen Thompson in representing her clients, but the two women had very different styles. Thompson was the warrior; she was on the verge of terminal burnout. Richards was the diplomat; she negotiated calmly with the prosecutor and judge and suggested reasonable alternatives to courtroom combat. Yet, the toll for her was high as well. She found it increasingly difficult to keep from being personally involved in the tragedies of her clients' lives.

"...the diagnosis," Richards continued reading aloud, "Mr. Freshour has bipolar affective disorder and is presently in a manic phase with grandiose, delusional thinking and very impaired judgment. He is on a locked unit on a fourteen-day hold for danger to others...."

Longo had heard that the new P.D. lived with a bearded musician in the bohemian beachfront community of Venice. She was, in fact, an accomplished musician herself, playing bass with a rock band in a Hollywood nightclub. A Quaker lawyer in a rock band, Longo thought. Only in L.A.

"What are you suggesting, Ms. Richards?" Bascue asked.

"What I am suggesting, your honor, is that the courtroom is not the appropriate place to deal with Mr. Freshour's problems. Little will be accomplished by prosecuting him and throwing him into jail for a few months. When he comes out, what then? This man needs help, professional help."

"Specifically?"

Richards told the judge that the defendant was not capable of making rational decisions. Under the law, he could not legally be prosecuted until he was mentally competent to understand the proceedings and assist in his own defense. She asked Bascue to suspend the case while the defendant was sent to Patton State Mental Hospital for treatment. When and if he was finally found to be mentally stable, he would be released from the hospital and returned to Department 127 to face the charges—even if that turned out to be years into the future. Since the charges stemmed from the mental condition, however, she was asking for a promise from the prosecutor to drop the charges when he was returned for trial.

"Mr. Torrealba?" Bascue said.

The young deputy D.A. looked down at his supervisor.

"Your call," Longo muttered.

"Your honor," Torrealba said, "I've reviewed the report, and I've discussed the matter earlier this morning with Ms. Richards. I believe that her suggestion is a reasonable one. However, I would ask for a stipulation."

"Yes?" Bascue said.

"Will the defendant stipulate that when he is returned, *if* he is returned, the case shall be suspended for a period of three years. If he stays clean, he can come back after the three years and we will not object at that time to charges being dismissed."

Bascue turned to the public defender. "Ms. Richards?"

Richards nodded slowly. "That sounds fair, your honor. On behalf of my client, I so stipulate."

The two lawyers seemed to have hit it off, Longo thought. In fact, it occurred to him that Richards and Torrealba made a handsome couple: His deputy, a slender, good-looking, thirty-one-year-old bachelor with an easy sense of humor and relaxed Latin charm, would be a good match for the new public defender. At least, he thought, an interesting match.

Leonard Torrealba, the only son of a wealthy Venezuelan cattle baron, had been born in Caracas, where his father ran the family's vast ranch—a multimillion-dollar empire to which Torrealba was heir. The Torrealba family had a long tradition of sending the sons to the United States for their formal educations. Leonard chose UCLA, then law school in Washington, D.C.

After working one summer as a clerk in the D.A.'s Office, Torrealba decided to turn his back on the family cattle empire and become a prosecutor, where he could have the excitement of trial work and possibly position himself for a career in politics. The novice prosecutor was quickly assigned to prosecuting cases in the barrios of east L.A.; because of his Hispanic appearance and his fluency in the Spanish language, victims and witnesses trusted the young Venezuelan.

Torrealba had been a deputy D.A. for eight years now. He still talked occasionally about vast cattle ranches and the lure of the political arena, but he loved the excitement of trial work and the power to find justice in a given case. "This is the greatest job in the world," he often said, "and the worst place to do it."

Torrealba shared an office on the seventeenth floor with Larry Boyle. It was an unlikely pairing: Torrealba, the privileged thirty-one-year-old with politically liberal views, and Boyle, a back-slapping, blue-collar Irishman with streetwise views of justice. The two had little in common.

Yet, surprisingly, they became best friends. A major reason for this was that they discovered one very important quality in common: a sense of humor. The two men spent a good part of their office time telling ethnic jokes and making fun of each other's trial abilities and cultural heritage.

A second reason for the success of this odd couple was that each gave the other a perspective that was lacking. Boyle educated Torrealba to the realities of the street, toughened him up for the rigors of the courtroom; Torrealba smoothed some of the older man's rough edges, softened him to the human side of a case. If Boyle was preparing for trial, the younger deputy would play the defense lawyer, attacking the expected testimony of the key witness. If it was Tor-realba's time for battle, the two men would argue the tactics of his case for hours.

"People versus Yamaguchi," Bascue announced. He looked out at the audience. "Ms. Iwakuni?*"

The blond *nisei* lawyer stepped forward, Mitsuru Yamaguchi beside her.

Richards gathered her case files into her arms and stepped away from the counsel table; as usual, she received no thanks from her client. Torrealba also began gathering the files that were sprawled across the table.

Longo stood up. He looked down the table at Yamaguchi, still seated. Yamaguchi had remained silent in his orange jumpsuit during the Freshour hearing, his head deeply bowed. He had not looked up once since he had entered the courtroom.

"As I understand it, Ms. Iwakuni," the judge continued, "you and Mrs. Yamaguchi are here to contest a subpoena."

"That is correct, your honor," Iwakuni said. "My client was served a subpoena from the district attorney to testify at the coming trial of her husband, Kazuhiko Yamaguchi."

Longo had realized that Mrs. Yamaguchi might appear in court with a lawyer. He had the feeling that Yamaki would get to his client's wife and tell her not to testify, to assert the marital privilege. It would be a conflict of interest for him to represent her, however, so a second lawyer would have to be brought in. Iwakuni was Mrs. Yamaguchi's lawyer, but Longo knew who was pulling the strings.

Mitsuru Yamaguchi's testimony was critically important: She was an eyewitness to the murder. Of course, Longo still had Carmona, the young man in the car across the street. But with Kariya dead and the defendant probably asserting his Fifth Amendment rights and refusing to testify, Mrs. Yamaguchi was the only one who could testify to what had happened among the three of them. Was jealousy the motive, or was there something more sinister? What if anything had Yamaguchi said to his wife during the thirty seconds he stood at the car after shooting Kariya? Had she been an accomplice in the murder? Or had Yamaguchi planned to kill her as well and changed his mind at the last minute?

Longo glanced back at Yamaki seated in the audience. The lawyer smiled back. The two men were acutely aware that they were deeply involved in a continuing game of chess.

The prosecutor had strongly suspected that Yamaki would get to Yamaguchi's wife and convince her not to testify against her lover's murderer. But he needed to know quickly; if she was going to hide behind the privilege, Longo needed to structure his case with the knowledge that she would not be available. Yamaki, on the other hand, wanted to keep Longo in the dark until the last minute; he would tell her not to take the privilege until the day she was called.

But there was risk in that for the defense. If the jury saw the defendant's wife appear and refuse to testify against him, they might well conclude the obvious: She had damaging evidence that she was holding back. If she asserted the privilege long before trial, however, the jury would probably never consider the possibility; they would simply assume that she was not subpoenaed, for whatever reason.

Longo had decided to issue an early subpoena to Mrs. Yamaguchi, forcing Yamaki into a decision. If she was not going to testify, at least the prosecutor could plan his strategy armed with that knowledge.

"Ms. Iwakuni," Bascue said, "what is your position?"

"It is my client's intention to refuse to testify against her husband," the woman said. "She claims the marital privilege under Evidence Code section 970."

Longo noticed that Yamaguchi had raised his head a few inches and turned slightly toward his wife. He glanced at her out of the corner of his eye. Mitsuru Yamaguchi, standing next to her lawyer, bowed her head almost imperceptibly.

"Very well," the judge said. "Mr. Longo?"

Longo shrugged, said nothing.

"Mrs. Yamaguchi," Bascue said, "you are released from the subpoena. It will not be necessary for you to appear for the trial."

Mitsuru Yamaguchi nodded silently. As she turned to leave, she glanced at her husband. Then she walked with her attorney out of the courtroom.

"Mr. Yamaki?" Bascue said.

The lawyer stood up, walked through the swinging gates, and

stood at the counsel table next to Yamaguchi.

"As I understand," Bascue said, "we are here for a discovery motion."

"Yes, your honor," Yamaki said. "The court has the original of my formal motion."

Bascue scanned through the file, found the document. "Yes," he said, scanning it, "yes . . . boilerplate . . ."

"The standard requests, your honor," Yamaki said. "All police reports, tape recordings, photographs, all statements, list of witnesses to be called . . ."

"Mr. Longo?" Bascue looked at the prosecutor. "Any problems turning over any of this to Mr. Yamaki?"

"He's already got it all," Longo said. "If I get anything more, he'll get it. But . . . I filed a discovery motion a while back myself."

"Yes."

"The deal is, Yamaki hasn't given me a thing."

Bascue looked back to the defense lawyer.

"Your honor," Yamaki said with a broad smile, "there just isn't anything to turn over."

You lying son of a gun, Longo thought.

"I have no written statements, no tapes, no photographs . . . nothing." Yamaki paused, looked at the prosecutor. "Of course, when and if such material becomes available, I'll be more than happy to turn over copies to Mr. Longo."

More chess play. California's discovery rules required both the prosecution and defense to turn over any material that might be evidence or lead to finding evidence. Longo had turned over piles of reports from Sakoda, the Montebello police department, the county coroner and other agencies, as well as dozens of photographs, diagrams, and drawings. On the other hand, he knew that Yamaki had talked with a number of witnesses personally, and his investigator had interviewed others. Yet, he was claiming that there was nothing. Either he was lying through his teeth, or . . . or he was being very clever.

The rules said that only *physical* items had to be turned over. This included any written statements from interviews of witnesses. But if neither Yamaki nor his investigator had written down what was told to them, or had asked the witnesses to write anything down, then there would be nothing physical to turn over. Yamaki could interview witnesses for days, coaching them in their testimony, and none of it was discoverable so long as he took no notes.

As for photographs, tapes, and other items, Yamaki could just tell the witness to keep them until they were needed for trial. Technically, the evidence would not be in his possession, and so he would not have to turn it over to the prosecution.

"I request a list of witnesses," Longo said.

Bascue looked at Yamaki.

"Your honor," the defense lawyer said, "I have not yet decided what witnesses, if any, I will be calling."

Baloney, thought Longo.

"When I do come to that determination," Yamaki continued, "I will of course immediately forward a list to Mr. Longo."

"Experts?" Longo asked.

The rules said that if any expert witnesses were to be called, their names had to be turned over long enough before trial to allow the other side to prepare rebuttal expert testimony. Unlike ordinary witnesses, if an expert's name did not appear on the discovery list he would not be permitted to testify.

Longo was forcing Yamaki's hand. The defense lawyer had something up his sleeve, something that made him think he could get a complete acquittal. It could be some self-defense theory, but there seemed to be no evidence of that. That left insanity, or some other state-of-mind defense. And that would require the testimony of a medical expert. If Yamaki wanted to call an expert, he had to give Longo his name and address. And then it would be a short step to finding out what the expert's specialty was—and, thus, what the defense would be.

"Your honor," Yamaki said, "may the record reflect that I am handing the prosecutor a list of possible expert witnesses." He handed a sheet of paper to Longo.

Longo quickly inspected the list. "Shoot," he said, "these guys are spread all over the country."

"Mr. Yamaki?" Bascue asked.

"Your honor," the lawyer said, "I'm not yet sure which of these expert witnesses I will be calling. They're very busy, and it's not apparent which of them will be available to testify at the time of trial. When it becomes clear who will be available, I will certainly notify Mr. Longo."

Longo knew that somewhere on the list was the name of the expert that would be called, maybe two experts. And Yamaki knew who they were. Longo would be chasing after phantom experts on irrelevant subjects for days. He was confident that the name of the "available" expert would not be pointed out until it was too late to do much about it.

He looked at the list again. Maybe Yamaki would call two or three experts; maybe there was a backup expert or two in case the primary expert could not appear. Longo made a mental note to put Sakoda on the list: find out if any of the names had fields of expertise in common.

Or was Yamaki being clever again? Longo was just guessing that there was an insanity or diminished-capacity defense. Maybe the defense was something else entirely, and there was no expert. Maybe Yamaki was just throwing a phony list at Longo, letting him waste time and resources on a wild-goose chase.

Queen's bishop to king's knight four.

"Anything else?" Bascue asked.

"No, your honor," Yamaki said.

"Mr. Longo?"

The prosecutor shook his head.

"Mr. Longo," the judge said, "any possibility of a disposition in this case?"

Longo looked at Yamaki, then at the judge. "Not a chance."

"Very well," Bascue said, sighing deeply as he stood up from the bench. "Court is in recess."

As the judge walked into his chambers, Longo and Yamaki looked at each other for a moment in silence.

The bulldog and the cobra.

Trial was two weeks away.

"Hey, Larry, you hear the news?"

Longo stopped in the corridor outside his office, sipping from the hot white cup in his hand. "What's that, Gary?"

"They got a new judge for the King trial."

The D.A.'s Office had been anxiously awaiting the naming of a new trial judge. The removal of the original judge was still a hot topic around the coffee machine.

The Rodney King case had quickly become a media sensation in Los Angeles, forcing the defense lawyers to move for a change of venue. The judge originally assigned to the case denied the motion, and the lawyers appealed. Learning that the appellate court was planning to reverse his ruling, the judge quietly called the court and asked for a chance to change it. He also secretly sent his clerk to the D.A.'s Office to explain why he was changing the ruling.

The attempt to influence the appellate judges and the secret contact with the prosecutor constituted clearly unethical conduct. Deputy D.A. Terry White appeared in the judge's court and, to the judge's considerable embarrassment, publicly revealed the clerk's visit. When the appellate court learned of the misconduct, it immediately removed the judge and began searching for a suitable replacement for the politically sensitive case.

"Yeah?" Longo said. "So who's the new judge?"

"Who do you think?"

Longo shrugged. "Lance Ito?"

"Weisberg."

Longo nodded slowly, thinking this over. Stanley Weisberg was a mild-mannered, reflective man, an intellectual who enjoyed the technical complexities of law. He looked and acted more like a benign professor of archaeology than the deputy D.A. who had successfully prosecuted the murderer of a beautiful model named Vicky Morgan, mistress of department store heir and presidential adviser Alfred Bloomingdale.

In taking over the King case, Weisberg was immediately faced with a critical decision: Where should the trial take place? After the appellate court ruled that venue had to be removed from Los Angeles, three counties were made available to him. The prosecution favored Alameda County, where a jury pool filled with blacks from Oakland would be unsympathetic to the officers. The defense preferred the largely white and conservative jurors of nearby Orange and Ventura counties.

Weisberg's decision was to have far-reaching consequences.

"They drew a good judge," Longo said. "Lousy poker player, but a good judge."

The deputy laughed. "So I heard."

The deputies in the D.A.'s Santa Monica office had regularly held a poker game, usually at the home of then–deputy D.A. James Bascue or John Ouderkirk, who later presided over the Reginald Denny trial. The scholarly Weisberg, who was helplessly sincere and incapable of bluffing, had gained some fame in the office for his almost unbroken losing streak.

"He was on the bench in the second McMartin preschool trial, wasn't he?" the deputy asked.

"Yeah."

"McMartin, now this." He shook his head. "What next?"

Weisberg's next case, as it turned out, would be the trial of the Menendez brothers.

Jimmy Sakoda was sitting in a chair as Longo entered the tiny office, wedged in among piles of transcripts and files.

"Hey, Jimmy," Longo said, "whaddya got?"

"Uchida. I went down there with his written statement, he wouldn't sign it."

Longo sighed as he sat down in his swivel chair. "Are you telling me our star witness is changing his story?"

Sakoda shrugged. "Looks like it, Larry."

Longo leaned back, propped his feet up on the overflowing desk, and pulled out a hard-boiled egg from a brown bag.

"I mean," Sakoda continued, "I had Connie type it up right from my notes, word-for-word from the interview. I give it to Uchida, and he starts waffling on me."

"Uh-huh."

"Says he's not sure now. All of a sudden, he doesn't recall so good what Hanemure said. Or Matsumoto, either."

Longo began peeling the egg.

"Maybe they told him Yamaguchi said he was going to 'finish' Kariya, maybe not."

"Uh-huh."

"Maybe Matsumoto told him Yamaguchi only said, 'I'm going to *do* it.' "

Longo continued peeling the egg.

"I asked him what he meant, 'I'm going to do it.' He says, like Yamaguchi was saying he was going to commit *seppuku*. You know, suicide."

"Uh-huh."

Sakoda shrugged again.

"Yamaki," Longo said quietly.

Sakoda nodded slowly in agreement.

"The son of a gun got to him," the prosecutor said.

"Looks like it."

"Jeez." He bit into the egg.

"By the way . . ."

"Yeah?"

"Just to be on the safe side, I ran a record check on our friend Uchida."

"He's got a rap sheet?"

"Nothing heavy. Just a little DUI case a couple years back."

"DUI."

"And you'll never guess who his lawyer was."

Longo looked up at his investigator.

"Yep," Sakoda said. "Mike Yamaki."

"I'll be . . ."

"Yep. Anyway, Uchida should be here any minute." The investigator glanced at his watch. "In fact, he's late."

"What'd you tell him?"

"Just said you'd like to have a little chat with him." Sakoda grinned. "He got real nervous, said he was too busy. I told him we could do this the easy way, we could do it the hard way. He decided to do it the easy way."

"Good."

Longo took another bite of the egg, mentally going over what was left of his premeditated murder case. Hanemure had already denied hearing Yamaguchi say he was going to kill Kariya, and now Uchida was backing off as well.

"Jimmy, you get ahold of that Matsumoto guy?"

"Yep, caught him at his jewelry store downtown. He wasn't too helpful, Larry. Real evasive."

"He talk to Yamaki?"

"I didn't ask. But I laid a subpoena on him."

"You ask him about the talk at the restaurant with Uchida and Hanemure?"

"Yep. Says he wasn't sure, couldn't recall."

"Sudden loss of memory."

"Yep."

Well, he still had the Carmona kid, Longo thought. And he could still put Hanemure, Matsumoto, and Uchida on the stand and work on them.

But there was no denying that Yamaki was doing a lot of damage. He had knocked Mitsuru Yamaguchi out of the trial, and he would probably keep his client off the stand as well. With Kariya dead, that left only Carmona as a witness to the shooting. Then Uchida, Hanemure, and Matsumoto had changed their stories.

Yet, this still left Yamaki facing at least a voluntary-manslaughter verdict. But he seemed confident of an acquittal. What was he up to? What kind of a defense was he putting together?

Longo's trial strategy in the Yamaguchi case was becoming clearer to him. He would have to be a counterpuncher. Yamaki was chopping up the prosecution case before they ever got into court, while keeping his own case completely hidden. Okay, Longo thought, we feint, draw him out, then counterpunch. We sandbag the son of a gun.

Longo would put on a skeleton case, just enough to avoid Judge Bascue's granting a motion to dismiss for lack of evidence. He would put on the coroner to show there was a dead body with a bullet hole through it. Then Carmona, to prove Yamaguchi had put the hole there and that he had spent half an hour lying in wait. Then the Chippy for the confession. Maybe throw the Three Stooges on the stand and rough them up a bit, hoping the jury would see through their cover. And rest the People's case.

It was not much, but there was enough there to survive a motion to dismiss. Then it would be up to Yamaki: He would finally have to show his hand. And Longo could do his favorite thing: cross-examination. When Yamaki finally rested his case, Longo would come back at him with rebuttal. He would lay the motive out clearly and then . . .

The motive. What *was* the motive? Was it just another jealous husband case? The problem with love triangles, he knew, was that jurors tended to buy into the heat of passion theory and vote for voluntary manslaughter, even where there was clear evidence of cold-blooded premeditation.

But Longo did not think this was a jealous husband, any more than it was a killing of passion. It had been fuzzy to him at first, but the picture was becoming clearer. The murder of Genji Kariya was not about jealousy or love. It was about territory. And *face.*

Yamaguchi was the old stud bull in J-Town. He was a powerful man and a recognized leader of the Japanese community. He owned a number of successful businesses, had a lot of money, and was widely respected. He had a nice home, a couple of good-looking kids, and a beautiful wife, a woman who still attracted men many years younger than she.

Kariya was the young bull, the one who wanted to knock off the aging king of the herd and take it all for himself. He had worked his way into Yamaguchi's business, gradually taking over more and more of the operation. He had challenged Yamaguchi in front of the old man's friends and family, bragging to his face that he had succeeded where the old man had failed. Finally, he had gone after his wife—and her community property; he was not just having an affair with her, he wanted to marry the woman. Kariya wanted the business, the wife, the house, everything.

Longo knew that appearances were important to the Japanese. Kariya had openly defied Yamaguchi, had even publicly humiliated him. He would have lost a lot of face in J-Town, Longo thought. He would have lost a lot of face with his wife.

Property. Pride.

Maybe, Longo thought to himself. Or maybe there was something else, something Yamaki knew and he did not. One thing was certain, though: He had to give the jury a motive for the murder.

Technically, motive was not a part of the *corpus delecti,* or "the body of the crime." To prove the *corpus* for first-degree murder, it was necessary to show only three things: a homicide, an intent to kill, and premeditation. It was entirely possible to convict a defendant of murder one without ever showing *why* he did it.

Longo knew that under the law he did not have to produce evidence of Yamaguchi's motive for murdering Kariya. But he also knew that no jury would ever convict Yamaguchi *without* knowing why he did it.

The prosecutor dropped his feet to the floor, began searching through the correspondence, documents, and files that were scattered randomly across his desk. He found a small piece of paper and handed it to Sakoda.

"Check it out, Jimmy."

The investigator looked at it. A phone number was written on the paper. He looked back at Longo.

"When I left court this morning," Longo said, "some lady came up to me in the hallway. Said she was a cashier at the Yamaguchis' restaurant. . . ." Longo stopped, seemed to think it over. Then he continued. "Said Yamaguchi and Kariya used to do a lot of drug deals at the restaurant. She saw a lot of money changing hands."

Sakoda nodded, saying nothing.

"Yeah," Longo said, "I know."

"Yamaki."

"Probably. But check her out."

"Sure."

It looked too good to be true: evidence that Yamaguchi killed Kariya over a drug deal gone bad. The perfect motive. But it did not sound right to Longo; it simply did not fit. Only on television did dream witnesses suddenly appear and dramatically hand you your whole case on a silver platter.

The incident smelled to Longo like a Yamaki "plant," an attempt to lead him off on a false trail. Maybe make him look foolish in trial. He could just imagine what the woman would say once she was on the stand in front of a jury.

The Japanese version of a Trojan horse, Longo thought.

"I located one of Yamaguchi's employees," Sakoda said, handing the prosecutor a three-page report. "This is the interview."

"Yeah?"

"Louis Bernal. Handyman. An illegal. Worked for the Yamaguchis on a house they were fixing up to sell over at Boyle Heights."

"Boyle Heights . . ."

"Yep, the one where Hanemure says Yamaguchi walked in on his wife and Kariya upstairs."

"Oh yeah."

"Well, I did some digging, figured the Yamaguchis weren't doing the work themselves, and I found this guy. And sure enough, he was working in the house that night."

"Yeah?"

"About eight or nine, he's doing some painting downstairs, and Kariya and Mrs. Yamaguchi walk in, go up the stairs. They go into the bedroom and close the door."

"Uh-huh."

"So about twenty minutes later, this guy Bernal says Yamaguchi comes storming in, doesn't say anything, just goes up the stairs. And then he hears something that sounds like a bunch of yelling for maybe a minute, then Kariya comes down the stairs, alone."

"Uh-huh."

"Kariya looks pissed, he's breathing hard. And he's got, like, a bruise or something around one eye."

Longo nodded, thinking this over. "Subpoena him."

"Okay."

Larry Boyle suddenly stuck his head into the small office.

"Hey, boss," he said. "Calendar's all wrapped up."

"Good," Longo said. "Leonard start that voodoo trial today?"

"Yeah. He's putting twelve in a box now."

"Voodoo?" Sakoda said.

"You know," Longo said, "chickens 'n' goats."

Torrealba was choosing a jury for a murder case in which the defendant was a "high priestess" in the Santería religious cult. Santería had evolved from the slaves in the Caribbean who had been converted by the Jesuits to Christianity. The religion was a strange mix of Catholicism and primitive African superstition, involving the ritual sacrifice of animals to a pantheon of gods.

"Reminds me," Longo said. "I ever tell you guys the voodoo story?"

"No," Boyle said.

"About crazy Judge Feder? Out in west L.A.?"

Sakoda shook his head, grinning in anticipation.

Longo propped his feet back up on the desk, pushing piles of papers out of the way.

"It was the first couple months I was in the office, greener than grass. Doing prelims out in west L.A., in Judge Feder's court, next door to old Judge Freund. Two guys hated each other." Longo started unwrapping a sandwich.

"One day, I'm doing a prelim on this voodoo case. Guy was sticking pins in these dolls, guy from Haiti or somewhere, I dunno. And next thing, there's dead bodies, right? Two guys just up and die, one after the other. I mean, real spooky. So, anyway, the bright boys down in Complaints file murder charges."

Longo took a big bite out of the sandwich, continued talking with his mouth full of tuna salad.

"So it's the morning recess, second day of the prelim, and Feder goes back to his chambers. Next thing, we all hear this scream. It's coming from back in the chambers." Longo shook his head, smiling at the memory. "So me and the bailiff, we run back there, into chambers. And there's Feder, standing there."

"Yeah?" Boyle said.

"He's standing there, and I mean his face is white as a sheet, you know? And his eyes, they're popping out of his head. And his mouth's wide open. And he's looking at his desk."

"Yeah?"

"Well, on top of his desk there's this voodoo doll."

"Yeah?"

"Dead ringer," Longo said, taking another bite from the sandwich. "I mean, it was *Feder,* you know? Bald head, pot belly, the whole thing. It was Feder. And sticking out of this doll was this long pin, stuck clean through the head. In one ear, out the other."

"So what happened?" Sakoda asked.

"Feder just stands there, making this kind of choking sound. And, jeez, I don't know what to do. So I go over and take the doll, and I pull the pin out of the head, you know?"

"Yeah?"

"And Feder, he gives out with another scream. And about this time, I hear this cackling sound down the hallway."

"Down the hallway?" Boyle asked.

"Yeah. Down where old Judge Freund's chambers are. There's this cackling sound, kind of like a screwed-up laugh."

Boyle laughed. "You gotta be kidding."

"Honest to Pete," Longo said. "Old Freund's down there, listening. And he's hysterical, just cackling away."

"You gotta be kidding."

Longo shook his head again, grinning. "Two old farts really hated each other."

"True story?" Sakoda asked.

"So help me," Longo said.

"Hey, Larry, I got to go," Boyle said. "I got some narcs up here want a search warrant."

"Hey, nice job on the Contreras trial," Longo said.

The verdict in the bandit tow truck case had come back the day before: guilty of second-degree murder.

Boyle grinned. "Thanks, boss." Then he disappeared down the hallway.

"Be a darned good lawyer," Longo said quietly, a touch of pride in his voice.

"I heard good things," Sakoda said.

"Okay, where are we?"

Sakoda checked some notes on a steno pad on his lap. "We got a rumor . . ."

"Yeah?"

"It's only a rumor, but . . . Well, there was this burglary at Ya-maguchi's house a couple of years ago."

"Uh-huh."

"Yamaguchi's son . . . Ken?"

"Yeah."

"Ken told me this gun his dad used to shoot Kariya, they kept it around the house for protection. Because of a burglary a couple years ago."

"Uh-huh."

"It seems Yamaguchi kept a lot of money and jewelry in the place. And these two kids, high school kids, came in and ripped him off for all of it. Maybe two hundred grand's worth."

"Two hundred grand . . ."

"Yep. And they seemed to know where everything was."

Longo looked at his investigator, waiting.

"Well, there's this rumor that Yamaguchi's son . . ."

"Yeah?"

"Maybe he was involved. Maybe he put the job together."

"Knocked over his own father?"

Sakoda nodded. "That's the rumor. Anyway, I called Holden over at Montebello P.D. The two kids got caught, pled out in juvenile court. Holden's going back over the burglary reports, going to call me back."

Longo thought about this for a moment. Could Ken Yamaguchi have masterminded a burglary job on his own father? And if he did, was there any connection with the Kariya murder? Or was this all another wild goose dreamed up by Yamaki?

"Yeah," Longo said. "Let me know."

"Meantime, I think I'd better give Uchida a call."

Longo grabbed the phone and handed it across the desk to his investigator.

Sakoda thumbed through the pad of paper on his lap, found the phone number he was looking for. He took the phone, dialed, then waited.

Longo watched as someone answered on the other end and, strangely, Sakoda jerked his head down in a reflexive half bow. He began speaking in rapid-fire Japanese. The investigator appeared to listen for a moment, then rattled off some more Japanese. Another pause. Then, again, the odd little bow of the head and he hung up.

"That was the manager at Uchida's store," Sakoda said.

"Yeah?"

"Mr. Takeshi Uchida will not be joining us today."

"Yeah?"

"It seems he left town a few hours ago. She doesn't know when he'll be back."

Chapter

12

"Do you, Rafael Diaz Santiago,* take this woman to be your lawfully wedded wife?"

The slender young prisoner in the orange jumpsuit grinned. "Yes, sir, I do."

"And do you, Maria Benitez,*" Judge Bascue asked, "take this man to be your lawfully wedded husband?"

The short, obviously pregnant woman in the blue calico dress nodded with a smile, her eyes fixed bashfully to the floor. "I do, sir."

"Then by the powers vested in me by the state of California, I now pronounce you man and wife."

The man and the woman glanced at each other shyly.

"Tom," Bascue said to the bailiff, "please take off Mr. Santiago's cuffs for a minute. I think he'd like to kiss his bride."

"Yes, your honor."

The bailiff unlocked the handcuffs. Santiago, still grinning broadly, leaned toward his new wife and kissed her gently on the cheek. The woman looked up at Bascue, embarrassed but happy. There was a tear rolling down from one eye.

Nancy Richards stepped toward her client. "Congratulations, Rafael." She smiled at the woman. "I'm happy for you both, Maria."

"Best of luck, folks," Longo said, standing a few feet away at the prosecution table.

The man and his wife nodded happily toward the prosecutor.

Deputy D.A. Craig Veals, standing next to Longo, said, "We wish you both well, Mr. Santiago, Mrs. Santiago."

The courtroom was silent for a long moment as Santiago and his new wife held each other's hands awkwardly.

"Well . . ." Bascue said finally. "As usual, we have a heavy calendar this morning." He looked at Longo and Veals, then at Richards. "Is your client ready for sentencing?"

"Yes, your honor," the public defender said.

"Rafael Diaz Santiago," Bascue said, "you have entered a plea of guilty to count one, grand theft auto. Is there any legal cause why sentence should not now be pronounced?"

"None, your honor," Richards said.

"No, sir," Santiago said, still grinning happily.

The bailiff gently led the woman away from Santiago and through the swinging gates. She stood at the banister, watching with tears welling in her eyes as the bailiff walked back and replaced the handcuffs on her husband.

"Then I hereby order you remanded to the Department of Corrections, there to begin serving the sentence imposed by law."

Santiago nodded, then looked back at his wife. The bailiff began to lead him away.

"Mr. Santiago," Bascue said.

The bailiff stopped as Santiago looked back.

"Mr. Santiago, I wish you and your wife a long and happy life."

"Thank you, sir."

"And if I may offer some advice . . ."

"Yes, sir."

"Look for a new line of work, son."

The young man grinned, then turned and continued with the bailiff to the steel door. As the door opened, he looked back a last time at the woman standing at the banister. Then he stepped inside and the door clanged shut.

Longo looked back as a slender, very attractive young woman in an expensive business suit stepped through the swinging gates. The fresh, innocent face of a sorority girl clashed oddly with the bored, heavy-lidded eyes of someone jaded by life. She was carrying a thick manila folder under her right arm, a D.A.'s case file.

The woman looked at Longo as she stepped into the jury box, then winked at him. This was Pam Ferrero, a deputy assigned to Special Trials. Ferrero had prosecuted the second McMartin pre-school trial, and was given first chair in the Menendez case. Longo knew that she was in Department 127 that morning for a sentencing hearing in the Theresa Saldana slashing case. He also knew that behind the cute, innocent face was a cold-blooded shark.

Ferrero had recently raised eyebrows in the office by announcing her engagement to Peter Bozanich, the head of Special Trials (the two had been living together for some time). In the competitive world of the D.A.'s office, this was seen by some as evidence that Ferrero was getting plum assignments for reasons other than merit. In fact, however, she had been originally assigned to the Menendez trial by the head of the Organized Crime unit; she and Bozanich had not even dated yet. Later, when Deputy D.A. Joe Martinez was handed the McMartin case to retry, Reiner promised him he could choose any deputy he wanted as second chair. Martinez chose Ferrero, and she was immediately reassigned to the retrial (after the McMartin fiasco had finally ended, the Menendez trial was returned to Ferrero).

Ferrero had been reluctant to accept the McMartin assignment. The case was a high-publicity career builder. But it was also a loser, a possible career ender. And there was another reason for her reluctance. In an amazing coincidence, Pam Ferrero had herself attended the McMartin Preschool Center for two years as a child. Although she could clearly remember Virginia McMartin from her days in the pre-school, she was confident no one would ever recognize her now. Nothing had ever happened to her there, and she was sure that the experience would not affect her ability to prosecute the case. If the media or the defense lawyers had ever discovered the fact, of course, she would have been in an awkward position.

"Ms. Ferrero," Judge Bascue said. "We are honored to have a member of Special Trials in our humble court."

"The honor is all mine, your honor," Ferrero said with a sardonic grin.

"Tom," the judge said to the bailiff, "would you bring out Mr. Jackson." He glanced back at Yamaki. "And Mr. Yamaguchi."

"Thank you, your honor," Yamaki said from his seat in the jury box.

Ferrero stepped over to Longo. "How go the wars, Larry?" she said.

"Piece of cake," Longo said, standing up and offering the woman his chair at the table.

"I see Yamaki's here." She looked out at the packed audience. "And his cheering section."

"Yeah."

"When's trial?"

"Three days. We're just clearing the decks today."

The woman nodded silently.

"By the way," Longo said, "congratulations. Peter's a good man."

"Thanks," she said.

"What're you doing here on the Saldana thing?" Longo asked. "I thought that was Susan Gruber's case."

"Susan just went into labor. But no problem. The P.O.'s report lays him out. And Saldana's here, wants to be heard on the sentence. I'm just going to sit back and direct traffic."

"Uh-huh. How's the big one going?"

"Menendez?" Ferrero shrugged. "Okay, I guess. We're waiting for a ruling from the Supreme Court on the tapes."

"Leslie Abramson keeping you entertained?"

She smiled wryly. "The woman's a raving bitch from hell."

Longo grinned. "So I've heard."

Ferrero looked at him for a moment. "Chinatown," she said quietly.

"Yeah."

Ferrero nodded again, slowly.

Longo walked over to the jury box, sat in one of the chairs. He glanced at Yamaki, then back at Ferrero. The woman was an anomaly, Longo thought as he watched her open the case file on her lap and begin studying it. A Wellesley graduate, had been raised in the exclusive Palos Verdes Estates area of Los Angeles, attending the best schools and living the privileged life of a corporate executive's daughter. The socialite prosecutor, the poor little rich girl with the killer instincts.

But the McMartin retrial proved to be a nightmare for Ferrero. Like Roger Gunson, Ferrero was convinced after talking with the children and the doctors that Raymond Buckey was guilty. Kids did not know enough to make up stories about "wiping the white stuff off my face." But like Gunson, she was also convinced that videotapes of highly suggestive interviews with the children made a conviction unlikely. Yet, she was under orders: retry Buckey.

The parents of the children were reluctant to undergo a second trial, and Ferrero found herself trying to talk them into it while knowing deep inside that it was a lost cause. "It was the worst thing I've ever done as a D.A.," she recalled later.

The three- and four-year-old children were now almost teenagers; what was left of their memories was discredited by the tapes. When the case was finally submitted to the jury after six months of testimony, they deliberated for fifteen days. Then, as the first jury had done, they announced that they were hopelessly deadlocked.

Soon after he was given the news, District Attorney Reiner called a press conference and announced that there would be no McMartin three; charges against Buckey were dropped.

The McMartin case took everything out of Ferrero, exhausted her. "It was emotionally devastating," she recalled later, "to be in charge of a sinking ship with kids on board."

Turning now to the Menendez case, Ferrero soon realized that the tape recordings of the brothers' sessions with their psychologist were the key to the case. She also knew that their admissibility was questionable. There was an exception to the privilege where the person making the statement constitutes a direct threat to the psychotherapist's life, but its application in the case was uncertain. Without the tapes, there was little evidence to convict the two sons.

If she got the tapes into evidence, Ferrero knew what the defense would be: voluntary manslaughter. The defense attorneys would portray their wealthy young clients as the emotionally abused children of a tyrannical monster (she would not discover until much later the allegations of sexual abuse). They would bring in a platoon of well-paid psychiatrists to testify that the years of oppression had so warped the two boys that they were incapable of meaningfully premeditating. The very viciousness of the shotgun slayings, they would say, was indicative of the rage that boiled within them—a rage that culminated in their finally lashing out at their tormentor in the heat of passion.

Ferrero knew that it would be a tough defense to overcome, particularly with Leslie Abramson on the other side. The defense attorneys would try to sell the jury on psychiatry, abusive parents, and diminished capacity. Ferrero, on the other hand, believed firmly that the murder was not caused by psychiatric disorders: It was caused by greed and *evil*. "Psychiatrists," she was fond of saying to juries, "cannot explain evil."

The Menendez case was widely expected to be one of the biggest trials of the decade. Once the media zeroed in on the case, Ferrero would become a household name. Yet, ironically, she no longer had any desire for success or fame or money. The woman had burned brightly, perhaps too brightly, and now she found herself weary of daily courtroom battle, unmoved by gruesome autopsy photos, hardened to violence and evil.

Like so many before her, Pam Ferrero was burning out.

The steel door to the lockup swung open and the bailiff brought out two men in jailhouse orange. One was Yamaguchi. The other was a thin, thirty-five-year-old man with thick dark hair, a deep scowl, and large, piercing eyes that seemed fixed in an angry glare.

Arthur Jackson was a drifter from Scotland who had been diagnosed as a paranoid schizophrenic. In 1982, he developed a fixation on movie actress Theresa Saldana after seeing her star in the film *Raging Bull*. He began approaching her in public places, then at her West Hollywood apartment. When she rebuffed him, he began following the woman, stalking her wherever she went. When she continued to ignore him, Jackson finally attacked her with a knife outside of her West Hollywood apartment, stabbing her ten times. The actress needed a transfusion of ten pints of blood and over one thousand stitches.

Jackson was tried and convicted of attempted murder and sentenced to twelve years in state prison.

In 1988, Saldana appeared on Geraldo Rivera's television show. The topic of conversation was fans who stalked Hollywood celebrities. Soon after the show aired, the associate producer received a letter from Jackson in prison. In the letter, Jackson vowed to kill Saldana, indicating that he would be getting out of prison soon and that a revolutionary hit squad would carry out the murder.

The producer quickly contacted Saldana and read the letter to her over the phone. Four other letters followed, each containing threats against the actress's life.

Saldana went to the district attorney with the letters. Charges were filed against Jackson under a new statute making it a felony to send death threats. A jury trial resulted in convictions on all five counts.

"This is the case of the People versus Arthur Richard Jackson," Judge Bascue announced. "For the record, Counsel?" he said to a lawyer stepping forward from the audience.

"Norman Kava, your honor," the man said. "Deputy public defender and counsel for Mr. Jackson."

"Ms. Ferrero?"

"Pamela Ferrero for the People, your honor," she said.

"This is the time for sentencing in this matter. I have reviewed the facts. I have read and considered the report from the probation department. Anything further?"

"Your honor," the prosecutor said, "Ms. Saldana is in the audience and would like to be heard."

"Of course." Bascue looked out into the audience. "Ms. Saldana?"

A slender woman with dark eyes and long curling dark hair stood up and stepped forward hesitantly. She glanced at Jackson sitting in his chair, then stopped at the swinging gates.

"Your honor . . . Before these threats, I had rebuilt my life. I was finally recovered from the attack and from all the surgery it caused. But when I was threatened again . . . I was terrified."

Saldana looked at Jackson again, then back at the judge.

"My father died of a stress-related heart attack only weeks after learning of this man's death threats. He had no prior history of heart trouble. I know that he felt helpless and sickened by the knowledge that I was living in a state of terror. He had lived through the events of 1982, he had watched me battle for my life. . . . As far as I am concerned, this man killed my father."

The actress suddenly turned to Jackson and looked directly at him.

"Mr. Jackson, I ask you to please leave me and my family alone. Take me out of your thoughts. I do not know you. You are a stranger. You do not know me. I am not your victim and I'm not anyone's victim any longer. You have caused not only me, but my entire family tremendous pain and suffering for many years."

She swallowed hard, then continued.

"I ask you to forget about me and I ask you to give our family some peace for once and for all."

She turned back to the judge.

"That's all I have to say."

"Thank you, Ms. Saldana," Bascue said as the woman turned back and sat down in the audience. "Anything further?"

"Your honor," the public defender said hesitantly, "Mr. Jackson wants to be heard."

"Go ahead, Mr. Jackson."

The wide-eyed man rose to his feet, his handcuffed hands held stiffly in front of him.

"I have a testament of truth and justice and also assurance by the defendant, I, Arthur Jackson. On this day, I recommend a special course of the proceeding known as the fourteen-stage arraignment and scenario to be put into effect, leading up to the mission's fulfillment. I am . . . If I am sent back to the prison other than by way of the fourteen-stage arraignment deal, I will regard it as a declaration of war—"

Bascue began his recitation of the state prison sentence.

"This is a catch–twenty-two," Jackson continued, "preventing me from being executed, a man-made paradox, artificially produced by bureaucrats . . ."

The bailiff pushed Jackson down into his seat and stood over him.

"Corrupt American justice," Jackson continued muttering as Bascue finished the statutory littany of sentencing. "Most crooked country in the world. Perverse, awkward in their contempt toward people of a vulnerable category . . ."

"People versus Kazuhiko Yamaguchi," Bascue announced.

Yamaki and Longo stood up in the jury box and walked to their seats at the counsel tables.

Longo stood next to Ferrero as she closed her manila file and prepared to leave. "Guy gave a real fine argument," he whispered to her. "Oughta be a lawyer."

Ferrero grinned. "Better than some I've heard," she whispered back. Then she turned and walked out of the courtroom.

"Gentlemen," Bascue said. "It is three days until trial. No possibility of a disposition?"

"No, your honor," Yamaki said.

Longo shook his head.

"Well . . ." the judge continued. "Any last-minute matters?"

"Yeah," Longo said. "Three days to trial and Yamaki still hasn't turned over a darned thing."

Yamaki smiled. "Your honor, until yesterday there was nothing to turn over. But now . . ." He opened his leather briefcase resting on the table, pulled out some papers. "Let the record reflect that I am handing over to the prosecution an affidavit of Takeshi Uchida and . . . a prescription."

The lawyer handed the papers to Veals, seated next to Longo.

"That's it?" Longo asked incredulously. "We're going into a murder trial and all the defense has is a lousy affidavit and some prescription?"

Yamaki shrugged.

"What about expert witnesses?" the prosecutor asked.

"I have still not been able to determine which of the experts will be available to—"

"Yeah, yeah, I know," Longo said, "they're all so busy you just can't say."

"Mr. Longo . . ." Bascue said ominously.

"Well, shoot, judge, talk about hiding the ball!"

"I assure the court," Yamaki said calmly, "that any expert who may testify will be one of those on the list submitted earlier to Mr. Longo."

"Gimme a break," the prosecutor muttered.

"Very well," Bascue said. "Is there anything else to resolve before trial?"

There was silence in the courtroom.

"Then I'll see you two gentlemen in three days."

Bascue stood up, walked down the stairs and into his chambers.

Longo grabbed the papers in front of Veals. One was a three-page affidavit from Uchida. A quick scan of the first page indicated what Longo had expected: The witness was recanting his story to Sakoda. The prescription was from the Kyoto Drug Store and was for Mitsuru Yamaguchi. It was dated November 17, 1990. The drug prescribed was Halcion.

What was Halcion?

"Triazolam."

"Uh-huh."

"Full name," Greg Dohi said, reading from his notes, "triazo-lobenzodiazepine. Made by the Upjohn Company. Halcion is their trade name for the drug."

"Yeah," Longo said, his back to the young intern as he sat staring out the window. "I'm listening, Greg."

"It's a hypnonarcotic," Dohi said, "one of a class of sedatives called benzodiazepines. A sleeping pill, basically."

"Yeah."

"Let me go back a bit. Twenty years ago, doctors were prescribing barbiturates for people who had sleeping problems or needed a tranquilizer. Seconal, that kind of thing. But the big problem with the barbiturates was that you could overdose very easily. Then in the seventies, the drug companies came out with the first benzodiazepines. Valium, Xanax, Restoril. With these new drugs, it was pretty hard to OD."

"Uh-huh."

"Well, these benzodiazepines still had a problem: They took a long time to clear out of the system. They left the person feeling groggy the next day. So then, about 1980, Upjohn came up with a new type of benzodiazepine that cleared out fast, that didn't leave you with a hangover the next day. Halcion."

"Uh-huh." Longo continued gazing absently out at the reddish brown sky, his thoughts on the latest news in the Rodney King case.

Judge Stanley Weisberg had finally picked a site for the trial. To the surprise of many, he had chosen Ventura County; the most important trial of the decade would take place in a small courthouse in suburban Simi Valley.

The choice of venue did seem a strange one. The removal to another county was caused by the extensive publicity the case received in Los Angeles. Yet, Simi Valley was next door to Los Angeles, sharing the same television stations; many residents subscribed to the *Los Angeles Times*. The impact of publicity on that community was the same as on any other L.A. suburb. And, Simi Valley was a solid white, conservative neighborhood, home to the Ronald Reagan Presidential Library. More important, it was known as a bedroom community of law enforcement officers, many of whom commuted to work in Los Angeles; a recent census indicated that over four thousand officers lived in the area.

It was a dream location for the defense.

What finally influenced Weisberg's fateful decision to choose Ventura County over Alameda and Orange counties is not known. Some said the travel expenses to Oakland would have been too high; others that Orange County did not have any open courts available. Alameda was heavily black; Orange predominantly white.

What *is* known is that Weisberg had been a loyal Philibosian man when Reiner defeated the former district attorney and purged his supporters. As a result, there were those who suspected that the judge would not be disappointed to see Reiner lose the King trial— and, along with it, the coming election. There was, they said, the McMartin incident.

Weisberg had been the judge in the second McMartin trial. Reiner was the district attorney at the time. He was also the heavily favored front-runner in the race for the Democratic nomination for state attorney general. And he realized that the case against Raymond Buckey was weak; another hung verdict or an acquittal in the McMartin case would damage his political future.

Reiner authorized secret plea-bargain sessions with Buckey's attorney, Daniel Davis.

At a meeting with Davis, John Lynch, Reiner's chief of Central Trials, offered the lawyer a deal: If Buckey would plead "no contest" the D.A.'s Office would see that he served no additional time in custody. Davis turned the deal down.

One month later, Reiner appeared in a televised debate with his underdog opponent. The candidate accused Reiner of being soft on crime. As an example, he said, Reiner had offered the McMartin child molester a "time served" plea bargain. Reiner hotly denied this.

His opponent then produced a tape recording of the plea-bargain session. Unknown to anyone, Davis had gone into the meeting with Lynch armed with a tape recorder hidden on his body.

Panicked, Reiner made a desperate attempt at damage control. He had his investigators track down Judge Weisberg on vacation in New York. One of his staff then secretly called Weisberg and told him that Davis had leaked information about the case, thereby violating a gag order the judge had imposed on the attorneys in the McMartin trial.

When Weisberg returned to Los Angeles, he called the Mc-Martin attorneys to an open hearing in his court. The media, alerted to an "event," turned out in force. Rather than holding Davis in contempt for violating the gag order, however, Weisberg lit into Deputy D.A. Pam Ferrero, angrily accusing her boss of unethically trying to influence the trial with the secret phone call.

Soon after the story hit the front pages, Reiner was defeated in the election.

Why was Ventura County chosen for the King trial? Weisberg's closest friends knew that the judge was a notorious homebody; setting the trial in nearby Simi Valley would permit him to commute daily. And valid arguments could be made for choosing Ventura over Alameda and Orange. It remains interesting, however, that Weisberg's judicial decisions were instrumental in both of Reiner's political defeats.

"Well," Dohi continued, "the FDA checked it out, and in 1982 they okayed Halcion."

"1982," Longo repeated, his attention returning to the Yama-guchi case.

"Now it's the most commonly prescribed sleeping pill in the

world, sold in over ninety countries, hundreds of millions of prescriptions a year." Dohi glanced at his notes again. "Last year, over eight million people took the drug. In the U.S. alone, there are over half a million prescriptions written for Halcion every month. But..."

Longo swung back around to face the young intern. "But?"

"There've been some problems."

"Go on, Greg," Longo said.

"There are claims that the drug has some bad side effects."

"Uh-huh."

"Like something called"—he glanced at his notes—"anterograde amnesia."

"Amnesia."

"Some people who take the drug, they do things and then they can't remember afterward what they did."

"Uh-huh."

"And there've been reports of..." He checked his notes again. "Paradoxical reactions."

"In English, Greg."

"Medical jargon for weird side effects. It seems there've been people who took the drug and they became nervous, agitated, hostile. Reports of depression, hallucination. Sleepwalking. That kind of stuff."

"Hostile," Longo repeated to himself.

"And suicidal."

Longo's mind flashed back to his talk with Hanemure. The man denied Yamaguchi had told him he was going to kill Kariya. His brother-in-law, he said, was going to commit suicide.

"There's even one case..."

"Yeah?"

"Well, they claim it caused a woman to commit murder."

Longo stared at the young law clerk.

Dohi checked his notes again. "The Grundberg case," he said. "Ilo Grundberg. A fifty-seven-year-old woman in Hurricane, Utah. Four years ago she shot her mother to death."

Longo said nothing.

"Well," Dohi continued, "there was no motive for the murder, and the woman didn't remember anything afterward. So she was examined by a couple of court-appointed shrinks. And they said she was under the influence of Halcion when she committed the murder. The drug made her agitated and paranoid and caused amnesia. It was like she killed her mother while she was sleep walking."

"What was the verdict?"

"No verdict. The prosecutor took a look at the shrinks' reports, and he dismissed the case. The woman walked in 1989."

"Jeez . . ."

"There's more. After the dismissal, this Grundberg woman's lawyer turned around and sued Upjohn for twenty-one million. Up-john denied there was anything wrong with the drug. But a few weeks ago, they settled the case. The terms of the settlement are secret."

Longo shook his head slowly.

"There's more," Dohi said. "After the FDA okayed Halcion, they started getting reports of bad side effects. Personality changes, aggressive behavior, that kind of thing. So they did a follow-up in 1987, did comparison studies with two other benzodiazepines . . ." He glanced at his notes. "Dalmane and Restoril. And they found that Halcion was getting a whole lot more complaints than either of the other drugs."

"Uh-huh."

"So, anyway, Upjohn decided to cut the recommended dose from a half milligram to a quarter milligram. And . . ."

Longo quickly began digging through some paperwork on his desk. When he found the photocopy of the Kyoto Drug Store prescription, he scanned the scrawled handwriting. The prescribed dosage was a quarter milligram.

"I'm listening, Greg."

". . . and they put a warning in a package insert, saying the drug could cause . . ." He read again from his notes. ". . . 'bizarre or abnormal behavior, agitation and hallucinations.' "

Longo swiveled in his chair and looked out the window. The twilight was gradually turning to darkness, giving life to a sea of tiny lights spreading across the city like phosphorescent plankton. Standing out in the glittering white tide were the bright neon colors of China-town only a few blocks away.

"Anything else, Greg?"

"Well, these were all just isolated reports, no studies or anything. So the FDA seemed satisfied the drug was okay. But there was this

Dr. van der Kroef in the Netherlands, he wrote a medical article, claimed that the drug caused paranoid behavior."

"Uh-huh." Longo recognized the name. It had been on the list of expert witnesses Yamaki had turned over to him.

"And there's a Dr. Ian Oswald, in Scotland. He claimed Halcion caused an obsession with suicide. So the sale of Halcion was banned by the government in Great Britain."

"Jeez."

"Then there's this Dr. Anthony Kales, the head of psychiatry at Penn State."

Another name from the list.

"Kales was involved in the FDA studies. He says that Halcion . . ."

Longo looked at the prescription again as Dohi continued filling him in on his hurried research. Why was the prescription in Mitsuru's name? he wondered. Was Yamaki going to try to show that the woman was getting the drug for her husband to use? He noticed that the prescribing physician was a Dr. Morimoto. He would have to put Sakoda on him. He noticed for the first time a small box labeled "NR" in the corner that was checked. It probably meant "not refillable," he thought. He would have to check on that too.

He looked at the date again: November 17, 1990. Yamaguchi shot Kariya on March 29, 1991—four and a half months later. How many pills were in the bottle originally? Was this the first prescription, or did Yamaguchi or his wife use the drug regularly? How long would the November prescription have lasted? How long would the pills have retained their potency? Was there another prescription after the murder?

Too many questions. Trial started tomorrow and, as always, there were too many things left to do. He had to educate himself on Halcion, on the effects of the drug. He would have to do a lot of reading, become familiar enough on the subject in the next few days to be able to cross-examine men who had international reputations in a highly technical field. He needed to get background information on those men—once he found out who they were. And he needed to find at least one reputable witness himself, to play the old "battle of the experts" game.

The prosecutor was still waiting for a call from Upjohn. He had contacted the pharmaceutical company, hoping to get information on the drug and on where to find expert witnesses. After talking with two receptionists, three secretaries, and a junior executive, Longo had finally been put through to a vice president. When he explained that a defendant in a trial was claiming that Halcion caused him to commit murder, the executive almost choked. The man promised to call Longo back as soon as possible.

Longo found himself wondering if it was all just a wild-goose chase. Was the prescription a clever feint by Yamaki, designed to keep him distracted from the real issues? He would have to play it by ear, reacting when—and if—it became apparent that the clever defense lawyer really was going to use the drug as a defense. Halcion might be a red herring, but he could not afford to ignore it.

Not enough time, Longo thought. There was never enough time.

This last-minute scramble before trial was the reality of being a deputy D.A. Hollywood left the public with the impression that murder cases were carefully prepared for months; the prosecutor on the screen had little else to do but investigate and prepare a single case for trial. In reality, a prosecutor never knew for sure which of the hundreds of cases in his court would eventually end up in front of a jury. Roughly 97 percent of them resulted in a plea bargain or other disposition. And it was difficult to tell until the last minute if a given case would be one of the 3 percent. It was simply impossible to prepare every case for trial; caught off guard, prosecutors often had only hours to get ready before a jury filed in.

Adding to the problem was a common defense tactic. Many lawyers liked to "play chicken," bluffing it out to the very day of trial to see if the prosecution really had a case and intended to go all the way. If the deputy D.A. announced ready for trial, the defense attorney pled his client to a last-minute negotiated deal. Longo was used to seeing lawyers suddenly agreeing to plead their clients guilty as the names of twelve jurors were being called.

Even if it was probable that a given case would go to trial, a deputy D.A. in Central Trials still had hundreds of other matters to deal with. He had a daily calendar call, with perhaps fifteen or twenty cases to deal with. After calendar, he had to review the files for the next day's cases. And there were witnesses to be subpoenaed for preliminary hearings, and cops who needed search warrants, and pretrial motions to draft, and meetings with supervisors, and lawyers who wanted to discuss cases. None of this just stopped because the deputy was in trial. Only prosecutors assigned to units like S.I.D. or Special Trials had the luxury of being able to focus on just one or two cases at a time.

Normally, one of Longo's junior deputies would be available to help with the calendar. But Torrealba was in the hospital for knee surgery. Veals was in trial on an arson case in Department 125; the case had been assigned to Department 127, but the Yamaguchi trial had forced Judge Bascue to transfer it to another courtroom. And Boyle had to cover the preliminary hearings in municipal court. That left Longo alone in 127.

To make matters worse, Longo knew that Yamaki and his investigators had been spending hundreds of hours preparing. The lawyer would be ready for trial. And he did not bluff.

"...On the other hand," Dohi was saying, "there are plenty of big names in the field who say Halcion is okay. This guy Dr. Roth says it's the safest sleeping pill made."

"Uh-huh."

"And..." The law clerk again looked at his notes. "...Dr. David Greenblatt, Harvard Medical, professor of psychiatry and pharmacology at Tufts Medical School, very big name, he says it's perfectly safe. And another expert, Dr. Stuart Yodofsky, he says—"

"Hey, Larry." A tall, long-faced man stood in the doorway, his sleeves rolled up and a club tie pulled loose. Deputy D.A. Bill Hodgman, the man who would later be named second chair in the O. J. Simpson case. His careful, methodical, low-key style would be considered a perfect complement to the piranha approach of first chair Marcia Clark; Hodgman was the detail man, Clark the street fighter.

"Hi, Bill," Larry said.

Hodgman looked at his watch. "It's past seven, my friend. Take the rest of the day off."

Longo snorted. "Starting a trial tomorrow."

"Oh yeah. That 187 down in J-Town, huh? How's it look?"

Longo shrugged.

Hodgman nodded silently.

"Hey, congratulations on the verdict," Longo said. Hodgman's victory in the Charles Keating trial had been a badly needed boost to flagging morale in the office.

"Thanks."

"How was Ito?" Longo asked. The judge in the Keating trial, Lance Ito, would be reunited with Hodgman in the O. J. Simpson trial.

"No complaints," Hodgman said. "Gave me a fair trial."

Longo nodded. "Hey," he said, waving toward Dohi, "you know Greg Dohi?"

Hodgman smiled, shook the law clerk's hand.

"Waiting for the bar results," Longo said. "Guy's going to be a star, Bill, you watch."

"No kidding?" Hodgman said, taking a second look at the young man.

Dohi shook his head in embarrassment.

The telephone rang.

"Hey," Hodgman said, raising his hand as he stepped back into the hallway, "good luck tomorrow, Larry."

"Yeah, thanks, Bill," Longo said, reaching for the phone. "Longo," he said gruffly into the receiver.

Dohi settled back in the folding metal chair.

"Yeah, well thanks for calling back," Longo said into the phone. "Yeah, we're kind of up against the wall here. Like I said, trial starts tomorrow. . . . Uh-huh . . . well, sure, we'd sure appreciate any help you could give. . . . Uh-huh . . ."

Longo covered the receiver for a moment. "The guy from Up-john," he said to Dohi. "The head honcho, I think. Calling from his home." Then he took his hand off the receiver and continued.

"Uh-huh. . . . What's his name?" Longo wrote something on the legal pad. "Uh-huh. Well, we sure appreciate the offer, but the problem is, if I put on some expert from Upjohn, the defense lawyer's just going to have him for lunch. . . . No, see, the problem is the jury's going to think the guy is biased, you know? I mean, sure the guy's going to say the stuff is safe. He's working for you guys, right? . . . Uh-huh."

Jimmy Sakoda suddenly appeared in the doorway. Standing

next to him was a small, middle-aged Japanese man in a gray flannel suit. He had a round face and a thin, wispy mustache and he wore plain eyeglasses.

"Uh-huh . . ." Longo put his hand over the receiver again. "Uchida?" he asked his investigator.

"Yep," Sakoda said.

"Hey, do me a favor. Take Mr. Uchida there to the coffee room, get him some coffee. And go down to Lew Ito's office, okay? Should still be there. I told him I wanted him to sit in." Lew Ito was a deputy in the office. Often confused with Lance Ito, he was not related to the judge.

"Sure." Sakoda left with Uchida.

"Uh-huh," Longo said back into the receiver. "Well, again, thanks for the offer but, see, even an independent expert like that, I mean, if you guys pay his fee and fly him out and all. You can see that doesn't look so good to the jury, you guys paying the freight and all, kind of blows apart his impartiality, know what I mean?"

Longo looked at Dohi and winked, then tilted back in his chair and propped his feet up on the crowded desk top.

"Yeah, well, we don't know yet who their expert is, or how many of them. . . . Right, trial's tomorrow. . . . Uh-huh, what's his name again?" Longo leaned forward and jotted something else down. "Uh-huh . . . could be, yeah . . . and you got transcripts from the testimony of all these guys? Yeah, great . . . uh-huh. Hey, that'd be great. What's his name? Lane D. Bauer?" He wrote the name on the pad. "Senior partner, Shook, Hardy and Bacon . . . Kansas City . . . What's that number? Uh-huh . . . New Otani, right . . ."

Longo sat up. "Well, we really appreciate it. . . . Uh-huh . . . well, sorry to bother you this late at night. Must be pretty late back there. . . . Uh-huh, you too. Thanks again. Good night." He hung up the receiver.

Dohi waited expectantly.

"Guy is having a fit," Longo said with a grin. "There is panic at Upjohn tonight."

"What did he say?" Dohi asked.

"Well, he offered me anything I wanted. The resources of the company are at our complete disposal, Greg. All the experts we can use, from anywhere in the world. All prepaid and delivered to our doorstep. Money is no object."

"Can't do it, huh?"

Longo shook his head. "Yamaki'd make it look like we were stooges for Upjohn."

"I guess so."

"And he wouldn't be far wrong. No, we gotta get our own man. But that doesn't mean we can't tap these guys for information. This V.P. gave me a couple names, big guys in the field." He ripped the top sheet from the legal pad and handed it to the law clerk. "Give them a call, explain the situation. See if either one's available. And find out their fees. The county won't go over a grand a day."

"Okay."

"Meantime, the senior partner of the law firm that represents Upjohn, he's flying out from Kansas City on the red-eye. He's been defending these Halcion lawsuits. Knows all the experts, the issues, everything. We're meeting tomorrow morning before trial. Then we'll go over transcripts of expert testimony and stuff in his hotel room tomorrow night. Instant education. I'd like you there, Greg."

"Sure. He's staying at the New Otani?"

"Where else?"

Sakoda stepped back into the office. Standing with him was a middle-aged Japanese man wearing a navy blue blazer, a blue button-down broadcloth shirt, and a red-and-black regimental tie.

"Hey, Lew," Longo said, "how you doing?"

"Pretty good, Larry," Lew Ito said. He looked around the disheveled office, shaking his head in disbelief. "I see you haven't changed your filing system much."

"Yeah, well, it's kinda complicated, see, but I got everything just where I want it."

"Sure."

"Oh yeah, that's Greg Dohi over there, Lew, one of our law clerks. He's half *samurai* himself."

"No shit?" Ito said, shaking the young man's hand. He turned to Longo. "The guy here yet?"

"Yeah. Cooling his heels in the coffee room." Longo looked at Sakoda. "You ask Uchida about the affidavit?"

"Yep," the investigator said. "He says after talking to me, Ya-maki came to see him. A couple of days later, Yamaki's investigator brought the affidavit to him, all typed up. And he signed it."

"You ask him why the change of story?"

Sakoda shrugged. "He says his memory got a lot clearer after talking to Yamaki."

"I'll bet," Longo said. "But he agreed to come here and talk about it."

"Yep. I think I mentioned something to him about making false statements to law enforcement officials."

Longo thought for a moment. "Anything on Yamaguchi's buddy, Matsumoto?"

Sakoda shook his head. "The guy's doing everything he can to avoid me, Larry. He's broken two appointments. Every time I find him, he's got to run somewhere on important business."

"Uh-huh."

"Oh, I gave Holden a call. The detective over at Montebello P.D.? On that 459 at Yamaguchi's home."

"Yeah?"

"A pretty heavy burglary for a couple of juvies. Thirty-five thousand in cash, fifteen thousand in Japanese yen, another fifty grand or so in diamonds."

"Wonder what Yamaguchi was doing with that kind of cash in his house?"

Sakoda shrugged. "Anyway, they caught the kids who pulled it off, two or three days later." He took out a small notebook from his vest pocket, thumbed through it. "One named Scott Ishida, the other named Darin Onishi. Copped out to the 459, but didn't say anything about Yamaguchi's son. Strange thing, though . . ."

"Yeah?"

"Well, Yamaguchi refused to press charges against the kids."

"No kidding?"

"Yep. So the charges were dismissed. Anyway, Holden's going to locate the kids and ask them about it."

"Good."

"But Holden did recall, when he questioned Ken Yamaguchi right after the shooting, he said his dad got the gun because of the burglary."

The phone rang again. Longo picked it up. "Longo," he barked.

Sakoda stepped farther into the crowded office. Dohi propped his feet up on a stack of files on the floor to give him more room. Lew Ito tried to squeeze in, then stepped back into the doorway.

"What's that?" Longo said into the phone. "Dr. Wenke? . . . uh-huh . . . well, thanks for calling . . . Uh-huh . . ."

The prosecutor put his hand over the receiver again. "A medical big shot from Chicago," he said to Dohi, "guy at Upjohn asked him to fill me in on Halcion. Take notes." He took his hand off the receiver.

"Uh-huh . . . If any adverse reactions to Halcion, will occur immediately, first time it is used . . . Uh-huh . . . If adverse effect, will be like sleepwalking. . . . Person will walk around in daze . . . unable to do much, can't carry on conversation. . . . Uh-huh . . . Effects will take place about one half hour after ingestion. . . . Lasts about three hours. . . . No long-term effects from using the drug. . . ."

Dohi was writing down Longo's words as fast as he could.

". . . uh-huh . . . well, tell me, Doctor, would a person who was having one of these reactions to Halcion, would that person become homicidal, would it make him try to kill someone? . . . It wouldn't, huh? . . . Would he be able to use a gun, point it and shoot? . . . He wouldn't. Okay, would he be able to drive a car? . . . No, okay, would he be able to carry on a conversation with, say, a police officer? . . . Not in that condition. Okay . . . uh-huh . . ."

Longo looked up at Sakoda, pointed in the direction of the coffee room. He mouthed the word "Uchida."

Sakoda stepped out of the office and disappeared down the hallway.

"Uh-huh," the prosecutor continued. "Uh-huh . . . oh yeah, sure, I guess it's pretty late there, I guess you're calling from home, huh? . . . Uh-huh . . . yeah, that'd be great. What's the number?" He wrote something down on the legal pad. "Uh-huh, well I'll probably take you up on that. . . . Uh-huh . . . okay, well thanks, Doctor, you've been a big help. . . . Uh-huh . . . yeah, I know. Good night."

Longo hung up the receiver.

Ito slid past his desk and stood next to the window. "So what do you want me to do with this Uchida?"

"I need this guy, Lew, I need him bad. But Yamaki got to him.

I figure he probably told Uchida to play games with the language thing when he testifies, or when I talk to him, you know?

"So if he starts that stuff, you can translate for the son of a gun. Plus, I could use a witness if he says something here and denies it later."

"Why not tape him?"

"Then I gotta turn it over to Yamaki. There's a discovery order in the case."

Ito nodded. "What about the—"

Sakoda and the man in the gray suit appeared in the doorway.

"Greg," Longo said to Dohi, "we can't squeeze everybody in here. Can you put in a couple more hours in the library? Maybe on that marital privilege stuff. Then head home. I'll see you tomorrow, six A.M."

"Sure," Dohi said. He stood up, stuffed his notes into a Samsonite briefcase, then squeezed through the door past Sakoda and Uchida.

"C'mon on in," Longo said to the two men. "Mr. Uchida, my name's Larry Longo, and this here is Lew Ito, he's a deputy D.A. too. He's going to sit in on our little chat."

Uchida bowed quickly toward Longo, then Ito.

"Why don't you grab that chair," Longo said, "and we'll get started."

Uchida glanced hesitantly at the folding metal chair, then sat down. He looked nervously around the crowded office.

"Now," Longo said, "I understand Mr. Yamaki asked you to sign an affidavit, that right?"

The man bowed his head sharply. "Yes, this is so."

"Uh-huh. How many times you talk with Yamaki?"

"We talk, maybe, two times."

"Uh-huh. And this was after you talked with my investigator here, Mr. Sakoda?"

"Yes, this is so."

"Well, Mr. Uchida, didn't you tell Mr. Sakoda that you were at the Mitsuru Cafe the day after Kariya was shot?"

Uchida nodded slowly, his eyes darting back and forth like a small trapped animal.

"And that you had a little talk with a couple guys named Matsumoto and Hanemure?"

Uchida nodded again.

"Didn't you tell him that Matsumoto told you he had a talk with Yamaguchi a few days before the shooting?"

Uchida kept slowly nodding his head.

"And Yamaguchi told him he was going to *finish* Kariya?"

Uchida stopped nodding. "I do not understand."

"You don't understand the question?"

"Yes, this is so."

"Did Matsumoto tell you Yamaguchi said he was going to finish Kariya?"

Uchida shook his head. "I am very sorry, I do not—"

"Lew," Longo said, not taking his eyes off Uchida.

Ito repeated the question to Uchida in Japanese.

Uchida was silent for a moment, then said something in Japanese back to Ito.

"He's not sure," Ito said to Longo. "He doesn't remember too clearly who said what."

"But did you tell *Sakoda* that was what was said?"

Ito translated. Again, Uchida paused, then replied in Japanese.

"Maybe so," Ito said.

"Did you tell Mr. Sakoda that Matsumoto told you Yamaguchi said he hired a private investigator to follow his wife and Kariya?"

Ito translated. Again, a pause and a reply in Japanese.

"I am not sure," Ito said. "My memory is not clear."

Longo leaned back in his chair and stared at Uchida in silence.

"Do you recall," he said finally, "telling Mr. Sakoda here that Hanemure also told you some things?"

Uchida studied the floor as Ito translated. He nodded slowly.

"And Yamaguchi told Hanemure the same thing, he was going to finish Kariya?"

Uchida listened to the translation, then replied in Japanese.

"My memory is not clear," Ito said.

"Hanemure said Yamaguchi told him he had been patient long enough, he was going to take care of the matter himself?"

Ito repeated the question in Japanese. Uchida paused, answered in Japanese.

"Maybe this is so," Ito said. "I do not remember very well."

Longo grinned at Uchida, said nothing for a few seconds.

"But you signed an affidavit for Yamaki?" he asked.

Uchida nodded, forgetting to wait for the translation.

"And in that affidavit, you said the statement you heard was 'I will do it' not 'I will finish him'?"

Ito translated. Uchida nodded.

"Yamaguchi said, 'I cannot take it anymore, I will do it.'"

Ito translated, and again Uchida nodded.

"You told Yamaki that?"

Uchida nodded.

"Did you tell him that this meant Yamaguchi was going to commit suicide?"

Longo waited as Ito translated. Uchida swallowed hard, then replied in Japanese.

"I believe this is so," Ito said.

"Uh-huh. Well, Mr. Uchida, you're going to be called as a witness in this case, and you're going to have to testify—under oath. Do you know what that means?"

Ito translated. Obviously miserable now, Uchida nodded.

"And your memory's gonna have to improve a whole lot before you—"

The phone rang.

The prosecutor picked up the receiver. "Longo," he growled.

"Larry," he heard the voice say, "this is Monty Holden."

"Yeah, Monty," Longo said, glaring at Uchida. "Whaddya got?"

"Bad news."

"Uh-huh."

"This Carmona guy? The eyewitness to the shooting?"

"Uh-huh."

"Well, I just went by his place to drop off the subpoena."

Longo said nothing.

"You there?" Holden asked.

"Yeah."

"Well, the guy's gone."

"Uh-huh."

"Yeah, cleared out. Place's empty."

"Uh-huh."

"Our eyewitness has disappeared, Larry."

Chapter

14

"Are there any further matters before my clerk calls for the jury panel?" Judge Bascue asked.

Longo rose from his seat at the counsel table. "I got a 402, judge."

"Mr. Longo," Bascue said, "what is the nature of your 402 motion?"

"Well, the way I see it, Yamaki here is gonna put on some kinda diminished-capacity defense. I think he's gonna offer evidence that Yamaguchi was under the influence of a drug called Halcion when he shot the victim."

"Halcion."

Longo looked across at the defense lawyer. "That about right, Mike?"

Yamaki smiled. The prosecutor was forcing him to tip his hand. Longo was making a pretrial motion under Evidence Code section 402 to exclude testimony unless it met certain foundational requirements. In this case, Longo was challenging the defense to prove that any planned medical evidence was relevant to the issues in the case. If Yamaki *was* planning to offer testimony that Halcion was taken by his client, he would now have to confirm that. He would also have to make some preliminary showing that the drug was, in fact, taken by Yamaguchi on the night of the killing and that it could have affected his ability to premeditate or to form the intent to kill.

"Your honor," Yamaki said, "I would request that the court reserve a ruling on this issue until the prosecution has rested its case."

"Mike," Longo said to the lawyer, "you gonna offer evidence of Halcion? Yes or no?"

The defense lawyer smiled, said nothing.

"Mr. Yamaki?" Bascue said. "In view of the 402 motion, I think that is a fair question."

Yamaki looked at Longo, then at the judge. "Yes, your honor, there will be evidence of Halcion usage by my client. But I request that any 402 hearing be postponed until after the People have rested."

"He's hiding the ball, judge. I mean, there's been a discovery order for over a month, and here we're about to start a trial, and he *still* hasn't given me the names of his expert witnesses."

"I have supplied the prosecution with a list of potential witnesses, your honor."

"There's over a dozen names on that list," Longo said. "How many you gonna call?"

"Your honor," the defense lawyer said calmly, "I have given the prosecution a list of possible witnesses. I assure the court that any witnesses who will testify will appear on that list. As to *which* witness . . ."

Longo snorted.

"I can't tell when the prosecution will rest its case," Yamaki continued, ignoring Longo. "So I can't really tell exactly when I can begin my case-in-chief. It could be in three days or three weeks. And these are very important men, with international reputations. They can't commit to flying out here to testify without knowing exactly when that will be. So I cannot determine at this point which witnesses will be available."

"That's baloney, Mike," Longo said, "and you know it."

"Well," Bascue said, "discovery issues aside, is there any reason why the court can't rule on the admissibility of this Halcion evidence today?"

"Not without an expert witness," Yamaki said, shrugging his shoulders helplessly. "We need his testimony on the effects of Halcion to show relevance."

"I see."

"Gimme a break," Longo said. "How do we know if Yamaguchi even took the stuff? There's nothing stopping Yamaki from putting on evidence today that his guy took Halcion that night."

"What would be the point, your honor?" Yamaki said. "The court still couldn't make a ruling on relevancy until it heard from the expert. Why hear the motion in two separate parts?"

Longo wanted badly to know how the lawyer was going to prove the drug was taken by Yamaguchi before the shooting. More important, he wanted to know if Yamaki's client was going to take the stand in the trial. If Yamaguchi testified in the 402 hearing that he had taken the pill, he would have to take the stand again during the trial to repeat the testimony to the jury. And once he was on the stand Longo could cross-examine him on any subject, including the circumstances surrounding the shooting.

But Longo had a feeling Yamaki was not going to let his client take the stand. Then how was he going to prove Yamaguchi took Halcion that night? Yamaguchi's wife could not testify she saw him take the drug: She was hiding behind the marital privilege. Who had been with him in the hours before the murder?

Bascue thought for a moment. "Very well," he said finally, "the court will hold off on the 402 hearing until after the People rest. At that time, Mr. Longo, you may renew your motion."

Longo snorted in disgust.

"But," the judge continued, "there will be no mention of Halcion or any other drug until it is ruled admissible. Neither of you will mention it during jury selection, or in your opening statements. Understood, gentlemen?"

"Understood," Yamaki said.

Longo nodded.

"Your honor," the defense lawyer said, "the defense also has a 402 motion to make."

"Yes?" Bascue said.

"I understand that the prosecution plans to put on a witness by the name of Takeshi Uchida."

Now what? Longo wondered.

"I understand further that the purpose of this witness is to elicit testimony that statements were made to him by two gentlemen to the effect that my client said he was going to 'finish' Mr. Kariya."

"What's this got to do with a 402?" Longo said. "The relevance of that kind of statement is obvious. You got a problem with the *credibility,* that's for cross-exam in trial."

"It's not a question of credibility, your honor. It's a question of relevance. If Mr. Uchida denies those statements were ever made to him, if the statements that *were* made related to other matters that are not relevant, then he should not be called as a witness."

It was a clever move, Longo thought grudgingly. If the lawyer could get a ruling before trial that Uchida had nothing relevant to offer, the witness would never take the stand—and the jury would never hear the critical evidence. But if Longo could put Uchida on the stand, he could get Yamaguchi's statements in even if Uchida denied hearing about them; Sakoda could testify to what Uchida had told him. Then it would be up to the jury to decide which of the two men was telling the truth.

"Judge," Longo said, "Yamaki wants to try this case *before* the jury gets here. I got a witness who says Uchida told him about the statement. If Uchida wants to take the stand and deny it, okay, I'll confront him with what he said to my witness." Longo looked at Yamaki. "Then it's a question of which one's a liar. And that's for the jury to decide."

Yamaki smiled. "Mr. Uchida's statements to another witness— I believe his name is Jimmy Sakoda—would constitute a violation of the hearsay rule."

"Naw," Longo said, "there's an exception to the rule. What we got here is a prior inconsistent statement, section 1235 of the Evidence Code."

Bascue nodded slowly. "If there is a prior statement that is inconsistent with Mr. Uchida's testimony, Mr. Yamaki, the prosecution would be permitted to confront him with it."

Yamaki was silent for a moment. Then he smiled again and bowed his head slightly. "I accept the court's ruling, your honor."

"Very well," Bascue said. "Anything further?"

Neither attorney said anything.

Bascue looked at the clock. "Well, I see it is already two forty-five. By the time the panel gets here, it will be after three." He looked down at the two men. "I have a couple of matters to attend to, gentlemen. Any objections if we get started with jury selection tomorrow morning? We've got a light calendar tomorrow, starts at eight-thirty, should be over by ten. Say, ten o'clock?"

"That would be fine, your honor," Yamaki said.

"Sure, judge," Longo said.

"Very well. The case of People versus Yamaguchi is trailed until ten A.M. Court is in recess."

Bascue stepped down from the bench and walked back into his chambers.

Yamaki placed some papers into his burgundy leather briefcase, closed it, and turned to leave. He paused for a moment, looked at Longo.

"Just like old times, Larry," he said.

"Yeah," Longo said. "Just like old times."

Yamaki smiled, then turned and left the courtroom.

Longo stepped out of the Criminal Courts Building and walked up to Broadway. It was dark now, and the downtown commuter traffic had already thinned out to a trickle. He waited for the green light, then crossed Temple Street and continued north on Broadway.

Lane Bauer, the senior law partner from Kansas City, had called that morning to tell Longo that he had missed the overnight flight to Los Angeles. He would catch another flight the following morning and meet with the prosecutor in the evening at the New Otani.

Halcion, Longo reflected as he walked. Could it be possible that Yamaguchi had really taken the drug? And if he had, could there have been side effects? Was it *possible* the drug could have caused him to commit a murder? No, Longo thought, shaking off the nagging doubts. Halcion did not cause people to kill.

But could Yamaki sell the idea to a jury?

Aggressive behavior. Paranoia. Sleepwalking. According to the doctor, the drug needed half an hour to take effect. Then it wore off three hours later. If Yamaguchi *had* taken the drug, any side effects would have occurred during that two-and-a-half-hour period. Ya-maki's defense, then, would depend on proving that the shooting happened during that time.

Longo worked out the time frame. Ken Yamaguchi had told Detective Holden that his father came home about one o'clock in the morning. There was apparently nothing unusual in his appearance or conversation to indicate either a semiconscious state or a homicidal rage; at least, the son mentioned nothing. Then, about half an hour later, Mitsuru pounded on the door, telling Ken his father just shot Kariya. Ten minutes later, Yamaguchi turned himself in at the Highway Patrol station. And according to the CHP officer, Yamaguchi was speaking clearly and coherently and there was nothing unusual about his appearance.

No symptoms of any side effects half an hour before the shooting, none ten minutes after. Or would Ken change his story when he testified in front of the jury? Would Yamaki now have him say that his father was acting "strangely"? Or would Yamaki's expert say that a homicidal impulse caused by the drug might not be detected by an observer?

If Yamaki was going to show that his client had taken Halcion, *where* had he taken it? It would not make sense to take a sleeping pill before going to a dinner party that evening. And he certainly would not take one when he was planning to confront his wife about her lover. Yet, he would have to have taken the pill in the three hours before the murder. When had that been?

And how was Yamaki going to prove his client *did* take Halcion that night? Longo was still confident that the lawyer would never subject Yamaguchi to his cross-examination. Was there a witness who would suddenly appear and claim to have seen Yamaguchi take the pill during the critical three hours before the shooting? And even if he had taken the drug, how was Yamaki going to prove that Yamaguchi was one of those rare individuals who suffered side effects? And that the side effects were so severe that they caused him to commit murder?

The Grundberg case, Longo thought. If Bascue ruled that evidence of Halcion was admissible, Yamaki would have his expert tell the jury all about the Grundberg murder. The prosecutor made a mental note to ask Judge Bascue for a suppression hearing. There had been no legal findings in the case, no conviction or acquittal, and the opinions of the two psychiatrists were no more than opinions, and hearsay at that. It was important that the jury not hear the unproven allegations about that homicide.

Yamaki's expert witness . . . Who was it? Would there be more than one? Dohi had contacted the witnesses on the list, but none had committed to testifying in the case. Longo was rapidly educating himself on the Halcion controversy, but he had a long way to go before he could challenge a psychiatrist in his own field of expertise. And time was running out.

Whoever the expert was, Longo thought, he would not have examined Yamaguchi before or shortly after the shooting. And that meant that Longo could keep him from testifying that Yamaguchi had, in fact, killed Kariya due to the effects of Halcion. Since there was no examination, Longo would object to the expert testifying to anything but hypothetical situations. He could not say that the defendant *was* suffering from side effects, or that he *did* kill while under the influence of the drug. He could only theorize that a hypothetical person who had taken the drug *could* have had an adverse reaction, *could* possibly even have committed murder.

Longo suddenly realized that he had walked past the lot where his old Toyota van was parked. He was now only a block from Chinatown.

He paused, then continued walking north on Broadway.

Where was Yamaki going with the Halcion defense? What was the legal theory he was constructing? Was he going for diminished capacity? This, he knew, could take one of two roads. The defense lawyer might try to show that the drug prevented Yamaguchi from "meaningfully premeditating" during the period before the shooting: Halcion diminished his capacity to premeditate. Since the jury could always return a verdict for a lesser crime than the first-degree murder charged, this would reduce the offense to second-degree murder.

The second possibility was that his mental capacity was so affected by the drug that he could not even form the mental intent to kill. If the jury bought this defense, they could return with a verdict of involuntary manslaughter—an offense that carried a very light sentence.

Or was Halcion all a clever ruse? Was Yamaki still going for the old-fashioned heat of passion killing? Was he going to present the classic lovers' triangle and argue for a verdict of voluntary manslaughter? Maybe even try for a sympathy acquittal? It was a long shot, but it would not be the first time a jury acquitted an enraged husband under the unwritten "law of the West."

Longo had a feeling that Yamaki was not aiming for voluntary manslaughter. Nor was he trying for involuntary manslaughter. And he would certainly not be satisfied with second-degree murder. No, the lawyer's strategy was much more ambitious. He was going for broke.

Sleepwalking.

One of the reported side effects of Halcion was sleepwalking. And amnesia. What had the Grundberg woman said? She did not remember killing her mother. It had been as if she killed her while she was walking in her sleep.

Actus reus.

The term suddenly flashed through Longo's mind. He had not heard the expression since his law school days. A crime had two elements: a state of mind, or *mens rea,* and a voluntary act, or *actus reus.* The state of mind was a common issue in criminal trials; premeditation, intent, and heat of passion were examples. The voluntariness of an act, however, was an extremely rare issue. Longo could not recall any case in his experience where the question was whether the defendant had control over his own physical movement.

If Yamaki could convince a jury that Yamaguchi shot Kariya while he was in a sleeplike state caused by Halcion . . . he would get a complete acquittal.

Longo found himself in the middle of Chinatown. The garish red and yellow and purple neon signs glowed brightly in the dark, lighting the street with a festive yet tawdry Asian flavor. WUNG FUNG TAI GINSENG. GOLDEN DRAGON RESTAURANT. TAI CHUN JEWELRY. VIET HOA BEAUTY SALON. NEW LUCKY RESTAURANT. VINH PHONG THA'I HERBS.

The prosecutor continued along Broadway, aware now where he was going.

Was it possible that he was wrong—that Yamaki *would* put his client on the stand? No, that would not be like the defense lawyer. Evasion, deception, stealth, surprise. He would avoid confrontation.

He would never give Longo the chance to cross-examine Yamaguchi in front of a jury. He had already shown one of his cards: Mitsuru was hiding behind the marital privilege. And then he had tried to keep Uchida off the stand too.

With both Yamaguchi and his wife refusing to testify, and Kariya dead, there were no witnesses to the shooting. Except Nicholas Carmona.

Holden had done some hurried checking and discovered that Carmona had suddenly moved with his new wife to a small town just across the state line in Arizona. There, he was safe from any California subpoena. Was it just coincidence, or had Yamaki somehow gotten to him?

Longo had sent Holden to Arizona to track Carmona down and try to bring him back voluntarily. But he felt like he was walking through a minefield, waiting for the next explosion. Mitsuru had taken the marital privilege. Uchida had changed his story. Hanemure now denied making his statements. Matsumoto was hiding. Carmona had left the state. What was left?

What was left was a dead body and a confession. Longo could prove that Yamaguchi shot Kariya—and little else.

The speedy loader meant nothing, and without Carmona's testimony the white sock was meaningless too. What was he doing with the speedy loader? And why was it empty?

And the sock: It had obviously been used to prevent fingerprints and in fact, there had been no prints on the murder weapon. But why do this and then turn yourself in? Carmona said Yamaguchi stood next to the car window for thirty seconds or so after shooting Kariya. Had Mitsuru told her husband during this period that she was going to turn him in? Or had Yamaguchi planned to kill his wife too, leaving no witnesses—and then lost his nerve? There had been *two* shots, one of them lodged in the roof on the passenger side—near where Mitsuru's head would have been.

The gun. It was a five-shot. Longo recalled that when Yamaguchi turned it over to the Chippy it had three live rounds and two spent ones. That checked with the evidence that there had been two shots fired. But the strange thing was the position of the hammer. If Yamaguchi simply fired twice and did nothing more, the hammer should still be resting on the second spent shell; the five-bullet cylinders would not have rotated until the hammer was brought back a third time. But the hammer was resting on a live round.

Yamaguchi must have cocked the hammer back a third time, then slowly eased it down. He had changed his mind. Why? For whom was the third bullet intended? Mitsuru? Himself? But if for himself, why wear the sock?

BAMBOO LANE the small sign read. The prosecutor turned left, walked slowly up the darkened alley.

There had been plenty of rumors in the Yamaguchi case, Longo thought. The murder was a Yakuza hit. Yamaguchi and Kariya were involved in heavy drug deals. Ken had engineered a burglary of his own home. And the latest: Kariya and Mitsuru were planning to kill Yamaguchi.

None of these rumors had checked out yet. And Longo could not afford to waste his time and Sakoda's on chasing down false leads. Particularly since he was not convinced they were not planted by Yamaki as diversions.

The usual strategy of the defense in criminal cases could be found in one word: delay. Faced with overwhelming evidence of guilt, most lawyers asked the court for repeated continuances and stalled as long as they could. The longer the case went on, the more likely witnesses would forget, move, or die. But Yamaki had done the opposite: He had pushed for an early trial. He had hurried the case to a jury before Longo could prepare, before he could react to esoteric medical evidence and witnesses who changed their stories or disappeared.

Longo stopped, looked at the simple storefront. JIN HING CO. the sign read. BY APPOINTMENT ONLY. The jewelry store was dark, the door locked. He looked up the alley for a moment, where Nagao had fallen in the rain.

The Chinatown case had seemed like a bottomless quagmire to Longo, slowly swallowing him. And as he stood there, he had the terrible feeling that it was happening all over again.

Chapter

15

"Is Mr. Yamaguchi guilty?"

"I do not understand, sir."

"Mrs. Vinh,*" Yamaki said, "as you sit there right now, do you feel that my client is guilty of murder?"

"I . . . I do not know," the small, frail Vietnamese woman said.

Yamaki stepped back from the wooden podium, smiling at the eleven other men and women seated in the jury box.

"At this very moment," he asked her gently, "if you had to cast a ballot of either guilty or not guilty, how would you vote?"

"I do not know, sir," she repeated, obviously confused.

"Do you understand that, under our Constitution, he is *presumed* to be innocent?"

The woman nodded slowly. "Yes, yes."

"Then, unless there is overwhelming evidence that he is guilty, you must vote to acquit, isn't that true?"

"I . . . I think so, yes, yes."

"At this very moment, then, how would you vote?"

The woman looked across the room at Yamaguchi, then to Judge Bascue for help. She looked back at Yamaki. "I . . . vote for . . . not guilty?" It was a question.

"Yes, Mrs. Vinh, the law *demands* that you vote not guilty."

"Yes, yes," she said, relieved.

Yamaki leaned forward and grasped the top of the wooden

speaker's podium, his eyes going from juror to juror. Then he looked back at the woman.

"The fact that he is here now, that he has been charged with a crime, does that make you think he must have done something wrong?"

She was confused again. "I do not know."

"You understand that he is here, in trial, because he insists he is innocent?"

"Yes, yes."

Yamaki smiled at the woman. "Mrs. Vinh, would you please look at Mr. Yamaguchi again."

The woman looked across the courtroom. Yamaguchi was sitting at the far end of the defense table, his head bowed deeply, his eyes closed. He was wearing a light blue suit, white shirt, and striped tie. A set of headphones covered his ears.

An older Asian man, wearing a rumpled black suit too large for his frail body, sat next to Yamaguchi, interpreting quietly into a small microphone. Yamaki had insisted that his client was both hard of hearing and in need of an interpreter.

A nice touch, Longo thought. Yamaki knew how to package his clients to get the most sympathy. But Yamaguchi had talked with officers at the Highway Patrol station and at the Montebello police department. And there had been no problems with his hearing or with understanding English. Longo would make the lawyer eat the package.

Yamaki turned to the other jurors. "Ladies and gentlemen, would each of you please look at my client."

All twelve men and women looked across the courtroom at the seated figure.

Longo recalled how they had looked at Yamaguchi earlier that day when the judge had read the charges to the jury. Disbelief. The older Japanese gentleman in the neat blue suit simply did not *look* like a murderer. And Longo knew that perception would be tough to overcome.

"Now, does any one of you feel he is guilty?"

There was no reply.

"Do any of you feel he is *probably* guilty?"

No reply.

"Would any of you have any difficulty in voting to acquit him, at this very moment?"

No reply.

"Do any of you have any trouble *saying,* right now, that he is not guilty?"

No reply.

"Let's try it," Yamaki said with a smile. "All of you together, please say 'not guilty.'"

There was a mumbled confusion of voices, some hesitant.

"At the end of the trial, you will have to vote together. Can you *say* it together? Once again, please."

The voices were louder and closer together this time, the words "not guilty" almost discernable.

"Thank you," Yamaki said, still smiling warmly.

Longo snorted under his breath. A childish trick. But an effective one. The son of a gun was clever, he thought. It was a standard defense tactic during the questioning of potential jurors, or *voir dire* as it was called by lawyers, to ask about the presumption of innocence. But Yamaki went further. He got them used to the idea of voting for acquittal, got them to conceptualize it, then to verbalize it. Then he got them acting as a group. It appeared foolish, but it was a useful psychological technique.

In theory, the questions asked during *voir dire* were designed to find out if any potential jurors held any prejudices or biases that might influence their verdicts. In fact, however, experienced trial lawyers knew such questions were seldom answered truthfully; very few jurors would ever admit to being biased or prejudiced. Instead, the procedure was commonly used as a form of subliminal persuasion; the "questions" were actually statements designed to influence the juror's views. Yamaki was not trying to find out if Mrs. Vinh would fairly apply the law on presumption of innocence or not. He was trying to alter her perceptions of the case.

The process, known as "preinstruction," was technically not permitted, but it was widely tolerated by judges because of the difficulty in determining whether a question was intended to ferret out a bias or to preinstruct. And it was a very effective technique. Jurors tended to be resistant during a lawyer's opening statement or closing argument, realizing he was trying to sell them something. During jury

selection, however, this resistance was all but gone; the juror believes
he is providing the information, and being new to the case and curious,
he is absorbing any information like a sponge.

Longo made a mental note to counter Yamaki's preinstruction
on the presumption of innocence when it came his turn to ask the
juror questions.

"You understand, Mrs. Vinh," Yamaki continued, "that my client does not have the burden of proof?"

"I understand, yes, yes."

"Mr. Longo is the prosecutor, he has the burden of proof."

"Yes, yes."

"He has to prove his case *beyond a reasonable doubt*, do you
understand that?"

"Yes, yes," the small, frail woman said.

"That's an awfully heavy burden, Mrs. Vinh. Do you think it's
fair to make the prosecution shoulder such a heavy burden?"

The woman shrugged. "I think so."

"Would you vote to convict if you had even a slight doubt, so
long as it was a reasonable one?"

"I . . . don't think so."

"Mrs. Vinh, what if you thought my client was *probably* guilty?
What if you were almost *sure* he was guilty? But you had this nagging
little doubt?"

"I . . . not guilty?"

The lawyer smiled, nodded approvingly. He looked around at
the other eleven men and women. Then he turned and quickly
scanned the sixty-five other potential jurors in the audience, waiting
to be called to replace anyone excused from the twelve in the
jury box.

"Mrs. Vinh, how do you feel about the Japanese?"

"Japanese?"

"Yes, how do you feel about Japanese people?"

"I . . . I do not . . . I do not feel anything."

"Many people, maybe some on this very jury, might want to
convict Mr. Yamaguchi simply because he is Japanese."

"Yes?"

"How do you feel about that?"

"I do not . . . That is not right."

"Would *you* be more likely to vote guilty because he is Japanese?"

He's playing every card, Longo thought. Get them sensitized to a nonexistent race issue. Get them hesitant to convict because of the possible racial overtones of a guilty verdict.

Longo had been stunned to learn from another deputy D.A. on the elevator that morning that Yamaki had been on television news broadcasts the previous night. Mayor Tom Bradley had held a press conference for the purpose of speaking out against the rising tide of racial prejudice. As a leader of the Japanese-American community and a Bradley appointee to the Police Commission, Yamaki had stood conspicuously at his side.

Except there was no rising tide of prejudice in Los Angeles of which Longo was aware. So what made it so newsworthy? Nothing, Larry thought. Except that Yamaki was married to Tritia Toyota, the most popular news anchor in Los Angeles.

Longo thought it was not coincidence that the press conference had been held on the eve of the Yamaguchi trial. He wondered how many of the jurors had seen the broadcasts.

The prosecutor checked his jury form again. This was a legal-sized sheet of paper, laid out lengthwise with a diagram of two rows of large boxes, six to a row. In each box, Longo had written the name of the potential juror sitting in the corresponding seat, along with any notes about that person's background or answers to the lawyers' questions. If a juror was excused, Longo attached a small yellow Post-it note over the box, then wrote in the name of the juror called from the audience to replace him. The form already had seven yellow notes covering various boxes.

Across the top of the sheet were two rows of twenty smaller boxes. This was for keeping track of peremptory challenges. Each lawyer had the right to excuse as many jurors as he wished if he could prove that the juror was biased; these were called "challenges for cause." In addition, he could exercise peremptory challenges against any juror, without giving any reason. But these were limited. In most criminal cases, each side had ten peremptories. In a murder case, however, the number was raised to twenty.

The use of peremptories usually resulted in each lawyer trying to maneuver the other into using up all of his challenges first. This was done by "passing" when it came time to exercise a challenge; if the other attorney then used a peremptory, he was left with one less than his opponent. Once a lawyer ran out of peremptories, his opponent was in the driver's seat; any juror, no matter how unacceptable to the lawyer left without challenges, would sit at the other lawyer's discretion. But passing was a gamble; if the second lawyer also passed, the game was over and the jury was sworn.

Longo counted twelve checks in the prosecution row of boxes. The defense row had only nine boxes checked.

"Now, Mrs. Vinh," Yamaki said, "do you watch television?"

"Yes, yes."

"And have you ever watched the show *60 Minutes?*"

"I think . . . Mike Wallace, yes, yes."

"Did you happen to see the segment about the drug Halcion that was on *60 Minutes*—"

"Objection," Longo growled.

Judge Bascue glared at the defense lawyer. "Mr. Yamaki—"

"I'm sorry, your honor," he said, "I withdraw the question."

"Ladies and gentlemen," Bascue said to the jurors, "you will disregard that question."

Sure, Longo thought, except that telling them to disregard it was like telling them not to think about a purple horse: They would then think about nothing else. Right now they were asking themselves, What's wrong with Halcion to make it a subject of *60 Minutes?* Did it have something to do with the murder? And Longo knew that those jurors who had seen the show would certainly fill in the others.

"I have no further questions, your honor," Yamaki said, walking back toward his seat. "I pass for cause."

Passing for cause meant there were no grounds to challenge the juror as unfit to serve. Yamaki had found no reason to believe Mrs. Vinh was biased; he was not challenging her for cause. But he could still use a peremptory challenge after Longo was finished questioning her; no reason was required for exercising one of the twenty peremptory challenges.

The prosecutor stood, smoothed down the lapels of his black Italian silk suit and adjusted his blood-red tie. He walked over to the jury railing in front of Mrs. Vinh, placed both of his hands on the rail and looked at the woman.

"Can you say 'guilty,' ma'am?"

"Can I . . ."

"Sure, go ahead, try it," Longo said with a grin. "Guilty."

"Guilty," she said.

"Now, does that make Mr. Yamaguchi guilty?"

She shook her head slowly.

"What if all of you say it together, all twelve of you folks. That make him guilty?"

She shook her head again.

"Heck, what if I play cheerleader like Mr. Yamaki? What if I ask all you folks to stand up and sing it together? Think then maybe you'll vote to convict him?"

"No, sir," she said, giggling.

Longo grinned again. "Will you make me a promise, ma'am?"

Mrs. Vinh nodded.

"Will you promise me that in this trial you'll just think for yourself?"

"Think for myself, yes, yes."

"Don't go chanting 'guilty' or 'not guilty.' Don't go doing what someone tells you to do, or what the group does. Just do what you think is right, okay?"

She nodded.

Longo walked across the front of the jury box, sliding his hand along the fake wood veneer.

"You know, ma'am, like Mr. Yamaki over there says, I got the burden of proof here. I got to show this guy committed a murder, and I got to show it beyond a reasonable doubt."

The woman nodded.

"And that's okay with me. I got no quarrel with that."

She continued nodding her head.

"*Reasonable* doubt," Longo repeated.

Nodding.

"You wouldn't make me prove *more* than that, would you, ma'am?"

"More?"

"Yeah. I mean, you wouldn't go and make me prove murder beyond *any* doubt, would you?"

The woman thought about this for a moment. "I do not know."

"Shoot, everything's open to *some* doubt, right?"

She nodded again, not entirely sure.

"You've got a young boy, don't you? Seven years old?"

She smiled, pleased that he remembered.

"Well, look, what if you walk into the kitchen one day, and right there in the middle of the floor is the cookie jar, all broken into a million pieces. And all those chocolate chip cookies that were in the jar? They're all gone. And there's crumbs all over the place. And sitting smack in the middle of the floor, crumbs all over him, and a big chocolate-smeared grin on his little face, is your son."

There were laughs from the jurors and audience.

"And there's nobody else in the house but you and him, see?"

She nodded, giggling again.

"Well, now, what do you think? Think maybe he got to those cookies and helped himself?"

"I think so," she said, laughing.

Longo laughed too. "You convinced *beyond a reasonable doubt?*"

She paused. "I think so, yes, yes."

"Me, too. But it's *possible* someone else did it, right? It's *possible* he knocked the jar off accidental-like, and when he picked them up, he got chocolate all over his hands, and then he wiped his hands across his face."

Mrs. Vinh thought about this. "It is possible, yes, yes."

"Think about it now, ma'am. Don't you have a nagging doubt that maybe he *didn't* go after those cookies? Maybe you're wrong and it was just an accident?"

She nodded.

"There's a doubt," the prosecutor said.

She nodded.

Longo grinned again. "But it's not a *reasonable* doubt, is it?"

"No, sir."

"And if your boy was on trial for swiping cookies, why, we'd just have to convict the little guy, wouldn't we?"

"Yes, yes," she said, smiling again.

"Sure."

Longo stepped back and walked toward the audience, then turned and leaned against the railing. He glanced up at Judge Bascue, noticed an irritated look on his face. The judge preferred attorneys to

ask their questions from the podium, as Yamaki had done. But Longo
was an inveterate pacer. He simply could not hold still when he was
talking to the jury or examining a witness, any more than he could
keep from waving his arms or using his hands when he talked. After
all, he would explain, he was Italian.

"Now about this moral certainty," Longo continued. "You know
what that means, ma'am?"

Mrs. Vinh pondered this, then shook her head.

"Well, all it means is, what's in your heart. It's just a fancy way
of saying, well, maybe I got some doubts in my head, but in my heart
I know he did it." He smiled. "Any problems with that?"

She shook her head.

"And this presumption of innocence, well, that's a good thing.
And I got no quarrel with that, either."

She nodded.

"But you understand, ma'am, once there's enough evidence
to show that Mr. Yamaguchi did it, that he committed murder,
why, that presumption disappears. It just flies out the window.
See?"

"Yes, yes."

Longo walked back to the woman, again grasped the railing in
front of her. "Think you'd like to sit in on this case, ma'am?"

"I think so, yes, yes."

"Well, it's okay by me." Longo looked at Judge Bascue. "Pass
for cause."

Longo walked back to his seat.

"You have both passed your challenges to this juror for cause,"
Judge Bascue said, shuffling some papers. "I believe the next peremptory challenge lies with the defense."

Yamaki stood. "Mr. Yamaguchi accepts the jury as presently
constituted, your honor."

Shoot! Longo thought.

"Mr. Longo?" Bascue asked.

The prosecutor studied the sheet, then looked back at the twelve
men and women. There were still five he wanted off the jury, and
two "maybes." And who knew how many more rejects there would
be as new jurors were called to replace those excused?

Every lawyer had his own theories on jury selection. The general view was that the defense in a criminal case wanted younger jurors, preferably blacks—individuals who tended to have less respect for authority. The prosecution, on the other hand, usually wanted older jurors, whites and Asians if possible. As for professions, a defense lawyer would favor teachers and social workers, while a prosecutor would typically look for engineers and retired military people. Of course, each case was different, and instinct played a large role in trying to predict who would be a sympathetic juror and who would not.

Longo, however, refused to use stereotypes in choosing a jury. He preferred to go entirely with his gut level feelings. With one strange exception: He never permitted a postal worker to sit on a jury. It was a prejudice that had roots buried many years earlier in his first few trials as a prosecutor. But it was a very deep-seated one and completely inflexible: Postal workers were unacceptable.

The prosecutor had another idiosyncrasy in jury selection. He focused his efforts on seating a leader on the jury, a person he felt would take command and be elected by his fellow jurors as the foreman. This individual was critical, Longo felt; he would guide the discussions and probably influence the votes of others. The prosecutor was willing to sacrifice two or three jurors in the challenge game to get the right kind of leader.

Once a trial was over and deliberations in the jury room had begun, Longo had a habit of loudly predicting who the foreman would be. And the prosecutor prided himself on usually being right.

There were two potential leaders sitting in the jury box, Longo felt, two individuals who would make good foremen. One was a middle-aged Mexican-American carpenter. The other was a black woman in her thirties, an office worker at the Long Beach Naval Shipyard. Traditional wisdom dictated that both be kicked off the jury. But Longo had a feeling about them.

The prosecutor looked up from his seat at the judge. "Eleven," he said.

"Juror number eleven," Bascue said, looking at his own chart. "Ms. Dobbs? You are excused, with the court's thanks. Please report back to the jury assembly room."

A young white woman in the back row stood, trying to hide her embarrassment, and carefully stepped over the feet of other jurors as she hurriedly left the box.

Angie, the court clerk, stood up behind her desk. "Frank Musaki," she announced loudly.

Oh great, Longo thought. A Japanese.

A man in his late forties stood up in the audience and walked toward the low swinging doors. He held one open as the woman excused by Longo walked out. Then he stepped to the jury box and took the vacant seat.

"Mr. Musaki," Bascue said, pointing to a large sign on the wall at the end of the box, "would you please answer those questions?"

The sign listed eight questions concerning area of residence, occupation, spouse, children, and prior jury experience.

The man took out a pair of eyeglasses and looked at the sign. "I live in Gardena," he said. "I am a supervisor in a shoe factory.... I have three children...." And proceeded to answer all the questions.

Longo drifted off, only half listening to the man. He found himself wondering how Holden was doing in persuading Carmona to come back and testify. The detective had called earlier that morning: He had found the eyewitness in Bullhead City, just across the Colorado River in Arizona. Carmona claimed he had gone there for a job, and was now reluctant to leave; his new wife was expecting a baby soon. Was it a cover story? Or was Yamaki behind it? Holden could not force Carmona to come, but he could talk with local authorities. There was a good chance they could convince the young man that it was in his best interests to cooperate.

Was Yamaki going for a complete acquittal with a "sleepwalker" defense? Was he aiming for a verdict of involuntary manslaughter? Or was it still all an elaborate feint, designed to cover the real thrust of the defense? Heat of passion from a romantic triangle? Or even self-defense?

Longo had long ago ruled out self-defense as an option. There was simply no evidence of a fight between the two men. But in going over the file, Longo had noticed a minor entry in the coroner's report. Kariya's corpse, according to the coroner, had a bruise on the cheek.

Could it have been from slumping forward and hitting the wheel after being shot? Had Yamaguchi struck him the previous night, when he caught him with his wife in the Boyle Heights house? Or had something happened just before the shooting, something Carmona had not seen? And if so, how would Yamaki prove it without the testimony of either Yamaguchi or his wife?

Longo had called the coroner's office, left a message to call him back.

The prosecutor knew he desperately needed Carmona. He knew that he could ask Judge Bascue for a continuance, gaining time to get an extradition order for the witness. But with jury selection already under way, the judge would never grant the request.

Then Yamaki asked, "Do you understand that my client does not have to take the stand and testify, Mr. Musaki?"

"Yes, I understand," the juror said.

"How would you feel if, perhaps because I instructed him, Mr. Yamaguchi did not testify?"

Longo wondered if Sakoda had any luck with Matsumoto. The investigator had staked out the man's jewelry store and . . .

". . . have something to say, your honor, and I think it's important."

The prosecutor's ears perked up. Something was wrong. The juror was talking directly to the judge.

"Mr. Musaki," Bascue said, "is this something that cannot be disclosed during questioning in open court?"

"I don't know, sir, but it's . . . well, I just don't think I can serve on this jury."

Bascue looked at Yamaki, then at Longo. "Gentlemen?"

Yamaki shrugged. "Bench conference with the juror?"

Bascue nodded. He turned to the juror. "Mr. Musaki, please come forward."

The man stood up, stepped out of the jury box, and walked up to the bench. Yamaki and Longo stood with him in front of the judge.

"Mr. Musaki?" Bascue said in a whisper.

"Well, my daughter . . ." The juror looked at Yamaki, hesitant. "I mean, I know this lawyer."

"You know him?"

"Yes, sir. My daughter was a witness in a case, two or three years ago. . . ."

"Yes?"

"Well, Mr. Yamaki was the lawyer for the defendant in the case. It was a reckless driving case. And . . ."

"Your honor—" Yamaki said.

Bascue held up his hand. "Go on, Mr. Musaki."

"Well . . . this man, this lawyer, he told my daughter not to testify." The juror looked down. "He told her not to testify against . . . against his client."

"I see." Bascue sighed deeply. "And do you think this will keep you from sitting as an impartial juror on this case, Mr. Musaki?"

The man nodded in silence.

The judge looked at Yamaki. "Do you wish to challenge for cause?"

"Yes," Yamaki said, glaring at the juror.

"Very well," the judge said, leaning back. "The challenge is allowed. You may return to the jury assembly room, Mr. Musaki. And thank you for your candor."

The juror nodded, then turned and walked away from the bench and out of the courtroom. Too bad, Longo thought to himself. There was a juror who would have understood all about Yamaki and witnesses who changed their stories. The prosecutor grinned to himself. He would love to have seen the man tell his story in front of the entire jury panel.

Returning to the counsel table as Angie was about to call the next name, Longo noticed a familiar figure walk through the door and take a seat in the crowded aisles. It was Jeff Jonas, a senior deputy D.A., wearing his trademark short-sleeve, button-down dress shirt and tweed sports coat. Jonas was an old friend. He was also Longo's immediate supervisor, the chief of CT-15.

The District Attorney's Office was structured in many ways like a military organization. Longo was in charge of Department 127, a "sergeant" supervising three junior deputies, or "privates," on the front line. Directly above him was Jonas, the "lieutenant" of CT-15, or unit 15 of Central Trials; CT-15 consisted of the deputy D.A.s from Department 127 and nine other courts. Above Jonas was Peter Bozanich, assistant director of Central Operations; this was akin to an executive officer. Central Operations (sometimes called Central Trials) covered the felony trial courts in the Criminal Courts Building (CT-11, CT-13, and CT-15), as well as the Child Abuse/Sex Crimes, Career Criminal, Night Court, and Special Trials units. Above Bozanich was the "colonel," or director of Central Operations, John Lynch.

At the top of the chain of command was the "general," District Attorney Ira Reiner, with his "chief of staff," Chief Deputy Greg Thompson. Reflecting the political nature of the D.A.'s Office, Thompson was a former lobbyist from the state capital.

"... and I live in Eagle Rock.... I have two children, ages five and nine.... My husband is a paramedic for the L.A. City Fire Department...."

Longo caught himself staring at Jonas and looked away.

The two men were markedly similar, almost like brothers in the view of many observers. The same age as Longo, Jonas had the same barrel-chested linebacker's build; in fact, both had been football players in their high school and college days. Both had thick necks and powerful hands, but the similarity was most striking in their faces, the square-jawed, pugnacious faces of a couple of worn-out prizefighters. They were blunt, honest, big-hearted family men with traditional values. And both were tough and dedicated prosecutors.

Jonas looked tired, Longo thought as he watched Yamaki question the new juror. There was a look in his eyes now, a look of ... defeat. Maybe it was finally taking its toll. He knew his friend was near the end of the road as a prosecutor. A few more months, maybe a year.

Longo felt a wave of sadness settle over him. It was too bad. Jonas was a good man, he thought, one of the best in the D.A.'s Office.

But the Morgan case had broken him.

On May 21, 1981, Nancy Morgan and her eight-year-old son had been found stabbed to death in the master bedroom of their Van Nuys home. The two were on the bed together, tightly clasping one another in a death grip. The woman had been stabbed forty-five times, the young boy twenty-one. From the location of the wounds, investigators concluded that the mother was trying to cover the boy with her own body during the attack. And the young son had been lashing out at the attacker, trying to protect his mother.

Los Angeles police detectives initially suspected burglary as the motive; various items were missing from the house, including some expensive guns and a valuable coin collection belonging to the husband and father, fifty-four-year-old Clifford Morgan. Morgan, who had been in Carson City, Nevada, during the incident, broke down in tears when he returned home to find that his family had been wiped out.

The gruesome murder scene had badly shaken the hardened homicide detectives. The sight of a mother and her young son butchered as each tried to protect the other touched something beneath their thick skins. It was an image that few of them would ever forget. In an unusual move, the detectives went to the District Attorney's Office and asked for Jeff Jonas to be appointed to the case.

The Brooklyn-born Mormon joined the detectives, forming a special task force to find the killer. And they soon found their first suspect. Morgan, an insurance salesman, had recently purchased a big policy on his wife's life.

Jonas learned that Morgan had hired Mark Reilly and James Hardy to kill his wife. With the evidence they had, Jonas was able to piece together a gruesome picture. On the night of the murders, Reilly had called Morgan in Carson City; Morgan had arranged for the murders to take place while he had an alibi in Nevada. Did he still want the job done? Yes, Morgan said. What about the boy? "If he's with his mother," Morgan said, "kill him too."

Reilly and Hardy broke into the San Fernando Valley home just before dawn. They crept into the master bedroom, where Morgan told them they would be. But something woke the woman up. She cried out as the two men set upon her. The woman grabbed her son, trying to protect him from the knives by covering him with her body. The boy was now wide awake, and trying to protect his mother from the knife blows by flailing out with his arms and legs. But the two men continued slashing at him and plunging the knives into the woman's exposed back.

"She wouldn't die," Reilly told a girlfriend afterward, "she just wouldn't die." At this point, with the woman and child near death, Reilly suddenly walked out of the house. He felt sick, he explained; he could not stand to watch them die any longer.

Hardy finished the job. With Nancy Morgan finally dead, he turned to the half-conscious boy, still tightly clasped to his mother. "He showed me how he grabbed the little kid," a friend recalled. "He kissed him on the forehead, and then shoved the knife in his chest."

After a two-month trial, the jury returned with verdicts of guilty as to all three defendants. All were sentenced to death.

Nancy Morgan's sixty-nine-year-old mother threw her arms around Jonas and buried her head in his shoulder. "Thank you, thank you," she sobbed.

There was no gratification for Jonas in the verdicts, no sense of victory. He felt only a sense of emptiness. Nobody had won.

Jonas loved the combat and competition of the courtroom; it reminded him of his football days. It was exciting and challenging. But the Morgan case changed all that.

Jonas found himself questioning the purpose of what he was doing. Being a prosecutor had meant far more to him than just playing games. Deep inside, he always felt that he was accomplishing some good, that in a small but important way he was changing the world into a better place. That world was made up of good and bad, he believed, and the bad could be redeemed. There was order to the universe, and someone like Jonas could make a difference.

With the Morgan case, Jonas's black-and-white world began turning gray. There was no sense to it, he began to think, no rational reason for it all. Morgan had all the benefits: a solid childhood, a good education, a high-paying job, a loving family, a nice home. How could he have been so completely evil? Where was the sense in it all?

Jonas had always believed that people made evil choices, but they also had free will; they could choose good. But Morgan had been evil, deeply and unalterably evil. Nothing could have stopped this evil, nothing would ever stop such evil. It existed.

The prosecutor came to realize that he could never stop men like Clifford Morgan, never protect innocent victims like Nancy

Morgan and her boy. All he could ever hope to do was clean up afterward.

Jonas went into an uncharacteristic depression after the death verdicts. The photographs were burned into his mind, the bloody bodies of the woman and the boy locked together in a death embrace, each trying desperately to save the other. He kept seeing Hardy kissing the little boy on the forehead, then plunging the knife into his heart.

A few months after the Morgan verdicts, Jonas was given a new assignment: spearhead a task force assigned to investigate over fifty unsolved gangland-style executions in the L.A. area. The murders were believed to have been committed by a group of Marielitos, former inmates of Cuba's jails and insane asylums set free by Castro. The investigation quickly focused on a refugee by the name of Roberto Lopez. Lopez, it turned out, had been a member of Batista's Los Tigros, a death squad dedicated to the elimination of the dictator's political opponents.

Jonas had Lopez arrested and charged with some of the murders.

Soon after this, detectives discovered that Lopez had put out a contract on Jonas, his wife, and three children. A photograph of the hit man, who was due to arrive any day from Panama, was circulated throughout the city. And twenty-four-hour police patrols were set up around Jonas's home in Burbank.

Then late one night, a man was caught by the patrol outside of a bedroom window in Jonas's home. The man turned out to be a peeping Tom, but the event had terrified the family.

Jonas's mind was still on the incident a few days later as he stood in line waiting to buy a tie in a department store. The next thing he recalled was being arrested outside the store by a security guard. He had left the store, the guard said, without paying for the tie.

District Attorney Reiner immediately suspended Jonas without pay for thirty days. When the manager of the department store learned all of the facts, he asked that charges be dropped. The standard policy in the D.A.'s Office was to dismiss shoplifting cases if the store did not want to pursue the matter. But Reiner insisted that Jonas be prosecuted for theft.

Reiner had defeated Bob Philibosian in the previous election for district attorney. And Jonas, who had been one of the former D.A.'s chief deputies, was well known to be a Philibosian man. More important, however, was the fact that Jonas was a star; he was widely considered one of the top prosecutors in the office and a favorite of the media.

The theft case finally went to trial in Glendale. The jury could not reach a verdict, hanging eight to four in favor of acquittal. Although the prosecutor was under orders to retry the case, the judge dismissed it.

Despite the dismissal, Jonas was taken off the Lopez trial. The case was given to Lester Kuruyama, who later served as second chair in the Menendez trial. Jonas was reassigned as chief of CT-15, an administrative position.

For years, Jonas had been immersed in the world of criminal justice, completely absorbed in finding dangerous people and putting them away where they could not hurt anyone. He was a man who felt a personal responsibility for weeding out evil and finding justice for the injured.

Now that was gone. What he believed so strongly in had been taken from him. Confused and disenchanted, he realized that all he had left was his family.

"Maybe it was the best thing that ever happened to me," Jonas said later, a touch of bitterness in his voice. "It made me realize what was important."

Yamaki's voice drifted back into Longo's thoughts.

"... and his honor will instruct you on the law at the end of the case, Mrs. Olguin," the lawyer said, smiling at the new juror. "And one of the things he will tell you is that if evidence has two different interpretations, both reasonable, you must adopt the one pointing to the defendant's innocence."

The woman nodded.

"Do you understand that instruction?"

"I'm not sure, uh-uh."

Jeff Jonas was a good man, Longo thought as Yamaki continued his *voir dire*. But the fire was gone. He had been beaten down and destroyed by the very system in which he believed so passionately and for which he had fought so hard. The system could not afford to lose such men.

The prosecutor looked back at the audience again, searching for the face of his friend.

Jonas was gone.

Chapter

16

"And what time was it you arrived at the scene, Mr. Browning?"

"One-thirty A.M."

"You alone?"

"No, sir. My partner was with me."

"He's a paramedic for the Montebello fire department too?"

"Yes, sir."

"Okay." Longo slid his hand along the jury railing as he walked back from the witness stand toward the podium. "How about if you tell the folks here just what you saw at the scene."

David Browning nodded, leaned back in the witness chair. He was a short, well-muscled young man with a surfer's tan and a laid-back air. Only the sunglasses were missing.

"Well, uh, after we got the nine-one-one call, like I said, we got there, and there was this guy, a young guy..."

"The name Ken Yamaguchi ring a bell?"

"Yeah, that was it. Anyway, he was just standing there, on the sidewalk, next to the car."

"Could you describe the car, Mr. Browning?"

"Uh, let's see, it was a blue car, light blue, and, uh, yeah, a Nissan, the fancy one... Maxima."

"Okay."

"Well, the car doors were open. And there was blood everywhere, all over everything. And inside, there was this older guy, sitting there behind the wheel, kind of slumped over, you know?"

"Uh-huh."

"And there was this woman, an older woman, she was kneeling on the passenger seat. And she was holding the guy's head in her arms, sort of cradling it."

Longo nodded.

"Well," the paramedic said, "I pulled the guy from the car and laid him out on the street. And I hooked up the EKG, but there was no heartbeat, no pulse, nothing."

"Uh-huh."

Browning shrugged. "He was dead."

"You see anything that looked like it might have caused the death?"

"Sure. A hole in the left side of his head."

"You get the name of the dead guy?"

"Genji Kariya."

"Thanks," Longo said. "Nothing further."

"Mr. Yamaki?" Judge Bascue asked.

"No questions, your honor," Yamaki said from his seat.

"You're excused, Mr. Browning," Bascue said. He looked at Longo. "Call your next witness."

"Dr. Eugene Carpenter, Jr.," Longo said loudly.

The bailiff walked out the door with Browning to summon the doctor. Yamaki and Longo had made a joint motion to exclude witnesses; anyone who might give testimony in the case was required to remain outside in the hallway until called. In theory, this kept witnesses from changing their testimony after hearing other witnesses.

A pale, thin man wearing a tan corduroy sports coat and a plaid tie entered and walked confidently through the swinging gates. He was about thirty-eight years old, with a light brown goatee and plain rimless eyeglasses that were secured by a cord wrapped around his neck. He looked like a middle-aged professor of English literature.

As the bailiff walked by Longo, he handed the prosecutor three telephone messages.

Longo read the first: "Department 100 called, will dismiss case if no D.A. here by 11:00." He crumpled the message in his fist; Boyle was running late, he thought.

The second: "Tea, Clarence? Barshop." The prosecutor grinned at the reference to Clarence Darrow. The note was from Steve Barshop, a deputy D.A. in the Santa Monica office. Probably downtown for another tongue lashing. But Longo would have no time for lunch with his old friend today.

The third message was from Sakoda: "Gruidl in Sacramento for CHP training. Trying to reach by phone." The Highway Patrol officer to whom Yamaguchi had surrendered had not shown up that morning for trial. Like Carmona, he had disappeared. But in this case, it was a fairly typical administrative screwup. The officer's court appearance had been overlooked when he was scheduled for training at the Highway Patrol headquarters in Sacramento, four hundred miles away.

Officer Gruidl was one of the first witnesses Longo was going to call, and an important one: It was to him Yamaguchi had confessed that he had shot Kariya. More important, if Yamaki raised Halcion as a defense, the officer's testimony of Yamaguchi's rational behavior only minutes after the shooting would be critical. And Yamaguchi's recollection minutes after the shooting would contradict any later claims of sleepwalking or amnesia.

Longo glanced back at the clock on the wall. Monty Holden had called late the previous night from Bullhead City. Carmona, he said, had been persuaded to accompany him to Los Angeles and testify against Yamaguchi. The two men would drive through the night to get to court for the morning session.

Longo had his eyewitness. And, with it, a shot at a murder conviction.

The prosecutor looked up as the thin man in the corduroy sports coat quickly repeated the oath and then took the stand.

"My name is Dr. Eugene Carpenter, Jr.," the man said in a quiet but confident voice.

"What's your job?" Longo asked him.

The doctor looked confused. "I beg your pardon?"

The doctor had expected Longo to ask the usual preliminary questions about his medical training and experience; expert witnesses loved to expound at length about their degrees and published articles. But the cause of death was not a big issue in the case. Longo knew that Yamaki would not waste time challenging the witness's qualifications to give an opinion on the cause of death.

"What's your job?" Longo repeated. "Whaddya do?"

"I am a medical examiner for the office of the coroner, county of Los Angeles."

"Doc," Longo said, "you do an autopsy on a guy by the name of Genji Kariya?"

"I did," Carpenter said, eyeing the prosecutor disapprovingly. "When and where?"

The witness glanced at a report lying on his lap. "March 30, 1991, at eleven A.M. At the coroner's office."

"Uh-huh. You decide what he died of?"

Carpenter again looked confused. He had never been questioned so bluntly, and it was vaguely irritating.

"I did."

Longo smiled. Carpenter expected the prosecutor to develop the details of the autopsy, concluding with a question such as, "Doctor, based upon your examination, did you have an occasion to formulate a professional opinion as to the cause of death?" After an affirmative answer, the script's next question was, "Doctor, based upon that examination and upon your training and experience as a medical examiner, what *is* your professional opinion as to the cause of death of the deceased?"

That was protocol. That was how lawyers and doctors liked to do it. But not Longo. He liked to "cut through the crap," as he would put it. He was there to present facts to the jury so they could understand, not to impress them with his vocabulary.

"So what killed him, Doc?"

Carpenter sighed. "The cause of death was a gunshot wound to the head, left temple. I retrieved a .38 slug from his head."

"Okay."

Longo continued his pacing, walking now along the banister that separated the court area from the audience. He looked out at the sea of elderly Japanese faces silently staring at him.

"Any idea how far away the shooter was at the time?"

"I would say the gun was approximately twelve to eighteen inches from the temple at the time of the weapon's discharge."

"Could you tell the folks here how you figured that out?"

Carpenter turned to the jury. "I observed stippling about the entrance wound, but no soot. 'Stippling' is the term for the small burns in the skin caused by partially burned gunpowder. If this is present, one can conclude that the gun was fired from a distance of between eighteen inches to two or three feet away. Soot, on the other hand, is caused by completely burned gunpowder which travels only six to twelve inches."

The medical examiner glanced at Longo, then looked back to the jury, comfortable now in his familiar role. He spoke slowly, carefully, a college professor lecturing a freshman class.

"Here, you see, there was no soot, so the gun had to be at least twelve inches away. But there was stippling, so it had to be less than, let us say, two feet. The farther away the gun is, the larger will be the spread of the burning pattern. In this case, we have a two-and-a-half-inch circumference in stippling, a relatively small pattern . . ."

Brick by brick, Longo thought as the physician continued. Presenting a case-in-chief to a jury was like building a house. First, the foundation. You showed the *corpus delecti* of the crime: There was a dead body and there appeared to have been a criminal cause for the death. The second step was throwing up walls and a roof: offering evidence that the defendant did it. And then, in the third and final stage, you filled it out with plumbing, electricity, and insulation. You proved what was in the defendant's head: the motive and the state of mind, in this case, premeditation. When the prosecution rested its case, the defense took a sledgehammer to the bricks, and maybe tried to build another, more attractive house next door. Then it was the prosecution's turn again; in its rebuttal case, it patched up the loose bricks and busted windows, then took a few kicks of its own at the defendant's new house.

"So . . ." Carpenter looked back at Longo. "We can conclude that the gun was held approximately twelve to eighteen inches from the temple when it was fired."

The prosecutor picked up an eight- by ten-inch photograph. An Asian man was lying on his back on a stainless-steel gurney. He was nude.

"Judge, I got a photo here of a corpse. Can we mark it People's one?"

"I assume Mr. Yamaki has seen it?" Bascue said.

"Yeah."

"It will be marked People's exhibit number one."

Longo picked up a second photograph. It was a shot of the left side of the man's face from the neck up. His eyes were closed, and there was a small, dark hole in his temple.

"Photo of a dead guy's face, close-up," Longo said. "People's two?"

"It will be marked People's exhibit number two."

Longo walked up to the medical examiner, handed the first photograph to him.

"That the guy?"

"Yes," Carpenter said. "This is the gentleman upon whom I performed the autopsy."

The prosecutor handed him the second photo. "Same guy?"

"It is."

"Thanks, Doc," Longo said, walking back. "By the way, you notice any other injuries to Kariya?"

Carpenter scanned his report again. "Yes. Abrasion to the upper right cheek. A lesion wound to the right lower lip. And the backs of both hands were scraped."

"Could any of the wounds be from a fist to the face?"

"The wounds are consistent with a blow to the face, yes."

"How old were they?" From his earlier review of the autopsy report, Longo knew the answer. And it would corroborate a fight between Yamaguchi and Kariya at the Boyle Heights house the night before the murder.

"From the early scabbing, I would say twelve to twenty-four hours."

"Uh-huh." Longo walked back to his chair. "Nothing further."

"I have no questions, your honor," Yamaki said.

"You are excused, Dr. Carpenter," Bascue said.

Carpenter stepped down as Longo called out the name of his next witness.

"Kenneth Yamaguchi."

Longo studied the jury as he waited for Yamaguchi's son to enter. It was a fairly good group, he thought. A wide geographic distribution. Nothing unusual in the professions or backgrounds. Six men, six women; four whites, four Hispanics, one Asian, three blacks. Yamaki had surprised Longo by exercising peremptory challenges against four jurors of Asian descent; only one, a Chinese woman, was permitted to sit on the jury. Why had the lawyer not wanted Asians sitting as jurors?

There were two jurors, maybe three, that the prosecutor would rather not have on the case. But, then, neither side ever got exactly what it wanted. He was satisfied that there were no "problems" sitting in the box. Most important, both of the jurors Longo had picked as possible foremen had made it past Yamaki's challenges. He was guessing that the black woman who worked at the naval shipyard would eventually be elected foreman.

Longo glanced again at the message from Steve Barshop. His old friend must be downtown for another chewing out by the bureaucrats, Longo thought. He was always in trouble with the front office. Barshop was a renegade. And a damned fine trial lawyer.

Barshop was a straight-talking Texan with all of the serenity and tact of a fox terrier. His combative personality and "loner" style were ideal for trial work. And trial suited him; he found the fast action and constant tension an addictive high. He became a complete insomniac when in trial, incredibly going for as long as three weeks without any sleep.

But Barshop, it was said, was not a company man. He was a loose cannon, refusing to follow rigid office policies. And when called on the carpet, the prosecutor would not back off. "I don't give a damn about policy," he said on one occasion. "I do what's *right*."

This attitude would have doomed the careers of most deputies in the office. But Barshop had one obvious thing going for him: He won trials. Even this, however, did not save him from the fallout of the *Twilight Zone* case.

When Gary Kesselman had accused Lea D'Agostino from the witness stand of suborning perjury in the highly publicized trial, the front office backed D'Agostino; Kesselman no longer had a future with the district attorney. But Kesselman was Barshop's friend, and Barshop, like Longo, was an intensely loyal man. He loudly denounced the front office for backing D'Agostino.

The next day, the prosecutor found himself transferred to Santa Monica. He accepted his banishment from the center of the universe as the inevitable cost of standing up for what was right. And, he thought, Santa Monica was not bad; at least, he was out from under the constant scrutiny of the bureaucrats.

Then, on May 16, 1990, Marlon Brando's son, Christian, shot a young Frenchman to death in his father's Hollywood Hills mansion. His twenty-year-old sister, Cheyenne, was four months pregnant at the time with the Frenchman's child and, he claimed, the Frenchman had been mistreating her.

Marlon Brando hired the most notorious defense lawyer in the country, William Kunstler. Kunstler had earned a reputation as an abrasive, thick-skinned radical who devoted his time to defending Black Panthers and Hell's Angels. He was a tough, no-holds-barred, no-quarter-asked brawler in the courtroom. And since the shooting occurred within the Santa Monica branch office's territory, the chief deputy countered with his own anti-establishment street fighter: Steve Barshop.

Barshop realized Kunstler's defense was going to be that there was no intent to kill; the shooting was accidental, the result of a struggle between Christian Brando and the Frenchman. But Cheyenne Brando's testimony would hang her brother: He had told her one hour before the shooting that he was going to kill her lover.

Then, suddenly, Cheyenne disappeared. She resurfaced a few days later in Papeete, Tahiti. Barshop was certain that Marlon Brando, who owned an island in Tahiti, had a hand in the disappearance. He also knew his case depended on the young woman's testimony.

The prosecutor managed to have a federal subpoena served on Cheyenne in Tahiti. But the French authorities would not enforce it. Because of her Tahitian mother, the young woman held dual citizenship, and as a French citizen she was being held while local police independently investigated the shooting. The authorities would cooperate with Barshop only if they received a *letter rogatory,* a document from the American judiciary formally requesting the French government's assistance.

Marlon Brando put on a continuing performance for the starstruck media, constantly accusing Barshop of prosecuting his son for personal motives. Then he fired Kunstler after the lawyer accused a pretrial judge of being "a black toadie for the white establishment."

His replacement, Robert Shapiro, began making inquiries to Barshop's superiors about pleading his client to voluntary manslaughter (Shapiro would later gain greater fame as O. J. Simpson's lawyer).

Barshop continued his battle to get his key witness back from Tahiti. Meantime, Cheyenne had given birth to the Frenchman's child, then twice attempted to commit suicide. When Shapiro presented evidence of the suicide attempts and of Cheyenne's deteriorating mental and physical health, the judge refused to issue the *letter rogatory*.

Without Cheyenne Brando's testimony, Barshop would not be able to prove the killing was murder. The best he could hope for was to prove an intentional killing in the heat of passion. Reluctantly, he and Shapiro agreed to a plea of guilty to voluntary manslaughter. But Barshop insisted that there were no deals on sentencing: He would argue for the maximum term of twelve years.

The sentencing hearing turned out to be another media zoo. Reporters and paparazzi climbed in through the windows to get pictures of the celebrities. Barshop put on witnesses who testified to previous acts of violence by Christian Brando; in one case, he had shot a party crasher in the head, seriously wounding him. Shapiro countered with his client's celebrated father, this time wearing a ponytail secured with a red band matching his tie. Marlon Brando, whom Barshop referred to as a "320-pound egomaniac," gave a rambling, sloppy performance from the witness stand in which he tearfully took the blame for his children's problems.

Unmoved, the judge sentenced Christian Brando to ten years in prison. But Barshop was disgusted with the entire affair. No one seemed interested in the truth or in justice. The media had sensationalized the case, distorting the facts and constantly misquoting Barshop. Lawyers, publishers, and movie producers were elbowing each other to sew up million-dollar deals. "Everybody who touched that case was lying, cheating, or trying to make a fast buck," he recalled later. "It was un-fucking-believable."

Barshop's disillusionment with the Brando prosecution told more about the prosecutor than about the case. Despite his cynical, tough-talking exterior, Barshop was at heart an idealist. But reality was wearing on him. Recently, he had turned to teaching part-time at UCLA's law school. And he found it oddly satisfying to deal with the law as an abstract concept. He discovered that he liked the *idea* of the law; he preferred teaching what the law *should* be more than dealing with the reality of what it was.

Longo looked at the note again. The Menendez murder case was widely viewed in the office as one of the biggest in recent years. But a top prosecutor, Elliott Alhadeff, had been taken off the case and replaced by Pam Ferrero. Barshop had, once again, loudly denounced the front office to everyone within earshot. (Many in the D.A.'s Office suspected that the popular Alhadeff had been replaced by Ferrero because she was living with assistant chief of Central Trials Peter Bozanich. In fact, however, Reiner removed Alhadeff over differences in his handling of the case. Reiner then reassigned Ferrero to Menendez because she had originally been assigned to the case before being taken off for the McMartin retrial.) It was probably no coincidence that, a few days later, the Russian Mafia case—widely seen as a career builder—was taken away from Barshop and transferred downtown to Marcia Clark.

Barshop shrugged off the slap. He had done the right thing. He had told the truth. "What are they going to do?" he was fond of saying. "Bureaucrats don't know how to deal with crazies like me."

But the last time Longo saw his friend, Barshop was wistfully talking about leaving the office. He had just bought some land in Texas, he said. He thought it might be nice to go back and raise some cattle, maybe teach school there for a while.

The truth was that talent like Steve Barshop's was often wasted in the L.A. District Attorney's Office. The simple reason was that the system was run largely by administrators, not prosecutors. Promotions within the office were based upon evaluations from supervisors, evaluations that depended upon a deputy's ability to get along with these supervisors and with judges. But trial lawyers were, by their very nature, aggressive and opinionated individualists. They were fighters, men and women who bridled at rules, who acted on their instincts, who insisted on going to trial despite pressure from judges more interested in expediting heavy calendars. Deputies who were promoted to supervisory levels, on the other hand, were those who did not rock the boat. It was these desk deputies who then formulated and administered the policies that handcuffed the real trial lawyers.

*   *   *

Longo looked up as Ken Yamaguchi walked behind him and stood next to the witness stand, his hand raised. He studied the young man as he took the oath.

Yamaguchi's son was twenty-two years old, slender, and of medium height. He wore a stylishly loose-fitting gray suit with baggy pants and a black silk shirt. And he had a habit of staring at people with a look of thinly veiled contempt. Asian-American cool. Longo rose from his chair.

"Mr. Yamaguchi, your father is Kazuhiko Yamaguchi, right?"

"Yes, sir."

Longo had the distinct feeling that this was the first time the young man had ever used the word "sir." Yamaki, he knew, had spent a lot of time preparing him for trial.

"Where do you work?"

"At Mitsuru Cafe ... sir."

"That's the one your folks own?"

"Yes, sir."

"Okay. You live at your folks' house, the one in Montebello?"

"Yes, sir."

"Now, were you home there the evening Mr. Kariya was killed?"

"Yes, sir."

"What time did you get home that night?"

"About twelve forty-five."

"You were driving a Honda, your sister's car?"

"Yes, sir."

"That was the car in the driveway when the shooting took place, right?"

"Yes, sir."

"Okay. Now, when you got home that night, was your dad there?"

"No, sir."

Ken Yamaguchi seemed cool, calm, almost supremely confident. Everything was a respectful yes or no; Yamaki had made sure that he would volunteer nothing. Longo noticed that the young man's eyes never left his own; his gaze was rigidly locked on the prosecutor. Most witnesses occasionally looked away, or down at their hands, or maybe glanced at the jury. He wondered if Yamaki had instructed him to maintain eye contact. Or was the young man simply very good at lying? The prosecutor knew that, contrary to popular belief, steady eye contact from the witness stand was no more a sign of truthfulness than evasive eyes were of deception.

"Mr. Yamaguchi, you saw your father sometime after you got home, right?"

"Yeah . . . yes, sir."

"When was that?"

"A few minutes after I got home."

Longo pointed at the jury. "Would you please tell the folks here what happened after he got home."

Break him out of the yes-or-no answers, get him talking.

"Well," Ken Yamaguchi said, shifting his steady gaze to the jurors, "he came in, you know, and he said, like, 'Is your mother home?'—something like that."

"Uh-huh."

"And . . . then he went into the bedroom. To use the phone."

"You could hear him?"

"Not what he was saying. Just, like, a low voice, you know?"

"Go on."

The young man shrugged. "He came out after a while. He still had the phone."

"Cordless phone?"

"Huh? Yeah . . . yes, sir, cordless."

"Go on."

"And he came in the kitchen, where I was. He seemed, like, edgy, you know? Then he walked out the door. With the phone."

Longo grinned. Yamaguchi's son had finally volunteered something: His father was "edgy." And it was not a slip. Yamaki was subtly laying the groundwork for a Halcion defense.

"Your dad own a gun?"

"Yes, sir."

"A .38 Smith and Wesson Special snub-nosed revolver?"

"I guess so . . . sir."

Longo picked up a blue steel revolver with walnut grips. He

looked up at Judge Bascue. "People's three, judge? It's been cleared."

It was a rigid rule that no weapons, whether evidence or not, were permitted in the courtroom without being checked by the bailiff to make sure they were not loaded.

"It may be marked People's exhibit number three, Mr. Longo," Bascue said.

Longo carried the gun to the witness stand.

"Recognize it?"

"Yes, sir," Ken Yamaguchi said, glancing at it.

"Your father's?"

"I guess so, yeah . . . yes, sir. My dad got it because of a burglary we had a while back."

Not if you were one of the burglars, Longo thought to himself. He wondered if Holden had talked yet with the kids who pulled off the job.

"Do you know where he kept it?"

The young man shrugged. "His bedroom, I guess. He kept it in a white sock."

Longo was confident that Yamaki had told him to mention the sock. The lawyer was going to claim that it was not intended to prevent fingerprints, it was just a wrapping for the gun. The prosecutor found it interesting that the young man was not sure where the gun was kept, but he was quite sure it was stored in a sock—and that it was a white sock. If it was kept in his father's bedroom, how would he know what it was wrapped in?

"Did you see your dad carrying this gun, or any gun, when he walked out the door?"

Ken Yamaguchi shook his head.

"Now, about half an hour later, you heard your mother outside, right?"

"Yes, sir."

"You want to tell these folks what happened?"

"Well, I heard her yelling, and pounding on the door."

"Uh-huh."

"And so I opened the door. And she was yelling, like, 'Call nine-one-one, call nine-one-one, Mr. Kariya's been shot.' "

"She say anything else?"

"I think she said, like, 'Your dad shot him, he's turning himself in to the CHP,' something like that."

Longo heard something from the defense table. He looked across the room. Yamaguchi was sitting in his chair, his head still deeply bowed. But his shoulders were heaving, and the unmistakable sounds of sobbing could be heard.

The prosecutor knew that Yamaguchi had been in court dozens of times, had even watched and listened as his son had testified to the same facts at the preliminary hearing. And there had never been any crying. But, then, there had never been any jury.

Longo could now hear the faint sounds of sobbing coming from the audience. He looked back. Two or three older Japanese women were crying.

Then he noticed Holden standing at the back door.

"Okay," Longo said, turning back to the witness. "What happened next?"

"I went out, to the car. And he was there, Mr. Kariya. In the car. I think he was dead."

Tears were beginning to well up in Ken Yamaguchi's eyes. He bowed his head for a moment.

"You want to take a break, Mr. Yamaguchi?"

The young man shook his head.

"Feel up to going on?" Longo asked.

"Yes, sir, I—"

"Was your dad wearing a hearing aid that night?"

"Huh? No . . . sir." He glanced at Yamaki, then quickly back at the prosecutor.

Longo knew that suddenly asking questions completely out of context often took witnesses by surprise, resulting in less rehearsed answers. He would make Yamaki eat the hearing aids and interpreters. And the tears.

"Nothing further."

Yamaki stood. "I have no questions, your honor."

Smart lawyer, the prosecutor thought as Yamaki sat down. Too many lawyers felt they had to cross-examine every witness, either for appearances or out of habit. But if there was nothing you wanted from the witness, it was wiser to ask nothing. "If you got nothing to say," the old trial adage went, "sit down and shut up." But Longo had a feeling he would be seeing Yamaguchi's son again before the trial was over.

Longo looked at Yamaki as the lawyer studied his notes.

"Nicholas Carmona," the prosecutor said loudly, watching for a reaction.

But there was no expression on Yamaki's face as the name was announced.

Chapter

17

The latest rumor in the Rodney King case had snaked through the hallways of the D.A.'s Office that morning, passing from one deputy to another with mercurial speed.

There were three decisions that would largely determine the outcome of the Rodney King trial. Two had been made: the selection of a prosecutor and the choice of a site for the trial. The third and final decision involved the tactical question of whether to put Rodney King on the stand. But it would not be the trial attorney, Terry White, who would decide. As he had done in the *Twilight Zone* trial, Ira Reiner would make the critical decision.

King was a big, powerfully built man who would be cross-examined about the wild car chase in which he was trying to avoid being sent back to prison for a parole violation. If he testified, he would also be questioned about an armed robbery conviction in which he nearly beat a grocer to death with a tire iron. Weighed against that was the conventional prosecution wisdom: It was difficult to win a trial without personalizing the crime with a living, breathing victim.

White reported yet another factor to his superiors, one that weighed heavily in Reiner's final decision. The deputy had met with King and his civil lawyer on five occasions. Each time, White said, King had changed his story, giving a different version of the events. If he took the stand, White feared, there would be yet a sixth account—and a seventh on cross-examination.

Reiner consulted with his advisers and, so the rumor in the hallways went, the decision had finally been made: Rodney King would not be called to testify.

The immediate consensus of the rank and file in the office was that the decision was a serious tactical blunder, yet another darkly ominous cloud on the horizon. But White continued in his preparation for the quickly approaching trial. His strategy was clear. "Race was never a factor in the beatings," he confided a few weeks before the trial. "The media created that issue." His approach would be to downplay race, avoiding a backlash from the white jury, and to present the incident for what it was: a few bad officers overreacting under the adrenaline rush of a wild car chase.

Despite the adverse venue and, now, the lack of a victim to show the jury, White felt confident of winning convictions against the four officers.

"The tape," he said only days before the trial, "speaks for itself."

Like most deputies, Larry Longo found his thoughts drifting to the King case throughout the day. He knew that a loss could destroy what morale was left in the office. Worse, the word in the streets was that an acquittal would trigger a bloody riot; the memories of Watts were not that distant.

As he stood at the counsel table questioning the eyewitness Nicholas Carmona, he willed himself to concentrate on the job at hand.

"I was just sittin' there, man."

"In your car," Longo said.

"Yeah."

"And this was at Eight Thirty-six North Vail Avenue?"

"I guess so, yeah."

"You alone in the car?"

Carmona shook his head. "It was like I told the cop, man, I was with this girl, you know?"

"Elizabeth."

"Yeah, right, Elizabeth."

"And this Elizabeth's a friend of yours."

"Yeah, man, you could say that. I was gettin' married, you know? So I was sayin' good-bye to . . . my friends."

Longo nodded, studying the young man. He was about twenty-five, tall, with short brown hair and wearing khaki jeans and a polo shirt. His slow speech and heavy-lidded eyes gave him a dull look.

Not a witness to hang a case on, the prosecutor thought.

"Okay, Mr. Carmona," Longo said, leaning against the jury railing, "now how long were you parked there before you saw this Mercedes drive up?"

Carmona shrugged. "Half hour, maybe."

"Uh-huh. Could you tell us what you saw?"

"Guy drives up, in this Mercedes."

Longo walked to the counsel table, picked up an eight- by ten-inch photograph.

"Judge, I got a photo of a Mercedes here. People's four?"

"It may be marked People's exhibit number four," Bascue said.

Longo approached the witness box and handed the photo to Carmona.

"That look like the car?"

Carmona glanced at it, shrugged again. "Yeah, could be."

Longo walked slowly back, running his hand along the jury railing as he did so often.

"The guy park the Mercedes?"

"Yeah. Parks across the street, maybe a hundred feet down the hill."

"There was just one guy in the car?"

"Yeah."

"Did you get a good look at him anytime that night?"

"Yeah."

"You see him in the courtroom now?"

Carmona looked toward the defense table, knowing that would be where the defendant was sitting.

"Yeah, man," he said, nodding at Yamaguchi, "that could be him."

"Okay. Now, some time later, another car pulled up and parked across the street, right?"

"Yeah."

"How long were you and Elizabeth parked there when that happened?"

"Another half hour, maybe."

"What kind of car was it, the one that pulled up?"

"Like I told the cop, one of them Japanese cars. Maxima, I think."

Longo picked up a second photograph from his table. "People's five?" he said to the judge.

"So marked," Bascue said.

The prosecutor handed the photo to Carmona. "This the second car?"

The witness shrugged. "Could be."

"Okay," Longo said, returning to the counsel table, "how many people were in this car?"

"Like I told the cop, man, a guy was drivin'. And there was this woman in the passenger seat."

"How far were they from you?"

"Oh, man, right across the street. Like from me to ..." He looked at the bailiff. "... to that cop over there."

Longo looked at Bascue. "Could the record reflect about fifty feet, judge?"

"About that," Bascue said.

"What'd you see then, Mr. Carmona?"

"Uh, this guy in the Mercedes, he gets out, and he starts walking real fast, then he starts running. He comes up to the car and—"

"Driver's side?"

"Huh? Yeah, right, driver's side."

Longo walked around the end of the jury box farthest from the witness stand. He stood there, leaning forward on the railing next to a juror. By standing on the far side of the jury, he forced the witness to talk more loudly. More important, the witness was looking toward the jurors as he testified. People paid closer attention when someone was speaking directly at them, rather than in another direction to a third party. It was a trick Longo had learned many years ago, and he used it whenever the testimony became critical.

"Did you see this guy carrying anything?"

"I don't know, looked like a rag or something, a white towel or a rag, you know? Looked like it was wrapped around his hand."

"Okay, what happened then?"

"He comes up to the driver's side, like I said, and he stops. And then he points his hand, the one with the towel on it? He points it right at the guy's head, the guy drivin'. And then there's this big flash, man, and then another one."

"Two flashes."

"Yeah. Lit the car up. Lit the guy's face up, guy drivin', you know? And you could see blood flyin' all over the place."

"Uh-huh."

"Then, this woman screams. She just screams. And the guy stands there."

"How long did he stand at the driver's window?"

"I don't know, fifteen seconds, thirty, maybe."

"Was he saying anything?"

Carmona shook his head. "I couldn't hear, man. He was standin' there, starin' at her. But I couldn't hear. Tell you the truth, after the shots, I was down in my seat, you know? I mean, peekin' out over the door."

"Where was your friend?"

Carmona shrugged. "She never saw nothin'. Elizabeth, she was down on the floor, you know?"

"Okay, what did you see next?"

"Well, this guy starts backin' away from the car. Toward me, you know? So, man, I duck down, got down real low. Next time I look up, he's down to his car, the Mercedes? And he's drivin' away."

Longo nodded. "That it?"

"Yeah."

"Thanks." He walked back to his chair. "Your witness."

Yamaki stood up and walked slowly to the podium.

"Good morning, Mr. Carmona."

Carmona nodded slowly, wary now.

"As I understand it, you were sitting in your car with this woman, Elizabeth?"

"Yeah."

"And you were . . . saying good-bye to her, correct?"

"Yeah."

"So . . . is it safe to say that your attention was on Elizabeth?"

"My attention?" Carmona grinned. "Yeah, I guess you could say that."

"You were not really focused on anything happening outside of the car."

The young man shrugged. "I guess not."

"In fact..." Yamaki read briefly from a document he was carrying. "You told the police you heard three or four shots, isn't that right?"

Carmona shrugged again. "Could be."

"Now you say there were only two shots."

"Yeah."

"Well, Mr. Carmona, which is it? Which is the truth?"

"Could be two, could be three, I don't know. Man, it happened real fast, you know? I wasn't countin'."

"The fact is, you don't really know how many shots there were, do you?"

"Could be two."

"Because you were paying attention to your ... friend."

"We was payin' attention to each other, yeah."

"You weren't watching what happened across the street, you were watching Elizabeth."

"I saw what I saw."

"You testified under oath that there were two shots."

"Under oath, yeah."

"In fact, didn't someone tell you that? Didn't someone tell you there were only two shots fired, rather than three or four?"

"I don't know, the cop might've said something. I don't know."

"Yes. Now, isn't it fair to say that there *might* have been something said between Mr. Yamaguchi and the driver of the Maxima?"

"Maybe."

"You wouldn't necessarily have heard any conversation, would you?"

Carmona shrugged.

"And if something had happened before the shots were fired, if the driver had done something to Mr. Yamaguchi, you wouldn't necessarily have seen it?"

"Maybe. Maybe not."

"I see." Yamaki glanced at his notes on the podium. "Did you notice if Mr. Yamaguchi was carrying a cordless telephone when he approached the Maxima?"

"A telephone?" The young man shook his head. "No, man, I didn't see no telephone."

"But you were not really paying attention to what he was carrying, were you?"

"Not . . . no."

"Now, Mr. Carmona, let's go back a few minutes. When Mr. Yamaguchi was sitting in the Mercedes. Before the Maxima arrived."

"Yeah."

"Didn't you tell the police that you saw him get out and walk up to a car parked in front of him?"

"Yeah, right, that's what he did."

"This was a Datsun 810, correct?"

"I guess so, yeah."

"And you saw him pick up a sheet of paper that had fallen to the ground from the driver's window."

"Yeah."

"The paper had been covering the driver's window, correct?"

"The driver's window, yeah."

"And Mr. Yamaguchi picked it up and replaced it over the window."

"Yeah, right, like I told the cops."

"Then he went back and sat down again in the Mercedes."

"Yeah."

"And waited."

"Yeah."

"In fact, this happened a second time, didn't it?"

"Like I told the cops, yeah, the paper falls down again, the dude gets out and puts the paper back up again."

"And then he went back to the Mercedes."

"Right."

"And then it happened a third time."

"I think so, yeah. Maybe three times, yeah."

"Mr. Yamaguchi got out, walked up to the Datsun, picked up the paper and replaced it, then returned to the Mercedes."

"Yeah, like I said."

Yamaki pondered this for a moment. "Didn't you think this was rather strange conduct, Mr. Carmona?"

The young man shrugged.

Longo knew the question was objectionable, of course: First, it called for speculation, and second, Carmona's opinion of what was "strange" was not relevant to the issues in the case. But the prosecutor knew that there was rarely anything to be gained by objecting. In most cases, the objection was overruled. And even if it was sustained, a good trial lawyer could usually find other ways to get the evidence in. Despite how television depicted trials, objecting to testimony usually accomplished only two things. It made the jury think you were trying to keep something from them. And it irritated the judge, making him less likely to later sustain a really important objection.

The simple fact was that most questions could be objected to on some legal grounds; the Evidence Code was filled with possibilities. The true sign of a novice or incompetent lawyer was making an unending series of objections; the more you made, it was felt, the more points you scored.

The art was in knowing how *not* to object. Longo knew this. So did Yamaki. It required some skill to recognize legal grounds for an objection in that one short second before the witness answered. It took much more skill to recognize it and then also weigh the tactical advantages of objecting versus remaining silent. The cardinal rule was that you did not object unless there was something important to be gained and the chances of being sustained were good.

But Longo was bothered by the question. What was Yamaki leading up to with the business about the sheet of paper over the window? He knew the Datsun was an extra car for Yamaguchi's kids. Was there something in the car that he wanted hidden? Or some*one*?

"I have nothing further, your honor," Yamaki said, collecting his notes from the podium.

"Mr. Longo?" Bascue said.

"Officer Phillip Gruidl," Longo announced.

A moment later a tall, lanky man in a dark blue suit walked into the courtroom and strode confidently to the witness stand. Sakoda had finally tracked Gruidl down at the Highway Patrol Academy in Sacramento. He had flown back to Los Angeles early that morning.

The patrolman took the oath, smiled at the jurors, then sat

down. "My name is Phillip Gruidl," he said. "G-r-u-i-d-l."

"Your occupation and assignment?" Longo asked.

"Patrolman with the California Highway Patrol. Currently assigned to the Montebello station."

"Assigned to Montebello on March 29, 1991?"

"Yes, sir."

"That night, Officer, about one-seventeen in the morning, anything unusual happen?"

"Yes, sir."

"Want to tell us about it?"

"I was inside the station, taking a breath sample from a DUI suspect. And I heard this loud knocking at the front door."

"Uh-huh."

"The station was closed. It's not open to the public at that hour. So, for reasons of safety, I went out the back door and circled around to the front. And he was there, the defendant."

"You see him in court, Officer Gruidl?"

The witness pointed to Yamaguchi.

"May the record reflect he indicated the defendant, your honor?"

"It will so reflect," Judge Bascue said.

"Okay, what happened next, Officer?"

Longo liked law enforcement witnesses. It was effortless; you wound them up and then let them go. They knew what to say and how to say it and rarely made a mistake. Once in a while you nudged them with a "What happened next, Officer?" just to make it look like question-and-answer rather than a recital.

"I asked if I could help him. The suspect, the defendant there, he said 'Help me, please help me.' I said, 'What's wrong?' He said, 'I just shot my friend.'"

"Uh-huh."

"And then he pulled out this gun from his coat pocket. I guess he was just going to hand it to me, but at the time it looked like he was going to shoot. Anyway, I yanked out my gun and dropped to the ground. And I told him to put the gun down. And real quick-like, he laid it down on the ground."

Longo walked up to the witness, the blue steel revolver held out sideways in front of him. "Showing you People's three, this the gun?"

The officer inspected the revolver. "Yes, sir."

"What happened next, Officer?" Longo asked, walking back to the audience railing.

"I picked up the weapon, using a pencil through the trigger guard. About this time, the defendant, he said, 'I found my friend with my wife.' Then I cuffed him and took him inside and got his name and address. And called Montebello P.D."

"Did you frisk Mr. Yamaguchi?"

"Yes, sir."

"Find anything unusual?"

"I found a white sock in his pocket, one of those tube socks."

"Uh-huh."

"And a speedy loader."

"How about if you tell the folks here what a speedy loader is."

"Yes, sir." Gruidl turned to the jury. "Basically, it's just an extra revolving cylinder with five cartridge chambers. After you've fired the five bullets, you normally have to take the empty cartridge out from each chamber in the cylinder and put in a new one. But with the speedy loader, you just pull out the original cylinder and put in a new one that's already been loaded with five fresh cartridges."

"So the purpose of the speedy loader is . . ."

"To get off five more shots fast."

"But the speedy loader you found on the defendant, it was empty, right?"

"Yes, sir."

"Uh-huh. Okay, thanks, Officer Gruidl. No further questions."

Longo walked to his seat and sat down as Yamaki stepped to the podium.

"Officer," the lawyer said, "isn't it a fact that when you first saw my client—"

"Aw shoot," Longo said, standing. "Judge, I got one more question, I clean forgot."

"Mr. Longo . . ." Bascue said impatiently.

Yamaki smiled in amusement. "I have no objections, your honor."

"Very well."

"Officer," the prosecutor said, "was there anything, well, unusual about how Yamaguchi seemed that night? I mean, did he seem dopey, speech slurred, anything like that?"

Gruidl shook his head slowly. "No, sir. He seemed pretty normal. Excited, but that's about it."

"Didn't seem to have any trouble talking to you? Understanding you?"

"No, sir, none that I could see."

"Didn't seem to be under the influence of alcohol or drugs or anything like that?"

"No, sir."

Longo nodded. He smiled and raised his hand in thanks to Judge Bascue, then to Yamaki.

The defense lawyer grinned, shaking his head. He was familiar with Longo's Columbo routine. He glanced at the jury, still grinning, inviting them to share the little joke.

"Now then, Officer," he said, "I think you testified that when you first saw Mr. Yamaguchi, he seemed very excited, upset?"

"Excited, yes, sir."

"Disturbed."

"Yes, sir."

"Definitely not calm and rational?"

"He was pretty excited."

"So excited and irrational that he didn't even realize that he was waving a gun at you?"

"He was pretty excited, sir."

"He asked you to *help* him."

"Yes, sir."

"And he referred to the person he shot as his friend?"

"Yes, sir."

"In fact, it was *not* his friend, was it?"

"I really don't know, sir."

"I see." Yamaki paused, referred to his notes at the podium. "Now, you said that you didn't need an interpreter."

"Yes, sir."

"Did you *ask* him if he needed an interpreter?"

"No, sir, it didn't seem necessary. He seemed to understand me."

"Do you *know* that he understood everything you said?"

"He volunteered information in English, answered my questions in English."

"But you can't say for sure, Officer, that he did understand everything, can you?"

"Not everything, no, sir."

"Nor that he *heard* everything."

"He seemed to."

"He *seemed* to?"

"Yes, sir."

"But, again, there is no way you could tell if he was actually able to hear everything you were saying."

"I suppose not."

"It's possible that he couldn't hear everything you were saying."

"It's possible."

The irony suddenly occurred to Longo that Yamaki was on the L.A. City Police Commission. He wondered what it was like for an officer to be cross-examined in trial by a police commissioner who represented the accused.

"Now, Officer Gruidl, you testified that Mr. Yamaguchi didn't seem to be under the influence of any drugs."

"Yes, sir."

"You have received some training in recognizing the effects of drugs, correct? For the purpose of arresting for driving under the influence?"

"Yes, sir."

"Drugs like cocaine, heroin, marijuana, that kind of thing?"

"Yes, sir."

"Amphetamines, sleeping pills . . ."

"Yes, sir."

It *was* Halcion! Longo thought as he sat back down. Yamaki was putting on some kind of diminished-capacity defense.

Longo wondered how Dohi was doing in his search for an expert witness. His young law clerk had been busily calling noted authorities across the country. But it was a difficult search. Either the physician was unavailable on short notice, or he was somehow associated with the Upjohn Company; three of the doctors had received funding from the pharmaceutical company for their research with the drug.

He had met with Lane Bauer after the trial had recessed the previous day. He and the senior partner of Upjohn's law firm had worked late into the night in Bauer's room at the New Otani, only one block from Yamaguchi's restaurant. Longo buried himself in FDA reports and waded through the transcripts of experts who had testified on both sides of the civil lawsuits.

"At any time did he refuse to cooperate with you?"

"No, sir."

"Thank you, Officer," Yamaki said, walking back to his chair. "No further questions, your honor."

"Any questions on redirect?" Judge Bascue asked.

"Just one more question," Longo said, standing up. "Officer Gruidl, the defendant over there said, 'Help me, help me.' "

"Yes, sir."

"He ever say, 'Help my *friend*'?"

"No, sir."

Longo nodded silently. Then, "Nothing further."

"Call your next witness," the judge said.

"Govan Yee."

Brick by brick, Longo thought as Officer Gruidl walked out of the courtroom.

As he waited for the witness to come in, he watched the new court reporter change the roll of paper in her stenotype machine. The usual reporter assigned to Department 127 was Cynthia Cartright. But a new one had been assigned to alternate with Cartright during the Yamaguchi trial. Her name was Ginny Ishida, a stunningly beautiful twenty-eight-year-old *nisei*. Longo had heard from the bailiff that her boyfriend was a Japanese-American lawyer. And the lawyer was a good friend of Yamaki.

Quite a coincidence, the prosecutor thought. Or was he becoming paranoid?

The entrance doors opened and a short Asian man in his forties, wearing a navy blue blazer and gray slacks, stepped into the room. He quickly walked up to the witness stand, took the oath, and sat down.

"My name is Govan Yee," he said. "G-o-v-a-n . . . Y-e-e."

"Occupation?" Longo asked absently as he sifted through some photographs on the table.

"Detective, Montebello police department."

"Detective Yee, back on March twenty-ninth of last year, you were at the Kariya murder scene, right?"

Yamaki rose. "Objection, your honor."

"The *shooting* scene," Longo said.

Yamaki sat down.

"I arrived at one forty-eight A.M.," Yee said.

"And you took a bunch of photos, right?"

"Yes, I did."

"Judge," the prosecutor said, holding up a photograph, "got a photo of the inside of a car. Mark it People's, uh, whatever's next?"

Judge Bascue nodded. "It will be marked People's exhibit number six."

"Okay," Longo said, approaching Yee. "You take this?"

The detective examined the photograph carefully. "Yes."

"Can you hold it up for those folks and tell them what it is?"

Yee held the photograph toward the jury. "It's a photograph of the victim's car, a 1984 Nissan Maxima, light blue in color. As you can see, I took it standing just outside the driver's door, with the door open. You can see the dark stains on the seats, which is the victim's blood."

"Uh-huh. Now, take a look at that tear in the ceiling, over on the other side, the passenger's side."

"Yes."

"What's that?"

"Yes, that's caused by the trajectory of a bullet. There were two empty casings found at the scene. One of the bullets was recovered from the victim's skull. The other I found myself, in the ceiling of the car. The tear is from where the bullet entered the upholstered ceiling. As you can see, it's on the passenger's side, just above the door."

"Uh-huh," Longo said thoughtfully. "That's just about where a passenger's head would be, wouldn't it?"

Yee nodded.

"So if Yamaguchi's wife was sitting there at the time, that bullet would have just missed her head, right?"

"Objection," Yamaki said quietly. "Calls for speculation."

"Sustained," Bascue said.

"Okay," Longo said, walking back to his chair. "That bullet they found in the autopsy..."

"Yes."

"You got ahold of that bullet and tried to make a match with the gun Yamaguchi turned over to the CHP, right?"

"Yes, I did. I had the gun test-fired at the police range, using one of the three unused cartridges found in the gun. I then had the spent bullet compared for striations with the bullet recovered from the victim's skull."

"Yeah?"

"They matched."

Longo sat down on the edge of the counsel table.

Judge Bascue closed his eyes, his patience strained. He sighed deeply.

"Okay, I understand you took a little drive from the defendant's house to the CHP station, that right?"

"Yes, I did."

"Why was that?"

"You asked me to determine the distance and the time it took to drive, at night, following the speed limit."

"So what'd you find out?"

Yee glanced at some notes on his lap. "One minute forty-four seconds. Distance, six tenths of a mile."

Longo nodded, then stood up and leaned his elbow on the speaker's podium.

"Now, you talked with Yamaguchi back at the station, didn't you? After he was picked up from the CHP?"

"Yes, I did. At two-thirty A.M."

"And while you were talking with him, you took a gunshot residue test."

"Yes, I did."

"Okay. So you swabbed the defendant's hands?"

"Yes, I did. The back of both hands and the palms."

"Results?"

Longo knew that, technically, the results were hearsay. If Yamaki objected, the prosecutor would have to bring in the laboratory technician to testify to the test results. But he also knew the defense attorney was not likely to object. The defense was not claiming that Yamaguchi did not shoot Kariya; he would not want it to look to the jury as though he had something to fear from the evidence.

"Analysis indicated the presence of antimony and barium on both palms."

"Both palms?"

"Apparently he was holding the gun with both hands when he fired it."

Longo nodded. So much for Carmona's testimony that Yamaguchi was pointing a single hand at Kariya when he fired, he thought. You took your witnesses as you found them.

"If the suspect was wearing a sock over one hand when he fired the gun, would there still be antimony and barium on that palm?"

"Yes, there would. It would penetrate the fabric."

"Uh-huh. By the way, you get a close look at the gun shortly after the defendant turned it over to the CHP?"

"Yes, I did."

"Was it loaded?"

"There were three live cartridges in the chambers and two spent."

"You notice if the hammer was resting on a live or spent cartridge?"

"Live."

"Uh-huh. Now, if I get this right, the hammer cocks back as the cylinder rotates, right?"

"Yes, it does."

"And then falls forward and hits the next live round, firing it."

"Yes."

"So, after firing, the hammer would be resting on a spent cartridge?"

"Yes, it would."

"But the hammer here was resting on a *live* cartridge."

"Yes, it was."

"What does that mean, Detective?"

"It would indicate to me that the hammer was cocked, rotating the chamber, and then eased back to a resting position by the person holding the gun."

"Okay. Now, you did a computer check on the gun's registration?"

"Yes, I did. The numbers were not registered."

"This was an unregistered gun?"

"It was an unregistered gun."

Longo seemed to ponder this. Of course, he already knew about the registration. Only an incompetent lawyer asked a witness a question to which he did not already know the answer.

"Now, you said you were talking with the defendant while you took the swabs."

"Yes."

"What were you talking about?"

"I was giving him instructions concerning the test, asking him when he last washed his hands, that kind of thing."

"Was this all in English?"

"Yes, it was."

"He have any problems understanding you, following your directions?"

"No, he did not."

"Uh-huh. By the way, did you ask Mr. Yamaguchi if he was taking any medication?"

"Yes, I did."

"Yeah?"

"He said he was not."

Longo walked back to his chair. "Nothing further."

Yamaki rose, walked quickly to the podium.

"Good morning, Detective Yee."

"Good morning."

The lawyer glanced at a document in his hand. "Did you fill out a report in this matter?"

"Yes, I did."

"And did you not write in this report, and I quote, 'Suspect appeared very sleepy and subdued'?"

"Yes, I did."

Halcion again, Longo thought.

"No further questions, your honor," Yamaki said.

"Mr. Longo?" Bascue said.

"Couple questions, judge." Longo walked over to the jury box, leaned against the railing. "What time of day was this that the defendant looked sleepy?"

"Two-thirty A.M."

"Weren't *you* a little sleepy at that hour?"

"I don't recall."

Longo nodded. "Detective, take a look over there at the defendant."

Yee looked across the room at Yamaguchi, still sitting with his head bowed and his eyes closed, the translator's earphones straddling his head.

"Now," Longo said, "as he sits there, would you say he looks 'very sleepy and subdued'?"

"Yes, I would."

"About the same as he did that night?"

"Yes, about the same."

"Uh-huh. Nothing further."

"Mr. Yamaki?" Bascue asked.

"No, your honor."

"Very well," the judge said, looking at the clock. "We will take our recess at this time. Ladies and gentlemen," he said, looking at the jurors, "you are excused until tomorrow morning at ten. As usual, I have a daily calendar of cases to dispose of, but I think we can get started by ten. As I have indicated before, please do not discuss this case with anyone."

The jurors stood, collected their belongings, and slowly filed out of the box. As they approached the swinging gates, Yamaguchi rose to his feet and, standing next to Yamaki, bowed deeply. He held the bow until the last of the jurors had left the courtroom. Then he turned back toward the judge, bowed quickly, and sat back down in his chair.

"Judge," Longo said, "one little thing."

"Yes?"

"The People move for a bench warrant."

Yamaki looked at the prosecutor.

"For the arrest of Kohei Matsumoto," Longo said. "He is a witness to certain statements made by the defendant."

"On what grounds?" Bascue asked.

"The guy's been subpoenaed, but he hasn't shown up. And he's dodging my investigator."

"You have proof of service?"

"Yeah. Affidavit from Jimmy Sakoda."

"In that case . . ."

"Your honor," Yamaki said, "I would ask the court to hold the warrant for two days. I know Mr. Matsumoto has been very busy, and his court appearance has probably slipped his mind. I'm sure I can locate him."

Longo grinned. He had expected this. It would not look good for the defense if Yamaguchi's close friend took the stand while under arrest for trying to avoid testifying.

"Mr. Longo?"

The prosecutor shrugged. "Thanks for the help, Mike."

Yamaki said nothing.

"Fine," Bascue said, standing. "Then, gentlemen, until tomorrow."

Phase one and two were over, Longo thought as he collected the notes, reports, and photographs scattered across the table. He had shown the jury a dead body, shown that it was dead from a bullet, shown that Yamaguchi was the shooter. That was the easy part. Yamaki had not even wasted time contesting the fact that his client shot Kariya.

Now it was time for phase three: proving motive and premeditation.

This was where the battle would be fought.

Chapter

18

At 9:00 A.M. Longo sat at the counsel table, working his way through the daily calendar before trial resumed. Craig Veals and Deputy Public Defender Nancy Richards were speaking to the judge at the bench.

"He wants Folsom Prison, your honor," Richards said in a hushed voice. "He'll plead straight up if you recommend Folsom."

"That's it?" Judge Bascue said, leaning forward, his voice almost a whisper. "That's the whole deal? He pleads guilty to robbery if I agree to send him to Folsom?"

Richards sighed. "My client got out of Folsom a few weeks before he got arrested on this charge. The thing is, he just couldn't cut it in the outside world. He's been in too long. Can't cope, can't deal with it all. He wants to go back. So he pulled that liquor store job. Never intended to get away with it. He just wanted to get caught and sent back."

Bascue shook his head. He looked at the defendant standing at the defense table, one arm handcuffed to the prisoner seated next to him. Richards's client was a thin, frail man, maybe sixty, with a bald head and heavy bags under watery blue eyes. He seemed completely disinterested in the proceedings around him.

"Mr. Veals?" Bascue whispered.

Veals shrugged. "The man's got a right to plead guilty, your honor."

Bascue looked back at Richards. "Why Folsom?"

"He worked in the library there," she said. "He likes the library at Folsom."

"He likes the library," Bascue repeated incredulously.

"Look, your honor," she said, "to tell you the truth, I feel funny about this. I mean, he wants me to plead him guilty. But I think the guy's got a defense."

"What defense?" Veals asked.

"No intent! This guy never *intended* to knock off that liquor store. He went through the motions, but there was no way he ever planned to pull it off. It was all a scam to get back to prison."

"You have a dilemma, Ms. Richards," Bascue said.

"I mean, my job is to *defend*. And I *can* defend this guy, I honest-to-God think I can get him off."

"But he doesn't want off," Bascue said sympathetically.

"Right. So what do I do? Do I follow my client's orders? Or do I take it to trial, with him kicking and screaming all the way? And if I go to trial, do I put him on the stand, knowing he's going to perjure himself and say he intended to rob the store?"

Bascue looked down at Longo sitting at the counsel table, then back at Veals. "Would Mr. Longo consider a dismissal?"

Veals shook his head. "We got a guy walking into a store, points a gun at the lady behind the counter..."

"It wasn't loaded," Richards said.

"She didn't know that. And then he takes all the money and walks out with it. That's called robbery."

"Yeah, and then he waits outside for the cops to show up."

Veals shrugged again. "What can I do, Nancy? Just pretend it didn't happen?"

"I don't know. What would I do with a dismissal anyway? He'd just go out and do it again." She shook her head slowly. "They don't tell you about these things in law school."

"Ms. Richards, if your client wants to plead guilty, I'll certainly recommend that he be sent to Folsom. Beyond that, I don't know what I can do. Or what Mr. Veals can do, for that matter."

Richards nodded, then looked back at her client, studying him for a moment. "At his age, it's a life sentence," she said quietly.

There was a long moment of silence.

"Okay," she said. "Let's get it over with."

Richards stepped away from the bench and walked back to her client. Veals returned to the prosecution table.

"Problem?" Longo asked his junior deputy.

"No," Veals said. "I'm just real grateful I'm not a public defender."

Longo glanced down the table at Richards, whispering now to her client. Then he looked behind him at the clock on the back wall: 9:40. The jurors were supposed to take their seats in the box at 10:00. But the calendar that morning was heavy. The trial would be starting late.

Once again he scanned the audience of Japanese faces staring passively back at him.

"Henry Simpson Earhardt,*" Veals began his litany, "you are charged in Information number A010879 with violation of Penal Code section 211, a felony, in that on March twenty-seventh . . ."

As Veals recited the language necessary for a guilty plea, a tall, heavyset young man in a navy blue pin-striped suit walked through the swinging gate and approached Longo. He was followed by a sullen young black man with a bow tie and a trim mustache and goatee. The tall one leaned down and handed Longo a business card.

Longo took the card, glanced at it. John T. Mahoney,* it read. Assistant United States Attorney. Longo nodded, stood up, and walked past the jury box and into the jury deliberation room. The federal prosecutor and the man in the bow tie followed, closing the door behind them.

Longo grabbed a chair and sat down. Mahoney sat across the table from him. The third man remained standing.

"This is Mohammed Tanney,*" Mahoney said, nodding at the man with the bow tie. "Counsel for Mr. Reed."

Tanney stared darkly at Longo, saying nothing. The angry young black lawyer, Longo thought to himself wearily.

Mr. Reed was Charles Edward Reed, a seventeen-year-old member of the Crips. He was on the next day's calendar for arraignment, charged with committing eleven bank robberies within a period of one week.

The more enterprising gangs in Los Angeles had recently developed a new technique for robbing banks. The older, hard-core members, called O.G.s for "original gangsters," recruited young kids for the gangs who were under eighteen. To "earn their bones," these recruits were armed and then taken to banks and ordered to rob them at gunpoint. If the young recruits pulled off the robbery, they brought the money to the O.G.s. waiting a few blocks away. If they got caught, however, they benefited from a quirk in the law. Bank robbery was a federal offense, but the federal government had no laws for juveniles. If the robber was under eighteen, he was referred to the state authorities where he became a ward of the juvenile court. By using juveniles there was very little risk; the worst that could happen if the recruit was caught was that he would spend two or three years in a youth camp.

But there was a flaw to this new bank robbery technique. And Reed had fallen victim to it. Under California law, anyone over sixteen could be prosecuted as an adult if a judge found at a hearing that he was "unfit" to be dealt with by the juvenile system. And Reed, after robbing eleven banks in the L.A. area, had been caught and found unfit.

Meanwhile, the FBI had arrested the O.G.s responsible for these and dozens of other bank robberies where juveniles had been used. The U.S. attorney filed bank robbery charges against the adults. The problem was that the juveniles were all refusing to testify that the adults had put them up to the robberies. And faced with the threat of nothing more than a couple of years in a youth camp, there was nothing that could be done to pressure them to testify.

Frightened by the prospect of a long term in an adult prison, however, Charles Edward Reed told his court-appointed lawyer to work a deal in exchange for his testimony. Tanney had gone to the assistant U.S. attorney prosecuting the case, Mahoney, and offered a deal: Reed would testify against the men in federal court if he was given immunity for the adult charges he was facing in state court.

The problem was that the U.S. Attorney's Office had no authority over the state prosecution. And so Mahoney had approached Longo, asking him to give Reed immunity so that he could testify against the O.G.s in federal court. But Longo was the wrong man to approach: He hated the very idea of immunity.

"Have you had a chance to consider my proposal?" Mahoney asked.

"No deal," Longo said.

"Longo . . ."

"I don't believe in immunity, Mahoney. It's against my religion."

"It's against your—"

"My religion."

"Look, Longo," Mahoney said, "let's be realistic. These guys are real bad actors. Reed's a kid, a first-timer."

"This kid's already got a rap sheet the length of your arm," Longo said. "He shot up one bank and pistol-whipped a teller at another."

"Believe me, next to these assholes, he's a fucking angel."

"Uh-huh. Well, you got your problems, Mahoney, I got mine."

"Look, Longo, I'd like to handle it at this level, you understand what I mean?"

Longo grinned. Mahoney was threatening to go over his head. But Longo knew that his supervisors were no more fond of bowing to the federal prosecutors than he was. The D.A.'s Office rarely got cooperation from the U.S. attorney; there was a long history of mistrust between the offices.

"Handle it at whatever level you want, Mahoney. Nobody gets immunity in my court."

Longo glanced at Tanney. The defense lawyer just sat there, glaring back at him in silence. Still eye fucking after four years of college and three years of law school, Longo thought.

"Look," Mahoney said, "whaddya got, eleven counts? How about, you knock one count down to grand theft, kid pleads to it, gets probation. You get a conviction, we get a witness. Everybody's happy."

Longo shook his head. "Mr. Reed's going to prison."

Mahoney sighed loudly. He looked at Tanney, then back at the deputy D.A. "Longo, we need this kid. Whaddya want?"

"Fifteen years."

"Fifteen *years*!"

"Fifteen years. And if I don't like how he testifies in the federal case, the deal's off and he'll do twice that."

Mahoney glanced at Tanney. The defense lawyer shook his head slightly.

"Look, Longo," Mahoney said, "this kid's not going to risk his life testifying against these clowns for any fifteen years in prison."

"Then you got a problem."

"Look, midterm for state robbery is, what, four years? How about, Reed cops to one count, you recommend low term to the judge. That's three years, all right?"

Under California's complex sentencing laws, a felony was punishable by a "base" prison term; for robbery, the base or "midterm" was four years. This could be increased or reduced by one year depending upon such factors as the defendant's record and any violence involved.

"Tell you what," Longo said, "I'll let him plead to three counts. Twelve years."

Mahoney rolled his eyes. "Look, Longo, we're on the same team, right? We're both trying to put away the bad guys, right? Let me do my job, huh? Look, how about . . . how about he cops to the one count, he does the midterm, four years."

Longo shook his head. He looked directly at Tanney. "Two counts, high term. Ten years."

Longo was confident that Tanney had already told the federal prosecutor what it would take to get his client as a witness. Now Mahoney was low-balling Longo in the hopes of reaching a compromise acceptable to the defense lawyer.

The assistant U.S. attorney shook his head in exasperation. "Look, you want two counts, okay, you got two counts. The kid pleads to two counts, you recommend low term, he does six years." He looked quickly at Tanney, then back at Longo. "We got a deal?"

"I got a calendar to run," Longo said, standing up. "And I got a jury waiting out in the hallway. You want a deal, this is it: two counts, midterm, he does eight years. End of story."

"C'mon, Longo, eight years, there's no way . . ."

Longo started to walk out of the room.

Mahoney looked quickly at Tanney. The defense lawyer nodded almost imperceptibly, his eyes still locked on the deputy D.A.

"Awright, awright," Mahoney said. "Eight years, it's a deal."

Longo stopped, looked back at the assistant U.S. attorney. "Always a pleasure to help our federal friends." Then he turned and left the room.

As Longo walked back into the courtroom, he saw a woman standing at the prosecution table and addressing the court. It was fairly common to have deputy D.A.s from other courts appear in Department 127. Some cases had deputies assigned specially to them, such as those in Special Trials or in the Organized Crime unit. Others had their cases transferred to 127 because a judge was sick or on vacation. But Longo did not recognize this deputy.

Veals was sitting in the jury box, studying some case files. Mike Yamaki was sitting in the second row, reading his trial notes.

Longo sat down in the chair next to Veals. "How's the calendar?"

"The bull-and-cow case was the last one. It got continued for a month, so we're all clear."

The case involved a crooked lawyer who staged car accidents and then made insurance claims for personal injuries. He would fill one car with five or six illegal immigrants from El Salvador; this was the "cow." Next, he put another El Salvadoran behind the wheel of a second car, the "bull." Then he ordered the driver of the bull to crash into the cow at thirty or forty miles an hour. After everyone was taken to the hospital, he filed lawsuits and then quickly settled with the insurance companies. In an average accident, he would pocket fifty thousand dollars. When they were released from the hospital, each of the immigrants was sent back to El Salvador with five hundred dollars.

Longo studied the woman talking to Judge Bascue from the prosecution table. She was maybe forty, short, freckle-faced, with long, tangled hair, and no makeup or jewelry, and wearing a sweater, pleated khaki pants, and brown penny loafers. When she spoke, her words were charged with wide-eyed enthusiasm and an almost child-like energy. The woman looked and sounded more like a hyperactive schoolgirl than a prosecutor.

"Who is she?" he whispered to his junior deputy.

"Katherine Mader," Veals said. "From Santa Monica."

"Mader . . ."

"Yeah. The Hillside Strangler case?"

"Oh yeah . . ." Longo looked at the woman again, studying her carefully now. This was the deputy D.A. who had been the defense attorney for the Hillside Strangler.

* * *

Mader had started her legal career as a public defender, then quit to hang up her own shingle. Sometime after this, one of the top criminal attorneys in the city, Gerald Chaleff, approached her with a proposition. He had recently been appointed by the court to represent Angelo Buono, accused of the sex-torture murders of ten young women and girls. Facing the gas chamber, Buono was entitled under California law to a second appointed attorney to handle the death penalty phase of the trial. Chaleff asked Mader if she would be interested in a court appointment to be co-counsel in what promised to be the "trial of the year," and she jumped at it.

The Hillside Strangler case consumed Katherine Mader's life for the next four years. From early in the morning until late into the evening, she and Chaleff researched, investigated, and prepared. The trial ended up taking two years and over fifty-six thousand pages of testimony. In the end, the jury convicted Mader's client of the murders.

Mader and Chaleff now entered the second phase: the death penalty trial. In a surprise move, Buono told his lawyers that he *wanted* the death penalty; he was sure the conviction would be reversed and a death sentence carried an automatic appeal to the Supreme Court. When Mader and Chaleff would not agree to "lay down," Buono refused to cooperate further with either of them. He never spoke again to either of his lawyers.

At the death penalty trial, Mader gave an impassioned plea for the serial killer's life. The jury listened; an angry Angelo Buono escaped the gas chamber and was given a life sentence without possibility of parole.

The Strangler trial was finally over. But it had taken something out of Katherine Mader. She found that she had lost her enthusiasm for defense work, another victim of burnout. She was quickly offered two more murder cases. Mader accepted them, but as she later recalled, "I remember thinking to myself, 'This doesn't interest me in the slightest.'" Later, in trial on one of the murders, she was alarmed to find herself giving "only 95 percent." It was time for a change.

She put her law practice on hold while she had a second child and co-authored a book, *Fallen Angels*. Reflecting her lifelong fascination, the book was a collection of the most celebrated crimes and mysteries in Los Angeles; the Hillside Strangler case was included. She followed this with a second book, *Rotten Apples,* about famous criminal cases in New York.

But Mader eventually found herself wanting to get back into action. She decided to return to the courtroom—as a prosecutor. When she applied to the D.A.'s Office, however, she was rejected: The office did not want Buono's lawyer prosecuting cases. And her motives, she later discovered, were suspect. Some in the office suspected her of being a spy for the National Lawyers' Guild, a radical group of defense attorneys. Others felt she was trying to position herself to write a third book, an exposé of the District Attorney's Office.

Frustrated, Mader offered to serve as a volunteer without pay. James Bascue, who had recently been banished to the Santa Monica office after Reiner defeated Philibosian in the election for district attorney, agreed to let her work with his staff. Although she had already earned a strong reputation as a defense attorney, she now began to earn praise as a sharp, tough prosecutor. After one particularly difficult murder trial, homicide detectives wrote letters to Ira Reiner praising her. Bascue concurred, strongly recommending that she be hired as a regular deputy.

The front office finally relented, but Mader was given no credit for her experience; she was hired as a beginning grade-one deputy and assigned to Santa Monica permanently. Her roommate in her tiny new office was Steve Barshop. Ironically, Barshop had been the prosecutor in the last murder case she had tried. As a result of the experience, Barshop held no affection for the woman, nor did he trust her; to him, she was still "Buono's lawyer."

Bascue ignored Mader's grade-one ranking and continued assigning her to heavy murder cases. As she won conviction after conviction, her fellow deputies in the office slowly and grudgingly began to trust her. But it was not until she won a death penalty verdict against a woman that she was accepted into the fraternity. Mader argued to the jury that the defendant, a lesbian nurse, was "the most vicious, sadistic, cold-blooded human being that we will ever see in our lifetime." The jury voted for death, making her the only woman on California's crowded death row. Even Steve Barshop was won over after that, and the two roommates became closest friends.

The transition from defense attorney to prosecutor surprised many in the profession, but it seemed a natural one to Mader. "I'm not here because it's the side of truth and justice," she said recently. "As far as I'm concerned, neither side wears a white hat. There are good people with a lot of integrity on both sides of the fence. I just needed a change."

Longo continued studying the hyperactive schoolgirl as she argued a motion on a murder case to her former boss, Judge Bascue. Katherine Mader, he thought to himself. He had never met her. With almost one thousand deputies now in the D.A.'s Office, he no longer knew most of them.

"... if there are no more cases," Judge Bascue said, "then the bailiff will please call in the jury."

Longo stood up, stepped out of the jury box, and walked toward the prosecution table.

Mader was stuffing pleadings and documents back into an old leather satchel.

"Katherine Mader?" Longo said.

The small woman looked up. "Yes?"

"Larry Longo," he said, extending his hand.

She looked blank for a moment, then suddenly smiled broadly.

"I'm very happy to meet you." She was studying his face intently now, as if trying to find something there.

"Same here."

Jurors began walking by the two prosecutors and taking their seats in the jury box.

"In trial?" Mader asked.

"Yeah. What was that case you were arguing to Bascue?"

"Oh, Beverly Hills dentist, falls in love with his assistant, wife has to be removed." She grinned. "Old story. You?"

"Guy knocks off wife's lover." He grinned back. "Old story."

She nodded.

"In the case of People versus Kazuhiko Yamaguchi," Judge Bascue announced, "let the record reflect that the defendant is present, both counsels are present, and all of the jurors are in their seats."

"Good luck, Larry," Mader whispered, squeezing Longo's hand.

"You, too, Katherine."

Mader turned toward the swinging gates. She looked back briefly at Bascue.

The judge winked at her.

She smiled at Longo, then walked out.

"Call your next witness, Mr. Longo," Bascue said.

"Kiyoji Shimaya."

The bailiff left the courtroom, then returned a few seconds later with a short, slender fifty-five-year-old man in a light blue polyester leisure suit. The man took the oath, then sat in the witness stand and looked around the courtroom in confusion.

"Mr. Shimaya?" Longo said.

"Ah yes," the man said, bowing his head slightly.

"Mr. Shimaya, you know Mitsuru Yamaguchi, right? Mrs. Yamaguchi, the wife of the defendant over there?"

"Yamaguchi-*san, hai,* yes, I know wife."

"In fact, you belong to Mrs. Yamaguchi's singing club, don't you?"

"*Yamabiko-kai,* yes, yes."

"Now, are you familiar with these variety shows that Yamaguchi put on?"

"*Tamasaburo,* yes, yes."

"And who was in charge of these shows?"

"Yamaguchi-*san.*"

"Now, at some point, Genji Kariya was hired by Yamaguchi to help out around the restaurant?"

"*So desu,* yes."

"And, later, he started helping out with the variety show too, right?"

"Yes."

"Did you notice, Mr. Shimaya, if Mr. Kariya's . . . attitude began to change at all?"

"Kariya-*san* . . . Mr. Kariya, he becomes . . . bold, more bold."

"Bold."

"He becomes like . . . boss man."

"You mean, he started taking over more and more, pushing out Mr. Yamaguchi?"

"Yes, yes. He say bad things to other people, make him small."

"He'd belittle Mr. Yamaguchi to other folks?"

"Yes. And he make big himself."

"He'd brag about things he'd done on the show himself?"

"Yes."

"Uh-huh . . . So, Mr. Kariya, he pretty much took over from Mr. Yamaguchi, that right?"

"*So desu,* yes."

"And what did Mr. Yamaguchi think of this?"

"Objection, your honor," Yamaki said quietly from his chair. "Calls for speculation."

"Sustained," Bascue said.

"Okay," Longo said. "Mr. Shimaya, you went to a party at the Mitsuru Cafe, a couple of nights before the shooting?"

"Yes."

"This was a celebration, after the variety show was a big hit, right?"

"Yes."

"And do you recall an argument between Mr. Yamaguchi and Mrs. Yamaguchi during the party?"

"Yes."

"Could you tell the folks in the jury over there what happened?"

"Yes. Mrs. Yamaguchi is angry, she is angry at . . . Mr. Yamaguchi. He makes mistake, with singers from Japan. He makes bad . . . deal, I think. And she . . . scolds him."

"This is in front of everybody?"

"Yes."

"Did Mr. Kariya join in the argument?"

"Yes. Kariya-*san,* Mr. Kariya, he also scolds Mr. Yamaguchi. He brags that he . . . the show is successful because of what he does. He scolds Mr. Yamaguchi for the mistake. He talks about the show before, Mr. Yamaguchi's show, it is a big . . . failure. Mr. Yamaguchi does that show before, and it loses much money."

"So Mr. Kariya is taking the credit for the successful show, and pointing out that Mr. Yamaguchi's show a few months earlier was a failure?"

"Pointing out, yes."

"And this was also in front of everybody?"

"Yes."

"What did Mr. Yamaguchi do?"

"Yamaguchi-*san,* Mr. Yamaguchi, he is quiet, he says nothing. But his face is red, very red. I think his feelings are hurt."

"Uh-huh." Longo looked at the jury, then back at the witness. "Thanks, Mr. Shimaya. Nothing further."

Yamaki stood up and moved slowly to the podium.

"Mr. Shimaya, you testified that Mr. Yamaguchi said nothing during this incident?"

"Yes."

"He remained quiet."

"Yes."

"In fact, Mr. Yamaguchi is a very quiet person, is he not?"

"Yes."

"Mr. Shimaya, do you recall a conversation you had with investigators from the District Attorney's Office? Mr. Sakoda and Mr. Park?"

"Sakoda-*san,* yes, yes."

"Do you recall telling them that you knew Mr. Yamaguchi to be a quiet person, not violent?"

"Yes."

The son of a gun did it, Longo thought with glee. Yamaki asked a question about the propensity of his client for violence. Under California's evidence laws, a prosecutor could not produce evidence of a defendant's past violent acts to prove that he had a tendency to be violent and that, therefore, he was probably violent on the occasion in question. This was called "propensity evidence." But there was an exception: If the defense "opened the door" by asking questions to show the defendant was *not* violent, the prosecution could rebut this with evidence that he was. By asking Shimaya if Yamaguchi was a nonviolent man, Yamaki had made it possible for Longo to get in evidence that he was, in fact, violent. The prosecutor could now put on evidence about the shooting incident and the Nagano attack. Yamaki had committed a serious error.

Or had he? Yamaki was too smart to make that kind of a mistake, Longo realized.

"Mr. Shimaya, before testifying, you were sitting out in the hallway, weren't you?"

"Yes."

"You were sitting with Mr. Cheman Park, from the D.A.'s Office?"

"Yes."

"And didn't Mr. Park tell you how to testify?"

Shimaya looked confused.

"Didn't Mr. Park tell you to testify that Kariya was bragging? That he was taking over from Mr. Yamaguchi?"

"He reads the writing, from what I say before to him. Because my memory, it is not clear always."

"So he read to you what to say here in court."

"He reads what I say, yes."

"Nothing further."

Longo remained in his seat. "Mr. Shimaya, Mr. Park was reading from a statement you gave to him a few weeks ago, right?"

"Yes."

"And is what you told him in that statement the truth?"

"Yes, yes."

"And what you've testified to here today, do you recall it happening?"

"Yes."

"Nothing further."

"Thank you, Mr. Shimaya," Bascue said. "Call your next witness, Mr. Longo."

"Louis Hernandez," Longo said, rising to his feet.

A small, frightened-looking man in his twenties with a thin mustache and small, darting eyes came into the courtroom. He followed the bailiff hesitantly to the witness stand, took the oath, and sat down. He continued looking around the room, as if for a way to escape.

"Mr. Hernandez, you work for Mr. Yamaguchi, right?"

The man nodded quickly.

"You're gonna have to answer out loud, so Ginny there, the reporter, she can take down what you say."

Hernandez stared at Ginny Ishida. "Yes."

"Doing odd jobs, painting, stuff like that?"

He nodded again, then quickly, "Yes."

"Now, one night back in March of last year, you were working on a house in Boyle Heights that the Yamaguchis owned, right?"

"Yes."

"Painting, in the living room?"

"Yes."

"And Mrs. Yamaguchi came into the house?"

"Yes."

"She alone?"

"No, Mr. Kariya was with her."

"What happened?"

"Mr. Kariya and Mrs. Yamaguchi, they went up the stairs."

"And what rooms are upstairs?"

Hernandez shrugged. "Three bedrooms. Two bathrooms."

"Okay, now, did *Mr.* Yamaguchi come into the house a little later?"

"Yes."

"When was this?"

"Maybe . . . fifteen minutes."

"And where did he go?"

"Up the stairs."

"What happened next?"

"It is like I said to the officer, it is quiet. And then there is loud talking. And yelling. More yelling. And then Mr. Kariya comes back down the stairs very fast. He seems very angry and he goes out the door."

"Did you notice anything unusual about his face?"

"It was a little red," Hernandez said, touching his right cheek, "there."

"Redness, like he'd just been hit?"

"Objection," Yamaki said.

"Sustained."

"Nothing further, judge," Longo said, sitting down.

"Mr. Hernandez," Yamaki said as he stood up and walked toward the jury with a vague smile, "did you hear any sounds coming from upstairs before Mr. Yamaguchi arrived?"

Hernandez shook his head. "No," he added quickly.

"And in fact, you don't know where Mr. Kariya and Mrs. Yamaguchi were upstairs?"

"No."

"Or what they were doing?"

"No."

"Now, when you spoke with the investigators from the District Attorney's Office..."

Motive, Longo thought. Kariya was muscling Yamaguchi out of the business, and then making a move on the old man's wife. Not much, but enough for now, enough for the case-in-chief. It was time to move on to the real war zone: premeditation. It was time to take on Hanemure and Matsumoto.

Tomorrow.

Chapter 1

Longo recrossed his feet on top of the littered desk. He glanced at the day-old copy of the *Los Angeles Times,* already stained with coffee rings. The long-awaited endorsement for the district attorney's race had struck the office like a thunderbolt. The *Times* was backing neither Reiner nor Garcetti. The liberal newspaper had thrown its considerable weight behind the underdog law-and-order Republican candidate, Ernie Norris. Longo was still trying to adjust to the idea that the *Times* would back a candidate who was actually the best qualified.

The loss of the expected endorsement put even more pressure on an already nervous Ira Reiner. The Rodney King trial now became a do-or-die effort. Solid verdicts of guilty could still pull out a reelection victory. An acquittal would mean the end.

And the pressure was being felt in places other than the front office. Tension was building in the streets too as the trial date rapidly neared. Gun sales were up, and there were rumors of secret gang treaties and Molotov cocktails being stockpiled. The King trial and verdict would be the matches that would blow up the powder keg of racial and ethnic tensions.

"I ask the kid," Holden said, "I ask him, 'How you guys know about that fifty thousand in cash in old man Yamaguchi's house?' "

"Uh-huh."

" 'How you know about the diamonds and all? I mean, where it's hidden and all.' "

Longo nodded.

"So I tell the kid, I tell him, 'You guys don't got the brains to pull off a job like that.' "

"Yeah."

"I say, 'Ken Yamaguchi put you guys up to the burglary, right?' "

"Yeah."

"And he just sort of shrugs, you know? I mean, I got his probation officer right there, so his balls are mine, right?"

Longo looked at Sakoda, sitting in the chair next to Holden, then at Dohi and Cheman Park standing next to the desk. The tiny office was crowded with three men; with five it was claustrophobic.

"So anyway," Holden said, sitting across the desk from the prosecutor, "make a long story short, the kid goes belly up, fingers Ken."

"He definitely says Ken Yamaguchi planned the job."

"Yeah."

"On his own father?"

"Yeah."

Longo pondered this. "When they caught the three kids, Yamaguchi wouldn't press charges, that right?"

"Yeah."

"So . . ."

"So Yamaguchi found out his son was behind it. That's what the kid says, anyway."

"When Ken was testifying a couple days ago," Longo said, "Yamaguchi started bawling for the jury. Then Ken gets teary-eyed. And the jury's eating up that father-son act. Real touching."

"Wonder what they'd think if they knew the devoted son ripped off his father?" Sakoda said.

"Why can't you just put Monty on the stand, or one of the kids who did the burglary?" Park asked.

"Not relevant," the prosecutor said. "An old burglary's got nothing to do with a murder. Unless . . ."

"The gun," Dohi said.

"Yeah. Ken testified his dad got the gun for protection, because of the burglary. But if Yamaguchi *knew* the burglary wasn't for real, if he knew it was his own son . . ."

"He wouldn't have no reason to go running out for a gun," Holden said.

"Yeah. Evidence of the burglary becomes relevant then to show that Yamaguchi didn't get the gun for protection, maybe he got it to kill Kariya. 'Course, without any registration, we can't say when he got it."

The telephone rang.

"Longo," the prosecutor growled. "Yeah ... well, good evening, Mr. Matsumoto, howya doin'?" He looked at Sakoda and grinned. "Yeah ... yeah ... sure, well, I understand how things are.... Yeah, real busy ..."

Longo spun around in his seat and looked out into the night. A blanket of sparkling multicolored lights spread out to the north, ending abruptly with the empty blackness of the San Gabriel Mountains. The river of red taillights snaking its way out of the city along the Pasadena Freeway was now thinning to a trickle.

"Yeah ... why, sure, Mr. Matsumoto, lemme tellya I understand completely.... That would be just fine.... Uh-huh, well then, I look forward to seeing you in court tomorrow.... You bet ... good night, Mr. Matsumoto."

Longo hung up the receiver and looked around the room with a grin.

"Mr. Matsumoto sends his profuse apologies. It seems there's been a terrible misunderstanding. The subpoena completely slipped his mind. Business has been very busy, and pressing personal matters ..."

"He'll be in court tomorrow?" Sakoda asked.

"Ten sharp."

"Be careful of him, Larry," Sakoda said. "Him and Hanemure, they're a couple of snakes."

Longo nodded, then looked at Park. "Okay, give it to me again, Park. This guy ... what's his name?"

"Seki," the Korean investigator said. "Patrick Mitsuo Seki. Owns a jewelry store in Honda Plaza, down in J-Town."

"Uh-huh."

"This is the first guy who's willing to talk, Larry. Down in J-Town, there's a bamboo wall, understand? Nobody's talking."

"Uh-huh."

"Until Seki. He says Matsumoto told him some stuff about the Kariya murder. And he says Yamaguchi's a pretty violent guy, has a couple stories to tell about him."

"So why's this guy ready to talk all of a sudden?"

Park shrugged.

Was he another plant? Longo wondered. Or was he the real thing, a break in the case? And if he was, would Yamaki get to him? Would he tell the prosecutor one thing, then change his story in court?

"And this guy's waiting in the coffee room?" Longo asked.

"Yeah. Want me to go get him?"

"No, gimme a couple minutes."

Longo opened a desk drawer, pulled out a small tape recorder, and opened it. A blank tape was inside. He closed the recorder and placed it behind a stack of files on the desk so that it could not be seen from the door or chairs. If this witness changed his story like the others, Longo thought, he would be ready for him.

"Greg," Longo said, "anything on the experts?"

"I think so," Dohi said. "I had a guy from Johns Hopkins, but he wanted two thousand a day, and the county will only pay twelve hundred."

"Yeah."

"But I think we've got one of the best, Larry. Dr. David Greenblatt. Harvard Medical, eighty-page résumé, one of the biggest names in the field. He doesn't even want the money, donating it to some institute."

"And he can be here when we start our rebuttal case?"

"That's the thing. I couldn't tell him exactly when we'd be putting him on, and he's got a busy schedule. It's going to be tricky."

"Okay. Any ideas yet on who Yamaki's gonna call?"

Dohi shrugged. "Could be any of five or six men in the field."

"Fer cryin' out loud . . . halfway through the case-in-chief, and the slippery son of a gun still hasn't given me the name." Longo shook his head. "Lemme tellya, I don't get it tomorrow, I'm asking Bascue for sanctions. Gimme a break."

"What kind of sanctions?" Dohi asked.

"Keep Yamaki from putting on *any* expert, he doesn't give me the name. For that matter, we still haven't had a ruling on the admissibility of Halcion evidence."

"Think he's gonna get it in, Larry?" Holden asked.

"Who knows?" Longo said. "Could go either way."

The room was silent for a moment.

"Well, guys," Longo said, "anything else?"

There was no reply.

"Okay," he said with a grin, "Monty, you and Greg take the rest of the day off."

Holden laughed. It was 9:40 in the evening.

"Park, why don't you bring Seki in here. And, Jimmy, stick around. I can use another witness to what this guy says."

Park stepped out of the office with Dohi. Holden and Sakoda stood up. Sakoda yawned and stretched.

"Give my love to Yamaki, Larry," Holden said as he walked out.

"Yeah, I'll do that," Longo said.

Longo started sorting through a stack of mail and phone messages on his desk as he waited for Seki.

A lanky figure with a slender Huck Finn face leaned in through the doorway. With his open, boyish grin and wire-frame glasses he appeared to be a high school physics teacher in his early thirties. In fact, he was forty-nine, a deputy D.A., and the man Charles Manson hated most in the world.

"Still in trial, Larry?" Stephen Kay asked.

"Huh?" Longo looked up at the man. "Oh, hi, Steve," he said absently. "Yeah, still in trial."

Kay had recently been promoted to the position of assistant director of Branch and Area Operations. From his office down the hall from Longo's, he was responsible for running the over two dozen outlying offices of the district attorney. While central branch was "where the action was," the vast majority of deputy D.A.s worked in smaller offices scattered from the shores of Malibu to the high desert of the Antelope Valley, from the sprawling San Fernando Valley to the shipyards of Long Beach.

But Kay had a second assignment, one he had taken on many years earlier: keeping Charles Manson and his family in prison.

Kay had been a twenty-seven-year-old deputy D.A. when he was assigned to serve as second chair to Vincent Bugliosi in the carnival known as the Manson trial. He emerged from the trial a man with a mission, obsessed with protecting the public from Manson and his family. In the following years he prosecuted Charles "Tex" Watson, then Bruce Davis, and finally Leslie Van Houten in a retrial after her original conviction was overturned.

Then, in 1978, a few years after the first convictions, Kay heard that Patricia Krenwinkle was up for parole; a "lifer" hearing was scheduled before the parole board in a few days. To his amazement, he also heard through the grapevine that the preliminary reports submitted to the board were favorable: Krenwinkle was reported to be a model prisoner and no longer a danger to society. Kay could not accept the idea of any of the Manson family ever being set loose on the public again. He was well aware that the charismatic Manson continued to control his followers from prison, and he refused to believe that the women who committed the atrocities at the Tate and LaBianca homes could ever be "harmless." Yet what could he do? The district attorney had no authority with the board. In fact, there was no precedent for a member of the D.A.'s Office taking part in the parole proceedings.

Kay decided he would set the precedent. He traveled to the prison where Krenwinkle's parole hearing was to be held. He reviewed the reports and recommendations submitted to the members of the board. They were surprisingly brief and completely inaccurate, glossing over the details of the grisly murders and depicting Krenwinkle as a reformed prisoner who had cut all ties with Manson.

Kay identified himself to the board, then asked for a chance to set the record straight. For the next hour, the deputy D.A. recounted the gruesome facts of the case for the amazed members, then told them of Van Houten's continuing association with Manson. When he finished, the board voted to deny Patricia Krenwinkle parole.

Stephen Kay attended forty-two more parole hearings in the following years. In only one of those was he unsuccessful: Over his objections, Steve Grogan was paroled a few years after his conviction for the murder of Shorty Shay.

Kay's crusade had not been without cost. He and his family had repeatedly been threatened. "Squeeky" Fromme screamed death threats at him, and Charles Manson on three separate occasions promised that he would die. At one parole hearing for Manson, Kay was confronted at the San Quentin gates by a mob of devil worshippers dressed in black and chanting, "Steve Kay, go back to L.A." As a result, Kay had an unlisted phone number and a secret voter registration; when he was in his car, he constantly checked for anyone following him.

But the prosecutor's work was not finished. His calendar continued to be carefully marked with the dates of every scheduled parole hearing involving Manson or a family member, dates that stretched on for years. It would never be over for Kay, not as long as he was a deputy district attorney.

Kay stepped aside as Park walked through the door. A short man in his forties, wearing spectacles and a gray suit, followed him, bowing slightly as he entered the tiny office.

Longo casually reached over to the hidden tape recorder and pushed the record button.

Kay winked as he backed out of the office. "Hang in there, guys."

Longo waved. "Say hello to Charlie."

Park stood against a wall as his charge glanced nervously around the cramped, disorderly office.

"Larry, this is Mr. Mitsuo Seki," Park announced.

"Mr. Seki," Longo said, rising to his feet.

"Mr. Longo," the man said, bowing again.

Sakoda stood. "We've met," he said as he and Seki nodded their heads to each other.

Longo pointed at the second chair. "Why don't you grab that seat right there and we'll get down to business."

Seki bowed quickly, then sat down.

"Now," Longo said, sitting again, "I understand you know the defendant in this case, Mr. Yamaguchi."

"Yes."

"And you might have some information about the case."

"Yes."

Longo nodded, studying the man carefully. "I'd like to hear what you have to say, Mr. Seki."

"As I explained to your investigator, Mr. Park, I have known

Mr. Yamaguchi and his wife for ten years. A business relationship. And also Mr. Kariya."

"Uh-huh."

"Of course, I attended the ceremony for Mr. Kariya. . . ." He looked at Sakoda, said something in Japanese.

"A wake," Sakoda said.

"*So,* yes, a wake," Seki said. "I was at Mr. Kariya's wake. There, I had a conversation with Mr. Matsumoto. I believe you know this gentleman?"

"Yeah," Longo said.

"Mr. Matsumoto told me that he spoke with Mr. Yamaguchi, before . . . before Mr. Kariya's death. He told me that Mr. Yamaguchi believed that his wife and Mr. Kariya were . . ." He searched for the word.

"Having an affair?" Longo said.

"*So,* yes, they were having an affair. Mr. Yamaguchi hired a detective to follow them. And the telephone, he . . ." Seki again spoke to Sakoda in Japanese.

"He had their telephone lines tapped," Sakoda said.

"Tapped the lines, yes. And there was a tape recorder, for the lines."

Longo wondered if Seki suspected he was also being tape-recorded.

"On the telephone," Seki continued, "Mr. Kariya asked Mrs. Yamaguchi to marry him."

"To marry him," Longo repeated.

"*So,* yes. And Mrs. Yamaguchi said she would have to think about this."

"Matsumoto said that Yamaguchi told him this."

"Yes."

Motive, Longo thought. But he was already mulling over the evidentiary problems with this testimony. Seki's story, if he decided to use it, presented the same problems as Uchida's. His testimony would constitute "double hearsay": Seki would be recounting a statement by Matsumoto about a statement by Yamaguchi. Any statement made outside of court that was offered to prove the truth of its contents was legally barred by the hearsay rule. But there were dozens of technical exceptions to the rule. The statement by Yamaguchi to Matsumoto was hearsay, but there was a clear exception for statements made by a defendant. It was also probably admissible under another exception: to show Yamaguchi's state of mind.

The problem was the second statement, by Matsumoto to Seki.

"Mr. Yamaguchi said he found them together," Seki continued. "Mr. Kariya and his wife. They were at a house they owned, upstairs in a bedroom. The detective followed them and called Mr. Yamaguchi, and he came to the house and found them. He said Mr. Kariya had his shirt off...."

There was a way to get past the second hearsay hurdle, Longo realized. When Matsumoto took the stand, he would probably deny that Yamaguchi told him about the detective and the taped phone calls. Longo could then use the "prior inconsistent statement" exception to the hearsay rule: Hearsay was admissible if it was an earlier statement by a witness that contradicted his own testimony. By denying that Yamaguchi told him about the detective, Matsumoto made it possible for Longo to get in Seki's testimony that he had.

"... then Mr. Matsumoto told me that Mr. Yamaguchi said he was going to finish Mr. Kariya."

"That's the word he used? *Finish?*"

"*So,* yes. And Mr. Matsumoto, he said to Mr. Yamaguchi, 'Maybe you should do it to him before he does it to you.'"

"Matsumoto told you that?"

"Yes."

"Uh-huh. He tell you anything else?"

Seki thought for a moment, then shook his head. "Mr. Hanemure was also at the ... wake."

"Hanemure?" Longo said.

"Yes. Mr. Hanemure and I also had a conversation at that time."

"Uh-huh."

"Mr. Hanemure told me that he advised Mr. Kariya to stay away from Mrs. Yamaguchi. He told him that Mr. Yamaguchi was a dangerous man. He—"

"Hanemure said Yamaguchi was dangerous?"

"Yes. You must realize, Mr. Longo, Mr. Yamaguchi has a reputation in Little Tokyo as a very dangerous man. He has a violent temper. I, myself, warned Mr. Kariya that it was unwise to be ... to have the affair."

"Uh-huh."

"There have been incidents. . . ."

"Incidents."

"A Mr. Nagano, a teacher at Mrs. Yamaguchi's singing club ... "

"Nagano, uh-huh."

"They stayed late many nights at the club, Mr. Nagano and Mrs. Yamaguchi. Mr. Yamaguchi, he became very angry. One evening, he came to the club with a gun and a knife. And he tried to shoot Mr. Nagano. But Mr. Nagano ran away."

"Where'd you hear this from, Mr. Seki?"

The man shrugged. "It is common knowledge in Little Tokyo."

"Uh-huh."

Longo looked at Sakoda. The investigator nodded slightly; he would find Nagano.

"There was another ... incident. Maybe two weeks before Mr. Kariya's death. Mr. Yamaguchi was with Mrs. Yamaguchi, in their house. And Mr. Yamaguchi pulled a gun from a paper bag. He threatened to kill her with it. Then he fired the gun into the ceiling, to frighten her."

"Hanemure tell you this?"

"I believe so, I am not sure."

The guy was a gold mine, Longo thought. If he was for real. The prosecutor glanced at the tape recorder.

"Mr. Yamaguchi is very good with guns," Seki said. "He takes businessmen from Japan, he takes them to a ..." He turned to Sakoda, spoke in Japanese.

"Shooting range," Sakoda said.

"*So,* yes, he takes them to a shooting range when they come to this country to visit. When Yamaguchi was young, living in Japan, he was in the military, he went to a military school."

"Uh-huh."

Seki smiled, bowed his head. "That is all I have to say."

Longo nodded back. "Well, Mr. Seki, I sure appreciate your coming forward with this information. I hope you'll be available to testify at the trial."

Seki's brow furrowed. "This is necessary?"

"Yeah, it'd be real helpful."

This time Longo was not going to let Yamaki get to his witness. Under the discovery order, Yamaki always knew who Longo's witnesses were. When Sakoda or Holden found a new witness, they summarized the interview in a report—and a copy had to be sent to Yamaki. Then Yamaki or one of his investigators went to the witness. And the witness suddenly changed his story.

Longo decided to set a trap for the lawyer. He would have Sakoda write a report summarizing the interview, then turn it over to Yamaki as required by the discovery order. But he would not turn over the tape, would not even let the lawyer know it existed. If Yamaki got to this witness too, and he changed his story . . . well, the tape would prove strong evidence of witness tampering.

It was a gamble: Longo could be held in contempt, even jailed, for violating Bascue's discovery order if the tape ever came to light. But it was worth the risk, he thought. Seki was the prosecutor's ace in the hole. And no one was going to get to him.

But was it all too easy, this sudden gift from the skies? There it was again, he thought, the paranoia. He had tried enough cases to know that trials took surprising twists, some good, some bad. Still, there was something uncomfortably familiar about the setup, something that troubled the prosecutor.

Chapter

The old interpreter repeated the question in Japanese as Hanemure, with dark, brooding eyes, watched the pugnacious deputy D.A. slowly pace along the audience railing. Yamaguchi's brother-in-law was wearing a black double-breasted suit with a green silk dress shirt and a wide floral tie. The short, powerfully built man with the black swept-back hair looked like a careful Japanese copy of George Raft.

"The last time I saw Mr. Kariya alive was at my restaurant," the interpreter repeated in English, "in Little Tokyo."

"This was after the dinner party at the Yamaguchis' restaurant?" Longo asked. "The Mitsuru Cafe?"

"*So desu,*" Mamoru Hanemure replied.

"This is so," the interpreter said.

"And this was the night Kariya was killed?"

"*Hai,*" Hanemure replied.

"Yes," the interpreter said.

"Awright, about nine that night, while Kariya was at your restaurant, you got a phone call from the defendant."

Again, the old man translated. And, again, Hanemure replied in Japanese and the answer was translated back into English.

"Yes."

"What'd Yamaguchi say?"

Slowly, the process was repeated and the answer finally translated back into English. Longo knew that Hanemure understood English perfectly well, but the man had insisted to Judge Bascue that he was not familiar enough with the language to testify "accurately."

"He was at the Mitsuru Cafe," the interpreter said. "He asked me to come to the restaurant."

"And did you go to the Mitsuru Cafe and meet Yamaguchi?"

"Yes."

Slowly, laboriously, the translations continued.

The process was frustrating to Longo. The prosecutor normally used a slow, easy pace in his questioning. If a witness was being untruthful, he increased the tempo, relying on an aggressive, rapid-fire style of interrogation to get at the truth; under fire and with not enough time to think, witnesses began to make small mistakes, then larger ones. But the plodding process of translation slowed his examination down to a crawl, giving the witness the luxury of time to consider the question and fabricate an answer.

The game continued.

"Was your sister, Mrs. Yamaguchi, at the dinner party?"

"Yes."

"Now, right after you got there, Mrs. Yamaguchi left the Mitsuru Cafe, right?"

"I believe so."

"And did the defendant say anything to you when she left?"

"He asked me if Mr. Kariya was at my restaurant, the Albatross."

"You told him he was?"

"I believe so."

"What else did he say?"

"He suspected that my sister was going to see him."

"So what'd you say?"

"I told him I would go back and keep an eye on them."

"Did you leave the Mitsuru Cafe and go back to your restaurant?"

"Yes."

"*Was* Mrs. Yamaguchi there?"

As the old man translated the question, Hanemure continued studying Longo as he would an irritating insect.

"Yes."

"With Kariya?"

"As I recall, they were at a table in the back of the restaurant."

Longo leaned against the jury railing, looked at Jimmy Sakoda sitting in his tweed sports coat at the prosecution table.

"Okay, they left your restaurant a little later, right?"

"When I closed."

"What time was that?"

"I believe that was about ten."

"They were still together?"

"I believe so."

"And did you see either of them again that night?"

"No."

"But you got a phone call from Yamaguchi."

Hanemure nodded.

"When was this?"

"I believe it was about one half hour after midnight. It was at home."

"This was a half hour or so before he shot Kariya."

"I suppose so."

"You want to tell the jury what he said to you?"

"Mr. Yamaguchi said that my sister called him to say she would be home late. She asked him to buy some cold drinks for their daughter. She told him that Mr. Kariya would give her a ride home."

"She told him she was with Kariya?"

"Yes."

"That was all she said to him?"

"Yes."

"What else did the defendant say to you?"

"He said, 'The same thing is happening, it's going to continue.'"

"Uh-huh."

"He said, 'Please take care of things.' He was going to commit suicide."

"Suicide," Longo repeated. "You talk with a Detective Holden couple of hours after the shooting?"

"Yes."

"You told him about this statement, 'The same thing is happening, take care of things'?"

"I believe so."

"But you never mentioned anything about him saying he was going to commit suicide, did you?"

Hanemure continued to watch the prosecutor as the interpeter repeated the question in Japanese.

"Maybe, maybe not. I am not sure."

"You also had a little chat with an investigator from the D.A.'s Office, Mr. Sakoda, right?"

"Yes."

"But, again, you never said anything about suicide, did you?"

"I do not recall."

"After talking with Detective Holden and Mr. Sakoda, you had a little powwow with Mr. Yamaki over there, didn't you?"

The interpeter looked puzzled. "Powwow?" he repeated to the prosecutor.

"A get-together, a meeting, you had a meeting with Yamaki, right?"

The man bowed slightly, then translated.

"So desu."

Longo suddenly pointed a finger at Hanemure. "And it was *after* you talked with Yamaki," he growled, "that you first came up with this story about a suicide!"

Hanemure glanced across the courtroom at the defense lawyer seated at the counsel table. It was the first time his eyes had left Longo since he had taken the witness stand.

Longo waited for the objection from Yamaki, the righteously indignant protest. But none came.

Hanemure quickly looked back at the prosecutor. When the translation was finished, he answered.

"I do not believe this is so," the old man translated.

"How many times have you had conversations with Yamaguchi's lawyer before testifying here today?"

"I am not certain. Maybe three."

"You talk to Yamaki yesterday?"

"I believe so."

Longo smiled. He would not ask the next question, "What did Mr. Yamaki tell you to say today in court?" He recognized the classic defense trap. Yamaki would have prepared the witness to reply, "He told me to tell the truth."

"You know a guy named Uchida?"

"I believe I met Mr. Uchida the evening after Mr. Kariya's death."

"At the Mitsuru Cafe?"

"Yes."

"You had a conversation with Uchida and a man named Matsumoto, right?"

"There was a conversation."

"Didn't you tell Uchida that Yamaguchi told you on the phone he couldn't be patient any longer, that he was going to *finish* Kariya?"

Hanemure shook his head. "No, I never said this."

"You never told him that?"

"I never said this."

"Mr. Hanemure, you ever tell anyone that they should stay away from Yamaguchi, that he was a dangerous man?"

"I never said this."

Longo nodded silently. He knew Hanemure would deny it, of course. But, like so many questions, the question had a hidden purpose. Hanemure's denial set up the later admission of Seki's testimony as a "prior inconsistent statement" exception to the hearsay rule.

"Didn't you tell Uchida that Yamaguchi shot a gun at your sister a couple weeks earlier, to scare her?"

"No. I believe I mentioned something about Mr. Yamaguchi *showing* a gun to her, not shooting it. The gun was in a paper bag. And seeing the gun scared her."

Longo looked at the jury, then back at Hanemure.

"He was just showing a gun to his wife, for no reason?"

"He was thanking her for a good life. He was going to kill himself with the gun."

"Uh-huh. And he just wanted to give his wife a little preview, show her how he was going to do it?"

"I cannot say."

It was frustrating, Longo thought as he walked back to his seat. He was sure that the suicide story came from Yamaki, to win sympathy from the jury and to show irrational behavior—behavior that he would later show was caused by Halcion. But the translation process shielded Hanemure from effective cross-examination.

Still, the prosecutor had accomplished what he wanted. The jury heard the facts, even if denied; it was a trial axiom that the question could be as effective as the answer. He had also laid the foundation for getting the testimony of both Uchida and Seki over the hearsay hurdle as prior inconsistent statements. And he had taken the first step in showing the jury a pattern of witnesses changing their testimony.

"Nothing further," Longo said as he sat down.

"Mr. Yamaki?" Judge Bascue said.

The defense lawyer rose and approached the podium. He smiled at the jury, then at Hanemure.

"Mr. Hanemure—"

"Oh, one more thing," Longo said, jumping up.

Yamaki's smile broadened. He bowed facetiously toward the prosecutor.

"You say Yamaguchi told his wife he was going to kill himself with the gun in the paper bag?" Longo asked.

"Yes."

"And then he told you a couple weeks later he was going to shoot himself?"

"Yes."

Longo paused. "Yamaguchi never *did* commit suicide, did he?"

Yamaki shook his head in amusement as the question was translated. Hanemure did not answer.

Longo sat down.

"Mr. Hanemure," Yamaki continued patiently, "what time did you say it was when you spoke with Detective Holden?"

"It was about three."

"Three. So is it fair to say that you were very tired?"

"Yes."

"I assume you were awakened to come to the station for questioning?"

"Yes."

"And I assume you were also very upset, learning about Mr. Kariya's death, and Mr. Yamaguchi's involvement?"

"This is so."

"Is it possible, Mr. Hanemure, that your mind was not, shall we say, fully alert when you spoke with Detective Holden?"

"This is so."

"Then it is possible you neglected to mention Mr. Yamaguchi's comment about committing suicide?"

"It is possible."

"Mr. Hanemure, have you ever known your brother-in-law to threaten suicide before?"

"No. This is not in his character."

"Something happened to change his . . . character?"

"Objection, judge," Longo said. Yamaki was steering it toward Halcion. Until Bascue ruled that it was admissible, no mention could be made of it in front of the jury.

"Sustained," Bascue said.

Yamaki smiled, looked down at his notes on the podium for a moment.

"This Mr. Uchida, he was a friend of Mr. Kariya, is that not so?"

"Yes."

"And did you ever tell anyone that Mr. Yamaguchi said he was going to *finish* Mr. Kariya?"

"I never said this."

"Now," Yamaki said, looking at Longo, "the prosecutor has suggested that Mr. Yamaguchi is a dangerous person. Would you consider him dangerous?"

"No. Mr. Yamaguchi is a quiet, very peaceful man."

Longo felt his heart suddenly quicken. Yamaki had just made another error. He had asked if Yamaguchi was a dangerous man, and Hanemure had replied that he was "peaceful." In doing this, the lawyer had again "opened the door": Longo could now offer evidence to contradict this. If he could find Nagano, the singing teacher, he could give the jury evidence of the defendant's violent temper, evidence that would otherwise be inadmissible.

"I see. And how would you characterize your sister's marriage to Mr. Yamaguchi?"

"They were very happy together. They were a good couple. It was a textbook marriage."

"Mr. and Mrs. Yamaguchi were very happy, then, until the last month before the shooting incident?"

"Yes."

"Now, it was in the last month that Mr. Yamaguchi began to

suspect that his wife, your sister, was having an affair with Mr. Ka-riya?"

"Yes."

"How would you describe his appearance during this time, his manner?"

"He seemed very upset, very worried."

"Did he talk to you about any problems he was having because of this worry?"

"Mr. Yamaguchi told me that his nerves were . . ."

The interpeter stopped, asked Hanemure something, then continued.

". . . raw. His nerves were raw. He was having trouble sleeping."

"He was having trouble sleeping?" Yamaki repeated.

The old man translated the question into Japanese.

As Hanemure answered in Japanese, Sakoda suddenly leaned toward Longo. "He's saying Yamaguchi started taking some sleeping pills," he whispered.

"He told me that—"

Longo rose from his chair to object.

"Withdraw the question, your honor," Yamaki said, looking at Sakoda with a vague smile.

Cute trick, Longo thought to himself. The son of a gun would have slipped in testimony that Yamaguchi took Halcion before the judge had a chance to rule it was inadmissible. Thank God for Sakoda.

He glanced again at the name on the slip of paper lying in front of him. "Dr. Martin B. Scharf," it read. "Director, Center for Sleep Disorders, Mercy Hospital, Cincinnati."

Yamaki had finally turned over the name of his expert witness. And the defense was now clear: Halcion.

"Mr. Hanemure," Yamaki continued, "I would like to direct your attention to the telephone call from Mr. Yamaguchi, the one from his home a half hour before the shooting incident."

"Yes."

"You testified that Mr. Yamaguchi said, 'The same thing is happening, it's going to continue'?"

"Yes. He was referring to my sister's affair with Mr. Kariya."

"Then Mr. Yamaguchi said, 'Please take care of things'?"

"Yes."

"What did you understand this to mean?"

"He was going to kill himself."

"And what did you say?"

"I said, 'Don't do anything foolish.' "

"I see." Yamaki looked at the jurors. "Did Mr. Yamaguchi sound . . . unusual on the phone?"

"He sounded very tired, disoriented. He was a very different man."

"A very different man," Yamaki repeated, speaking toward the jury. "Thank you, no further questions."

Yamaki walked back to his seat as Longo stood up to begin redirect examination.

"I got this problem, Mr. Hanemure," the prosecutor said, a puzzled look on his face. "I mean, there's something I just can't figure."

Longo walked over to the jury box, seemingly lost in thought.

"You and Yamaguchi, you're pretty close, right? I mean, you're his brother-in-law, he comes to you with his problems?"

"We are friends."

"You're the guy he calls at twelve-thirty in the morning, right?"

"He called me."

"And he tells you he's gonna knock himself off."

"Yes."

"See, the thing I can't figure . . . How come you didn't try to talk him out of it?"

Hanemure continued looking at Longo as the old man translated the question. He answered calmly in Japanese.

"I said, 'Don't do anything foolish.' "

"That's it? Just, 'Don't do anything foolish'?"

"Mr. Yamaguchi hung up the telephone before I could say anything more."

Longo nodded, apparently considering this answer. "And then you just calmly went to bed," he said.

Hanemure said nothing.

"I mean, you said you got woke up by the cops a couple hours later, went down to the police station all sleepy, right?"

"Yes."

"See, that's what I don't get," the prosecutor said, shaking his head slowly as if confused. "Your good buddy, he says he's gonna blow his brains out...and you don't go over and try to *stop* him? You just calmly go to sleep?"

Hanemure looked quickly at Yamaki as the question was translated, then back at Longo.

"See what I mean?" Longo said. "Doesn't figure, does it?"

"Objection, your honor," Yamaki said.

"Sustained."

"Nothing further," Longo said.

The courtroom was silent as the prosecutor returned to his seat.

"You are excused," Judge Bascue said to the witness.

Hanemure glanced uncertainly at Yamaki, then stepped down from the witness chair.

"Ladies and gentlemen," the judge said, "the court has one small matter to dispose of, a case left over from this morning's calendar. It will just take a minute. Please feel free to stand up and stretch while we handle the matter."

Longo looked back, saw Harry Stein* sitting in the front row. The Friel* case. Stein, as he always did, had called the court and informed the clerk that he would be late. He often got away with it; the tiny, shriveled-up old lawyer was a contributor to the reelection campaigns of many judges on the criminal bench. Judge Bascue, however, was not one of those judges.

"People versus Friel," Bascue announced. He looked at his bailiff. "Please bring in the defendant."

Longo shuffled through the case files scattered across the prosecution table, half buried among the transcripts, documents, and photographs from the Yamaguchi trial. Finally he found the Friel file. He quickly scanned the summary sheet on the inside cover, then recalled the facts.

It was another of Los Angeles's recurrent stalker cases, but with a twist. The victim who was being followed was a very attractive forty-eight-year-old woman. The enamored defendant was a twenty-three-year-old from a wealthy family. And a woman.

The media had immediately dubbed the Friel case a lesbian "fatal attraction."

The story was a sad one, with an ironic beginning: Marlene Friel's own stepsister had been murdered by a stalker. Devastated by the loss, Friel turned for sympathy to the older woman, a design consultant for her father. The woman took pity on Friel, consoling the distraught girl and letting her cry on her shoulder. Grief and compassion soon turned to sexual attraction. The two women embarked on a passionate affair.

After four discreet liaisons at her house, however, the older woman called the relationship off. It had been a mistake, she explained; she had never done this before and she was uncomfortable with it.

But Friel could not let go. For the next year she constantly followed her former lover, shadowing her every movement and harassing her male friends. At one point, the victim called a plumber because of noises she was hearing beneath her floor. When the plumber crawled underneath the house to investigate, he found blankets, a pillow, and woman's clothing.

Events reached a climax one evening when the woman threw a dinner party for a group of friends. In the middle of the dinner she heard a sound at the front door and stepped out into the foyer. Friel was standing just inside the front door, a revolver in her hand. The woman ran screaming into the dining room. When Friel threatened her guests with the gun, they fled through the back door. A police SWAT team quickly arrived on the scene and surrounded the house. After a ten-hour standoff, Friel finally surrendered.

The steel door swung open and the bailiff stepped out alone. "Miss-out, your honor," he said.

Bascue sighed. "Mr. Stein, it would seem that the sheriff's department has once again misplaced one of our defendants. We will have to continue the case. What is your pleasure?"

"Three months, your honor?" the lawyer said with his patented ingratiating smile.

"No way," Longo growled. "This case's already been stalled for over a year."

"It is not my fault that Ms. Friel is not here today," the lawyer said indignantly.

"No, but you were gonna ask for a continuance anyway."

Stein was an expert at delaying cases until witnesses tired of coming to court and waiting for hours in crowded hallways. When the delays ran out, he became a "cop-out artist." One thing was certain: With Stein as counsel, the Friel case would never go to trial. If the lawyer ever had to actually try a case, it was said, he would not know at which table to sit.

Longo respected defense lawyers who fought for their clients. He had nothing but contempt for a man like Stein who hid behind lies, practicing law like a used car salesman and then selling out his defendants when it finally came time to strap on the guns. The prosecutor found it difficult to keep his assessment of the merits of a case from being influenced by his distaste for the lawyer.

"Three months *is* a bit long, Mr. Stein."

"Your honor, I appreciate that fact, and I understand Mr. Longo's concern. I, too, am anxious that this matter be resolved in the most expedient—"

Longo snorted.

There were titters from the jury. Bascue sighed again.

Stein ignored the prosecutor. "If the court could see my trial calendar for the coming months . . ."

"I understand, Mr. Stein," Bascue said. "Can we all agree to a continuance of, say, thirty days?"

"Your honor," Stein said, "would *two* months be acceptable? I'm sure that Mr. Longo and I can come to an acceptable resolution of this matter."

"Mr. Longo?"

"The People have a right to speedy trial too, judge," Longo said. "And, yeah, I got an acceptable resolution for Mr. Stein . . . so long as his client pleads straight up."

Bascue looked at the calendar on the wall behind his clerk's desk. "Forty-five days," he said. "And this will have to be the last continuance, Mr. Stein."

"I understand, your honor," the lawyer said.

"Time for speedy trial is waived?"

"Time is waived, your honor."

"Mr. Longo, call your next witness."

"Kohei Matsumoto," the prosecutor announced. He dug through the jungle of legal pads on the table as Stein and the bailiff left the courtroom. Matsumoto was the buddy of Yamaguchi and Hanemure who had evaded Longo's investigators for weeks.

A file fell off the table, spilling its contents on the floor in front of the jury. He and Sakoda began collecting the paperwork as a short, stocky man in his early forties stepped into the courtroom. The man was wearing a double-breasted gray-striped suit with a flashy red tie, another Asian caricature of a thirties gangster.

The man glanced at the audience of Japanese men and women, bowed slightly several times, then walked through the swinging gates. He bowed again as he walked past the jury, then took the oath and sat down in the witness chair.

"Mr. Matsumoto," Longo said, "you're a friend of the defendant in this case, Kazuhiko Yamaguchi, right?"

The elderly interpeter repeated the question in Japanese. Matsumoto, it seemed, had also asked for help in translation.

"*Hai,*" Matsumoto said.

"Yes," the interpeter said.

"In fact, a pretty close friend?"

"Yes."

"Awright, you recall Yamaguchi telling you that he hired a detective to follow Kariya and Mrs. Yamaguchi?"

"No."

"You say he didn't tell you that?"

"He did not."

"Uh-huh. And did Yamaguchi tell you that he taped phone calls between Kariya and Mrs. Yamaguchi?"

"No."

Longo nodded silently. "You knew Kariya?"

"Yes."

"Okay, the evening after Yamaguchi shot Kariya, you were at a get-together—a gathering—at the Mitsuru Cafe, right?"

"Yes."

"And during that evening, you had a talk with a guy by the name of Takeshi Uchida?"

"Yes."

"And during part of this conversation, a friend of yours, guy named Mamoru Hanemure, he joined in, right?"

"Yes."

"Awright, you recall telling Uchida that Yamaguchi said he had a detective following Kariya and his wife?"

"I did not say this."

"Did you tell Uchida that Yamaguchi said he taped phone calls between the two?"

"No."

Longo looked at the jurors as he walked away from the witness box. Then he turned and looked back at Matsumoto.

"So if Uchida takes the stand here and says you *did* tell him that, why, he'd be a darned liar, right?"

"He would be mistaken."

"Mistaken. And I don't guess anything was said about Yamaguchi telling you he was going to *finish* Kariya, either."

"I did not hear this."

"Uh-huh. You ever talk with your buddy, Hanemure, about this case?"

"We have discussed the matter."

"You talk with him about what you guys were going to testify to?"

"I do not recall such a conversation."

"Didn't try to get your stories together?"

"Objection, your honor," Yamaki said, rising to his feet. "Mr. Longo persists in trying to impeach his own witnesses."

"There's no rule against that," Longo said.

"There is a rule against cross-examining your own witnesses," Yamaki said. "I have been very tolerant, your honor, but Mr. Longo continues to ask leading questions."

"It's pretty obvious I got a hostile witness here, judge," the prosecutor said.

A "leading question" was one that suggested an answer and was normally permissible only on cross-examination. Thus, on direct examination, a lawyer was limited to asking "What time did you arrive?" On cross he could ask "Isn't it a fact that you arrived at three-oh-seven P.M.?" The Evidence Code contained an exception, however, where the witness was clearly hostile. In such cases, the lawyer could ask his questions as if it were cross-examination, even though he had called the witness himself.

"The witness would appear to be hostile, Mr. Yamaki," Bascue said.

The defense lawyer nodded graciously, then sat down.

"You got an answer to that last question, Matsumoto?"

"Please repeat the question," the old man in the baggy suit translated. "I do not understand."

The heck you don't, Longo thought.

"Did you and Hanemure get your stories together before coming here to testify?"

"No."

"Didn't I see you and Hanemure sitting together out in the hallway this morning?"

"We are friends, as I have said."

"Uh-huh. How many times you talk with Mr. Yamaki over there before testifying?"

Matsumoto looked briefly at the seated lawyer, then back at Longo.

"Two times. Maybe three."

"Uh-huh."

"I told him what I knew, he told me to tell the truth."

"I didn't ask a question, Mr. Matsumoto."

"I am sorry."

"Did Mr. Yamaki tell you what the other witnesses were going to say?"

"No."

"You sure, Mr. Matsumoto, that maybe the two of you didn't sit around his office and go over reports from the D.A.'s Office that mentioned your name?"

"This did not happen."

Longo started sifting through the piles of paper on the counsel table. Another file fell to the floor. "Gimme a second, judge," he said.

Yamaki smiled at the jurors, shaking his head once again in continued amusement at the loutish prosecutor's antics.

"Awright," Longo said triumphantly, holding up a document. It was an affidavit signed by Matsumoto that Yamaki had turned over that morning.

Longo approached the witness, handed him the affidavit. "That your signature?"

Matsumoto studied the affidavit for a moment.

"Yes."

"You sign that for Yamaki?"

"He requested it."

"Look at paragraph number five. You say there that you didn't tell Uchida about Yamaguchi saying he was gonna finish Kariya."

"Yes."

"See, I'm confused. I mean, how'd you *know* Uchida said you told him that?"

"I do not understand the question."

"You say Yamaki never told you what other witnesses said. You guys just talked about what *you* heard and saw."

"Yes."

"But then you sign an affidavit, you swear that what Uchida is telling our investigator here, Jimmy Sakoda, is flat-out wrong. I don't get it: How did you *know* Uchida told Sakoda that?"

"When Mr. Sakoda interviewed me, he asked me about the statement. He told me then about Mr. Uchida's statement."

"Uh-huh, so you're saying Sakoda here told you what Uchida said?"

"Yes."

"You didn't learn about it from a D.A.'s report."

"This is correct."

"Want to take a closer look at that affidavit, Mr. Matsumoto?"

"I do not understand."

"Read a little further. In there, under oath, you say that you read Sakoda's report about your statement to Uchida, and that it's not true."

Matsumoto began reading the affidavit again.

"You need any help from the interpeter reading that?" Longo asked.

The witness looked up at Longo, then at Yamaki, finally at Judge Bascue.

"You understand what perjury is, Mr. Matsumoto?" Longo said.

The witness looked back at Longo. "You are saying I will be prosecuted."

"Have you been lying here?"

"There was one thing I misunderstood."

"Uh-huh."

"I believe there was a report."

"Uh-huh."

"Mr. Sakoda's report, about Mr. Uchida."

"And who was it that gave you a copy of this report?"

"Mr. Yamaki."

Longo nodded his head. "No further questions."

Yamaki rose slowly, again smiling and shaking his head in amusement.

"Mr. Matsumoto, the fact is, you and I ran into each other at the Mitsuru Cafe, isn't that so?"

"Yes."

"And we talked, and I mentioned Uchida's statement."

"Yes."

"And I showed you the report and asked you if that was really what you told Mr. Uchida, isn't that so?"

"Yes."

"And you denied ever telling Mr. Uchida that Mr. Yamaguchi said he was going to kill Mr. Kariya."

"Yes."

"And I asked you to put this into an affidavit."

"Yes."

Yamaki smiled at the jurors. "There was nothing sinister about any of this, was there?"

"No."

"Did I ever *tell* you what to say here in court?"

"No."

Yamaki put one hand on the podium, his other casually in his front pants pocket.

"By the way, Mr. Longo pointed out that you are a friend of Mr. Yamaguchi. You were also a friend of Mr. Kariya, were you not?"

"Yes."

"Mr. Matsumoto, one last thing. I would like to be very clear. Did Mr. Yamaguchi ever tell you that he was going to finish Mr. Kariya?"

"No."

"Did you ever tell Mr. Uchida—or anyone—that he said this?"

"No."

"Thank you," Yamaki said, returning to his seat. "No further questions, your honor."

"Mr. Matsumoto," Longo said, standing up, "who typed out the affidavit?"

"I do not understand."

"Well, Mr. Yamaki over there says he asked you to put your denial in an affidavit."

"Yes."

"Was that affidavit typed on your typewriter, or was it done at Mr. Yamaki's office?"

"I told him what happened. He wrote the affidavit, and I read it and I signed it."

"Uh-huh. And this was based on what you told him at the Mitsuru Cafe?"

"Yes."

"When you just happened to run into him there."

"Yes."

"Just coincidence."

"As you say, coincidence."

"And he just happened to have a copy of the Uchida report on him at the time."

"It seems so."

"Nothing further."

"Call your next witness," Bascue said.

As Matsumoto stepped down from the witness stand, Longo again began shuffling through the chaos on the counsel table. He had set up Hanemure and Matsumoto, he thought as he looked for another report. Now it was time to knock them down.

"Takeshi Uchida," he said.

Chapter

21

"She was pretty loud, wasn't she, criticizing her husband in front of everybody?"

"I don't know if I would characterize it that way."

"She was blaming Yamaguchi for double booking a group from Japan for the variety show, right?"

"I believe Mrs. Yamaguchi made some comments to that effect."

"And didn't Kariya join in?"

"Mr. Kariya made some comments."

"Wasn't there some heated talk by Kariya about how Yamaguchi's show was a failure, and his, Kariya's, was a big success?"

"I wouldn't call it 'heated.'"

"Didn't Kariya blame Yamaguchi for the failure?"

"He may have said something to that effect."

Longo studied the small middle-aged man. Uchida had a round face, gray hair, baggy eyes, thick eyeglasses, and a sickly mustache.

And he had a habit of avoiding the prosecutor's eyes.

Longo knew that the testimony was not going to go well as soon as Uchida asked Judge Bascue for an interpeter. Two days earlier, the prosecutor had talked with Uchida and confirmed that he would not need one. Then, after Longo called him to the stand and loudly announced to the judge that an interpeter would not be needed, Uchida calmly sat down and said that this was not true; as with the others, he would need the assistance of a translator.

"Mr. Uchida, didn't you hear Kariya tell Yamaguchi, in front of the guy's friends and associates, that he screwed up the booking for the show?"

"I recall some mention of a mistake."

"And wasn't Yamaguchi angry at this public humiliation by his wife and Kariya?"

"It is difficult to say."

"Uh-huh." Longo pointed to Sakoda, seated at the prosecution table. "You recall talking with my investigator here, Mr. Sakoda?"

"Yes."

"And you told him that Yamaguchi's face was flushed, and he was trying to control his anger."

"I doubt that I said that."

With a sick feeling, Longo realized that Yamaki had gotten to another of his witnesses.

"Awright, you ran into Kariya the next day, at the Albatross restaurant, right?"

"Yes."

"Kariya was pretty unhappy with Yamaguchi, wasn't he?"

"I believe so."

"Why was that?"

"I believe he said that Mr. Yamaguchi tried to fire him."

"This was after he humiliated Yamaguchi at the Mitsuru Cafe?"

"It was after the incident we spoke of."

"But Mrs. Yamaguchi kept him from being fired."

"I could not say."

"Yeah." Longo walked to the counsel table. "Yamaguchi hired Kariya to do odd jobs around the restaurant, to help out around the place, right?"

"I am not certain of their arrangement."

"Isn't it a fact that Kariya started interfering with Yamaguchi's role, edging him out as producer of the variety shows?"

"I am not aware of this."

Longo picked up a small, white card from the confusion of paper covering the counsel table. He held it up toward Judge Bascue.

"People's, uh . . ."

"It will be marked People's exhibit number seven," Bascue said patiently.

Longo approached Uchida and handed him the card.

"Recognize it?"

Uchida studied the card carefully. "Yes."

"It's your buddy Kariya's business card, right?"

"It would appear so."

"And what does it say?"

"Mitsuru Enterprises, Incorporated."

"And below that?"

"Genji Kariya, Producer."

"He had those printed up himself, didn't he? Without Yamaguchi's permission?"

"I could not say."

Longo stepped back from the witness stand, walked over to the counsel table. He whispered something to Sakoda, then sat down on the edge of the table, facing the jury. Sakoda got up and walked out of the courtroom.

"Let's talk about the gathering the night after the shooting, the wake."

"Yes."

"At some point, you were talking with your buddy, Matsumoto, right? Outside of the Mitsuru Cafe?"

"Yes."

"Okay, and Matsumoto tells you that he talked with Yamaguchi a couple days before the shooting, right?"

"I believe he may have said something like that."

"And Yamaguchi says to him, 'I'm gonna *finish* Kariya,' right?"

"Would you repeat the question?"

"Didn't Matsumoto tell you outside the cafe that Yamaguchi said he was gonna finish Kariya?"

"Outside the cafe?"

"Anywhere."

"I do not believe so."

"Didn't you tell Sakoda he said that?"

Uchida shifted in his seat. "Would you repeat the question?"

"Didn't you tell Sakoda that? Matsumoto told you Yamaguchi said he was gonna finish Kariya?"

"If I said that, I was mistaken."

"Mistaken."

"Yes."

"Awright, didn't Matsumoto also tell you that Yamaguchi hired a detective to follow his wife and Kariya?"

"I am not certain. There may have been something said to that effect."

"And that he taped phone conversations between his wife and Kariya?"

"It is possible. I do not recall."

"And in one of the calls, Kariya asked her to marry him."

"I do not recall this. It is possible, but I do not recall."

The slippery son of a gun was playing it very cute, Longo thought. The answers were vague, noncommittal. He was giving the prosecutor nothing, yet stopping just short of outright provable perjury. Someone had coached Uchida very carefully.

"Okay, now after you and Matsumoto talk, a guy named Mamoru Hanemure walks over, and your buddy introduces him to you, right?"

"Yes."

"Says he's Yamaguchi's brother-in-law?"

"I believe that was mentioned."

"Now, didn't this guy Hanemure say that Yamaguchi called him on the phone the night before?"

"He may have mentioned that."

"Just before the shooting?"

"It is possible."

"Uh-huh. And didn't Hanemure tell you guys that Yamaguchi said he'd been patient long enough, he was gonna take care of the matter himself?"

"I cannot recall the exact words."

"You recall him telling you that Yamaguchi then said, 'The same thing is happening, I'm gonna finish Kariya, please take care of things'?"

"Could you repeat the question?"

"He tells you that Yamaguchi says, 'The same thing is happening, I'm gonna finish Kariya, please take care of things.'"

Uchida shook his head slowly, answered again in Japanese.

"I do not recall Mr. Hanemure saying that Mr. Yamaguchi was going to finish Mr. Kariya," the interpeter repeated.

"Do you recall this: Matsumoto said that Yamaguchi told him the same thing he told Hanemure, that he was gonna finish Kariya?"

"I do not recall this."

Longo studied Uchida for a moment. He would have to put Sakoda on the stand to testify that Uchida *had* told him about the statements. But Sakoda was also going to testify to earlier statements made directly to him by Hanemure and Matsumoto. Now it would be his word against that of three respectable businessmen. And, as Yamaki would be quick to point out, Sakoda was working with the prosecutor to convict Yamaguchi.

But Longo had his ace in the hole: Mitsuo Seki. And if anyone got to Seki, he had the tape recording to confirm his story—and a possible pattern of witness tampering.

"I'm gonna ask you one more time, Uchida," Longo growled, walking back to his seat. "Did you hear either of those men tell you that Yamaguchi said he was gonna finish Kariya?"

"I do not recall this."

Longo nodded slowly, glowering at the witness. Then he sat down.

"Mr. Yamaki?" Judge Bascue said.

The defense lawyer stood. "Good afternoon, Mr. Uchida," he said with a smile.

"Good afternoon."

"I understand that you were a close friend of the deceased, Mr. Kariya."

"Yes."

"I see." Yamaki stood in an easy stance behind the podium, his hands resting on the edges. "Now, Mr. Longo seems to think statements were made about 'finishing' Mr. Kariya."

"I believe Mr. Longo is mistaken."

"Yes. Did either Mr. Hanemure or Mr. Matsumoto ever use the word 'finish'?"

"No."

"Did *you* ever use that word in talking with Mr. Sakoda or anyone else?"

"No."

"In fact, Mr. Uchida, you were speaking to Mr. Sakoda in Japanese, were you not?"

"Some of the conversation was in Japanese."

"And when you were talking with Mr. Hanemure and Mr. Matsumoto, you were speaking in Japanese."

"I believe so."

"Now, Mr. Longo seems to think that the words used were, 'I'm going to finish him.' What were the actual Japanese words you used?"

"*Yarukara ato'o.*"

"And how would you translate these words?"

"It is difficult to translate. It is a vague expression. It can mean many things, depending upon the context in which it is used."

"Can you give us a rough translation?"

"It can mean, 'I will do it.' "

"I will do it?"

"Yes."

"And does the context change the meaning?"

"Yes. When Mr. Yamaguchi says, 'I have been patient long enough, I am going to handle the matter myself, please take care of things' ... well, if you believe this means he is going to harm Mr. Kariya, then the words *yarukara ato'o* can mean 'I will finish him' or 'I will kill him.' "

"So if Mr. Sakoda heard the words *yarukara ato'o*, knowing that Mr. Yamaguchi did, in fact, later kill Mr. Kariya ... he could take the words to mean 'I will finish him'?"

"I believe so."

"Suppose there was a *different* context, Mr. Uchida?"

"Yes?"

"If you knew that Mr. Yamaguchi had recently attempted suicide, what could the words *yarukara ato'o* mean?"

"It could mean, 'I will finish myself.' "

" 'I will commit suicide.' "

"Yes."

Yamaki glanced at the jury, then at Longo.

The prosecutor was studying Uchida. Mighty smooth testimony for cross-examination, he thought. A regular dog-and-pony show.

"Mr. Uchida, you were interrogated by Mr. Longo, were you not?"

"Yes."

"In his office?"

"Yes."

"He questioned you about the statements?"

"Yes."

"And did you tell him that you were not clear in your recollection of the events?"

"Yes."

"What did Mr. Longo say to this?"

"He became angry. He said I *must* be sure, I must act like I'm sure when I testify. He said I must never say maybe, I must always say yes or no."

Longo leaned back in his chair, scowling darkly at Uchida. He was aware that some of the jurors were now looking at him rather than at the witness.

"Did you feel he was trying to tell you how to testify?"

"Yes, it was my feeling that I was being forced to testify as he wished."

"Gimme a break," Longo muttered.

Bascue frowned. "Mr. Longo..."

"That's all right, your honor," Yamaki said, smiling, "I have nothing further."

Longo sprang to his feet as the defense lawyer walked back to his chair. He stepped toward the witness.

"Uchida—"

"Oh, one more thing," Yamaki said. "Did you ask Mr. Longo about using an interpreter?"

"Yes. He told me not to use one."

"Thank you." Yamaki sat down.

"Uchida," Longo growled, "you ever talk with Yamaki over there, before today?"

Uchida glanced at the defense lawyer, then back at Longo. "Yes."

"This was *after* you talked with my investigator, Jimmy Sakoda?"

"I believe so."

"You and Yamaki sat down and talked about this case, right?"

"He asked me what I saw, what I heard."

"Uh-huh. And you talked about what you were gonna testify about here today?"

"We . . . discussed what I saw and what I heard."

"And those Japanese words you said . . . What were they?"

"Yarukara ato'o."

"Yeah. You guys talk about that too?"

"I believe we discussed the words."

"Yeah. And he tells you, if Yamaguchi attempted suicide recently, why, the words could mean he's gonna do it again?"

Uchida's gaze was fixed on the clock in the back of the courtroom. "In view of the attempted suicide, the words could take on that meaning."

"Did Hanemure ever mention suicide?"

"I do not recall it."

"Matsumoto ever mention suicide?"

"I do not recall it."

"In fact, the only person who ever mentioned suicide was Yamaki, right?"

"I . . . do not recall."

"He *did* tell you Yamaguchi attempted suicide some time before making this statement?"

"I believe so."

"What if I tell you Yamaguchi *never* attempted suicide?"

Uchida continued his study of the courtroom, averting Longo's glare.

"I do not understand your question."

"Yamaguchi never attempted suicide."

"I see."

"Now, those words still mean he's gonna knock himself off?"

"I could not say."

"If the context was, Yamaguchi's known to be a violent man, what do those words—"

"Objection," Yamaki said.

Judge Bascue nodded. "Sustained."

The entrance door opened and a small Japanese man in an olive suit stepped in with Sakoda. The two men stood at the rear of the audience.

"Uchida," Longo said, "you know what perjury is?"

"Yes."

"Uh-huh. See that guy standing in the back there? The one next to my investigator?"

Uchida looked toward the back of the courtroom. The eyes of the jury and the audience swung to the back.

"Yes."

"Recognize him?"

"I believe I have seen him before."

"That's Deputy D.A. Lew Ito. He was in my office when you and me, we had our little chat, remember?"

Uchida nodded silently.

"Now . . . Did I ever tell you what to testify to?"

Uchida coughed lightly. "Could you please repeat the question?"

"Did I ever tell you what to say?"

"I felt pressured."

"Did I ever tell you what to say?"

"Maybe not in words." Uchida looked down at his hands crossed in his lap. "But I felt pressured."

"Did I tell you that you couldn't use an interpreter?"

"I believe you said that I did not need one."

"From talking with me, in English, I said you probably wouldn't need a translator, right?"

Uchida said nothing.

"And you agreed?"

Uchida said nothing.

"By the way," Longo said, walking toward his chair, "you knew Yamaki before this case, didn't you?"

"I do not understand."

"Yamaki was *your* lawyer at one time, wasn't he?"

Uchida quickly looked across the room at the defense lawyer.

"Objection, your honor," Yamaki said, rising quickly to his feet. "This is irrelevant to the case."

"The heck it is," Longo said.

Judge Bascue leaned toward the witness, whispered something. Uchida whispered back. The judge pondered for a moment.

"He may answer," Bascue said finally. "But that is all. The reason *why* Mr. Yamaki represented the witness is not relevant."

"Well?" Longo asked Uchida.

"Mr. Yamaki was my lawyer."

"Nothing further, judge."

"Mr. Yamaki?" Bascue asked.

The lawyer shook his head.

"Very well," the judge said. He looked at the clock, then at the jury. "Ladies and gentlemen, I think this would be a good time to recess."

Bascue stepped down from the bench and disappeared into chambers. The jurors stood up and began to file out. The courtroom was quickly filled with a low roar as the audience of Japanese spectators was released from its silence.

Longo began piling the files and papers into a cardboard box as Sakoda walked up.

"Yamaki's getting personal, huh, Larry?"

"Old trick," Longo said. "Attack the prosecutor, shift the focus away from the defendant."

Longo stacked the box on top of another cardboard box resting on a luggage cart, then wheeled it out of the courtroom. Sakoda followed.

The two men walked down the hallway toward the elevators, Longo lost in thought.

"They got to Uchida," Sakoda said.

"Yeah."

"Well, Larry, I can testify to what these guys told me before they changed their stories."

"Yeah."

"And we still got Seki and Nagano."

"Yeah."

The doors opened. The two men squeezed into the crowded elevator.

"Hey, Larry," a voice said from the back.

Longo looked back. "Hey, Lester, howya doin'?"

"Great," Deputy D.A. Lester Kuruyama said. "How's that trial going?"

"Lemme tellya," Longo said, shaking his head. "Hey, whatcha doin' here? I heard the surf was up."

Kuruyama chuckled. "You know, Leslie's really starting to cut into my time on the waves."

"Yeah, I'll bet."

"Leslie" was Leslie Abramson, the criminal defense lawyer whom Longo had faced in the Chinatown trial. She was now the attorney for one of the Menendez brothers. When Deputy D.A. Pamela Ferrero was assigned to the Menendez case, she was told that she could have any deputy in the office to sit as second chair. She chose Kuruyama. He was a hard worker and he had a rapport with juries, she explained.

Kuruyama was one of the best-liked deputies in the office, an outgoing and perpetually cheerful man with an always ready sense of humor. He was also the only good trial lawyer Longo knew who lacked an oversized ego. The self-effacing prosecutor would rarely talk about his own courtroom exploits; when pressed about a big courtroom win, he would only say that he "got lucky." One of six kids in a family supported by a father who made ninety dollars a week and a mother who took in laundry, Kuruyama felt genuinely grateful to be a deputy district attorney. He was particularly grateful to the man who, as chief deputy, had hired him: James Bascue.

Kuruyama had the fresh, youthful face and broad, muscular shoulders of a college athlete. Much of this was attributable to his activities: Kuruyama was still an avid weight lifter, gymnast, and featherweight boxer. But the secret to his youthful energy, he would jokingly say, was surfing; after twenty-two years of riding the waves, he still found time to take his surfboard to Redondo Beach at least twice a week.

The elevator door opened on the seventeenth floor and Longo, Kuruyama, and Sakoda stepped out.

"What's going on with Menendez?" Sakoda asked. "You guys ever going to trial?"

"Gosh, I don't know, Jimmy. They haven't even been arraigned yet. We're still tied up in the Supreme Court."

It occurred to Longo that Kuruyama was the only man he knew who still said "gosh."

"The tapes?"

"Yeah."

The California Supreme Court was in the slow process of deciding whether the tape recordings of the brothers' confessions to their psychotherapist were admissible evidence. Until that critical decision was made, all courtroom proceedings had been suspended.

The three men passed the armed security guard sitting at his desk, then punched in the combination to the lock on the door and walked into the District Attorney's Office.

"I heard Weisberg might try the case," Longo said.

"That's what I heard, too," Kuruyama said. "But there's nothing official yet."

It was rumored that the presiding judge of the superior court was having trouble finding someone to sit in the Menendez trial. Few judges wanted the headache; the case would be a media circus, and Leslie Abramson was known to be a firebrand who ran wild in the courtroom—a firebrand whose husband was an editor at the *Los Angeles Times*. The latest rumor was that Stanley Weisberg would be assigned to the celebrated case, the same judge who had presided over the second McMartin preschool trial and who was now sitting on the bench in the Rodney King case.

"You guys going for special circ?" Longo asked.

"Special circ" was prosecutor jargon for the death penalty. If special circumstances were present in the case, such as torture or multiple murder, then the state was authorized to seek a death sentence.

"Front office hasn't decided yet, Larry." Kuruyama shook his head. "You know the juries downtown. . . . And the time and expense of a penalty phase."

"Yeah, and then if you do finally get 'em shipped off to death row, they sit there for ten, twenty years."

"I hear they got over four hundred guys up there on the row now. I guess you can't blame the front office if they decide to go for L-wop, but, gosh, it doesn't seem right. Not in a case like this."

"L-wop" was slang for life without the possibility of parole.

The men walked down the stark beige corridors that honeycombed the floor to a juncture of more corridors.

"See you guys later," Kuruyama said, turning right.

"Yeah," Longo said. "Give Leslie a kiss for me, huh?"

Kuruyama laughed.

Longo and Sakoda continued on down the corridor. As they

approached Longo's office, they passed a conference room in which a group of deputies was crowded around a television set.

The two men stopped.

Longo leaned into the room. "What's goin' on?" he asked one of the prosecutors watching the screen.

"The trial," the man said simply.

Longo and Sakoda looked at the television screen. They could see a man sitting in a witness stand. A lawyer was asking him a question. The lawyer was immaculately dressed in a three-piece navy blue suit, white dress shirt, burgundy club tie, and cordovan wing tips. It was Terry White.

The Rodney King trial had finally started.

As Longo looked at his fellow deputies locked on the small screen, he realized again the trial's importance to the office. More than the position of district attorney was at stake. There was morale. In the combative and highly competitive world of the courtroom, prosecutors took great pride in winning. And although notoriously individualistic, they had a very real sense of being part of a team, of "us" against "them." And playing on a team that blew the big ones was something that slowly ate away at professional pride and confidence.

Morale was not just an abstract concept. The L.A. branch of the Association of Deputy District Attorneys had recently voted overwhelmingly to back Reiner's opponent and former chief deputy, Gil Garcetti. And the endorsement was widely reported in the media.

Longo pulled himself away from the television set. He was in trial himself; there was no time to watch television.

"What do you think, Larry?" Sakoda asked as they made their way down the beige corridor. "The cops have a chance?"

Longo snorted. "Tough jury panel. And how you gonna convict if the jury never *hears* from the guy they beat up?"

Cheman Park was sitting in Longo's office.

"Hey, Park," Longo said.

The investigator jumped up. "Bad news, Larry."

"Yeah?"

"Yeah." He looked at Sakoda, then back at the prosecutor. "I talked to Seki . . ."

"Jeez, don't say it . . ."

"Yeah, he's changing his story."

"Gimme a break."

"And he don't want to testify anymore."

Longo shook his head slowly.

"That's not all."

Longo stared at the investigator in silence, waiting.

"Nagano?" Park said.

"Yeah?"

"He's gone."

"Gone?"

"Yeah. He left for Japan a few days ago."

"Do you give up the right to confront your accusers?"

Longo watched from his seat in the jury box as the tall deputy
D.A. standing at the prosecution table recited the litany for a guilty
plea.

A squat, powerfully built black man in jailhouse orange stood
at the far end of the defense table, his red-tinted eyes fixed malevolently on the prosecutor. He nodded steadily as an elderly woman
standing on his right translated the words into a language Longo did
not recognize. Another black man, a high-priced attorney well known
in the criminal courts, stood to the defendant's left. The defendant
growled something back to the interpeter in the same strange language.

"I do this, sir," the interpeter said to Judge Bascue with a slight
British accent.

"Do you understand," the prosecutor continued, "that you also
have a right to a jury trial, a trial wherein your guilt or innocence
will be determined by twelve of your peers?"

"I understand this, sir."

"Do you give up your right to a jury trial?"

"I do this, sir."

The defendant was an illegal immigrant from Nigeria, one of
a large Nigerian car-smuggling ring that stole luxury cars in Los Angeles, then shipped them out on freighters to Africa for resale. Another

African car-smuggling gang was also operating in Los Angeles, that one from Ghana. The leader of the Nigerian group, deciding to frighten his competition off, had ordered the defendant to eliminate one of the Ghanaians. The defendant obediently kidnapped one of the gang and, in an apartment in fashionable Westwood, tortured him to death.

Witnesses had fled back to Africa, leaving the prosecution with a badly weakened case. Reluctantly, the tall deputy D.A. had agreed to a deal: a plea to murder, with an agreement to drop the special circumstances of torture that could lead to the gas chamber. Then he called the Immigration and Naturalization Service, making sure they would be aware of the killer's eventual release from prison.

"Do you understand that you have a right under the Fifth Amendment to remain silent, to refuse to incriminate yourself?"

"I do understand this, sir."

"And that by pleading guilty here today, you are giving up that right?"

"I understand this, sir."

"Is it your desire, then, to give up your right to remain silent?"

"I do give it up, sir."

As Longo watched, he found himself wondering what kind of constitutional rights the defendant would have enjoyed in Nigeria. He shifted his gaze to the tall prosecutor as the chorus continued. The man was at least six four in height, with a prominent nose and huge ears jutting out from a long, angular face. He wore a plain blue serge suit with a white button-down oxford shirt, an outdated narrow club tie, wire-rimmed eyeglasses, and enormous wing tip oxford shoes. In one of his massive hands was an empty straight-stemmed briar pipe.

The man looked every inch an oversized computer engineer. But his hard, steady gaze met the Nigerian's dark glare without flinching, and when he spoke, it was in a deep, powerful voice filled with conviction.

Dinko Bozanich was a true believer, Longo thought. And one of the best trial lawyers in the office.

Bozanich was the same man who had helped teach Lea D'Agostino her trade in the infamous Alphabet Bomber trial. The son of an immigrant Slav fisherman, he and his brother, Peter Bozanich, had been raised in San Pedro, a tough L.A. harbor community of Croatian and Italian fishermen, longshoremen, and merchant seamen. He was a fire-and-brimstone evangelist, a crusader who hated anyone who got in the way of his ridding the streets of "bad actors." Usually this meant the desk lawyers in the front office. And, like Steve Barshop in Santa Monica, he was not reticent in expressing his feelings about incompetent supervisors and idiotic policies.

This did not endear Bozanich to the power brokers in the office. Not surprisingly, the prosecutor had long ago been banished to Norwalk, a courthouse in the eastern part of the county. But it had probably been this independent streak that got him assigned to the Robert F. Kennedy investigation.

In 1968, Senator Kennedy was gunned down in the pantry of the Ambassador Hotel in Los Angeles, minutes after delivering his victory speech following the California Democratic presidential primary. The assassin, a twenty-four-year-old Arab named Sirhan Sirhan, was immediately arrested, confessed, and was subsequently convicted by a jury of first-degree murder.

As happened with the John F. Kennedy and Martin Luther King assassinations, however, the RFK case soon spawned dozens of conspiracy theorists. The most prominent of these was Paul Schrade, a labor union official who co-chaired Kennedy's campaign and who was himself shot in the head by Sirhan during the attack on Kennedy. Schrade, insisting that there was a "second gun," retained Vincent Bugliosi to conduct his own investigation of the events surrounding the assassination. At the time, the former Manson prosecutor was campaigning for district attorney against the incumbent, John Van de Kamp. And the media was always interested in evidence of another Kennedy conspiracy.

Bugliosi visited the scene where Kennedy was shot and found what appeared to be previously undiscovered bullet holes. The evidence seemed to indicate that thirteen shots were fired rather than only the eight from Sirhan's .22-caliber revolver. This evidence was reenforced by the new claims of a Pasadena criminalist who compared the bullets introduced at the trial with photographs of those found in Kennedy's body. The bullets, he told reporters, could not have been fired from the same weapon.

District Attorney Van de Kamp now had to find a prosecutor

on his staff to reopen the investigation. But the political pressures and claims of a cover-up meant that the prosecutor had to have a reputation for toughness, integrity, and independence from the front office.

The natural choice was Dinko Bozanich.

Seven experts from around the country were gathered to examine the recovered bullets, test-fire Sirhan's gun, and review the trial evidence. In the course of his career, Bozanich had developed a deep skepticism of experts generally, but of ballistics experts particularly. He wanted to give the seven men a test of their abilities, making them compare known bullets for matches. All but one refused. When he pressed the matter, the prosecutor found that his own superiors were also against the test; they were afraid that the publicized results would impair the credibility of ballistics evidence in the public eye.

As the experts conducted their analyses of the Sirhan gun and bullets, Bozanich continued to interview witnesses to the assassination and examine the evidence introduced at the trial. He got a search warrant for the Ambassador Hotel and sealed off the kitchen and pantry (an incident he refers to as "the pantry raid"). With his own photographers and experts, the prosecutor inspected the holes that were claimed to be caused by bullets. None proved to have been caused by bullets.

When the seven ballistics experts finally presented their separate sealed findings, Bozanich found that almost none of them agreed on specific matches. But they did agree on one negative finding: "There is no substantive or demonstrable evidence to indicate that more than one gun was used to fire any of the bullets examined."

The investigation into the Robert F. Kennedy assassination was finally closed.

"And are you now pleading guilty because, in truth and in fact, you are guilty of this offense, and for no other reason?"

"I do this, sir," the interpreter said.

"To count one in the Information," Bozanich continued, oblivious to the defendant's glare, "alleging a violation of Penal Code section 187, murder, how do you now plead?"

After a flurry of translations, the interpreter said, "I am guilty, sir."

"Very well," Judge Bascue said, "this case is referred to the probation department for a report." He looked at the calendar on the wall behind his clerk, then at the defense attorney. "Can we set this for the seventh, Counsel?"

"That would be fine, your honor," the lawyer said.

"Mr. Bozanich?"

"Sure," the prosecutor said.

"Then the case is continued for sentencing to the seventh." Bascue shuffled the file onto a stack to his right, pulled another from a smaller stack to his left. "People versus Johnny Kee," he announced.

Bozanich shoved the case file into a large briefcase as Longo walked up to the counsel table.

"How's Norwalk, Dinko?" Longo said in a low voice.

Bozanich shrugged, then smiled. "The air's cleaner."

"Yeah." Longo grinned. "The eastside's always had great air."

"I hear you got a good one going."

It was Longo's turn to shrug.

"Yamaki, huh?" Bozanich asked.

"Yeah."

"Well—"

"Gentlemen," Bascue said ominously from the bench, "we're trying to run a calendar here."

Bozanich winked at Longo, then turned and walked out through the gate. Longo sat down next to his junior deputy.

"Mr. Torrealba?" Bascue said.

"People's motion to continue," Torrealba said.

"We oppose the motion," Nancy Richards said, stepping forward. "My client is ready for trial."

Longo grabbed the file in front of Torrealba, scanned the fact sheet. Kee was a Korean bricklayer charged with two counts of mayhem. He had returned home early one day to find his wife and best friend in a compromising situation. Incredibly, Kee had grabbed the man's jaw and, with his powerful bricklayer's hands, ripped almost half of the teeth out of his head. When his friend lost consciousness, Kee pulled his screaming wife into the bedroom and tied her spread-eagled to the bed. Then he poured lighter fluid inside and around her vagina. And lit a match.

"Grounds for the continuance?" Bascue asked the deputy D.A.

"We're having some problems locating the male victim," Torrealba said. "And the female victim is still recuperating."

"Come on, Leonard," Richards said, "is she willing to testify against Mr. Kee?"

Torrealba shrugged. "We subpoena her, she doesn't have a choice."

"Get real," the public defender said. She turned back to the judge. "My client has a right to a speedy trial, your honor."

"Yes," Bascue said, "and the prosecution has the right to rearrest him if I dismiss, Ms. Richards. Then we start the whole thing all over again."

"So how long do we keep this up? Mr. Kee has been in jail waiting for his jury trial for over six months now."

Bascue looked at Longo, then Torrealba. "Gentlemen?"

"This will be the last continuance," Torrealba said, glancing at Longo. "Next time, we'll go with what we've got."

"Boys and girls," Bascue said patiently, "I'd take it as a personal favor if you would get together and talk this over. I'm sure you'll find some mutually agreeable way to resolve this matter and not take up the court's time with a needless trial."

Richards and Torrealba said nothing.

Two counts mayhem, Longo thought. No criminal record. One witness missing, probably gone from the jurisdiction. Another unwilling to testify; who knew what her testimony would be if she were forced to take the stand. Translation: The case was worth a GBI, with time served. Let Kee cool his heels for another month or two, then offer Richards the deal: plead to a reduced charge of "assault with force likely to produce great bodily injury" and walk out of jail a free man.

It was not justice, Longo thought with a sense of resignation. It was reality.

"The People's motion is granted," Bascue said, writing in the file. "Case continued to the tenth. But the record will reflect that this is the last such continuance."

"Thank you, your honor," Torrealba said.

Longo leaned back in his chair. He absently patted his left coat pocket again, felt the small, hard bulge of the audiotape.

Judge Bascue closed the file, threw it on the stack to his right. "Angie," he said to his clerk, "bring in the jury."

The clerk pushed a button, signaling the men and women waiting in the jury deliberation room.

Mike Yamaki stood up in the back row of the audience and stepped forward as the bailiff brought Yamaguchi out of the holding cell. As always, Yamaguchi entered the courtroom with his head bowed. He walked toward the counsel table, turned to the audience and bowed from the waist, then bowed a second time. Then he adjusted his tie and sat down next to his lawyer.

The door to the deliberation room opened and the jurors filed out. When they were settled in their seats, Bascue turned to them.

"Ladies and gentlemen, I apologize for the delay." He turned to Longo. "Call your next witness, Mr. Longo."

"Patrick Mitsuo Seki," Longo announced loudly.

As the bailiff stepped out into the hallway to get the witness, Longo glanced down the table at Yamaki. There was a confident, almost serene, smile on the lawyer's face.

The morning session of trial had gone about as expected. Monty Holden had taken the stand to testify about his brief interrogation of Hanemure and Ken and Mitsuru Yamaguchi. Then it was Jimmy Sakoda's turn. The D.A.'s investigator recounted the damning statements made to him by Hanemure, Matsumoto, and Uchida, statements that contradicted their testimony in court. And Yamaki had smoothly cross-examined Sakoda, emphasizing the language difficulties and suggesting possible motives for Longo's investigator in "creative recollection." Was it not strange, the lawyer asked, that every one of these honorable businessmen contradicted his testimony? Did he have any evidence to corroborate *his* version of the truth?

The courtroom door opened and Seki stepped in with the bailiff. The small, round-faced man walked hesitantly down the aisle, bowing to the audience repeatedly. The bailiff escorted him to the witness stand. After taking the oath, Seki sat down and looked around apprehensively.

"Mr. Seki," Longo said, rising to his feet, "where do you work?"

"I am the owner of Seki Jewelers," Seki said, "in Honda Plaza."

"That's in Little Tokyo?"

"Yes."

"You know the defendant sitting over there, Kazuhiko Yamaguchi, right?"

Seki bowed his head toward Yamaguchi. "Yes."

"And you also know a guy called Mamoru Hanemure?"

"Yes."

"Awright. And you had a little chat with this Hanemure, didn't you? A day or two after Yamaguchi shot Kariya?"

"Yes."

"You recall what Hanemure told you?"

"We discussed many things."

"He tell you anything about warning Kariya just before he was shot?"

"I do not recall such a thing."

Longo snorted. "You don't remember him saying that he warned Kariya to be careful? That Yamaguchi was a dangerous guy?"

"I do not recall such a thing."

Longo took a step toward Seki. "You don't remember sitting in my office and telling me that?"

"I do not recall."

"You remember telling me that you also warned Kariya that Yamaguchi was known to be a dangerous guy to fool with?"

"I do not recall."

Longo glared at the man for a moment. Then he turned to Judge Bascue.

"Judge, I request a short recess."

"A recess?" Bascue asked.

"Yeah. *In camera.*" The prosecutor was requesting a confidential meeting with the judge in his chambers. "With the reporter," he added. He wanted everything on the record; it was serious.

Bascue studied the prosecutor for a moment, then nodded. "Very well," he said finally. He turned to the jury. "Ladies and gentlemen, I realize we just got started, but these things happen. Please take this opportunity to stretch your legs, get a drink, whatever. And please be back here in fifteen minutes." He glanced back at Longo for another moment, a this-better-be-good look on his face.

Bascue stepped down from the bench and disappeared through the door. Longo strode past the clerk's desk and through the door. Yamaki's eyes narrowed in puzzlement.

Longo entered the chambers. The room was spacious, with a

long picture window looking out over east L.A. fifteen floors below.
Three upholstered chairs stood in front of a large desk, and a well-
padded couch rested under the window. One wall was lined with a
huge bookshelf stacked with legal treatises and appellate reports. The
other two walls were covered with dozens of mounted diplomas,
framed letters, and bronze plaques. A second door behind the desk
led to a private restroom.

Bascue was hanging his black robe on a tall wooden coatrack
as the prosecutor entered. He sat down in a plush swivel chair behind
the desk, his eyes fixed on Longo, waiting.

Ginny Ishida stepped into the room, carrying her stenotype machine. She sat down near the desk and set the machine on a collapsible
metal stand.

Longo sat down.

"Well?" Bascue said, breaking the silence.

The prosecutor reached into his pocket and pulled out the audiotape. He placed it on the desk in front of Bascue.

"So?" Bascue said.

"It's my interrogation of Seki in my office a few days ago." He
paused. "I had a tape going. Seki didn't know."

Bascue said nothing.

"Sakoda was in the room at the time," Longo continued. "He
wrote out a report, a complete summary of the interrogation. I turned
a copy over to Yamaki as soon as it was available."

"Let me see if I understand this. You have a tape from your
meeting with Seki, right? And I assume on the tape, he makes statements that contradict his testimony here today."

"Sure does."

"I assume he says that Hanemure *did* tell him he warned Kariya
about Yamaguchi being dangerous."

"That, and a lot more."

"And I assume you were aware of your obligation to turn over
any relevant material to Mike, as soon as it was available to you?"

"Look, judge, every time I get a witness in this case, he tells my
investigator one thing. Then I turn over the report about the interview
to Mike. Next thing I know, the guy's pissing backward on me. Every
time."

Bascue sighed, then looked at the reporter. "For the record, I find no evidence indicating any witness tampering in this case. Now, as for the discovery order . . . you'll agree you're in violation of the order?"

"Well, I mean technically, yeah, but it was the only way to prove what's been going on. And Mike got a written report of everything that was said. If I turned that tape over to him, lemme tellya he'd have told Seki about it before the sun set and—"

"I assume you've got more questions of this witness."

"Yeah," the prosecutor said. "A lot more."

"And you plan to introduce the tape, play it for the jury to impeach him?"

"Lemme tellya."

"Was there any *Brady* material on the tape?"

If the taped interrogation contained any evidence that tended to point to Yamaguchi's innocence, then withholding the tape would be in violation of *Brady* v. *Maryland,* a landmark U.S. Supreme Court decision.

"No."

Bascue closed his eyes, then massaged them slowly with the fingers of his right hand. After a long moment he opened his eyes. He picked up the tape and stared at it.

"For the record," he said finally, looking at Longo, "I find that there has been a violation of the court's discovery order. There has also been a violation of the terms of the discovery provisions of Penal Code section 1054. Pending a review of the tape, however, I find that there has been no *Brady* violation."

The possible sanctions began running through Longo's mind. Contempt of court, followed by a short jail sentence. Dismissal of all charges against Yamaguchi. Suppression of some critical testimony. A damning instruction to the jury that the prosecutor has been guilty of unethical and illegal conduct.

The judge said to the reporter, "I further find that Mr. Longo acted in good faith. Assuming the tape is as represented, it would appear that this witness may have changed his testimony. And if Mr. Sakoda is to be believed, perhaps other witnesses have also changed their stories. I do not pass judgment on this. I only say that there appears to be reasonable grounds for Mr. Longo's belief that it was necessary to withhold the tapes. I simply find that he did not act in bad faith." He looked at the prosecutor. "Stupidly maybe, but not in bad faith."

Well, Longo thought, at least he would not have to call Aelina and ask her to bring his toothbrush.

"Nevertheless," the judge continued, "there must be an appropriate sanction for the violation. It is up to this court to fashion such a sanction. And it is this: The tape will be suppressed."

"What?" Longo said incredulously.

"The prosecution will not be permitted to use the tape for any purpose."

"Judge," Longo said, "this tape is critical evidence. I mean, everybody's changing stories left and right. This tape's the only thing the jury's got that proves who's doing the lying."

"That is the court's ruling," Bascue said. "There's nothing to prevent you from recalling Sakoda to testify to what Seki said in your office."

Longo looked at the tape in the judge's hand. He knew that putting Sakoda back on the stand might finally destroy his investigator's credibility; it would then be his word against that of *four* respected members of the business community.

"Okay," the prosecutor said, "I can't play the tape for the jury. But how about if I play it for Seki, in private? Let him listen to it before testifying any further." And threaten the son of a gun with perjury, Longo thought.

"The tape can't be used for *any* purpose in this trial," Bascue said.

"Can I at least *tell* him there's a tape?"

"There will be no mention of any tape." Bascue threw the tape back on the desk. "Larry, you're lucky you're not in jail."

Longo snorted loudly. "One other thing," he said. "I got evidence that Yamaguchi shot a gun at his wife a couple weeks before he killed Kariya. To scare her."

"Seki?"

"Yeah," the prosecutor said. "Hanemure told him."

"I assume he will just deny it, then?"

"I still wanna ask the question."

"Larry, evidence of shooting a gun at an earlier date is propensity evidence. You can't offer it."

"But—"

"That's my ruling. Of course, if Mike offers evidence during his case that his client had a reputation for being non-violent . . ."

"Judge," Longo said, "he *did* offer it. He—"

"No," Bascue said, "that's the ruling." He glanced at his watch, then stood up and began putting his judicial robe back on.

Longo rose to his feet, followed the reporter out of the chambers. His mind had quickly shifted to damage control, assessing now what was left of his case. He had a dead body, with Yamaguchi the killer. Minor evidence of premeditation. Speculative motives. The shooting incident was out. Nagano had fled to Japan. Hanemure and Matsumoto had changed their stories. Followed by Uchida. Then Seki had joined the parade. Now the tape was useless. And Sakoda's credibility was stretched to the breaking point. And Yamaki had not even started his Halcion defense. . . .

Then it suddenly occurred to Longo; there had been a fourth person in the office during the Seki interrogation! It was someone he had come to take for granted, someone who had become his constant shadow for almost a year. And that person had been writing down everything that was said. Me.

I was talking to the bailiff when Longo reentered the courtroom. He walked quickly over to me.

"Larry," Longo whispered, "you remember the session in my office with Seki?"

"Sure."

"Wanna testify?"

"Testify?" I said. "Me?"

"Yeah. You know, what you heard Seki say."

I took a deep breath, let it out. "What about Sakoda?"

Longo shook his head. "Used him too much already."

"Testify . . ." I repeated, shaking my head. "I don't know, Larry, that kind of puts me in the middle of what I'm writing about, you know? I become a character in my own book. I mean, there goes my credibility as outside observer."

"Yeah."

"You really need my testimony, huh?"

"It'd help. In rebuttal, after Yamaki puts on his case."

"Damn." I sighed deeply. "Okay."

"Look," Longo said, "you took notes, right?"

"Sure."

"You got 'em here?"

"No, they're at home. Buried somewhere in a couple dozen notebooks."

"Find 'em, okay? The notes on Seki. They'll corroborate your testimony."

"Yeah . . ."

" 'Course, I gotta give a copy of your notes to Yamaki." Longo winked. "*You're* not gonna waffle on me, are you?"

I smiled.

"All rise," the bailiff announced as Bascue entered the courtroom and mounted the three steps to his bench. "Department 127 is again in session."

"Ladies and gentlemen," Bascue said, looking at the seated jurors, "again, my apologies. I can only assure you that the interruption was a necessary one." He looked at the prosecutor. "Mr. Longo?"

Longo returned to the counsel table, fixed his eyes on Seki sitting forlornly in the witness box. The man looked thoroughly miserable.

"No further questions," Longo said. He would wait for my notes, he decided, then recall Seki to the stand during his rebuttal case. If Seki continued to deny the statements, he would put me on the stand to testify and produce the notes.

"Mr. Yamaki?"

The lawyer rose to his feet, smiling. "I have no questions of this witness, your honor."

"Very well," Bascue said, looking back at the prosecutor, "call your next witness."

"Judge," Longo said, "the People rest."

The prosecutor eased the old Toyota van forward in the evening traffic, his eyes locked hypnotically on the red taillights flashing in the darkness ahead of him. There was an oddly comfortable numbness in being swallowed by the surging tide of traffic. He felt an overwhelming sense of fatigue, of physical and mental exhaustion, as he inched along the Santa Monica Freeway.

It was going all wrong, he thought. Everything was going all wrong.

Chapter 23

"Based upon Mr. Yamaki's offer of proof concerning what Dr. Scharf will testify to," Judge Bascue announced from the bench, "I find that testimony about Halcion is relevant and admissible evidence of diminished capacity."

"Judge," Longo said, bouncing up from his chair at the counsel table, "Dr. Greenblatt's gonna testify that the stuff *doesn't* have the effects Yamaki claims. He's gonna—"

"Then the effect of Halcion is for the jury to decide. They can weigh the conflicting testimony of the two experts and decide. I simply find that evidence that the drug is capable of affecting the defendant's mental state is relevant.

"You've charged him with murder. If the jury believes that Halcion prevented him from being able to meaningfully premeditate, then he's not guilty of first-degree murder. And if he was sufficiently impaired that he couldn't even form an intent to kill, he's not guilty of second-degree murder either. That, of course, leaves manslaughter."

"If I may add, your honor," Yamaki said, rising to his feet, "the jury is also permitted to find that Halcion prevented Mr. Yamaguchi from having conscious and voluntary control over his conduct."

Bascue nodded slowly, considering this. "Yes. If the jury finds that this drug impaired the defendant's conscious control . . ."

"Then he is not guilty of *any* offense," Yamaki said.

"I believe that is a correct statement of the law."

"Awright," Longo growled, "but Yamaki can't put this guy Scharf on the stand if there's no evidence Yamaguchi actually *took* the stuff."

"Mr. Longo is correct," Bascue said, looking at the defense lawyer. "As I said, I find that evidence of Halcion is relevant to the issue of diminished capacity. But there is no relevance to *this* case unless the defendant actually consumed the drug, and at a time proximate to the shooting."

"Again, your honor," Yamaki said, "by way of an offer of proof, there will be testimony that my client did take the drug shortly before the incident."

"Yamaguchi'll testify to that, Mike?" Longo asked.

Yamaki smiled. "I don't have to tell you if my client is going to take the stand, Larry."

"And what happens if the jury hears all this talk about Halcion," Longo said, "and it turns out there's no evidence Yamaguchi actually took the stuff? Or that it has the effect Yamaki says? The jury's heard all about it. It's been on the cover of *Newsweek,* and that TV show, *60 Minutes*. They're gonna jump to their own conclusions."

"In that case," Bascue said, "I will instruct the jury that they must disregard any evidence of Halcion."

Yeah, Longo thought, unring the bell.

Bascue looked at the two lawyers. "Anything else before I bring in the jury, gentlemen?"

Neither said anything.

Longo sat down. The ruling had not come as a surprise to him, and he had put up only token resistance. It had become clear early in the hearing that Judge Bascue was going to let in evidence of Halcion. Longo would have to make his stand on the question of whether Yamaguchi actually took the drug on the night of the murder. And on what effect it could have had, if any.

"Angie?" Bascue said.

The clerk pushed the button. Within seconds, the twelve men and women filed out of the deliberation room and quickly took their seats in the jury box.

Longo scanned the faces of each, searching for some clue, some body language or facial gesture that would give him a hint of how they were leaning. But there was nothing. He saw only enigma staring back at him.

"Good morning, Ladies and gentlemen," Bascue said. "As you know, the People have rested their case. It is now time for the defense, if they wish, to present evidence. When they are finished, the People may present what is called rebuttal testimony. So, you see, we are moving right along." He turned to the defense lawyer. "Call your first witness, Mr. Yamaki."

"Tom Okita," the lawyer announced.

The bailiff brought in an elderly gentleman with the prim, pained look of an accountant. The man crossed to the witness stand, bowing slightly as he passed the audience, then took the oath. He sat perfectly erect, again bowed his head to the jurors, and adjusted his perfectly arranged tie.

"Mr. Okita," Yamaki said from the lectern, "what is your profession?"

"I am a pharmacist."

"In fact, you own a pharmacy, is that correct?"

"That is so. Kyoto Drugs."

"This is in Little Tokyo?"

"Yes."

No translator, Longo noted wryly.

"Mr. Okita," Yamaki continued, "do you have a customer by the name of Mitsuru Yamaguchi?"

"Yes."

"Your honor," the lawyer said, holding a small paper object in his hand, "I have a prescription label from Kyoto Drugs, dated May 8, 1990. May this be marked defense exhibit A?"

"It will be so marked."

Longo had already seen a copy of the prescription label when Yamaki had finally turned it over in discovery. Once again he found himself wondering why Yamaki was using a prescription not for Yamaguchi but for his wife. And the date, May 8, 1990, was almost a year before the murder.

"Thank you, your honor." Yamaki approached the witness, handed him the label. "Do you recognize this, sir?"

Okita pulled a pair of eyeglasses from his vest pocket, put them on, and studied the exhibit. "Yes," he said slowly, still reading it.

"That is a label for a prescription you filled for Mrs. Yamaguchi, is that correct?"

"Yes."

"The label designates the name of the prescribed drug, does it not?"

"Yes." Okita took his glasses off and returned them to his pocket.

"And would you please tell the ladies and gentlemen of the jury the name of that drug?"

"Halcion."

"Halcion," Yamaki repeated ominously.

"Yes."

The lawyer stepped back, looked at each of the jurors in turn.

Longo was also looking. And he could see signs of recognition in the faces of some of the men and women. There were at least four on the jury who knew of the drug, possibly from the television show. And they would tell the other jurors.

"What are the instructions on the label, Mr. Okita?"

Okita pulled out his glasses again, read the exhibit. " 'Take one before bedtime as needed.' "

Yamaki produced a second label, held it up toward the judge. "Your honor, another label from Kyoto Drugs, again with the name Mitsuru Yamaguchi. This one is dated November 19, 1990. May this be marked defense exhibit B?"

"It will be so marked."

November 19, Longo thought. Still over four months before the murder.

"Mr. Okita," Yamaki said, "do you recognize this?"

Again, Okita took out his eyeglasses and studied the second exhibit. "Yes," he said finally.

"It is also for Halcion?"

"Yes."

"To be taken at bedtime as needed?"

"Yes."

"Now, Mr. Okita," the lawyer said, walking back to the podium, "would you please describe what these Halcion tablets look like?"

"Halcion comes in two doses. The .125-milligram pill is white. The .250-milligram pill is blue. Both are oval-shaped, scored across the middle."

"Thank you," Yamaki said, walking back to his seat at the defense table. "Your witness."

"Mr. Okita," Longo said, rising to his feet, "these labels look pretty new to me."

"They are duplicate originals," Okita said.

"Duplicate originals," the prosecutor repeated. "Could you explain that?"

"Yes. Mr. Yamaki asked me to prepare a second set of labels. He explained that the original labels were thrown away with the bottles, when the tablets were used up. He needed another set prepared to use as evidence."

"So these labels, they're not the real thing?"

"They are duplicates."

"You just made them up for Yamaki?"

"Yes."

"Awright." Longo walked to the witness stand, picked up one of the labels and glanced at it. "I see where the label has a couple letters on it, 'NR.' What's that mean?"

"Not refillable."

"So these two prescriptions for Mrs. Yamaguchi, they were one-shot deals, huh?"

"One-shot deals?"

"Yeah, you know, use them up, and you can't get any more without another prescription."

"Yes. One-shot deals."

"Uh-huh. How many pills were there in the first prescription, the one from the year before the murder?"

"Objection," Yamaki said. "Mr. Longo is drawing a legal conclusion that it was murder."

"Sustained," Bascue said. "Rephrase your question, Mr. Longo."

"Yeah, sure," Longo said. "So, Mr. Okita, how many pills were in that first bottle—the one from the year before the defendant here blew Kariya's brains out?"

Yamaki rolled his eyes to the ceiling, while the judge tried hard to suppress a grin.

"The first prescription was for fifty tablets."

"That was the .125-milligram size, the small ones?"

"Yes."

"And I guess she must have used them all up, huh? I mean, she came back and got another prescription six months later."

"I assume so."

"Awright, so how many pills were in the second bottle, the one in November?"

"Thirty tablets."

"Same size? The little ones?"

"Yes."

"Uh-huh. And this was over four months before the . . . shooting."

"I believe so."

"Awright, you remember my investigator, guy named Jimmy Sakoda?"

"I recall Mr. Sakoda."

"He came and talked to you, right?"

"Yes."

"He ask you about any other prescriptions?"

"Yes. I explained to Mr. Sakoda that I filled a prescription for Mrs. Yamaguchi on September 14, 1991. This was for thirty tablets."

"About six months *after* the . . . shooting."

"I believe so."

"Uh-huh."

Longo was not sure what the relevance was of the third prescription, if any. But it still seemed strange to him. Yamaguchi's wife used fifty tablets over a six-month period. Then she used only thirty more over the next ten months, during which the murder had taken place. It would seem that she would have increased her use of the sleeping pills in the traumatic days and weeks following the murder. Instead, she appeared to have used fewer of the tablets—did not even need a refill of the smaller prescription until fully half a year after the murder.

"Mr. Okita, you described the pill to us a minute ago."

"Tablet."

"Right, tablet. You remember if there was a name on the tablet? The name of the drug, or the manufacturer?"

The pharmacist furrowed his eyebrows, trying to recall the image of the white tablets.

"No," he said finally, "I cannot recall at this time. There may be a name, I cannot recall."

"Uh-huh." Longo walked back to his seat. "By the way, your pharmacy's in the same building as Hanemure's restaurant, that right?"

"Mr. Hanemure, yes."

"You're good buddies with Hanemure?"

"We are friends."

"Uh-huh." The prosecutor sat down. "Nothing further, judge."

"You are excused, sir," Bascue said to Okita. Then he turned to Yamaki. "Call your next witness."

The lawyer rose. "Ken Yamaguchi."

It was going to be the son, Longo thought. He was going to testify that he saw his father take Halcion pills the night of the murder. He had already testified he saw his father walk into the house and make a telephone call a half hour before the shooting.

What did Dr. Greenblatt say over the phone? It took half an hour for Halcion to kick in. Yamaki had it set up pretty well.

Ken Yamaguchi came through the door with the bailiff. He was wearing baggy black trousers, a black dress shirt, and a loose-fitting gray sports coat rolled up at the sleeve in the style popular among the young. He moved down the aisle without acknowledging the audience, crossed to the witness box, and sat down.

"Mr. Yamaguchi," Bascue said, "do you understand that you're still under oath?"

"Yes, sir."

"Ken," Yamaki said, "you testified here earlier for the prosecution, but let me just repeat the question: You are the son of Kazuhiko Yamaguchi, the defendant in this case, are you not?"

Ken nodded, his heavy-lidded eyes locked on the lawyer.

"Now," Yamaki said, standing confidently at the lectern, "you recounted in your testimony the events surrounding the unfortunate incident with Mr. Kariya. I would like to go back to those events."

"Sure."

"Your father came home about one that morning, is that correct?"

"Yes, sir."

"And you said he went into the bedroom and used a mobile phone to call someone, presumably Mamoru Hanemure?"

The young man shrugged. "I couldn't tell who it was."

"At some point, he came out of the bedroom, didn't he?"

"Yeah . . . yes, sir."

"Was he still talking on the phone?"

"Yes, sir."

"Could you hear what he was saying?"

"Not really."

"All right. Now, where did he walk to as he was talking on the phone?"

"Into the kitchen."

"The kitchen. And where were you at this time?"

"I was in the kitchen too. Getting something to eat."

"I see. Now, Ken, did your father do anything while he was in the kitchen?"

"Yes, sir."

"What was that?"

"He took some medicine."

Yamaki paused, looked at the jury. "Some medicine," he repeated slowly. "And where was this medicine he took?"

"In a bottle. On the table."

"Had you seen this bottle before?"

"Yeah. It'd been there for a month or so."

"Did you ever get a close look at this bottle?"

"Yeah."

"Would you describe the bottle for the ladies and gentlemen, please."

"It was, you know, a little plastic bottle, sort of brown. It was round, about the size of a quarter across."

"Was there a label?"

"Yeah . . . yes, sir."

"What did it say?"

"It had my mom's name on it. And Halcion. And something about taking it when you go to bed."

"You clearly recall the word 'Halcion' on the label?"

"Yeah."

"I see. Now, Ken, when your father came into the kitchen at about one that morning, did you see him take any of the pills?"

"Yeah, I did."

"Would you please describe for the ladies and gentlemen of the jury just exactly what you saw?"

"He poured a glass of water from the sink, and then he grabbed a couple of tablets from the bottle and . . . he swallowed them."

"*Two* tablets," Yamaki said, studying the jurors.

"Yeah . . . yes, sir."

"Two Halcion tablets?"

"Yes, sir."

Yamaki nodded. "All right, Ken, what did your father do after taking the Halcion?"

"He walked out the front door."

"Was he still talking on the phone?"

"Yes, sir."

"Did you see him again that evening?"

"No, sir."

"And it was about half an hour after he walked out the front door that you heard your mother crying out that your father had shot Mr. Kariya?"

The young man lowered his gaze and nodded.

"No further questions," Yamaki said, collecting his notes from the podium and returning to his chair.

Longo rose to his feet and approached the jury box. He ran his hands along the wooden railing, studying it for a moment.

"You mind if I call you Ken, too?"

Yamaguchi's son shrugged, his eyes wary now.

"Ken, you said you saw the pills that your dad took."

"Yes, sir."

"And you were watching him as he took them out of the bottle?"

"Yeah. Yes, sir."

"And swallowed them?"

"Yes, sir."

"And you saw the two pills in the palm of his hand?"

"Yes, sir."

"Standing there in the kitchen, you were concentrating on his palm, and you could see that there were *two* pills—not one, not three."

"Yes, sir."

"Think you could describe them for us?"

"Yeah. They were long, kind of oval, like a football, you know? And there was a line, like a stripe, across the middle."

"What color were they?"

"White."

"Did they have any name on them?"

"Yeah, there was some name on one side."

"Now, let's see if I get this right. From seeing a bottle of your mother's medicine in the kitchen, you can recall that the bottle was plastic, the width of a quarter, brown in color?"

"Yeah."

"And the label had your mother's name on it, and instructions to take it at bedtime?"

"Yeah."

"And it said 'Halcion'—you remember that word?"

"Yes, sir," Ken Yamaguchi said, his voice developing an edge.

"And these little pills, you were able to notice that they were white, and oval, shaped like a football?"

"Yes, sir."

"And there was a line across the middle?"

"Yes, sir."

"And there was a name on it?"

"Yes, sir."

"Are you aware that even the pharmacist, Mr. Okita, could not tell us if there was a name on the pill?"

Ken Yamaguchi shrugged.

Longo turned, walked slowly back to the audience railing, looked out at the dozens of hostile Japanese faces staring back at him.

"You noticed all of this detail at the time," he said, turning to face the witness, "and you are able to remember it a year later?"

"I guess so."

"Why didn't you mention any of this during your testimony here a few days ago?"

"You didn't ask me."

"Uh-huh. And what about your testimony at the preliminary hearing?"

Ken Yamaguchi shrugged again. "Nobody asked me."

"Uh-huh. So, tell me, whatever happened to this bottle?"

"I threw it away."

"You threw the bottle away?"

"Yeah."

"When?"

The young man shrugged. "Six o'clock, when I got home from the police station."

"Let me guess: the bottle was empty."

"Yeah."

"Uh-huh. You didn't think maybe your mom might need it to get a new prescription?"

"I didn't think about it."

"When you threw this bottle away, did you realize that it might be important evidence?"

"No, sir."

"When did you realize Halcion might be important?"

"Mr. Yamaki asked me if my father was taking any medication."

"When was this?"

"September, maybe October, last year."

"This was a month or so after the preliminary hearing?"

"I guess so."

"Yamaki tell you, 'Gee, that would be a great defense, if your dad was taking your mom's Halcion'?"

"Objection!" the defense lawyer said.

"Sustained," Judge Bascue said.

"Awright," Longo said, walking back to the jury box. He leaned against the railing and folded his arms across his chest. "So your dad had the phone to his ear the whole time he was taking the pills?"

"Yeah . . . yes, sir."

"Had the phone to his ear while he was turning on the faucet?"

"Yes, sir."

"Pouring the water into the glass?"

"Yes, sir."

"This took two hands, didn't it?"

"He was holding the phone between his head and his shoulder."

"Uh-huh. And he unscrewed the bottle with two hands, and took out the pills with two hands?"

"I guess so."

"By the way," Longo said, walking over to the podium and leaning against it, "did you know that the booking report in this case says your dad told the booking officer he hadn't taken any medication?"

Ken Yamaguchi again shrugged.

"This gun your dad had," the prosecutor continued, stepping now around the jury box so that the witness had to speak toward the jurors, "did that belong to you?"

"No, sir."

"Belonged to your dad, huh?"

"I guess so."

"You know why he got the gun?"

The young man glanced quickly at Yamaki, then back at the prosecutor. "I think it was for protection."

"Protection? Against what?"

"There was a burglary a few years ago."

"Oh?" Longo said, sounding surprised. "In your house?"

"Yeah."

"Did the burglars get away with anything?"

"Yeah. I think there was a lot of money and stuff."

"In fact, Ken, there was over fifty thousand dollars in cash and over a hundred grand in jewelry, right?"

"I guess so," the young man said, shifting slightly in his seat.

"They caught these burglars, didn't they?"

"I think so."

"You *think* so? Weren't they your best friends, Ken?"

"Objection," Yamaki said, rising to his feet. "Relevance."

"Weren't *you* the guy that set up the burglary, Ken?"

"Objection!"

"Sustained," Bascue said. "Move on to another subject, Mr. Longo."

"No more questions, judge," the prosecutor said, returning to his seat.

"Mr. Yamaki?"

"Nothing further, your honor," the lawyer said, glaring at Longo. "The defense calls Dr. Martin Scharf."

"You are excused," Bascue said to Ken Yamaguchi. The young man nodded, stepped down, and tried to act nonchalant as he left the courtroom.

The bailiff stepped outside, then reentered immediately with a strikingly handsome, square-jawed man wearing a gray silk sports coat and a designer tie. His thick, carefully styled hair was fashionably gray at the temples, and an open, ingratiating smile showed almost perfect teeth. Oozing confidence and charm, Dr. Martin Scharf looked as though he had stepped right out of a perfume ad in *Cosmopolitan.*

Longo studied Yamaki's expert as he walked confidently through the gate and flashed his winning smile at the jurors. As Scharf took the oath, the prosecutor thought back over Ken Yamaguchi's testimony. The prosecutor was confident that the father had never taken any Halcion. But why did the young man say he threw the bottle away? Why did he not just produce a bottle? And how was he able to describe the bottle, label, and tablets with so much precision?

There probably never was a bottle that night, Longo thought. Yamaguchi's wife had used up whatever tablets she had from the November prescription months earlier. Yet, Ken was able to describe everything in detail. Even though he testified he did not realize it was important until Yamaki asked him about medications in September or October of last year. How had he been able to . . .

The *Newsweek* article! Longo suddenly thought. He bent down and began digging into the cardboard box lying next to his chair, throwing documents and notes out onto the courtroom floor. Some of the jurors turned their attention from the witness and watched the prosecutor with amusement.

Longo finally found an article Greg Dohi had given him on the controversy about Halcion. He pulled it out and set it down on the table where the jurors could not see it. Featured prominently on the cover of the weekly news magazine was the feature story: "Halcion—Sweet Dreams or Nightmare?" The prosecutor looked at the date. It was August 19, 1991—four days after the preliminary hearing had been completed.

So that's where Yamaki had got the idea about Halcion, Longo thought. The defense lawyer probably knew that Yamaguchi's wife was taking the drug. But he also knew that he had to keep his client off the stand during a trial; someone else had to testify to his taking the drug. Yamaguchi's son was the only one who might have been with him in the hour or so before the murder—the only one who *could* testify he saw him swallow the pills. And Ken had testified that he discussed Halcion with Yamaki in September or October.

The third prescription! Of course, Longo thought; it was in September that Yamaguchi's wife got another prescription for Halcion—shortly after Yamaki would have seen the cover of *Newsweek*. The prescription was not for Mrs. Yamaguchi; it was for Ken. The September prescription was to prepare Yamaguchi's son for his description of the bottle and pills.

". . . and after receiving my bachelor of arts degree from UCLA, I attended Pennsylvania State University where I was awarded a doctorate in pharmacology."

"And what is your present position, Doctor?"

"I am presently the director of the Center for Sleep Disorders at Mercy Hospital in Cincinnati. I also teach in the Department of Psychopharmacology at the University of Cincinnati."

Dr. Scharf paused, waiting for the next question in the carefully rehearsed drama.

"Have you published any articles on sleep disorders, Doctor?" Yamaki asked from the lectern.

Scharf turned again to the jury and smiled. "I have published in excess of one hundred articles in various medical journals on the subject of sleep disorders and pharmaceuticals associated with the problem."

"And have you been associated with any research, any studies in the area?"

"I worked with Dr. Anthony Kales, who wrote the first draft for the Food and Drug Administration on hypnonarcotic drugs. I was also involved in the NASA study on sleep for astronauts in space."

"The Kales study was the first to test Halcion, is that not so?"

"Yes," Scharf said, still smiling to the jury. "And I have been interviewed extensively concerning Halcion. I have appeared on the

Today show, on *Good Morning America,* on *20/20,* and on the *MacNeil/ Lehrer NewsHour.*"

"Thank you, Doctor." Yamaki scanned his notes. "Now, could you please tell the jury just what Halcion is?"

"Of course." Scharf turned to the jury again, his face suddenly grave. "Halcion is the Upjohn Company's name for triazolam, a member of the benzodiazepine family. It is—"

"Excuse me, Doctor." Yamaki interrupted.

"What?"

"Do you see a representative of the Upjohn Company in the audience at this time?"

"Yes, yes, there is," Scharf said, pointing to the back of the courtroom. "The attorney for Upjohn."

"Would you please stand, sir," Yamaki said toward the audience, "and identify yourself?"

An older man in a plain brown suit and yellow bow tie stood up. "My name is Lane Bauer," he said, "and I am a senior partner with the law firm of Shook, Hardy and Bacon in Kansas City."

"And you are the attorney for Upjohn?"

"We represent Upjohn, yes."

Yamaki nodded, glanced at Longo, then turned his attention back to the witness. "I apologize, Doctor. Please continue."

Longo was angry at himself. He had asked Bauer to sit in and take notes during Scharf's testimony. Bauer had cross-examined Scharf in civil suits; his comments might prove helpful during Longo's cross-examination. But the prosecutor realized that he should have foreseen that Yamaki might point Bauer out. Now it looked to the jury as though Upjohn was hounding and spying on critics of their drug. Worse, it made Longo look like a stooge for the giant pharmaceutical company.

"The benzodiazepine family of drugs includes such tranquilizers as Valium and Xanax," Scharf continued, "and such sleeping aids as Restoril and Dalmane. Halcion was introduced by Upjohn in the late 1970s, and was finally approved by the FDA in, I believe, 1982. And, of course, it grew to become quite popular in dealing with sleep disorders."

"I see. Now, tell me, Doctor, have there been any problems with Halcion?"

This was the flag question, Longo realized. It was a signal to the expert witness that he was now free to launch into his discourse.

Scharf turned back to the jurors with his professionally concerned look. "In 1977, before the drug was approved by the FDA, a Dutch psychiatrist reported that Halcion was causing depression, anxiety, amnesia, paranoia, and hallucination in his patients. In some cases, even verbal and physical aggression."

"Aggression?"

"Absolutely. As a result, in 1979 the Dutch authorities suspended the drug. They later authorized its use, but only in the smaller .250-milligram size. It had previously been prescribed in half-milligram doses."

"I see."

"After similar findings in Great Britain, that country banned the sale of Halcion altogether."

"What has been the experience in the United States, Doctor?"

"In 1987, the FDA reported that there were between eight and thirty times as many adverse reactions to Halcion as to Restoril and Dalmane combined. And in 1989, the FDA's Psychopharmacological Drugs Advisory Committee announced that they had examined six years' worth of reports on side effects from using the drug. They focused on six side effects: anxiety, amnesia, confusion, hostility, psychosis, and seizures. They found that Halcion was eight to forty-five times more likely to generate these reactions as Restoril."

Scharf paused, looked back at Yamaki.

"You mentioned amnesia," the lawyer said.

"Without question, Halcion can cause anterograde amnesia."

"You mean, an individual who takes Halcion might not have a memory of what he is doing?"

"Basically, yes."

"Tell me, Doctor, have there been any instances reported of automatic behavior? Or of sleepwalking?"

"Yes. These have occurred with all sleeping pills, of course, but they have been reported more frequently with Halcion."

"So Halcion can cause someone to act automatically—to commit an act, without having any control over that act?"

"Yes."

"And to commit an act while not conscious that he is doing it, as if he were sleepwalking?"

"It is possible, yes."

Yamaki paused to look at the jurors, letting the significance of this sink in. Longo knew he would pound it home during his closing argument.

"Doctor, in your articles you have mentioned 'paradoxical reactions.'"

"Yes. This refers to reactions that are the opposite of what is expected. Halcion is, of course, supposed to make one sleepy. In some individuals, however, the opposite reaction takes place: He can become agitated, irritable, aggressive, even hostile, as I indicated a moment ago."

"All right, Doctor," Yamaki said, "can you tell us how long it takes for Halcion to take effect?"

"About half an hour."

"And how long will it last?"

"Halcion has a half-life of about three hours. That is to say, every three hours, it will lose half of its strength. It will generally take five half-lives to be eliminated from the body altogether. So, perhaps fifteen hours before all effects are gone."

"Thank you. Now, Doctor, have you had a chance to interview Mr. Yamaguchi?"

"I have."

"And you have read the reports in this case? Police reports and statements of witnesses?"

"I have."

"Based upon your interview with Mr. Yamaguchi, and your review of these reports, do you have an opinion about this case?"

Scharf again turned to the jury. "Of course, I cannot say that Mr. Yamaguchi *did* take Halcion on the evening in question. Nor can I say that he did, in fact, have adverse side effects. I was not there. But based upon his statements, and the reports, I can say that he exhibited all of the symptoms of a paradoxical reaction to Halcion."

"And what were some of those symptoms?"

"I believe one of the officers reported that he was sleepy at the police station, subdued. And then there was the incident with the paper."

"Yes?"

"Well, I understand that while he was waiting in his car for his wife and the deceased to arrive, an eyewitness saw him repeatedly get out of his car and walk over to another car and replace a piece of paper over a window. This type of irrational conduct is symptomatic of a paradoxical reaction to the drug."

"I see." Yamaki glanced at the jurors, then back at Scharf. "Hypothetically, Doctor, if a man of Mr. Yamaguchi's age takes a double dose of Halcion while under a great amount of stress ... might such a man act aggressively, even homicidally—and not be aware of what he is doing?"

"In my opinion, yes, this is very possible."

"Based upon your review of the reports and your interview of Mr. Yamaguchi, is it your opinion that this type of homicidal reaction was possible in this case?"

"Based upon the reports, and Mr. Yamaguchi telling me he took a double dose of the drug, it is my opinion—"

"Objection," Longo growled. Clever, he thought. Yamaki got in Yamaguchi's statement that he took two pills, corroborating Ken's testimony—without his client ever taking the stand.

"The objection is sustained," Bascue said, "and the answer as it relates to what the defendant said to Dr. Scharf is stricken. The jury is instructed to disregard the witness's testimony as to what the defendant told him."

Unring the bell.

"Doctor," Yamaki said with a slight smile, "are you saying that from what you've seen and heard, it is your opinion that Halcion could have driven Mr. Yamaguchi to kill someone—without even knowing it?"

"That is my professional opinion."

"I see." Yamaki looked at the jurors. "Tell me, Doctor, have there been any confirmed instances of Halcion causing someone to commit murder?"

"Yes. The Grundberg case." Scharf again turned to the jury with a concerned look. "In that case, a fifty-seven-year-old woman shot her mother to death. The woman was arrested and charged with second-degree murder. Before trial, however, she was examined by two psychiatrists. They discovered that she had been taking Halcion to help her sleep for about a year before she shot her mother. During this period, she had grown increasingly agitated and paranoid. And when questioned about the murder, she had very little memory of it."

"What was the psychiatrists' diagnosis, Doctor?"

"The two psychiatrists were both of the opinion that Halcion caused the woman to become involuntarily intoxicated."

"Involuntarily intoxicated," Yamaki repeated slowly, his eyes still on the jurors.

"Yes. Mrs. Grundberg had not been acting voluntarily when she shot her mother to death. She was not in control."

"I see. And, tell us, Dr. Scharf, whatever became of the Grundberg case?"

"After the prosecutor reviewed the reports of the two psychiatrists, and could find no motive for the shooting, he dismissed the murder charges."

"Thank you, Dr. Scharf. No further questions."

Judge Bascue looked at the prosecutor. "Your witness, Mr. Longo."

Chapter 24

The next morning Longo sat at the counsel table, reviewing the list of cases left on the court's morning docket. Of an original sixteen, there were still seven left to dispose of. Four, he knew, would be continued; with a jury waiting in the wings, Judge Bascue would be unlikely to deny the defense requests. That left three cases, one a possible plea, another a probation violation. Both would probably be trailed by the judge to the afternoon session as soon as he got off the phone in chambers and resumed the bench. The third case was a suppression motion, but it was a "special," a case being prosecuted by a deputy from one of the units like S.I.D. or Special Trials.

The prosecutor looked at the courtroom clock: 9:40. The jury had been ordered back for 10:00. When trial resumed, he would begin his cross-examination of Dr. Martin Scharf.

Longo's interrogation of the doctor would be a pivotal point in the trial. If the jury accepted Scharf's testimony, Yamaguchi would win a manslaughter verdict—or even walk out of the courthouse with a complete acquittal. If his testimony raised even a reasonable doubt, the case would be lost.

Longo knew this. And he had been up most of the night preparing his cross-exam.

The prosecutor yawned, then stood up and stretched mightily. He tugged on his lapels, straightened his broad mauve tie, then re-adjusted the matching scarf blossoming from his pocket. Satisfied, he wandered over to the empty jury box, where his junior calendar deputy was talking over a case with a defense lawyer.

"... plead straight up to one count," Larry Boyle was saying.

"I'm telling you, Larry," the defense lawyer said to the junior deputy, "you got no case, no specific intent. She wasn't trying to kill him. Anyway, the guy won't testify against her. Marital privilege."

"The privilege doesn't apply if the spouse is the victim, Arnie."

"C'mon, Larry, this is a piece of shit. You know it, I know it."

"Hey, what am I supposed to do? We can't just sit by while your client keeps trying to turn her husband into ashes."

Longo slapped the defense lawyer on the back. "Hey, howya doin', Arnie?"

"Hey, honcho," the man said.

Arnold Swanson* was a former deputy D.A., and he had been a good one. After nine years in the office, he was lured into private practice by the promise of big money. The word was that he was now clearing over a quarter million dollars a year. Much of his success came from the simple fact that he had a reputation for being a man of his word; there were few criminal lawyers whom prosecutors trusted. Trust and respect translated into better plea bargains, and that meant more clients.

"Whatcha got?" Longo asked.

"Christ," the lawyer said, "a real piece of shit, believe me."

"Yeah?"

"Honest-to-God dog meat, Larry. Can't figure why you guys filed it."

"Harriet Smith,*" Boyle said, handing the case file to the senior prosecutor. "One count arson, seven counts attempted murder."

The case sounded only vaguely familiar to Longo.

"Defendant's an older woman," Boyle continued, "about fifty—"

"Fifty-two," Swanson said. "And no rap sheet."

"Yeah," Boyle said. "But she's got this nasty little habit. She keeps trying to barbecue her husband."

"Christ," Swanson said, turning to Longo. "What it is, Larry, my client has a bit of a temper..."

Boyle snorted.

"What happens," the defense lawyer continued, "Mr. Smith has some buddies over for poker games, watch football, that kind of thing.

And there's some drinking, and sometimes they get a little obnoxious. Anyway, Mr. Smith and Mrs. Smith usually end up in a fight, and Mrs. Smith, she stomps out of the house."

"Yeah?" Longo said.

"And then she sets fire to the house."

"With her husband and his pals inside," Boyle added.

Longo broke out laughing. "You gotta be kidding."

"Honest to God," Swanson said, trying to remain serious. "I mean, you tell me where you guys get intent to commit murder out of that."

"This is the sixth time, Arnie," Boyle said. "What do we do, cite her for not having a fire permit?"

Longo shook his head, still laughing. "Reminds me of a case couple years back. This guy, he's at this wedding reception, over in east L.A. Big Mexican blowout, you know? Mariachis, the whole enchilada. And he's drinkin' like a fish and dancin' with whatever's wearing a skirt."

Longo paused, recalling the facts with a widening grin.

"So his wife, very hot-tempered senorita, she's just sitting there on the sidelines, doin' a slow burn, right? And the guy, he just keeps getting sloppier and sloppier, and he's makin' moves on a couple of the ladies, the whole thing. So anyway, the shindig finally winds down, and the guy and his wife drive back home and the guy passes out on the bed."

"Yeah?" Swanson said.

"Yeah, so a couple hours later, the guy wakes up, he's got this sharp pain down between his legs. And he looks down, and there's blood all over the place, all over his legs, the sheets, everywhere."

"Aw, man," Boyle said, grimacing.

"Yeah. And she's standing there at the foot of the bed, this bloody straight-edge razor in one hand . . ."

"Aw, man," Boyle repeated.

". . . and the family jewels in the other."

"Mother of God," Swanson said.

"Yeah. Just looks at him and says, next time she cuts off the rest."

"Cold," the defense lawyer said.

"So we filed ADW on her. Or was it mayhem? Anyway, it gets to trial—"

"He wouldn't testify against her, right?" Swanson said.

Longo nodded. "Learned his lesson, the guy says." He paused. "Funny," he said, shaking his head again. "Real quiet, kinda mousy guy . . ."

"Man," Boyle said, shivering.

"Yeah."

"I remember one . . ." the defense lawyer said.

"Yeah?"

"Yeah, back when I was in the office."

"No kidding?" Longo said. "You used to be a lawyer?"

"Believe it." Swanson grinned. "Anyway, some homicide dick brings in this case for a murder filing. Seems LAPD out in the Valley gets a phone call, shots fired. They go to this real nice house, there's this guy lying on the floor in the hallway, three bullet holes in him. But he's still alive, see?"

"Uh-huh," Longo said.

"So they ask him, 'What happened? Who shot you?' And the guy says to them, he says, 'My wife shot me.' He tells these cops that his wife found out he's ballin' his secretary or somebody, and she ambushes him in their house, drills him when he walks through the front door."

"Yeah?"

"So he falls to the floor, and she just stands over him. He's looking up at her, begging her to get a doctor. And, cold as hell, she just pumps a couple more shots into the guy. Then she just walks out."

"Uh-huh."

"Well, one of the cops, he's going to law school at night, see. And so he knows this guy's statement about who killed him is hearsay, right? Never get into evidence. But he also knows about the exception for dying declarations."

"Yeah?"

"But he knows the exception works only if the guy *thinks* he's dying, right? If the guy doesn't think he's dying, it's not a dying declaration, even if he does end up croaking."

"Right, right," Boyle said.

"Well, the guy's not long for this world. He's taking his last few breaths. So the cop, real smart-like, he says to the guy, 'You realize you're dying, don't you?' And the guy looks up at him, and you know what he says?"

"What?" Boyle said.

"Guy says to the cop, 'Hell no, I'm not going to die.' He says, 'I'm going to live and I'm going to kill that fucking bitch!' "

Longo laughed.

"So what happened?" Boyle asked.

"He died. Cops arrested the wife, but she clammed up, got a high-priced lawyer." He shrugged again. "No witnesses. Never found the gun. Without the guy's statement, there was no evidence. I had to tell the homicide dick to let her go."

"You're kidding," Boyle said.

"True story."

"Man."

"So what are we going to do about Mrs. Smith, guys?" Swanson said.

"You see any evidence of intent to kill?" Longo asked his junior deputy.

"Naw," Boyle said, "I think it got overfiled. But we got a right-eous arson."

"It's her own house," the lawyer said. "No insurance claims, the husband fixed the fire damage himself, same as always. No harm, no foul."

"I dunno," Longo said. "What do you think, Larry?"

Boyle shrugged. "Plead to a misdemeanor, say a 452, something like that. Time served, she walks out today."

"Sounds fair," Longo said.

"Yeah," Swanson said.

"But we want a long tail, Arnie," Boyle said. "Three years. She torches the house again, she does a bullet."

The deputy D.A. was offering to accept a plea of guilty to a charge of recklessly causing a fire, with an agreement that the judge would sentence her to the time she had already served while awaiting trial. But he would place her on probation for three years; if there was a recurrence, the judge would find her in violation of the probation and send her to jail for one year.

Boyle suddenly turned to Longo. "Damn, I forgot about the memo, Larry."

A memorandum had been circulated a few days earlier to all deputies in the office. The memo, entitled "Special Directive 91-03," was from District Attorney Ira Reiner and ordered all prosecutors to demand maximum sentences in any cases involving violent crimes.

"We get those memos every four years, a few months before the election," Longo said with contempt. "Right off, they get leaked to the media. Makes the incumbent look like he's tough on crime. After the election's over, the memo's buried and it's back to business as usual."

"Maybe so," the junior prosecutor said, "but an order's an order. And we got an arson and seven counts of attempted murder here."

"I'll talk with Bascue," Longo said with a wink. "If he wants to accept a misdemeanor plea over my strenuous objection, why, there's not much we can do about it, right?"

"I see the office hasn't changed much," Swanson said.

"Naw, same old games," Longo said.

"I hear you're in trial, huh?"

"Yeah."

"Yamaki?"

"Yeah."

Swanson nodded. "He's good."

"Yeah." Longo glanced back at the clock, then at the door to the jury deliberation room.

A woman in a beige business suit finished checking in with the clerk, then strolled confidently over to the three men. She was in her late thirties, with hard good looks and a trim figure that reflected her onetime profession as a ballet dancer and actress. But it was her eyes that drew attention, bright, flashing brown eyes that seemed to radiate an intense energy.

This was Deputy D.A. Marcia Clark, later to gain fame in battle against the all-star defense team assembled to defend O. J. Simpson.

"Hey, *hombres,*" she said. "*¿Qué pasa?*"

"Hey, Marcia," Boyle said.

"What're you doing in 127, Marcia?" Longo asked. "Slumming?"

"Shit," the woman said, "the front office just thought you guys needed to see what a real prosecutor looks like."

"Looks pretty good," Swanson said.

"Well, *muchas gracias,* stranger," she said.

"Marcia, you know Arnie Swanson?" Longo asked.

"Sure," Clark said. "How's life on the outside, Arnie?"

Swanson shrugged. "It's a living."

"Damned good one, I'd say." She ran her hand down the silken fabric of the defense lawyer's sleeve.

"Crime's a growth industry, Marcia," Swanson said. "Totally recession-proof."

"Hey," Boyle said, "I understand you got the Russian Mafia case, Marcia."

"Yeah," Clark said.

"Congratulations."

The woman shrugged.

Boyle sensed a sudden tension in the air. He looked at Longo. Then it dawned on him. The career-building murder case had been taken away from Steve Barshop and given to Clark. And Barshop was Longo's friend.

Deputy sheriffs in West Hollywood had found a car left idling in front of a house near Sunset Strip. When they knocked on the front door of the house, a man answered; his clothes were soaked in blood and he was carrying a semiautomatic handgun. The deputies wrestled the gun away, then found another man inside. They also found two dead bodies; each of the recently killed corpses had its fingertips cut off to avoid identification.

The two men turned out to be former soldiers in the Soviet Army—and members of the *organizatsiya,* the so-called glasnost gangsters who had recently infiltrated the United States. Los Angeles, home to the nation's second-largest Russian population, had quickly became a primary target. This so-called Russian Mafia, which some detectives believed was run by KGB officers, was extremely violent and ruled by terror. Victims often had their tongues or eyes cut out, or the skin burned off their bodies with acid.

Since the double murder occurred in West Hollywood, the investigating detectives went to the D.A.'s Santa Monica office to file charges. The head of the branch office quickly assigned the case to his best prosecutor: Barshop. But Barshop was still in disfavor among the powers downtown for his criticism of the *Twilight Zone* trial. Word came down from the front office: The Russian Mafia case was being transferred downtown to Special Trials and given to Clark.

The awkward silence was suddenly interrupted by the bailiff announcing that court was again in session.

"Ladies and gentlemen," Judge Bascue said loudly to the attorneys as he took the bench, "we have a jury in the back room and a trial set to resume at ten. Any cases that cannot be resolved in the next ten minutes will have to be trailed until the one-thirty calendar. With that in mind, are there any matters that are ready?"

Clark stepped forward. "People versus Mohammed Tyrell Jordan,*" she said, her voice confident and businesslike. "Marcia Clark, deputy district attorney."

"Good morning, Ms. Clark," Bascue said as he shuffled through the stack of files on the bench. "Always a pleasure to entertain Special Trials."

Clark curtsied facetiously.

A young black attorney wearing an African turban on her head stepped forward. "Elizabeth Wilkens,* your honor, for the defendant."

"Good morning, Ms. Wilkens."

"Morning."

"Miss-out, your honor," the bailiff announced.

Bascue sighed. "Just as well, we really don't have time for the hearing today. Well, since your client seems lost somewhere in the jail system, Ms. Wilkens, can we agree on a date for a court's continuance?"

Longo watched from his seat in the jury box as the two attorneys checked their pocket calendars and conferred. Clark was a rising star in the office. Ambitious, profane, hair-triggered, aggressive, even cocky. A tightly wound street fighter, a female bantam with a taste for the jugular. The district attorney's answer to Menendez attorney Leslie Abramson. What a donnybrook *that* would be, Longo thought with a grin.

The traditional view among lawyers was that the D.A.'s Office was no place for a female; women were simply not cut out for the rough-and-tumble of courtroom battle. This view was rapidly changing as women like Lea D'Agostino, Pam Ferrero, Katherine Mader, and Marcia Clark racked up one trial victory after another. The prevailing view now seemed to be that a lawyer's gender made no difference; skill, not sex, was the critical factor.

Clark, however, firmly believed that women were *better* trial lawyers than men. Men were too objective and "fact-oriented," she felt; they were taught to repress feelings and deal with facts in the abstract. Women, on the other hand, were better at relating to witnesses and juries on an emotional level. A male prosecutor would ask a witness, "And after the defendant raped you, what happened next?" A woman would ask, "What did it *feel* like when he raped you?" And, as any good trial lawyer knows, feelings and emotions are much more powerful weapons than mere facts.

Men were also the more fragile sex when it came to trial combat, Clark felt. It was men who burned out after a few years of trying cases, not women. This, she believed, was because men repressed emotions, creating the internal pressures that eventually caused the occupational disease of trial lawyers: burnout. Women were better adapted to trial work because they dealt openly with emotions and problems; they had not learned to keep fear, anger, pain, and frustration bottled up inside. "The oak breaks," she would remind her male associates, "the willow bends."

Marcia Clark had originally set her sights on a career in the State Department. But after graduating magna cum laude from UCLA, she quickly discovered that the only women in that agency were secretaries. Abandoning her plans to become a diplomat, she turned to acting and dancing. She appeared in a number of off-Broadway plays, then began using her ballet training to work as a dancer with jazz groups. When those jobs could not pay the rent, she joined the Romanian Folk Ballet and spent the next few months touring the United States and Canada.

Clark finally grew tired of constantly scratching for money. Being an actress and dancer was a fine dream, but the reality of life was that she needed to make a living. She took a job as a cocktail waitress.

Then late one night, after a long evening of serving drinks in a short skirt and high heels to inebriated customers, Clark sat down and took stock of herself. She started by making up a list of what she was good at. She was a logical thinker, she decided, enjoyed research, and loved to argue. That sounded like a lawyer to her and she immediately enrolled in law school.

Being a lawyer to Clark meant being a criminal lawyer. She longed for the action and excitement of trial, the variety of colorful characters, the drama of human tragedy. Being a criminal lawyer, she decided, was a lot like being an actress.

After graduation, Clark was offered a position by Gerald Chaleff, the criminal defense attorney who, along with Katherine Mader, would later represent the Hillside Strangler. But she soon found that defense work bore no resemblance to the worlds of Matlock and Perry Mason. Being a defense lawyer, she discovered, had little to do with championing the wrongfully accused; most of her clients were guilty.

Clark applied for a position with the district attorney and when the offer came, she quickly accepted.

Clark loved being a prosecutor. And she was good at it. But it was not until the Schaeffer case that her name became known to the front office.

Rebecca Schaeffer was a rising twenty-one-year-old actress who co-starred in the television series *My Sister Sam* and the movie *Scenes from the Class Struggle in Beverly Hills*. And, like most popular stars, she attracted the attention of thousands of fans. One of these, it turned out, was Robert Bardo, a young, bookish fast-food worker from Tucson who was completely obsessed with the beautiful young woman's wholesome girl-next-door image. Bardo hired a private investigator to find where the actress lived, then showed up one morning and rang the doorbell. When Schaeffer politely asked him to leave, Bardo walked to a nearby restaurant. An hour later he returned and again rang the bell. Schaeffer, who was expecting a television script to be delivered, came down to the security door and opened it. As she looked around for the package, Bardo stepped out and grabbed her by one arm. Then he shot her to death as he held her.

The defense at trial hinged on the testimony of the psychiatrist who had testified in the Hinckley case. Bardo was a schizophrenic, the doctor explained; his feelings toward Schaeffer vacillated wildly between love and hate. The killing had been one of sudden impulse, a spontaneous emotional response to the actress's rejection of the young man. The defendant was not responsible for his actions. Certainly, there had never been any meaningful intent or premeditation.

Marcia Clark refused to play the courtroom game of "battle of the experts," countering the defense psychiatrist by calling one of her own. Instead, she relied on a vicious cross-examination of the doctor to make her case. From her experience both as defense attorney and prosecutor, Clark had developed a deep contempt for the psychiatric profession. Psychiatry was an undisciplined and unprincipled pseudoscience, she believed; its practitioners were nothing more than "medical whores," willing to testify to anything for the right price. "*Nobody* can tell what's in the mind of someone when they kill," she said. "Anyone who puts a shrink on the stand is suborning perjury."

Shortly after the prosecutor finished her attack on the psychiatrist, Robert Bardo was convicted of first-degree murder.

"All other matters are trailed until one-thirty this afternoon," Bascue announced. "Tom," he said to the bailiff, "after you've returned Mr. Jordan to the holding cell and brought out Mr. Yamaguchi, please bring in the witness, Dr. Scharf. Then signal the jury."

Longo and Boyle stood up in the jury box and returned to the prosecution table as Clark finished stuffing the case file back into her briefcase.

"You catch that cross-exam of William Kennedy Smith, Marcia?" Longo asked innocently.

Clark snorted, shook her head in disgust. The Smith rape trial in Florida had been televised live nationally. Many in the Los Angeles D.A.'s Office had watched the trial with professional interest. The performance of the prosecuting attorney in the case, Moira Lasch, had been the subject of coffee talk throughout the office for days. The broad consensus was that she had conducted the most incompetent job of cross-examining a defendant any of the deputies had ever seen.

Longo knew that the Florida prosecutor's highly visible bumbling was a source of considerable embarrassment to Clark. It certainly did not help her view of female superiority in trial.

Longo glanced away from Clark, his eyes now on Dr. Scharf as he strode through the gate.

"Good morning, Mr. Longo," he said confidently.

"Top of the morning to you, Doc," Longo said.

Scharf sat in the witness stand as the door to the jury deliberation room opened and men and women began to file out.

"Your jury?" Clark asked.

"Yeah."

She nodded. "Break a leg."

"Thanks."

Longo sat down at the counsel table as Clark turned and passed toward the gate.

Mike Yamaki placed his burgundy leather briefcase on the defense table, opened it, and began taking out legal pads and documents. Then he sat down and whispered something to Yamaguchi, seated next to him in a dark blue suit.

"Dr. Scharf," Bascue said to the witness, "you are reminded that you are still under oath." He looked at the deputy D.A. "You may proceed, Mr. Longo."

"Dr. Scharf," Longo said, rising to his feet and ambling toward the jury box, "how long you been a physician?"

"I . . . am not a physician," Scharf said. "I have a Ph.D."

"Yeah?" the prosecutor said with mock surprise. "You don't have an M.D.?"

"No."

"So you don't really have patients, huh?"

"Yes, I have . . . clients. Individuals who are referred to me with sleep disorders."

"But you can't really prescribe medicine for them, drugs, that kind of thing?"

"That is the province of physicians."

The prosecutor nodded. "You said something to Mr. Yamaki about being a professor somewhere?"

"I am on the faculty at the University of Cincinnati, in psychopharmacology."

"Full professor?"

"Associate professor."

"Uh-huh. And how many hours a week would you say you teach there, Doc?"

"I . . . it's difficult to say."

"Well, let's just take this last year. How many hours a week did you teach?"

"I can't recall exactly."

"Well, how many for the entire year, then?"

"I would have to . . ."

"Isn't it a fact, Dr. Scharf, that you only taught for *two hours*— for the entire year?"

"That is possible."

"Uh-huh. And you also said something about being the director of something?"

"I am the director of the Center for Sleep Disorders at Mercy Hospital."

"That center isn't a part of the hospital, is it?"

"Actually, the center is affiliated with it, as am I."

"This center of yours is in the same building as the hospital, right?"

"That is correct."

"Who owns that building, Doctor?"

"I do."

"And you rent it to the hospital, right?"

"That is correct."

"Uh-huh."

Longo turned away from the witness, looked out across the audience.

"You mentioned working with Dr. Kales," the prosecutor said, his back still to Scharf, "when he was doing the FDA work on Halcion."

"Yes."

"You weren't a Ph.D. then, were you?"

"I was working on my doctorate."

"So, I guess you were just a student at the time, huh?"

"I was a graduate student, Mr. Longo."

The prosecutor turned around to face the man. "Has the FDA banned Halcion, Doc?"

"What?"

Longo was using the "scatter-gun" technique of cross-examination, suddenly changing subjects with no apparent method. Faced with sudden, illogical shifts in topics, expert witnesses accustomed to order often became flustered and even angry.

"Halcion," Longo repeated. "You were talking about how the stuff was dangerous, and the FDA was doing a bunch of studies. I figure the FDA must have banned the stuff, huh?"

"No."

"No?"

"But Upjohn reduced the dose."

"The original dose was .500 milligrams, right? Half a milligram per pill?"

"That is correct."

"And Upjohn reduced it to .250- and .125-milligram sizes?"

"Yes."

"These pills Mrs. Yamaguchi was taking, they're .125 milligrams, right?"

"I understand Mr. Yamaguchi consumed two of the tablets."

"You don't *know* that, do you, Doctor? I mean, you've only been told that, right?"

"That is correct."

"Even if he did take two of the pills, that only adds up to .250 milligrams, right?"

"That is correct."

"By the way, you mentioned that the Dutch banned Halcion."

"Yes."

"Fact is, they only banned the .500-milligram pills, right? The .250 pills were okay?"

"I believe that is correct."

Longo slowly walked toward the witness, his hand trailing along the jury railing.

"Awright, you mentioned that there were a lot more complaints about Halcion than about other sleeping drugs."

"Yes."

"Well, there's a lot more Halcion *sold,* right? I mean, there's, what, a half-million prescriptions for the stuff every month in the U.S. alone?"

"That's true," Scharf said patiently, "but the larger sales cannot explain the vastly larger number of complaints."

"Well, fact is, new drugs always get a lot more reports to the FDA, right? I mean, after they've been out there a few years, the number of reports dies down. Isn't that the normal pattern?"

"There is ... I suppose so, yes."

"And Halcion's a lot newer than those other drugs?"

"Yes, but, again, I do not believe that accounts for the higher number of reports."

"You ever meet Mr. Yamaguchi before this week, Doc?"

"What?"

"The defendant, Yamaguchi, you get a chance to examine him right after the shooting?"

"No, of course not."

"First time you ever saw him was this week, right?"

"Yes."

"So how many studies has the FDA done on the effects of Halcion?"

"Studies?"

"Yeah. They get these reports, so I guess they must be pretty worried, huh? I guess they must conduct some kind of studies on what the stuff does?"

"I am not aware of any such studies."

"There aren't any studies by the FDA on Halcion?"

"No."

"Nothing indicating that the drug causes depression?"

"No."

"Or paranoia?"

"No."

"Or aggression?"

"No."

"Violent behavior?"

"No."

"No FDA studies showing Halcion causes homicidal acts?"

"Obviously, that would not be possible, Mr. Longo."

"How much they paying you?"

"I beg your pardon?"

"Mr. Yamaki over there, he's paying you to testify, right?"

"You, as an attorney, should know that is perfectly appropriate."

"How much?"

Scharf sighed. "My fee is a thousand dollars a day, plus expenses.

And two hundred and fifty dollars an hour for preparation time."

"And how much preparation was there?"

"Eight hours."

"So . . . three thousand bucks to testify?"

"That is correct."

"What about your own studies?"

"My own . . ."

"You do any studies of your own on the effects of Halcion?"

"Yes, yes, I have conducted such studies."

"How many of them show that people taking the stuff commit homicides?"

Scharf shook his head patiently. "None, Mr. Longo. You know that is not possible."

"Well, these studies of yours, you ever observed depression that was caused by Halcion?"

"No."

"Paranoia?"

"No."

"Psychotic behavior?"

"No."

"Dr. Scharf," Longo said, walking around to the far side of the jury box, "has *any* study ever found violent behavior resulting from taking Halcion?"

"I . . . am not aware of any."

"Has *any* study found a link between the drug and homicide?"

"No."

"Yamaguchi told the cops he wasn't taking medication."

"I beg your pardon?"

"The police reports you read. They say that after the defendant was arrested, the cops asked him if he was taking medication. He said he wasn't."

"Yes?"

"You remember reading that?"

"I seem to recall that, yes."

Longo nodded thoughtfully, then walked over to the prosecution table and sat on the edge.

"The Grundberg case . . ."

"Yes."

"Halcion wasn't the only drug Mrs. Grundberg was taking when she shot her mother, was it?"

"I believe there were others."

"Fact is, she was also taking Valium, right?"

"I believe that is correct."

"And other drugs?"

"As I said, I believe there were other drugs."

"Do you know what dosage she was taking of Halcion?"

"No."

"Fact is, her doctor kept increasing the dosage when her symptoms didn't improve, that right?"

"I believe that is correct."

"So she was taking pretty heavy doses of the stuff, along with the Valium and the other drugs, right?"

"That is my understanding, yes."

"You know Dr. David Greenblatt?"

"Doctor . . . yes, of course."

"He's a medical doctor, a physician, right?"

"I believe so."

"Professor of pharmacology, psychiatry, and medicine at Tufts University School of Medicine?"

"I believe so."

"He's pretty well known in the field, isn't he?"

"He is, yes."

"Written a few books on the psychological effects of drugs like Halcion?"

"Yes."

"In fact, wouldn't you say he's recognized all over the world as an authority on Halcion?"

"He is well recognized, yes."

"Would it be fair to say that he's considerably better known than you are?"

"He is well known," Scharf said. "I cannot really make a comparison."

"Uh-huh. Yamaguchi had a paradoxical reaction, huh?"

"What? . . . yes, yes. In my professional opinion, Mr. Yamaguchi displayed symptoms of a paradoxical reaction to the ingestion of Halcion."

"And by that, you mean a witness saw him pick up a sheet of paper and replace it over the open window of a car."

"This was done repeatedly, Mr. Longo."

"You know *why* he did that, Doc?"

"I could not say. But it certainly appears to be the kind of repetitive, irrational conduct that can be caused by Halcion."

"Or maybe it was his car, and he didn't want dust getting inside?"

"I could not say."

"But based on this evidence, covering an open window, you're prepared to say he was having a paradoxical reaction to Halcion?"

"Done repeatedly, it could be evidence of such a reaction, yes."

"Amnesia."

Scharf stared at the prosecutor.

"Amnesia," Longo repeated. "You said Halcion can cause amnesia."

"Yes, yes."

"Guy does something, he can't remember about it afterward, huh?"

"Basically, that's correct. The individual will have immediate recall, but once the drug wears off, he will have no recollection of events."

"So, guy kills somebody, and he's got amnesia from Halcion, he won't remember it later?"

"Essentially, yes."

"But he knows what he's doing *at the time*."

"He ... in usual amnesia cases, he will be aware of his actions at the time, yes. But—"

"He can form the intent to kill at the time, can premeditate the killing."

"Yes ..."

"And it's only later, *after* the killing, after the drug wears off, that he forgets."

"Yes."

"You said you read the police reports in this case?"

"I did."

"Then you know Yamaguchi told the cops that he just shot Kariya?"

"I believe that is correct."

"So, some time after the shooting, Yamaguchi was still able to remember what he did, huh?"

"I cannot say."

"You weren't there, right, Doc?"

"As you say."

"Nothing further."

Chapter

25

"You got the wrong man, Larry."

"Uh-huh."

"I'm telling you," the lawyer* said as he polished his bifocals, "I got a witness puts my guy in Alhambra at the time of the shooting, fifteen miles away."

"Tell it to the jury, Sammy," Longo said as he shuffled through the stack of case files on the prosecution table. The diminutive lawyer was vaguely irritating to the prosecutor; the man reminded him of a Chihuahua on speed. Longo glanced behind him at the six lawyers waiting to discuss their cases with him.

"C'mon, Larry," Chihuahua continued, "your victim didn't even get that good a look, am I right? These freeway shootings, what kind of ID can you expect?" He shrugged. "I mean, what we got here is a race thing, right?"

"A race thing . . ."

"Sure. Your guy's white, mine's Korean. . . ."

Longo shook his head. "Gimme a break."

There it was again. The race thing. Racial conflict had always been present in the courts, but since the Rodney King trial had begun the polarization in the city had intensified dramatically. Longo could feel the hostility and anger in the hallways of the courthouse as the trial ground toward judgment day.

But it was not just black versus white. It was Korean against black, El Salvadoran against Samoan, black against Jew, Vietnamese against Arab. The so-called melting pot was nearing a boiling point and all eyes were on Simi Valley.

A few days earlier, a black man had been arraigned in Superior Court for "ADW," assault with a deadly weapon. He had pulled an Asian woman out of her car, smashed in her windows with a baseball bat and then beaten the helpless woman. "I don't like fucking Koreans," he had screamed at her, "and I don't like that fucking sentence." He was referring to the Latasha Harlans case, in which an elderly Korean grocer had shot a teenage black girl during an attempted theft; the jury verdict of manslaughter rather than murder, and the resultant sentence of probation, had infuriated the black community and ignited long-simmering resentments. Yet, the rage that the Harlans case unleashed seemed directed beyond just the Koreans. It probably would not have mattered to the man with the baseball bat had he known that the woman he sent to the hospital was, in fact, not Korean but Thai.

The case had been sent to the D.A.'s Organized Crime and Anti-Terrorist Task Force. The main focus of the task force was the myriad ethnic gangs in L.A. with roots in the old country, especially Chinese, Vietnamese, and Iranian. But the unit was also responsible for hate crimes, which were loosely classified under "terrorist activity."

The deputy assigned to the case was Dave Conn, a Marine veteran of Da Nang who had been raised in the Bronx. Conn had gained headlines with his successful prosecution of the *Cotton Club* murders, involving the Mafia and drug deals in the financing of the Richard Gere feature film. Conn was later named to retry the Menendez brothers. When the highly coveted O. J. Simpson case broke, however, he was reassigned to lead that prosecution team.

But Conn made a costly mistake. Reporters came to him asking for copies of the 911 tape in which Nicole Simpson had called the police for help during one of O. J.'s rages. Since the incident had been handled as a misdemeanor by the City Attorney's Office (inside the city, the district attorney prosecuted only felonies), Conn simply told the reporters to get the tape from that agency. When the city attorney was advised by reporters that Conn had referred them to him, he assumed that the D.A.'s Office was not opposed to releasing the tape and so provided them with copies.

Conn was immediately called on the carpet by the media-sensitive front office. As lead prosecutor he should have taken a strong position with the reporters: No evidence was to be turned over without prior approval from the front office. If he had shown poor judgment in this situation, it was felt, then he could not be trusted with the media circus that was sure to revolve around the Simpson case.

Conn was removed from the prosecution team. Bill Hodgman, riding a victory in the Charles Keating trial, was given the Simpson case to try with Marcia Clark (the judge in the Simpson case, Lance Ito, had also presided over the Keating trial). A disappointed Dave Conn returned to his preparation for the Menendez retrial.

Conn would later gain some satisfaction from winning first-degree murder convictions against the brothers—shortly after the Simpson prosecution team had gone down in highly publicized defeat. In reporting the Menendez verdicts, the *Los Angeles Times* commented that "District Attorney Gil Garcetti, who stands for reelection next Tuesday, could cite the verdicts as evidence that his office actually can win a big one." Boosted by the desperately needed victory, Garcetti won enough votes against a lackluster field of challengers to force a runoff election in November. Two days after the verdicts, however, the *Times* had run a front-page story touting Conn as the next District Attorney of Los Angeles. Garcetti, the article added, "said he isn't threatened by Conn's skills and rising star."

"My guy picked your client out of the lineup, Sammy," Longo said. "Positive ID."

"Hey, how positive can he be? They're going, what, sixty, seventy miles an hour when your guy changes lanes, cuts my guy off? He's got his eyes on the road, am I right? The shooter pulls up in the next lane, your guy looks over, sees him for, what, a second, maybe two, before he gets shot at? What kinda ID is that, fer Chrissake."

"He IDs the car, too, Sammy. And three letters from the license plate. DMV records show they match your client's plates."

"Sure they do, Larry. No question. But like I told you, he wasn't driving the car that day. Honest to God. He loaned it to a friend."

"So gimme the name of the friend."

The lawyer shrugged helplessly. "Like I told you, Larry, I can't do that."

"Oh yeah, I forgot," Longo snorted. "The friend's gonna kill your client if he snitches." He opened another file, began skimming the fact sheet on the inside of the cover.

"Look, Larry," the lawyer persisted, "let's be realistic...."

"Sure."

"Your guy's a Vietnam vet, had some emotional problems after he got back. Spent some time at the V.A. out on Sawtelle. Am I right?"

"What's your point, Sammy?" Longo said, still reading the fact sheet on the next case. "I got one heck of a calendar to get through this morning, I got no deputy to help me, and I got a substitute judge about to take the bench who's in the middle of a trial in his own courtroom and who doesn't know squat about these cases. On top of that, I got a jury coming back tomorrow that I gotta get ready for."

"Yeah, sure. Point is, Larry, my guy's Korean."

"So?"

"So they all look the same to a white guy, you know? I mean, Asians, they all look the same to this guy."

"Gimme a break. There were six Asians in that lineup, Sammy."

The lawyer shrugged again. "Vietnam vet, emotional problems, guy has an attitude about Asians, know what I mean? Hey, what's a jury going to think, Larry? Specially, you know, kinda juries we got around here nowadays? I mean, your guy's white, am I right?"

"Let's put twelve in a box and find out," Longo said.

"Yeah, sure, fine, but the thing is, maybe we can work something out, save us both a lot of time."

The prosecutor looked up from the file he was reading. "What'd you have in mind, Sammy?"

The lawyer studied his fingernails for a moment. "Say, a 242, with time served."

Longo laughed. "A misdemeanor battery? You gotta be kidding. Lemme tellya, Sammy, your guy's pleading straight up to the ADW. And he's looking at hard time."

"C'mon, Larry, it's not like your guy got hit or anything. I mean, a lousy car window, no big deal. Look, maybe we—"

"All rise," the bailiff announced loudly. "Department 127 is now in session, the Honorable John Ouderkirk presiding."

Judge Ouderkirk stepped into the courtroom, grinned, and waved to an old friend he recognized among the waiting lawyers. Then he leapt up the three stairs to the bench and sat down. He was in his early forties, but a boyish face, a ready smile, and a lighthearted manner gave the impression of a much younger man. Dressed in flowing black robes and with a laughing twinkle in his eye, Judge Ouderkirk looked like a mischievous kid caught playing a grown-up game.

"Okay, folks," he said, "I guess you all know Judge Bascue's a little under the weather today. But I talked to him on the phone a couple minutes ago, and he's pretty sure he'll be back tomorrow. Meanwhile, I have a trial going on across the hall. So if you'll just bear with me, we'll try to get through this calendar as fast as possible. Now, who's got first ups?"

"Your honor," Nancy Richards said, standing, "I'm in trial in Department 129. Could the court call the Manning case?"

"You bet," Ouderkirk said.

"Custody, your honor," the bailiff said loudly.

"Could you bring him out, Tom?" the judge said.

Longo knew the boyish looks were deceiving. John Ouderkirk had been a widely respected prosecutor before receiving a judicial appointment from the governor. He had started in the D.A.'s Office as an investigator, one of two assigned to the small Santa Monica branch office, while attending law school at night. James Bascue used the investigator in many of his Santa Monica cases, as did Stanley Weisberg (who later served as judge in the McMartin and Rodney King trials; Ouderkirk would himself soon be named as the judge in the sequel to the Rodney King case, the Reginald Denny trial). It was Ouderkirk who, as an investigator assigned by Roger Gunson, had uncovered the dark background of the mysterious Dr. Raymond LaScala. LaScala, the so-called physician to the stars, was a tiny, soulful, enigmatic man who counted some of the biggest names in Hollywood as his patients. He was also a concert pianist, the author of a published novel, and an artist whose portrait of Ronald Reagan hung in the White House. And he had an unfortunate habit of hypnotizing his patients, getting them to leave him everything in their wills, then murdering them with insulin injections and completing the death certificates himself.

But it was Chinatown that was in Longo's mind as he stood at the prosecution table. John Ouderkirk was the deputy D.A. from the CAPO (Crimes Against Police Officers) unit who first responded to the bloody scene at the Jin Hing jewelry store.

Longo sorted through the stack of files, found the Manning case as the bailiff brought the defendant in.

Frederick Manning was a short, slightly built young man, about twenty-five, with a baby face, intelligent eyes, and a pleasant smile. There was an all-American look about him that seemed oddly out of place with the orange jail uniform and handcuffs. He was charged with kidnapping small boys in his van, then torturing them in the back of the vehicle with an electric Tazer gun and sodomizing them.

Longo recalled the "torture van" case that Manson prosecutor Stephen Kay had tried a few years ago. And Ernie Norris's Freeway Strangler had sodomized and murdered teenage boys in his van. The more he thought about it, the more these heinous crimes seemed to be an L.A. phenomenon. Did they somehow reflect the city's mobile lifestyle, its car-oriented culture? Did criminals in other parts of the country use their automobiles to commit torture and murder?

"People versus Frederick Manning," Ouderkirk announced.

"People's discovery motion, judge," Longo said, glancing at a document in the file.

Ouderkirk began reading his copy of the written motion Craig Veals had filed. He suddenly looked up. "Pubic hair?"

Longo nodded, ignoring the titters in the courtroom.

"Let's see if I've got this right, Mr. Longo," the judge said, returning to the file. "You're asking the court . . . to order the defendant . . . to produce a sample of his . . . pubic hair."

"Judge," Longo said with a sigh, "the cops found pubic hair in the back of the defendant's van, where he committed the acts, and on one of the boys. The victims in this case are too young to have pubic hair. We want a sample from the defendant, try for a match."

"We object, your honor," the public defender said.

"Grounds?" Ouderkirk asked.

"Fifth Amendment," she said. "Forcing my client to provide a sample of his own pubic hair constitutes compulsory self-incrimination."

"Self-incrimination."

"Yes, your honor. It's forcing him to incriminate himself."

"Mr. Longo?"

"Judge, Supreme Court only says you can't make a guy *talk*. But you can sure as hell force him to give *physical* evidence. Look at drunk-driving cases. We make them give blood or breath samples. And forgery cases, we can get court orders for handwriting samples. And fingerprint samples. Same thing here."

"Your honor, there is no precedent, no appellate cases on the subject of pubic hair."

"I would guess not," Ouderkirk said.

"Same principle as fingerprints and blood samples, judge," Longo repeated.

"Sounds right," Ouderkirk said. "Motion granted. The defendant is hereby ordered to provide..." He looked at the prosecutor. "How many hairs you want, Mr. Longo?"

Longo shrugged. "Half dozen?"

"... six hairs from the pubic region of his body, said hairs to be turned over to the Sheriff's Department within five days of this order." Ouderkirk closed the file. "Next case?"

An attorney stood up as Richards whispered something in Manning's ear. "Your honor," the attorney said, "could the Court please call the Rodriguez case? I'm scheduled for a hearing in Long Beach at ten and Rodriguez is just a motion to continue."

"People versus Enrique Rodriguez," Ouderkirk announced, searching through the stack of files.

Longo shuffled through his own files, looking for the case. He found his thoughts returning to the Yamaguchi trial, to his cross-examination of Dr. Scharf the previous afternoon. He felt he had done some damage to the doctor's credibility, but how much? How many on the jury were wondering if Halcion had driven Yamaguchi to kill? How many were asking themselves if he was another Grundberg?

Yamaki had conducted a good redirect examination of his expert, patching up some of the holes Longo had punched in the witness's testimony. Then, suddenly, he had rested the defense case.

Now it was time for Longo to put on a rebuttal case. It was time to counterpunch.

Longo went over it again. Dr. David Greenblatt would arrive from Philadelphia this evening. Park would meet the physician at the airport, then Longo was scheduled to meet with him at the New Otani Hotel to go over his testimony. Tomorrow, when Judge Bascue returned, the prosecution's Halcion expert would take the stand.

Then what?

Longo once again pondered his strategy. He could recall Patrick Seki, again ask him about Yamaguchi's plans to kill Kariya. If Seki still denied it, Longo could confront the man with my notes from the Seki interview in his office; I had turned the notes over to Longo and copies had been given to Yamaki. And then, Longo thought, he could put me on the stand to testify to what I heard Seki say.

But there was a risk. Longo had already put on three witnesses who had denied making statements to his investigator. Now he was putting on a fourth respectable businessman who would also deny the prosecution's claims.

And what about my testimony? If he put me on, Yamaki would bring out the fact that I was a former deputy D.A. To make matters worse, the lawyer might point out that I had served in the Santa Monica office with Judge Bascue. Would the jury begin to think that even the judge was part of a D.A. conspiracy? And then there was the joker in the deck: How would the jurors react to knowing that they would be exposed to public scrutiny in a book?

Meanwhile Longo had lost his chief investigator, Jimmy Sakoda. As the trial neared its end, the D.A.'s overworked Bureau of Investigation had reassigned him to another murder case. That left Longo with Sakoda's partner, Park.

Greg Dohi, too, had been lost. The young law clerk had made the list of those passing the California bar exam. Immediately after being sworn in as an attorney, Dohi had been appointed a deputy D.A. grade one and assigned to the east L.A. office.

Park had located Nagano after his return from Japan and confronted the singing teacher: Had Yamaguchi threatened him with a gun? No, a nervous Nagano replied, no such assault ever took place. But Park then hunted down another lead and finally hit pay dirt. An elderly woman named Masaye Oshita had witnessed the gun incident.

A crack in J-Town's bamboo wall, Longo thought. Or would she also fold, like Uchida and Seki?

"Any objections from the People?" Ouderkirk said.

"What?" Longo said.

"Any objections to the defendant's request for a continuance, Mr. Longo?"

"No, no objections."

"Okay, People versus Rodriguez is continued to the eighteenth." The judge closed the file. "Any other requests for priority?"

There was silence in the courtroom.

"Okay, folks, let's go down the calendar." Ouderkirk grabbed the top file from the stack on the bench.

Longo felt a tap on his shoulder. He looked around. A short, stern-faced man with a stubby salt-and-pepper beard stood behind him, his brow furrowed into a constant frown.

It was Longo's old friend Phil Halpin, a deputy D.A. assigned to the San Fernando branch office. Halpin was a top trial lawyer, one of the few battle-scarred veterans in the office who still fought the wars in the trenches.

"Hey, Phil," Longo whispered with a grin, "what're you doing downtown?"

Halpin shrugged. "Mind-fucking the front office."

Longo's grin broadened. Halpin, like Steve Barshop in Santa Monica, was a rebel who did things his own way. And like Barshop, he had been banished to an outlying branch. Anytime Halpin was downtown, it was a good bet it was because the higher-ups had once again called him on the carpet.

Phil Halpin had reached the top of the D.A.'s ladder years earlier when he tried two ex-cons for the kidnapping and cold-blooded execution of an LAPD officer. Defense lawyers turned the case into an endless circus, making it the longest criminal trial in California history until the McMartin preschool fiasco. When Halpin finally won a hard-fought death penalty conviction, the case was overturned on appeal. Another long trial ended in another conviction and death verdict; this time the state Supreme Court changed the death penalty to life imprisonment. The case later gained fame as the subject of Joseph Wambaugh's book *The Onion Field*.

"Okay," Judge Ouderkirk said as the heavy steel door clanged open and a slender black man with a short Afro stepped out with the bailiff. "People versus John James."

"What're you doing for lunch?" Halpin whispered to Longo.

"I was gonna work out at the Y," Longo whispered back. "Whaddya got in mind?"

"Your office at twelve?"

"You got it."

"Mr. Longo," Ouderkirk said with a familiar nod and wink to Halpin, "if I could interrupt your busy social life for a minute?"

"No problem, judge," Longo said. He found the James file, read the fact sheet. The defendant, a thirty-one-year-old man, had had a heated argument with his wife. In the middle of the argument, he had grabbed their five-month-old baby from his crib and violently shaken him. The shaking had caused hemorrhaging in the baby's brain; the infant died hours later. The man had been charged with second-degree murder and Leonard Torrealba had taken the case to trial. The jury returned with a verdict of guilty as to a "lesser-included" offense: felonious child endangering.

"This is the time for sentencing in the case of People versus John James," Ouderkirk said. "Would the People like to be heard?"

"Judge," Longo said, "the mother of the victim is in the court. She'd like to say a couple things."

"Of course."

The prosecutor looked out at the audience as Halpin left through the swinging gate. "Mrs. Sarah James?" Longo announced loudly.

A tall, slender black woman in a dark gray suit stood up. She walked down the aisle and through the gate, her gaze carefully avoiding the man in the jail uniform at the table to her left. She stood next to Longo, holding four sheets of paper in her hands.

"Mrs. James," Ouderkirk said softly, "the law gives any victim of a crime the right to address the court at the time of sentencing. I find that for the purposes of that law, ma'am, you are a victim. Is it your wish to be heard?"

"Yes," she said with a tremor in her voice.

Ouderkirk settled back in his chair.

The woman stiffened her posture, then began to read from the sheets of paper.

"My name is Sarah James. I was the wife of the defendant in

this case, John James. And I am the mother of . . ." She paused for a second, swallowed hard. "And I was the mother of . . ." Tears began to form in her eyes, and again she swallowed hard. "I was the . . ." She closed her eyes tightly, put her right hand over her mouth. Tears began to flow down her cheeks.

Longo pulled the pink scarf from his breast pocket and placed it in the woman's left hand. She clutched at it, nodding rapidly.

"Mrs. James . . ." Ouderkirk said quietly.

The woman shook her head violently, then held one finger up. She opened her eyes, took a deep breath, then carefully folded the sheets of paper in half, then in half again.

"Yes, I would like . . . to make a statement," she said, her voice quavering. "I would like to make a statement."

Sarah James looked for the first time to her left, looked at her husband in the orange jumpsuit and handcuffs. With her eyes locked on his, she shook her head slowly for a moment. Then she looked back at the judge.

"He was my . . . our only child," she said softly. "I loved him so much. So much. It has been a year now. . . ." She took a deep breath, let it out. "I think of him all of the time. All of the time. There is not a day . . ." She looked at Longo, then back at the judge. "A few months ago, I attempted suicide. I tried to kill myself. I could not go on. It hurt so much. My life was over."

Longo felt a terrible sense of helplessness, standing there and watching this woman in such pain.

"Since then," she continued, struggling for control, "I found God. And He has given me the strength to go on."

Sarah James again looked at her husband, her lips trembling. Then she looked back at Judge Ouderkirk.

"I am trying to forgive John. I am trying to forgive him for what he has done. I hope God will someday give me the strength to do that. But I cannot do that now." She sighed deeply. "John is filled with hate. He has shown no sorrow for what he has done. He must accept responsibility. Even if God forgives him. Even if, someday, I can forgive him. He must accept responsibility for what he has done."

She looked down at the paper in her hands for a moment. Very softly, she said, "The Lord hates one who sheds blood and who lies."

She looked up. "Proverbs." Then she turned around and, her eyes fixed straight ahead, walked out of the courtroom.

The room was silent.

Judge Ouderkirk coughed finally, breaking the silence. "Is there anything further from either side?"

Longo shook his head.

"Your honor," the defense lawyer said, "our position is set out in the memorandum on file with the court. I would only reiterate at this time that Mr. James has a spotless record, and that there was no intent, at any time, that the child be injured. It was a tragic accident. Mr. James acted in a foolish manner, a reckless manner, but there was never any evidence that he intended to hurt his own baby."

"Anything further?" Ouderkirk said.

"Submitted, your honor," the lawyer said.

"Okay, Mr. James," the judge said, looking directly at the defendant, "I've read the probation officer's report. And I'm bothered by the fact that you've apparently shown no remorse for your actions. None at all."

The defense lawyer started to speak. "Your honor—"

Ouderkirk held up his hand, stopping her. "I figure you were real lucky, Mr. James. You were lucky the jury didn't get you for second-degree murder. In any event, it's my job now to sentence you on the child-endangering conviction." He paused, glancing again at the file. "For violation of Penal Code section 273a, I hereby sentence you to the high term, the maximum permitted under the law. I order the Sheriff's Department to remand you to the Department of Corrections and . . ."

Longo sat down, recorded the sentence on a sheet of paper inside the case file. Six years in prison, he thought. Maybe it would bring Sarah James some small measure of peace.

The prosecutor looked at the stack of case files. Then he turned around in his seat and glanced back at the clock on the wall: 11:40. Judge Ouderkirk would break for lunch at twelve. Either the judge would have to continue the remaining cases, or return for an afternoon session.

"The case of People versus Randolph Waring," Ouderkirk said.

"Defense motion to continue," a lawyer said, rising to his feet. "My investigator is still trying to—"

"Granted," Ouderkirk said, glancing at Longo for any objection. Seeing none, he jotted down a date suggested by the attorney, then threw the file on the growing stack and hurried on to a new one. "People versus Jesus Torres."

Longo's mind wandered back to Phil Halpin as he searched for the D.A.'s file on Torres. He tried to think of a good place to go for lunch. Maybe Olivera Street, he thought. It was a tourist trap, but it had a certain sleepy charm to it. And he knew a restaurant there that made decent *chiles rellenos*.

Phil Halpin. Longo had not seen his old friend for nearly a year. But he looked older, much older. The Night Stalker trial had taken its toll.

In the summer of 1985, Los Angeles had been terrorized by a Satanic serial killer who came to be known as the Night Stalker. Fifteen homes were visited by the Stalker during that frightening summer—and fourteen men and women lost their lives. A near panic swept the L.A. area. Sales of guns, ammunition, locks, and window bars skyrocketed; attendance at firing ranges in the county almost tripled. The Night Stalker Task Force was created, consisting of over forty officers from a dozen law enforcement agencies. Halpin was asked to head the task force.

Unknown to anyone, the prosecutor had a serious heart condition. Largely as a result of the marathon *Onion Field* trial he was hypertensive, had high blood pressure, and had suffered a heart attack. His physician advised him to leave the D.A.'s Office, or at least avoid any major stress. The strain of prosecuting another high-profile murder case could prove fatal.

Halpin knew that once the Stalker was found the case would take years to prosecute. He knew that, like the *Onion Field* trial, there would be unending eighteen-hour days, with defense lawyers constantly attacking him, reporters hounding him, and bureaucrats interfering at every stage. The pressure would be intense and constant.

In the end, though, Halpin finally decided to accept the assignment. "I *couldn't* turn it down," he recalled to a friend later. "There was this guy running around killing people. . . ."

The Night Stalker, Richard Ramirez, was finally caught. And, as had the *Onion Field* case, the investigation and trial took over the prosecutor's life for the next five years. The jury eventually returned with verdicts of guilty and a unanimous recommendation for the death penalty.

Six months later, Halpin was hospitalized with another heart attack.

The Night Stalker case was not over. Halpin spent the next year correcting and cataloging trial transcripts for use in the endless appeals to follow. His office is filled with stacks of transcripts and appellate briefs. The appeals, he is confident, will continue for many years.

Halpin's reward for convicting the Night Stalker was not long in coming. Concerned that the prosecutor's highly publicized courtroom victories would make him a future political threat, the front office banished him to the San Fernando branch office. Like others before him, Halpin fell victim to the Bugliosi Syndrome.

Ironically, Halpin hated publicity and had little but contempt for the media. He refuses to give any interviews about the Night Stalker case, and declines invitations to appear on talk shows, telling one persistent representative of Geraldo Rivera to "go to hell." He is a prosecutor, he tells them, not an entertainer. "If I wanted to be an actor," he growls, "I'd join the goddamn Screen Actors Guild."

The Night Stalker trial left Phil Halpin a bitter and cynical man. Defense lawyers dragged the case on for years, attacking him personally in court and in the media. Reporters hounded and misquoted him. The most aggravating to the prosecutor, however, were the hated bureaucrats in the D.A.'s Office who constantly interfered with their petty politics.

Like Jeff Jonas and Steve Barshop, Halpin was a totally dedicated prosecutor, an idealist who believed in the value and dignity of seeking justice. And as with them, that belief was battered and finally broken—not by the horrors of the dark side of human nature, but by the very men entrusted with that system of justice.

Phil Halpin looks back on his twenty-seven years in the D.A.'s Office with a deep sense of regret. He has watched his two daughters grow up from a distance, often without the attention of their father. He feels that his years as a prosecutor have been wasted, that he has, in the final analysis, accomplished very little. If he had to do it over again, he thinks, he would be a rancher, or perhaps a construction worker. Something outdoors. Something where he could work with his hands. Something where there are no bureaucrats. He stays, he continues to fight so hard for justice, because, he says with a shrug, *someone* has to do it.

"There being no objection from the People," Judge Ouderkirk said, looking at Longo, "the Franchant case is continued for pretrial motions to the twenty-ninth." He threw the file on the stack to his right, grabbed another from his left. "People versus Frank Towson McBride."

Longo looked back at the clock, sighed, then shuffled once again through his own stack of files.

Should he put Nagano on the stand, Longo wondered, knowing that he would deny the gun incident? No, there were already too many denials. He would just put Mrs. Oshita on to testify to what she saw.

A copy of Park's report on his interview with Mrs. Oshita had been turned over to Yamaki. And the prosecutor knew he would object to Oshita testifying; the witness's story of Yamaguchi assaulting Nagano with a gun was propensity evidence. But Longo was sure that Yamaki had opened the door with Hanemure's testimony that Yamaguchi was a peaceful man.

Yamaki had already managed to keep Seki from testifying about Nagano. Nagano himself was now denying the incident. And evidence of Yamaguchi shooting a gun at his wife had also been suppressed; Mrs. Yamaguchi was hiding behind the marital privilege and Hanemure denied describing it to Uchida. If Bascue now kept Oshita off the stand as well, Longo would have nothing to show that Yamaguchi was a violent person. The jury would only see an old man sitting sadly in the courtroom, his head bowed in apparent shame.

Longo knew he was facing the "unwritten law of the Old West": It was open season on those who fooled around with a man's wife. And he had an unappealing victim; some jurors might feel that the ambitious Kariya "needed killing." The prosecutor had to show the jury what kind of man Yamaguchi really was. And that he killed not for passion but for possession, for power.

It was critical that Mrs. Oshita testify.

Greenblatt, Longo thought, then Oshita. Then . . .

Then it was up to the jury.

Chapter

26

Dr. David Greenblatt sat stiffly in the witness box, clearly uncomfortable in a courtroom. He was a tall man with a short, efficient
haircut and a humorless air. He wore the usual academic uniform, a
gray herringbone sports coat, button-down white oxford shirt, and
burgundy club tie.

"If an individual takes Halcion," the physician said, "he will
become drowsy. He will have difficulty concentrating, his coordination
will become somewhat impaired, his speech will be slurred, and there
will be some loss of memory."

"Loss of memory," Longo repeated.

"A temporary loss, usually."

"The guy won't remember afterward what happened?"

"He may remember some things, not others. Later, of course,
after the effects of the drug are gone, he will regain his memory."

"Would the guy know what's going on *at the time?*"

"Yes, of course. It is only that he may not recall events a few
moments later."

"Tell me, Doc, would the guy's *judgment* be affected by the
drug?"

"No, absolutely not. As I said, there is some memory loss later,
but there is complete awareness and control at the time."

Longo stepped back from the counsel table, leaned with both

elbows on the speaker's podium. He glanced at the jury, then back at the witness.

"Awright, you know a Dr. Martin Scharf?" Longo asked.

"I do."

"This guy an M.D.?"

"He is not."

"Is he qualified to prescribe drugs, treat patients, that kind of thing?"

"He is not."

"Okay, you know he testified here, right?"

"Yes."

"One of the things he told the folks here, there's this reporting system with the FDA."

"Yes. These are isolated reports of side effects, sent in to the FDA from patients, doctors, and other sources."

"Dr. Scharf says Halcion has eight to forty times more of these reports than other sleeping pills."

"Yes. First, you must understand that the reporting system is random and voluntary. There are no attempts to verify the accuracy of these reports. Nor is there any attempt to determine the actual causes of the reported side effects."

"Uh-huh."

"Second. Halcion far outsells other drugs in this category, so naturally there will be more reports. There have been hundreds of millions of prescriptions for the drug. In 1990, for example, it was taken by over eight million people."

"Okay."

"Third. Most of these spontaneous reports are received by the FDA in the first two years or so after the drug is released. So, again, it is natural that Halcion will receive proportionately more reports than the older drugs."

Longo nodded, waiting for Greenblatt to indicate that he was finished with his short lecture.

"Fourth, the so-called Lever Report, a study conducted by the FDA, concluded that the spontaneous reporting system could not be used to draw any conclusions concerning cause and effect. There must be controlled clinical studies to accomplish that."

Longo nodded again. "So, Doc, any clinical studies ever show Halcion to cause violence?"

"No."

"Any studies ever show Halcion causes paranoia?"

"No."

"Automatic behavior? Where you don't have control over yourself?"

"No."

"So what *does* Halcion do?"

"It makes you sleepy."

Longo stepped toward the jury box, slid his hand along the wooden railing as he approached the witness.

"Awright, this Dr. Scharf, he mentioned something called paradoxical reactions. He told the folks here that this drug can make a person get violent."

"Absolutely not. It is possible that Halcion can relax an individual so that his social inhibitions are down, and he may *verbally* vent his anger or frustration. But the drug will never cause him to be *physically* violent. Unless, of course, he was already so disposed."

"Scharf also mentioned that it can make a person commit murder."

"That is patently ridiculous. There is not one single documented case of Halcion causing an individual to kill another."

The prosecutor considered this, then sat on the edge of the counsel table. He pondered the Grundberg case for a moment, then decided to leave it for Yamaki's cross-examination.

"What if I tell you some guy took Halcion, and then a half hour later he sees this sheet of paper covering an open car window, he sees it fall down. And he picks it up and puts it back. A few minutes later, it falls down again. And he puts it back. This happens maybe three times. Does this mean the guy's having a paradoxical reaction?"

"Of course not. It means he's trying to place a sheet of paper over an open window and it keeps falling down."

Longo chuckled. "What if someone took a higher dose, say two .125-milligram pills, instead of one? Could that cause him to have a weird reaction?"

"It will only make him sleepier."

Longo jumped off the table, leaned against the podium.

"Doc, we got something called voluntary manslaughter. It means the guy killed someone in a sudden heat of passion. It means the guy's judgment was overcome by impulse and rashness."

"I understand."

"Can Halcion cause a guy to lose his judgment, to kill someone out of blind rage?"

"No."

Longo nodded, pondering this. "We also got something called *actus reus*. That's fancy lawyer talk, means you're not responsible if you can't control your own body movements. Like sleepwalking, for example."

"I understand the concept."

"Awright, can Halcion make you commit acts you're not even aware of?"

"Absolutely not."

"Can it cause you to lose conscious control of your body?"

"Of course not."

"Can this stuff keep a guy from being aware of the law? From obeying the laws of society?"

"No, Halcion will not do that."

Longo nodded, again seeming to consider this. He glanced at some of the jurors, then looked back at the witness.

"Doc, lemme give you a hypo, okay?"

"A hypothetical set of facts."

"Yeah."

"All right."

"Take a guy sixty-two years old. About twelve-thirty in the morning, he walks out of his house and sits in his car. He's got a gun in his pocket and a sock on his hand to keep from leaving fingerprints. He gets out maybe three times to put that paper back over the window we talked about."

"Yes."

"About half hour later, car drives up. This guy with the gun gets out of his car, runs maybe a hundred feet up a hill to the car that just drove up, pulls out the gun, and puts a bullet in the driver's head. You with me?"

"Yes, yes."

"So then, this guy takes off in his car and drives straight to a

Highway Patrol station, five minutes away. And he tells a cop there that he just shot his best friend, and turns over the gun. He looks normal to the cop, a little excited, but normal."

"Yes."

"Half hour later, he's at another police station, answers a lot of questions for another cop. Name, address, where he works, if he's taking any drugs, that kind of thing. Cop says he looks normal, maybe a little sleepy."

"Yes."

"So, whaddya think? Could this hypothetical guy have taken Halcion just before walking out of the house with the gun?"

"No."

"You don't think so?"

"No. He would have been experiencing the effects of the drug by the time the car drove up. At that point, a sixty-two-year-old man under the influence of a sleeping pill like Halcion would probably not have the presence of mind to use a sock on his hand. He would have difficulty running up a hill. He would have difficulty aiming a gun and shooting with any accuracy. He would have difficulty driving his car to the Highway Patrol station."

"Uh-huh."

"Furthermore, the drug would have been reaching peak effect at the police station. The officers would have noticed objective symptoms, such as slurred speech, uncoordinated body movement, difficulty in understanding and answering questions."

"So this hypothetical guy, you're saying no way he took any Halcion?"

"That is my opinion."

"Thanks." Longo walked back to his chair, sat down. "Nothing further."

"Mr. Yamaki?" Judge Bascue said.

The defense lawyer stood up, the confident smile in place. He straightened his tie as he walked toward the podium.

"Good morning, Dr. Greenblatt."

"Good morning, sir."

"I just have a few questions, if you don't mind."

"Of course."

Darned civilized, Longo thought.

"Now, Doctor," Yamaki said, "you are being paid for your testimony here, just as Dr. Scharf was, are you not?"

"Yes, the county of Los Angeles is paying me."

"How much is that?"

"Twelve hundred and fifty dollars an hour, plus expenses."

"I see."

"I have requested that the money be paid to the National Institute for Mental Health."

The lawyer turned to Judge Bascue. "Your honor, could the witness be instructed to limit his testimony to the questions asked?"

"Dr. Greenblatt," Bascue said, "please do not give any testimony that is unresponsive to a question."

"Of course," Greenblatt said. "I apologize."

"Now," Yamaki said, looking at the jurors, "isn't it a fact that Mr. Longo was not the first person who contacted you to testify in this case?"

"That is correct."

"You were first contacted by Mr. Lane Bauer, the attorney for Upjohn, were you not?"

"That is correct."

"He told you that there was a murder case in Los Angeles, one involving Halcion, and that the D.A. needed your help?"

"Words to that effect, yes."

"You've worked for Upjohn in the past, have you not?"

"I have consulted for them, but again, the money was paid—"

"Thank you, Doctor. Incidentally, you've never examined Mr. Yamaguchi, isn't that true?"

"That is true."

"So your testimony here is somewhat speculative."

"I have been asked to testify concerning the effects of the drug Halcion."

"Yes. Now, didn't you conduct a study in 1984 about adverse reactions to the drug?"

"I did."

"And Upjohn provided some of the money for this study, did they not?"

"They did not. We received ninety-five percent of our funding from the National Institute for Mental Health. Five percent was from other sources. Upjohn only provided the raw data on Halcion."

"Are you familiar with a recent newspaper article that says Up-john withheld data in studies on Halcion?"

"I have heard the allegations."

Yamaki glanced at his notes, then again looked at the jurors as he asked the questions.

"Are you familiar with a Dr. Ian Oswald of Edinburgh University?"

"I am."

"Hasn't he reported that he observed an obsession with suicide among some users of Halcion?"

"He has made that claim."

"And a Dutch psychiatrist, Dr. van der Kroef, isn't it true he has described seeing some patients on the drug suffer anxiety and depression, even suicidal tendencies?"

"I believe so."

"And, in fact, the drug has been banned in Great Britain, is that not so?"

"That is correct."

Yamaki smiled, glanced again at his notes. Then he leaned forward on the podium and looked directly at the witness.

"Are you familiar with the Grundberg case, Doctor?"

"I am."

"In that case, a woman was charged with the murder of her aged mother."

"Yes."

"And the woman had been taking Halcion, had she not?"

"Yes."

"This woman was examined by two different psychiatrists, as I understand."

"Yes."

"They concluded that she was involuntarily intoxicated when she committed the act?"

"Essentially, yes."

"And, after reviewing the two reports, the prosecutor dropped the murder charges."

"That is correct."

"Then, Dr. Greenblatt, we would seem to have at least one

documented case of Halcion causing someone to kill another."

"No."

"Dr. Greenblatt," Yamaki said, "are you claiming to know as much about that case as the two psychiatrists?"

Gotcha! Longo thought.

"I am saying, sir, that I was an expert witness in the civil lawsuit that was filed by Ms. Grundberg against Upjohn. I studied the police reports, the patient's medical history, and the reports of the two psychiatrists. I am intimately familiar with the facts of the incident. I gave a deposition in the case. And I can state with some authority that there was never any study done to determine the effects of Halcion or any other drug on Ms. Grundberg. All that can be said of the incident is that the woman had been taking many different drugs when she shot her mother, including Valium and excessive doses of Halcion. Whether there was a cause and effect cannot be determined from the facts available. For that matter, there was never any jury verdict."

"Doctor—"

"It is inevitable, when over eight million individuals are taking the drug each year, that there will be isolated incidents of violence committed by some of those individuals. But it would be erroneous to conclude that those incidents were *caused* by the drug."

Yamaki had stepped squarely into the trap, Longo thought. The physician's testimony about the Grundberg case was much more dramatic during cross-examination than it would have been on direct.

"Nevertheless," the defense lawyer continued, "after reviewing the evidence in the Grundberg case, the prosecutor dismissed the murder charges, isn't that so?"

"For whatever reason, yes."

"By the way, Doctor, which side hired you in the Grundberg civil suit?"

"The defendant."

"Upjohn?"

"Yes."

"I see. Now, you once wrote an article on the effects of Halcion on older people, did you not?"

"I did."

"And did you not conclude that older people, such as Mr. Yamaguchi, could experience greater effects from the drug?"

"Yes."

"In some cases, nearly twice the effect as on younger people?"

"In some cases."

Yamaki again glanced at his notes on the lectern, then looked at the jurors.

"You also wrote an article about a passenger on an airplane who took .125 milligrams of Halcion, slept on the flight, then later could not recall anything about the flight?"

"I did."

"That passenger was yourself, was it not?"

"It was."

"So, apparently, you are living proof that Halcion *can* cause a person to suffer permanent amnesia."

"As I have said, the drug—*any* benzodiazepine—can cause temporary loss of memory. This was an unusual incident in that I apparently suffered a more permanent loss of recollection. But we are talking about *afterward. During* the flight, I was behaving in a perfectly normal manner, aware and in control."

"Ah, Doctor." Yamaki smiled, turning to the witness. "If you cannot recall, how do you *know* you were in control and behaving normally?"

"From extrinsic evidence, sir. From what my associates later told me."

Yamaki looked back at the jurors, the smile still there. "Doctor, have you read reports of sleepwalking where Halcion had been taken?"

"Yes."

"Then a person who has taken Halcion might sleepwalk?"

"As might a person who has *not* taken Halcion. Or a person who has taken, say, Valium."

"And during this sleepwalk, the person will not be conscious of his conduct?"

"Of course not."

Yamaki nodded, his eyes again on the jurors.

"Can alcohol and Halcion have a heightened effect together?"

"Yes."

"By the way," Yamaki said as he gathered his notes and walked back toward the defense table, "the FDA now requires Upjohn to put warning inserts into packages of Halcion, isn't that so?"

"Yes, but, of course, that is true of most drugs."

"This insert warns the user that Halcion can cause anxiety, paranoia, depression, suicidal tendencies?"

"The FDA requires manufacturers to warn buyers of reported side effects, even if isolated or unsubstantiated."

"One last thing, Dr. Greenblatt..."

"Yes?"

"The FDA did a study in 1990, comparing the number of violent acts associated with three hundred and twenty-nine different prescription drugs, did they not?"

"Yes."

"And, Doctor, what drug ranked first in that study?"

"Halcion."

"Thank you. I have no further questions."

Yamaki had done a good job, Longo thought. The expert witness had been hurt. The prosecutor quickly considered whether to ask a few questions on redirect examination, giving Greenblatt a chance to explain some answers, patch up some ragged holes. But that would mean more cross-examination. And the longer the witness was on the stand, the more confused the jury would become about his testimony. Longo knew that the key to making sure a jury understood expert testimony was KISS: "Keep it simple, stupid."

"No questions, judge," the prosecutor said.

"Very well," Bascue said, "call your next witness."

"Masaye Oshita," Longo announced.

Dr. Greenblatt stepped down from the witness box. With his head high he walked through the swinging gate.

At the same time, Cheman Park entered the courtroom and motioned to the prosecutor.

Yamaki stood up. "I request a bench conference, your honor."

"Very well," Bascue said, waving the two lawyers toward him. "Ladies and gentlemen," he said to the jurors, "now would be a good time to stand up and stretch. We have a procedural matter to discuss. I assume it will only take a few minutes."

Longo and Yamaki moved toward the bench as the jurors stood and began chatting among themselves.

Park stepped through the gate and pulled the prosecutor aside. "Larry, Mrs. Oshita's outside, in the hallway."

"Yeah."

"She tells me Ken Yamaguchi approached her a few minutes ago. Hanemure was with him."

"Yeah?"

"Says Ken told her not to testify against his father."

Longo said nothing.

"Says he told her Nagano's all through, and just testify she doesn't know anything."

Longo nodded, then looked down at his own shoes for a moment. Then he turned and joined Yamaki at the side of the judge's bench farthest from the jury.

"Your honor," Yamaki said in a hushed voice, "I would like to inquire into the relevance of Mrs. Oshita's testimony."

"Larry?" Bascue whispered.

"Judge," Longo said, "I don't gotta clear my witnesses with Mike. If he's got an objection during the testimony, let him make it then. But I'll be doggoned if I'm gonna let him screen my witnesses ahead of time to make sure they meet with his approval."

"Mike," Bascue said, "what *is* your point here?"

"I believe Larry's going to put Mrs. Oshita on to testify about the Nagano incident."

"Refresh my memory," the judge said.

"There is a rumor that my client once fired a gun in the presence of a Mr. Nagano. He's a singing instructor at Mrs. Yamaguchi's academy. It is a rumor, nothing more. I have spoken with Mr. Nagano, and he absolutely denies such an incident ever took place."

"And this Mrs. Oshita?"

"Judge," Longo said, "she *saw* this incident that never took place."

Bascue sighed. "Mike, I assume you're objecting on grounds of propensity evidence?"

"Yes, your honor. This is the same situation we had with Patrick Seki, with the rumor that my client fired a shot at Mrs. Yamaguchi a few weeks before Kariya was killed. It's just offered to show propensity for violence, and that's barred by the Evidence Code."

"Larry?"

"First off, judge, Mike opened the door when he had Hanemure testify what a great marriage they had and what a quiet, peaceful guy Yamaguchi was. The code is real clear: If the defense offers evidence of peaceful character, the prosecution can offer evidence of violent character to rebut it."

Bascue slowly massaged his eyes with thumb and forefinger.

"But I'm not putting on Oshita just to show propensity for violence," Longo continued. "I'm also showing M.O."

"M.O.?" Yamaki said with a sneer.

"Yeah. The code says evidence of prior acts is admissible if it shows a *modus operandi*. And here, Yamaguchi's got an M.O.: Every time he gets pissed off at someone, he grabs a gun and shoots at them."

"That's ridiculous," the defense lawyer said.

Bascue leaned back in his chair, closed his eyes for a moment. Then he opened them, leaned forward.

"I'm sustaining Mike's objection," he said. "I don't want this trial to get off onto collateral issues. I don't want a series of mini-trials on whether the defendant did or didn't shoot at his wife, or at this Nagano, or whatever."

"Judge—"

"That's my ruling, Larry. Call your next witness."

Longo looked at Park, sitting at the prosecution table. Then he looked at the jurors. He could tell that some of them were trying to hear what was being said at the bench conference.

"Ken Yamaguchi," Longo said in a lowered voice.

"What?" Yamaki said. "What for?"

"There you go again, Mike, wanting a preview of my witness's testimony."

"Gentlemen!" Bascue said. "Mike, Larry's right. Unless he foresees a significant problem with calling the witness—"

"There *is* a problem," Longo said.

Bascue looked at the prosecutor expectantly.

Longo looked directly at Yamaki. "Ken Yamaguchi just told Mrs. Oshita to testify that she doesn't know anything."

"What?" the defense lawyer said.

"Out in the hallway a few minutes ago."

"Larry," Bascue said, "do you know what you're saying?"

"Yeah. I'm saying there's been an attempted intimidation of a witness. And that's a felony."

Yamaki shook his head. "I don't believe—"

"Believe it or not, Mike, I got a witness who says it happened. Now, I'm gonna call Ken Yamaguchi, and I'm gonna ask him, point-blank: 'You try to silence my witness?' "

"God . . ." Bascue said, shaking his head in frustration.

"But first, judge," Longo continued, "I think I gotta give him a Miranda warning or something. And if he takes the Fifth, refuses to testify . . ."

Longo knew he was making it up as he went along. He might have to Mirandize Yamaguchi's son, since he would be asking him if he had just committed a felony in the hallway. And if he took the Fifth . . . then the prosecutor had to make a choice. He could accept that and ask no more questions; Ken Yamaguchi's credibility before the jury would be damaged. Or he could give the young man immunity, even if he did not want it. That would eliminate the possibility of self-incrimination. Then he would *have* to answer, or be held in jail for contempt.

What if he *did* answer the prosecutor's question—and simply denied trying to intimidate Mrs. Oshita? Then Longo could call Mrs. Oshita to testify what happened. And later prosecute Yamaguchi's son for perjury, another felony.

This time they got caught with their hands in the cookie jar, Longo thought. Yamaguchi's son had grown too bold. Now he finally had Yamaki in a vise.

"This is ridiculous," Yamaki said angrily. "Your honor, what's the relevance of all this to the issues in the case? Even if it *did* happen, what's the relevance to my client's state of mind at the time he shot Kariya?"

"Ken Yamaguchi's a key witness," Longo said. "Without him, there's no evidence the defendant took Halcion. And if he tries to intimidate a prosecution witness, that goes directly to his bias and credibility."

"Very well," Bascue said wearily, "you may call Ken Yamaguchi. But you will advise him of his rights first."

"And Mrs. Oshita?" Longo asked.

"Yes, yes. But only for the limited purpose of testifying to the attempted intimidation, if any. Nothing more." The judge glared at Longo. "If there is even a *hint* of the Nagano incident from her, I'll declare a mistrial. Is that understood?"

"Yeah."

"Very well." Bascue sighed again. "Mike, I'll give you a couple of minutes to talk with Ken Yamaguchi if he's still out in the hallway. Then, gentlemen, let's try to wrap this up."

Yamaki and Longo stepped away from the bench. The defense lawyer quickly walked out of the courtroom.

"Ladies and gentlemen," Bascue said to the jurors, "we are again in session. I apologize for the delay."

Longo grabbed Park by the arm and whispered in his ear. "Tell Mrs. Oshita she can't say anything about Yamaguchi shooting at Nagano. Just answer my questions about what happened in the hallway, nothing else. Got it?"

"Yeah," the investigator whispered back, "she doesn't mention the shooting."

"Tell her, if she's gotta refer to the Nagano shooting, just call it 'the incident.' But no names, no testimony about what she saw."

"Okay."

Longo walked over to the jury box as Park stepped out of the courtroom.

"Ken Yamaguchi," Longo announced loudly.

There was an awkward silence as everyone waited for the next witness. Then the doors behind the audience opened and Yamaki stepped into the courtroom. He managed a confident smile for the judge and jury, then walked through the gate and sat down at the counsel table.

A moment later, Yamaguchi's son walked through the doors. He was wearing a loose-fitting beige suit, with a black silk shirt and a red tie. He looked calm, almost bored, as he approached the witness stand.

"Mr. Yamaguchi," Judge Bascue said, "you have testified here twice before, so you are still under oath."

"Yes, sir," the young man said. He sat down in the witness chair.

"Ken," Longo said, walking toward the jury box, "you know a woman by the name of Masaye Oshita?"

"Yeah . . . yes, sir."

"Did you have a little talk with her a few minutes ago? Out in the hallway there?"

"Yes, sir."

"Awright." Longo leaned his elbows on the podium. "Didn't you tell Mrs. Oshita that Nagano didn't know anything? That he was all through?"

"No. Mrs. Oshita seemed nervous. And she said something about Nagano. And I said that he'd been interviewed and he didn't know anything."

"Uh-huh. Did Yamaki here tell you about my investigator's interview with Nagano?"

Ken Yamaguchi glanced at the defense lawyer, then looked back at Longo. "Yes."

"Uh-huh. Now, did you tell her to testify in here that she didn't know anything either?"

"Could you repeat that, please?"

"Yeah. Didn't you tell her to testify that she didn't know anything?"

"No. I said, 'If you don't know anything, just say you don't know anything.' "

"Uh-huh." Longo sat down. "One other thing, Ken. Who was with you when you were having this talk with my witness?"

"Mr. Hanemure."

"Nothing further, judge."

"Mr. Yamaki?" Bascue asked.

"No questions, your honor," the lawyer said.

"You are excused, Mr. Yamaguchi," the judge said. "Call your next witness," he said to the prosecutor.

The young man quickly stepped down from the witness chair, his expression still stoic.

"Masaye Oshita," Longo said loudly.

Ken Yamaguchi walked through the gate and out of the courtroom.

As the doors swung shut, a tiny, slightly bent-over Japanese woman in her sixties stepped in and quickly bowed twice. She had a kindly smile on her face and there was humor in the wrinkles of her eyes.

The woman looked around at first, confused, then shuffled toward the swinging gate. She followed the bailiff to the witness stand, took the oath, and laboriously climbed into the witness box. She turned to the jurors, her smile growing as she bowed her head slightly.

"Morning, Mrs. Oshita," Longo said.

The witness nodded rapidly.

"You know the defendant here, Kazuhiko Yamaguchi?"

She looked toward Yamaguchi, bowed her head again.

"Mrs. Oshita, see, the court reporter here, she's gotta take down what your answer is. So would it be okay if you answered out loud? It makes it a lot easier on her."

"*Hai* . . . yes, yes."

"Okay. Now, my investigator in this case, Mr. Park, he asked you to come here and testify today, that right?"

"Yes, yes, Korean gentleman."

"Right. And, so, you came here this morning to testify?"

"Yes, yes."

"Weren't you sitting outside of the courtroom a few minutes ago, waiting to testify?"

"Yes."

"And while you were waiting out there, did you have a conversation with a young man?"

She nodded.

"Remember the reporter, Mrs. Oshita?"

"I am sorry, yes."

"What was this young man's name?"

"Ken Yamaguchi."

"The defendant's son?"

"Defendant?"

"Kazuhiko Yamaguchi, his son?"

"Yes, yes."

"Now, Mrs. Oshita, would you please tell the folks here what Ken Yamaguchi said to you."

"Yes." She turned to the jurors, still smiling pleasantly. "Ken Yamaguchi, he said to me, 'Mr. Nagano doesn't know anything. He's all through.'"

"Uh-huh. And by Nagano, he meant a witness to an incident that you were here to testify about?"

"Yes, the time when Yamaguchi-*san,* Mr. Yamaguchi, when—"

"Right, the incident."

"The incident, yes."

"And so Ken Yamaguchi said that Nagano didn't know anything, that he was all through?"

"Yes."

"What happened next?"

"I told him that Mr. Nagano was there, he saw it. I told him that it would be difficult for me, because Mr. Nagano's name will come out. I said, 'What should I do?'"

"What did he say?"

"He said, 'Just say you don't know anything at all about anything.'"

"Ken Yamaguchi told you to testify that you didn't know anything about the incident?"

"Yes."

"And is that true? That you know nothing about the incident?"

"No, no, I saw it. I saw Mr. Yamaguchi—"

"You saw the incident."

"Yes."

"And then what happened, Mrs. Oshita?"

"I said, 'But I already told the truth to the man from the district attorney last night.'"

"And what did Ken Yamaguchi say to that?"

"It was then that the Korean gentleman walked toward us. And Ken walked away."

"Uh-huh." Longo leaned against the audience railing. "By the way, Mrs. Oshita, was there anyone with Ken Yamaguchi when he told you to testify falsely?"

"Mr. Hanemure."

"Mamoru Hanemure? Mr. Yamaguchi's brother-in-law?"

"Yes, yes."

"Uh-huh." The prosecutor walked back to his chair, glanced at Yamaki. "Your witness."

The defense lawyer rose to his feet.

"Good morning, Mrs. Oshita," he said with a friendly smile.

The witness nodded, smiling back.

"Now, isn't it true, Mrs. Oshita, that Ken Yamaguchi never approached you? That you walked up to *him*?"

The woman nodded. "Yes."

"You were nervous about testifying here, isn't that so?"

"I was nervous, yes."

"And so you walked up to Ken Yamaguchi and Mr. Hanemure, because you knew them, isn't that so?"

"Yes."

"Now, think about this, Mrs. Oshita," Yamaki said, leaning on the podium and looking directly at her. "Didn't you say something like, 'I don't know anything about the Kariya shooting'?"

"Yes, I think so."

"And didn't you say something like, 'I don't know why I'm here, all I know is about the Nagano incident'?"

"I think so."

"And wasn't it *then* that Ken Yamaguchi said, 'If you don't know anything, just say you don't know anything'? Something like that?"

"Yes, something like that."

Shoot! Longo thought. Oshita had just done a complete reversal before his very eyes. Sakoda had warned him that the more traditional Japanese were reluctant to openly disagree with another person, particularly in public. Or was Mrs. Oshita just incredibly susceptible to suggestion? Or, maybe, afraid of Yamaki?

"No further questions, your honor," Yamaki said, smiling at the witness. "Your witness," he said to the prosecutor.

Longo stood up. "Mrs. Oshita . . . lemme get this straight. When Ken told you to testify that you didn't know anything, he meant about the Nagano incident, right?"

"Mr. Nagano, yes."

"You were talking about the Nagano incident, and you asked him what you should do when Nagano's name came up, right?"

"Yes."

"Uh-huh. And Ken Yamaguchi, he says, 'Tell them you don't know anything,' right?"

"Yes."

"Even though you *did* know something. You *saw* it."

"Yes."

"Awright." He looked at the jury, then at the judge. "Nothing further."

Yamaki stood up. "Mrs. Oshita, didn't Ken Yamaguchi tell you, 'If you don't know, then just *say* you don't know'?"

"Yes."

"No further questions, your honor," Yamaki said, sitting down. There was still an amused smile on his face.

"Nothing further, judge," Longo said, trying to hide his frustration.

"Thank you, Mrs. Oshita," Bascue said. "You are free to leave now, with the court's thanks."

The witness bowed her head, smiled broadly. Then she stepped carefully down from the witness box and shuffled out of the courtroom, bowing twice as she passed the jury and then the spectators in the audience.

It had gone like everything else in the trial, Longo thought. Truth, reality, everything shifting constantly, changing shape, taking one form now, another just moments later. Nothing was as it seemed. It was like living in a world of elusive shadows.

"Call your next witness," Bascue said.

Longo stood up.

"The People rest," he said.

Longo lay in bed, his eyes wide open and staring up into the darkness as the questions continued to flood through his mind.

Would Yamaki focus on heat of passion in his argument? Would he concentrate on getting a verdict of voluntary manslaughter? Or would he go for it all, a complete acquittal? Would he argue that Yamaguchi was under the influence of Halcion, unconscious at the time he shot Kariya?

What would *you* do? the prosecutor asked himself. I'd go for the acquittal, he thought; I'd argue the heck out of Halcion. But I'd also let the jury know that there was a middle road possible. If some jurors were buying the drug defense while others were holding out for first-degree murder, I'd make sure they had voluntary manslaughter available as a compromise verdict.

Longo sighed deeply, then looked over at Aelina lying asleep next to him. Since the trial had begun, he had seen little of his wife and kids. They were often in bed by the time he dragged himself home. There was little time in the early morning. A few brief moments at the breakfast table, then the long drive to the office to prepare for calendar call. He made a note to ask Jeff Jonas for some time off after the verdict came in. A week, maybe two. Take Aelina and the kids up to the cabin at Mammoth Lakes.

Longo looked to his right at the small, glowing numbers in the dark: 3:15 A.M.

Closing argument was set to begin at 10:00.

He massaged his eyes. Two more hours of sleep, he thought, then he would get up and make some coffee. He knew he needed the sleep; it was deadly to argue a murder case when you were physically and mentally fatigued. Two more hours.

He closed his eyes, tried to concentrate on a quiet, idyllic meadow near a crystal clear lake high in the mountains. It was a warm, lazy summer afternoon. White, puffy clouds floated by. Quiet. Peaceful. Sleep.

His eyes blinked open.

It all rested on the closing arguments tomorrow, he thought. No, not tomorrow. Today. In less than seven hours.

Longo used no outline in his argument, no carefully prepared notes to follow. Rightly or wrongly, he felt these detracted from establishing a rapport with the jury. Spontaneity was critical, he believed; jurors mistrusted a lawyer who had to rely on notes for the truth. They were more receptive to an unrehearsed talk than to a carefully prepared sales pitch.

There was no formula for presenting argument to a jury, no "right way" that was taught in law school. Each lawyer had his own unique style. Yamaki would be smooth, rational, and infinitely clever; eloquence and personal charm were his strengths. Longo would plow ahead, clumsy, tenacious, and unrelenting, relying upon his common touch and a sense of deep personal conviction to reach the jury.

The viper and the bulldog.

Longo once again went over his strategy as he lay in the dark bedroom. He would have to present his argument to the jury first, before Yamaki showed his hand. Should he focus his efforts on the heat-of-passion defense? Or on Halcion? Like a general in the field, he had to guess from which direction the enemy's attack was coming, then commit his forces to counter it.

One bullet had entered Kariya's head, Longo thought. The second had lodged in the roof, near Mrs. Yamaguchi's head. Had he been shooting at his wife, and missed? Or was he just trying to frighten her?

What was said between Yamaguchi and his wife in those fifteen to thirty seconds when the eyewitness watched them after the shots?

What would Mrs. Yamaguchi have testified to if she had taken the stand? Was it her decision not to testify, or Yamaguchi's?

Unlike the neat postmortems favored by Perry Mason and other Hollywood lawyers, life in a real courtroom was filled with enigma and dead ends.

He would wear the black double-breasted suit, Longo suddenly decided. A white dress shirt. And the wide, dark scarlet tie, with a matching handkerchief in the breast pocket. Yes, he thought, black and dark scarlet. The deep, rich color of blood.

Longo found himself wondering if it was possible that Halcion *could* drive a person to commit murder. He was not an expert: Why was he so sure it could not? Was he convinced—beyond a reasonable doubt—that the drug could not have this effect?

Was he really trying to find justice? the prosecutor asked himself. Or was he just trying to *win*?

Why *had* Mrs. Grundberg suddenly and for no apparent reason murdered her mother?

With a sinking feeling, the prosecutor realized that there was a small, nagging doubt buried deep inside somewhere. A tiny, squirming, ugly little doubt. And it would not go away.

It always happened that way to Longo. The last-minute doubts, the fear that he could be wrong, that he could be sending an innocent man to prison. But there would always be that doubt. What did the judge's jury instruction say? All things are subject to some doubt; nothing in human affairs is certain. The law requires proof only beyond a *reasonable* doubt—proof to a *moral* certainty.

Am I convinced beyond a reasonable doubt, Longo asked himself, that Kazuhiko Yamaguchi murdered Genji Kariya in cold blood? Am I morally certain of this? Will I sleep well if he is convicted?

Yes.

Longo rolled over to his right once again. He stared at the glowing red numbers in the darkness.

4:48.

Five more hours.

Chapter 27

"...and he *ran* to the car, ladies and gentlemen," Yamaki said, leaning on the jury railing. "He didn't calmly walk, he ran. Does that sound like a cold, calculated murderer to you? Or does it sound like a man who was acting in the heat of passion?"

Yamaki stepped back, turned and looked at Longo seated in his chair at the counsel table.

"In his argument, Mr. Longo told you that Mr. Yamaguchi carefully planned the shooting for days. He would have you believe that this distraught, elderly man cleverly plotted the murder, that he even wore a sock so that he would not leave any fingerprints on the gun."

He stepped closer to the prosecutor.

"If Mr. Yamaguchi planned so carefully to avoid being caught, then why did he immediately drive to the CHP station and turn himself in? Why didn't Mr. Longo explain that to you in his argument?"

Yamaki turned back to the jury.

"Because he cannot. Because Mr. Yamaguchi never intended to get away with the shooting. Because he never had conscious control over his own actions. Because there was never any premeditation."

Yamaki paused, looked down in thought for a moment. Then he looked back up.

"What *did* happen that night? What happened was that there was a man, a respected elderly businessman, who was experiencing intense emotional frustration. Mr. Yamaguchi loved his wife very much, and he was suffering through the agonies of her extramarital affair with Mr. Kariya. He had hired an investigator, he had tapped her phone conversations. He had caught them together at the Boyle Heights house. And then, that night, he discovered that they were together again."

The lawyer turned and studied his client in silence. Yamaguchi still sat at the table, his head bowed as it had been throughout the trial.

"Intense emotional frustration. Pain. Deep pain. And so what did Mr. Yamaguchi do? He took two of his wife's sleeping tablets to kill the pain. Two Halcion tablets. And he did this as he talked on the telephone to his friend and brother-in-law, Mr. Hanemure.

"Do you recall what he told his friend? 'It's happening again,' he said. Intense emotional frustration. And then he said, 'I'm going to do it.' Mr. Longo would have you believe that he said 'I'm going to finish him,' but that's not what Mr. Hanemure testified to. Nor Mr. Matsumoto. Nor Mr. Uchida. Nor Mr. Seki. Mr. Longo would have you believe that everyone is lying, that they are all liars, these respected members of the Japanese-American community."

Yamaki looked back at the prosecutor again. Longo was slouched in his chair, his eyes locked on the witness box in front of him.

"The truth is that Mr. Longo has no respect for Japanese Americans. You've heard him in this trial, he refuses even to pronounce their names correctly. He treats them with contempt on the witness stand."

There it is, Longo thought. Yamaki had played the race card. "You've seen how he and I get along," Yamaki continued, still looking at Longo. "He has no respect for Japanese Americans, no respect for their culture."

The lawyer paused for a moment, then turned and pointed out at the audience.

"Do you think all these people would be here if Mr. Yamaguchi was not a good and honorable man? Do you think they would come day after day?"

Yamaki turned back to the jury.

"Pain and intense emotional frustration. Then two Halcion tablets. And this drug pushed him over the edge."

Cleverly done, Longo thought. Don't dwell on Jap-bashing. Just plant the seed and let it grow.

Yamaki grabbed a magazine from the podium. He held it up to the jury. It was the copy of *Newsweek* with the bottle of Halcion featured on the cover. A bold caption read "Halcion: Sweet Dreams or Nightmare?"

"Halcion," Yamaki said. "These two tablets triggered what Dr. Scharf called a paradoxical reaction. You remember his testimony, how this drug, a drug that's been banned in some countries, how it triggers hostility, paranoia, aggression, even violence. You recall the Grundberg case . . . Halcion. Even Upjohn's expert witness, Dr. Greenblatt, admitted that this drug has more reports of violence than any others."

Yamaki paused now, his head bowed in thought. Then he looked up.

"Mr. Longo gave you his opening argument. Now this is my turn. Then he will have one more chance, what is called rebuttal argument. And that will be all. I get only one chance, I won't be able to talk with you again. Please remember that as he's giving his rebuttal argument. No matter what he says, I won't be able to reply. Please remember that. Ask yourselves, as you listen to him, 'What would Mr. Yamaki say to that?' "

The lawyer glanced again at the notes on the podium.

"Reasonable doubt. His honor will read you some jury instructions when we are finished with argument. Listen to them carefully. He'll tell you that if you're not convinced beyond a reasonable doubt that Mr. Yamaguchi acted with premeditation, you *must* acquit him of first-degree murder."

Yamaki looked at the judge, then back at the jury, his arms grasping the edges of the lectern.

"His honor will also tell you about circumstantial evidence. He'll instruct you that if it has two reasonable interpretations, one of which points to his guilt, the other to his innocence, you *must* adopt the one pointing to innocence.

"Think of these instructions when you ask yourself if, instead, he acted in the heat of passion. Think of them when you ask yourself, 'Was

Mr. Yamaguchi in conscious *control* when he pulled the trigger?' "

Yamaki leaned forward on the lectern.

"Because if he was not . . . if, as with Mrs. Grundberg, he was not in conscious control . . . then you must acquit him of any crime. You must find him innocent."

The lawyer took a deep breath, slowly let it out. He stepped away from the podium, walked over to the jury railing. He looked at each of the twelve jurors in turn.

"Ladies and gentlemen, you can hear a song a hundred times and still never hear the words. Later, in hard times, the words come back to you. I recall a song, a Lou Rawls song. The name of the song was 'You're Gonna Miss My Lovin'.' I remember the words now, the final words to the song."

Yamaki dropped his head for a moment in silence. Then he looked back up. He paused again, his eyes locked on the jurors.

" ' . . . Love is a hurtin' thing.' "

He stood there for a moment in silence. Then he bowed slightly, turned and walked back to his seat.

The courtroom was hushed.

"Mr. Longo?" Judge Bascue said finally, breaking the silence. "Are you prepared to give your rebuttal argument?"

The prosecutor rose to his feet.

"It's a real pretty song, folks. But, tell you the truth, I don't think Lou Rawls had Mr. Yamaguchi in mind when he sang it."

Longo looked back at Yamaki.

"Y'know, I been prosecuting a lot of years now. And one thing I've learned about defense lawyers' tactics. If you've got the law on your side, argue the law to the jury. If you've got the facts, argue the facts. But if you don't have either, then you attack the prosecutor."

He looked back at the jurors.

"Yamaki says I don't have any respect for his client. He says I don't show any respect for Mr. Yamaguchi. And you know what? He's right. Dead right. I don't have any respect for cold-blooded murderers. Never had, never will. I don't care if they're Japanese Americans, or Ukrainians, or Eskimos. I don't respect people who commit cold-blooded murder."

Longo looked back at the audience.

"Yamaki tells you his client is a great guy, a real pillar of the community. Why else do you think all these folks here come day after day?"

He turned back to the jurors.

"You think, maybe, just maybe, Yamaki had something to do with that? You think maybe Yamaki might have had something to do with all these folks being here?"

The prosecutor walked along the front of the jury, dragging a hand along the railing.

"My investigator, Jimmy Sakoda, he talks to Hanemure. Then Yamaki gets a copy of his statement and talks to him. Next thing, Hanemure changes his story. Awright, Sakoda finds another witness, Matsumoto, gets a statement. Yamaki gets the statement, talks to him. Guess what? Matsumoto changes his story too. Strange?

"Along comes Uchida, tells Sakoda what the two guys told him. What happens? Yamaki gets the report, and Uchida does a quick reverse too. And then Seki, same thing. He backs off, denies everything. Do you see any pattern here, folks?"

Longo walked over to the witness box. He stepped up into the box and sat down in the witness chair.

Judge Bascue sighed, leaned back.

"You remember when these guys testified? You remember Matsumoto? When I asked him a tough question, where did he look?"

The prosecutor sat forward in the chair, looked directly across the courtroom at Yamaki.

"And Ken Yamaguchi. I ask him something, he's not sure, where's he look?"

Again Longo turned his eyes to the defense lawyer. Then he stood up and walked back to the jury.

Yamaki smiled as he sat at the defense table, shaking his head in disbelief.

"Awright," the prosecutor continued, "so what happened that night? In my opening argument, we went back over the evidence. The gun. The sock. The speedy loader. The statement to Hanemure. The half-hour wait in the car. The lack of any symptoms at the police station. The clear memory. And that all adds up to only one thing: first-degree murder.

"Awright, so you know what *I* think happened that night. So what's Yamaki tell you happened?"

The prosecutor shrugged, threw both arms up in the air, palms up.

"I dunno. I dunno. On the one hand, he tells you his client shot Kariya in the heat of passion. He tells you there was this sudden, overwhelming rage, and so he's only guilty of voluntary manslaughter."

He shook his head in apparent confusion.

"But then he turns around and tells you he wasn't even *conscious* at the time, he had no control over his movements. He tells you Halcion made him do it, took over his mind and body. And so, no, it isn't voluntary manslaughter—he's not guilty of *anything.*"

Longo looked back at Yamaki.

"Which is it? Did Yamaguchi kill out of sudden, overwhelming passion, or was he completely unconscious at the time?"

He looked back at the jury.

"Reminds me of a case I had a couple years back, folks. This defense lawyer comes in, see, his client's charged with murder. And the judge wants to know what his plea is, right? Well, the lawyer says, 'My client didn't do it, judge. And besides,' he says, 'he was insane when he did.' "

Longo noticed faint smiles on two or three of the jurors as he turned and walked over to the podium. He leaned on it with one elbow, shaking his head in disbelief again.

"Halcion. Folks, did you all get a good look at that copy of *Newsweek* Yamaki flashed at you? Any of you notice the date? August 19, 1991—a few days after Ken testified at the preliminary hearing and never mentioned the drug. Then, a couple weeks after the magazine comes out, Mrs. Yamaguchi suddenly decides to get another prescription. And you know what? Now Ken not only remembers his dad taking Halcion, he can describe everything in detail—the tablets, the bottle, the pill, everything."

The prosecutor walked over to the counsel table, sat down on the edge.

"Yamaki mentioned reasonable doubt. Awright, let's talk about reasonable doubt . . ."

"I still think Terry screwed up not putting Rodney King on the stand," Longo said. "You gotta *humanize* it, let the jury see a living, breathing victim."

"I dunno, Larry," said the lean, sleepy-eyed man with the wicked grin. "Fact is, with King not testifying, Weisberg ruled that the defense couldn't tell the jury about his criminal record. What do you think the jury would think if they knew he did prison time for armed robbery? Maybe Terry made the right choice. Or," he added with a knowing wink, "the front office did."

The man's name was Richard Chrystie, and he was the deputy D.A. in charge of training. It was his job to take newly hired deputies and run them through a three-week "boot camp." During this period, the fledgling prosecutors were immersed in mock trials, preliminary hearings, and pretrial motions, dealing with make-believe forgetful witnesses and constantly under fire from tyrannical judges and treacherous defense lawyers. Few of the rookies had ever examined a witness before, even in law school; many had never seen the inside of a courtroom.

As a former public defender with a quick wit and a notorious sense of humor, Chrystie was the perfect choice for the assignment.

"You gotta humanize it," Longo repeated, rocking back in his chair and propping his feet up on the cluttered desk. "Any bets on the verdict, Dick?"

The man shrugged. "That videotape . . . I don't see how they could vote to acquit."

"Yeah," Longo said, "but how many times they played that tape? I mean, the jurors must have seen it a dozen times now. You play it enough times, it starts to lose the impact, you know? The jury gets used to it. There's no emotional reaction after a while."

Chrystie nodded. "And all that slow-motion replay. Real clever move by the defense. Take those split-second movements by King, slow them down, magnify them. Makes it look like he was resisting, attacking the cops."

"Yeah, and how many experts have testified so far on LAPD policy? A dozen? A dozen witnesses giving the jury a dozen different versions of what's the approved way to deal with the situation."

"Still . . . it's hard to get past that tape. You can slow it, and cut it, and bring in experts, but . . ."

"Yeah."

The two men were silent for a moment. Longo's thoughts began to drift from the King trial to the jury deliberation room in Department 127. He felt that familiar cold, empty feeling in his stomach. It had been two days now, and there was still no verdict in the Yamaguchi case.

"You been hearing the talk in the building?" Chrystie asked.

"What talk?"

"There's some that are saying we're trying to throw the King case."

"*Throw* it?"

"Yeah. Reiner wants good relations with LAPD and the other agencies. We got to work with the cops to get convictions, and . . . well, maybe good relations are more important than a conviction."

Longo snorted.

"Yeah, I don't figure that either." Chrystie paused. "But there's some that's wondering how come Reiner put Terry on the case. I mean, you don't gotta look very far to find more experienced guys in the office, right?"

"Terry's okay. . . ." Longo said halfheartedly, grabbing a ham and cheese sandwich from a drawer.

Chrystie nodded. Again the men lapsed into silence. And again

Longo's mind wandered to the small room where the Yamaguchi jury was deliberating.

"Oh by the way, Larry," Chrystie said, "you interested in doing a demonstration for the rookie class?"

"Sure, Dick," Longo said absently. "Any time." He took a bite out of the sandwich. Were they near a verdict? he wondered. Was it manslaughter? Or had they fallen for the Halcion defense?

"We're using an old rape case," Chrystie said. "You'll do the cross-exam of the defendant. I'll get the police reports to you a couple days before."

"Okay."

"We got a guy from USC's drama department, he's going to play the defendant. One of the rookies'll do the direct exam. Then you can cross. One hour okay?"

"Sure."

"After the demonstration's over, stick around. The class'll ask you questions. You know, Why'd you do this? Why didn't you do that?"

"How many new deputies in the class, Dick?"

"Eight. Lost three the first week."

"How do they look?"

"A good bunch, I think. 'Course, half of them can't sleep nights. Other half's throwing up out in the hallway. But couple weeks, they'll be ready for the courtroom."

Longo laughed. "How to be a trial lawyer, in ten easy lessons." He shook his head. "Things've changed."

"That's for sure."

"Boy, I remember the day I got hired. They handed me a bunch of misdemeanor files and pointed me to the courthouse. And that was it. Baptism by fire. Honest to Pete, I got in that courtroom, I didn't even know what table to sit at."

"Yeah, same here. But, y'know, they learn a lot in three weeks. I mean, you can't teach style, right? A good trial lawyer, it's an art. Probably born with it. But you can sure as hell teach technique, and procedures, and tactics."

"I guess so. Still, it seems funny to—"

The two men were interrupted by a towering sixty-one-year-old man with large eyeglasses and a broad smile. His jovial manner reminded one of a kindly grandfather, yet behind the smile were cool, probing eyes that were constantly studying, weighing, dissecting.

District attorneys came and went with the changing tide of politics, but Richard Hecht had been there for thirty-one years, always quietly behind the scenes, ever more firmly in control. He was known around the office as the Godfather.

"Morning, boys," Hecht said.

"Mr. Hecht," Longo said.

"Morning, Mr. Hecht," Chrystie said.

"What's the line on the King trial this morning?"

"We were just talking about that," Chrystie said.

"Ten years," Hecht said, still smiling.

Longo and Chrystie looked puzzled.

"It's been ten years since there's been a change of venue out of L.A.," Hecht said, smiling enigmatically.

Chrystie and Longo glanced at each other.

"Not even the Charlie Manson trial, with all that publicity, got a change of venue," Hecht said.

The men nodded slowly.

"Any word yet on *your* jury, Larry?" Hecht asked.

Longo shook his head. "They're still out."

"How long's it been now? Two days?"

"Yeah. Two days."

Hecht nodded silently. The same unspoken thought was in each of the three men's minds. A quick verdict often meant a conviction. But the longer the jury deliberated, the more likely it became that there was doubt and the defendant would be acquitted. Or that there would be a hung jury, the bane of all lawyers: If the jurors could not reach a unanimous verdict, the judge was forced to declare a mistrial. Then the case would have to be tried all over again with a new jury.

Longo tried not to think of that possibility.

"Well," Hecht said with a knowing glint in his eye, "and how is your old friend Yamaki, Larry?"

Longo shrugged.

"I understand he gave a hell of an argument," Hecht said.

"He knows what he's doing."

"Yes. He does."

Richard Hecht was feared and respected around the office. For Longo, however, he was a fond link with the past, a reminder of his own first days as a prosecutor during the Joe Busch era. A no-nonsense, whiskey-drinking, cigar-chomping trial lawyer, District Attorney Joe Busch was the last of the old-time prosecutors who would head the office. The crusty old warrior had died as he had lived, stricken by a heart attack while in the throes of ecstasy with a prostitute.

Longo recalled that it was Busch who had ordered Hecht, as chief of the D.A.'s Organized Crime unit, to step in when the "White House plumbers" case broke. Hecht had personally prosecuted Erlichman, Krogh, Liddy, and Young for the burglary of Daniel Ellsberg's psychiatrist's Beverly Hills office.

Longo's thoughts were suddenly interrupted by the jarring ring of the telephone. He sat straight up.

Hecht and Chrystie stared at the telephone, thinking the same thing. It rang a second time. Longo picked up the receiver.

"Longo," he said tentatively.

"Hey, Larry," the voice said. "Any verdict yet?"

Longo sighed heavily. It was Greg Dohi, calling from the east L.A. office. Longo looked up at Hecht and Chrystie, shook his head; it was not news of a verdict.

"No, Greg," Longo said. "Nothing yet."

"Oh. Well, let me know when it comes in, okay?"

"Yeah, I'll do that. How's everything going in the barrios?"

"Hey, this place is great! Mostly drunk driving and fights. One trial after another. Two or three weeks ago, I had two juries out at the same time."

"Way to go, Greg. I've been hearing good things."

"Really?"

"Yeah. You're a star."

"Sure." Dohi laughed. "Hey, good luck on the verdict, huh?"

"Yeah, thanks, Greg. I'll let you know when it comes in."

"See you later."

"Yeah." Longo hung up the phone. He leaned back in his chair again, listening to Hecht and Chrystie.

"...attitudes of the rookies," Chrystie was saying. "They first get there, they got these ideas, you know? I wish I could tape-record these kids, then play it back after they've spent a couple months in the courtroom."

Hecht said nothing, nodding with his broad smile.

"I mean, first off," Chrystie continued, "they're shocked when it dawns on them that most defendants are guilty as hell. Then, they find out that blacks and Hispanics are treated just like everybody else. And then, the big shocker, cops aren't a bunch of sadistic, lying Nazis."

"Hollywood," Hecht said. "The media."

"Yeah."

"There's nothing like a dose of reality."

Chrystie nodded.

"What do you see in the new ones that says you got a trial lawyer?" Longo asked Chrystie.

"Attitude, I guess," Chrystie said. "Willingness to work hard. A thick skin. Endurance. A killer instinct doesn't hurt."

"Attitude," Hecht said, nodding in agreement. "More than that, *compulsion*."

"Compulsion?" Longo said.

"Yes. I've seen the good ones come and go, boys, and they all have it: a compulsion to . . . to be the best. There's a need for perfection, a need to excel, to win."

Chrystie nodded. "You're right."

"You think that's a healthy thing?" Longo asked. "A compulsive personality?"

Hecht smiled. "A good trial lawyer is not necessarily a healthy human being."

Longo and Chrystie laughed, nodding in agreement.

The telephone rang.

Longo again stared at the telephone before answering it. Then he picked up the receiver.

"Longo," he said.

"Larry . . ." a woman's voice said. It was Angie, Judge Bascue's clerk.

Longo's heart began pounding. "Yeah?"

"We have a verdict."

* * *

The twelve men and women filed out of the deliberation room and took their seats in the jury box.

As Longo sat in his chair at the prosecution table, he studied their faces for some sign, any sign, of what the verdict was. At the next table, Mike Yamaki was doing the same thing.

When all of the jurors were seated, Judge Bascue walked out in his flowing black robes and took his seat at the bench.

"Ladies and gentlemen," he said, "have you elected a foreperson?"

A black woman in the second row stood up. "I am the foreperson, your honor."

Juror number eleven, Longo thought with satisfaction. Yolanda Jasmines. Worked at the Long Beach Naval Shipyard. He had predicted that she would be elected foreman.

"And has the jury reached a verdict?" Bascue asked.

"We have, your honor," the woman said.

"Please give the verdict to my bailiff."

The bailiff crossed to the jury box, took the folded sheet of paper from the woman. Then he turned and walked to the bench, handed it to the judge. Bascue accepted the paper, unfolded it, and silently read it to himself.

For the love of Mike, Longo thought, his heart now pounding heavily somewhere in his throat. It was all so slow, so agonizingly slow. Hurry up! Read the darn thing! How many times had he been through this barbaric, dragged-out ritual? It never got easier.

There had to be a more humane way, he thought.

Bascue finally looked up from the paper and glanced at Longo. Then he looked at Yamaki, then at Yamaguchi.

"Please rise as the verdict is read," he said.

Yamaguchi stood up slowly, Yamaki standing next to him.

Bascue handed the paper to Angie. "Madame Clerk, please read the verdict."

Angie stood up behind her desk, accepted the paper from the judge, read it quickly to herself. She cleared her throat.

"We, the jury in the above-entitled matter, find the defendant, Kazuhiko Yamaguchi, to be . . ."

She looked up quickly at the defendant, then back at the paper. "...guilty of the crime of murder in the first degree."

Longo eased the old Toyota van forward, merging with the crawling tide of cars on the Santa Monica freeway. The brakes again squealed loudly as he brought the van to another stop. The pads were probably worn out, he thought. He made a mental note to have the brakes checked. The oil probably needed changing, too. For that matter, a new paint job would not hurt.

He checked his watch: 6:40. It would be nice to have dinner with Aelina and the kids for a change. A quiet evening at home. No trial to prepare for. No jury to face. A long, peaceful night of sleep.

He eased the van forward again, then applied the brakes to the sound of shrill squealing.

Longo could see the sun in the distance, low in the sky now, turning reddish-orange as it settled into the Pacific off Malibu. It had been a long time since he had seen the sun setting on the way home.

A week in the cabin, he thought. Jeff Jonas had already approved his request for some time off. He would take the whole family. Clean air, clear blue lakes, the fresh smell of pine. A roaring fireplace, bacon and eggs in the morning. A little fishing with the boys...

Longo could not know that the Rodney King jury was about to postpone his vacation indefinitely.

Longo glanced at the towering stack of files on the counsel table, then back at the line of defense attorneys waiting to speak with him. His shoulders sagged as he looked back at the clock on the wall. It was already 11:15 and the monstrous court calendar had hardly been dented. Twenty-six cases to go.

The long-feared "wave" had finally hit. The flood of cases from the riots after the Rodney King verdict had moved through the legal system like a huge *tsunami*. Now they were finally crashing on the already swamped trial courts.

"Whaddya got, Dave,*" Longo said resignedly to the mousy public defender at the front of the line.

"Elijah Watkins,* one count of 459."

"Watkins, burglary," the prosecutor repeated as he shuffled through the stack.

"Gimme a trespass, we got a deal."

"Trespass!" Longo snarled, glancing at the cover of the file. "You gotta be kidding, Dave. We got your guy on burglary, and he's got priors. We're talking eight, ten years, and you want a lousy trespass?"

"You read that file, Larry? You know what a piece of shit this is?"

Longo sighed, opened the file, and began reading the summary.

"I'll tell you what you got, my friend," the public defender continued. "What you got is eight blacks standing outside this stereo store, arms loaded with goodies. All the windows been busted out and half the neighborhood is inside helping themselves, right? I mean, there's shit all over the sidewalks—TVs, boom boxes, Walkmans, you name it."

Longo grunted, still reading from the file.

"So a couple LAPD come running up, bust my guy and the other seven. Throw them in the van, scoop up all the stolen stuff and dump that in there too. Then they're running off after some more looters."

"Uh-huh."

"So they inventory the stuff later, back at the station, right? Only now they can't recall which stuff goes with which guy."

"Uh-huh."

"So, I mean, what do you got, Larry? You got my guy standing outside a looted store, and you got no evidence, no ID'd goodies you can put in his hands. I mean, you got a bunch of guys, and a bunch of goodies, but you can't put them together. Am I right?"

Longo continued reading.

"Hell," the attorney said, "I'm doing you a favor even taking the trespass, Larry. But my guy wants out today. Doesn't want to rot in jail waiting for an acquittal."

Longo nodded slowly, then looked up. "Trespass," he muttered. "Time served."

"Deal."

"Next," the prosecutor growled angrily at the line of attorneys.

The historic verdicts had finally been returned on Tuesday, April 28, 1992. Three of the LAPD officers charged in the beating of Rodney King were found not guilty; the jury was hung as to the fourth.

The verdicts were greeted in the District Attorney's Office with disbelief. Prosecutors walked the hallways in silence, shaking their heads. In the front office, Ira Reiner and his advisers were assessing the damage to his reelection campaign.

By late afternoon the riots had begun.

The racial powder keg that was Los Angeles quickly exploded into arson, looting, and murder. Thousands took to the streets. Random individuals were beaten and shot, passing cars were attacked, stores broken into and ransacked, buildings put to the torch. Raging fires burned through the night, witnessed live by millions on television. The next day, columns of smoke could be seen across the city, dozens of thin gray fingers reaching into the darkened sky.

Los Angeles looked like a scene from Kuwait.

The courts shut down later that morning; disruptions in the county jail had prevented the sheriffs from transporting any defendants to court. By noon, word spread that the riots were beginning again. The Criminal Courts Building was abandoned, save for a skeleton force of armed D.A.'s investigators left behind to defend it.

The acting chief justice of the California Supreme Court issued an emergency order: "It has been determined that because of the current civil unrest and consequent state of emergency which has been declared for the City and County of Los Angeles, there is danger to the buildings appointed for holding the court, and the orderly operation of the Los Angeles Superior Court is threatened." The chief justice then authorized the L.A. courts to hold sessions anywhere that was safe.

The Criminal Courts Building reopened the next day. Windows were shattered and the main floor had been fire-bombed. Piles of debris still smoldered in the streets outside. National Guardsmen were stationed around the building, their automatic weapons held at the ready. Hum-vees cruised the downtown streets along with LAPD black-and-whites.

An eerie calm surrounded the building as judges, lawyers, and court personnel filed silently inside. There was a strange, dreamlike quality to the scene, a sense that this could not really be happening in America.

Ira Reiner and his advisers were in one frantic meeting after another. Were looters to be treated as serious burglars, petty thieves, or mere trespassers? Were fires to be considered arson or simply malicious mischief? Should Officer Powell, on whom the jury had hung, be retried? If so, would it just be setting up another riot scenario later? If not, would the decision aggravate the existing situation? And how could political damage be minimized, perhaps even be turned to advantage?

Reiner finally issued Special Directive 92-02, entitled "Office Response to Civil Disorder in Los Angeles." The directive took a hard-line approach toward anyone arrested during the riots.

This "get tough" policy sounded fine in theory, of course; certainly it was an expected move in view of the approaching elections. But it was one thing to issue directives. It was quite another to carry them out in the harsh realities of the situation.

Over fifteen thousand people had been arrested during the riots. The jails were bursting; the computers that kept track of the massive jail system in Los Angeles County began to break down. Police officers could not keep up with the paperwork on their arrests, often could not even remember whom they had arrested or why. In the D.A.'s Complaint unit, dozens of deputies were overwhelmed by the avalanche of police reports; officers packed the lobby outside waiting to file more complaints.

The courts stayed open through the weekend to process the flood of arraignments. Prosecutors and public defenders ran hundreds of defendants through like cattle until midnight Saturday, went home to get some sleep, then came back Sunday morning and continued with the surrealistic scene. By late that evening, nearly twelve hundred suspects had been arraigned. But reports from the Sheriff's Department indicated that there were thousands more still packed into overcrowded cells awaiting arraignment. Incredibly, over five thousand of the individuals arrested had simply disappeared in the jail system; no records existed for them.

By Monday, judges, prosecutors, and public defenders were numb and exhausted. The system had simply broken down.

The courts were now fighting a constitutional time limit. Anyone arrested who was not arraigned by midnight Monday would have to be released. The specter of thousands of rioters set loose on the streets in the middle of the night was a chilling one.

In emergency session, the state legislature rushed through a bill extending the deadline for arraigning arrestees to seven days. The bill was flown from Sacramento to the governor in Los Angeles, where he signed it on the hood of a car one hour before the midnight deadline.

"Whaddya got?" Longo said to the next lawyer.

"Whittaker,*" the young woman said, a combative edge in her voice. "Carl Evans Whittaker."

Longo nodded, began thumbing through the stack of files again. "987?" he asked.

"Yes," she said. The lawyer had been appointed by the court to represent the defendant. The flood of post–King cases typically involved groups of looters; each case could only have one public defender. And that meant hundreds of private attorneys were being appointed, at considerable expense to the taxpayer.

"Got it," Longo said, opening a file. "Whittaker, burglary, one count, no rap sheet."

"Mr. Whittaker demands a jury trial."

"Uh-huh." The prosecutor continued to read the file.

"We refuse to waive our right to speedy trial."

By California law, a defendant in custody in a felony case had to be tried within sixty days of his arraignment. Unless he waived this right, he was entitled to a dismissal if a jury could not be sworn within this period. And the flood of cases from the King riots was straining the system's ability to meet these time limits.

"Whaddya got?" Longo sighed.

"I've got a winner," the lawyer said.

"So tell me."

"My client, along with a number of other individuals in the community, was arrested taking stuff from what was once a department store."

"Whaddya mean 'was once'?"

"I mean it was burned to the ground. They were just helping themselves to what they found in the smoldering ruins."

"So?"

"Well, Mr. Prosecutor, there was no structure left, correct?"

Longo shook his head slowly as the woman's legal theory dawned on him. She was correct, of course; Longo had no case. The definition of burglary was the entry into a structure with the intent to commit a theft. But the defendant had entered what *used* to be a structure. No structure, no burglary. The most he could push for was petty theft, a misdemeanor.

"Petty theft, time served?" he said.

"I'll discuss it with my client."

"Yeah, you do that." Then, loudly, "Next."

* * *

One of the hundreds of cases that rose from the ashes of the King riots was, of course, the assault on Reginald Denny. The image of the white truck driver being beaten by a group of blacks as he lay defenseless on the street was broadcast live from hovering news helicopters. As with the King beating, the Denny incident was caught on tape and seared into the minds of a nation.

The selection of a trial judge for the Denny case proved difficult. The case was originally assigned to Judge Roosevelt Dorn, an African American; with each side having one peremptory challenge, Dorn was removed by the prosecution. The next judge selected was white; he was challenged by the defense. Another white judge was then selected, but when the defense was given an additional peremptory challenge he was also removed.

The case finally found its way into the courtroom of John Ouderkirk. With no challenges left, the Denny defense team tried to remove Ouderkirk on the grounds of prejudice: The judge was dating (and later married) Ira Reiner's executive secretary. The attempt failed, and the highly publicized trial eventually began. The resulting verdicts of guilt on lesser charges proved as infuriating to L.A.'s white community as the King verdicts had been to the black.

The Rodney King verdict, coming after the disasters in the McMartin and *Twilight Zone* cases, spelled the end for Ira Reiner. But his disqualification of the black judge in the Denny case proved the coup de grace. Judge Dorn angrily addressed L.A.'s black community from the pulpit of the First African Methodist Episcopal Church: "I'm not telling you who to vote for, but Ira Reiner must go."

Three weeks before the elections, Reiner conceded to his former chief deputy, Gil Garcetti.

In the familiar game of D.A. politics, Garcetti immediately began to consolidate his position after the elections. Wholesale demotions, promotions, and transfers of personnel were ordered. Reiner men were removed from key posts, replaced by Garcetti backers. Anyone who was not seen as supportive of the new administration was shipped to outlying branch offices. A chance comment over coffee two years earlier could now mean a transfer to Pomona.

The third candidate in the district attorney campaign, Special Trials deputy Sterling "Ernie" Norris, had been endorsed by the *Los Angeles Times* and represented a future political threat. In a now-familiar move, he was transferred to the Pasadena branch office, isolating him from the power and publicity of the Criminal Courts Building.

"Yeah?" Longo said to the next lawyer in line. "Whaddya got?"

"I represent Maria Ortiz,*" the man said, wiping sweat from his forehead with a handkerchief. "But you have no case."

"Uh-huh," Longo said. "Why don't you tell me why I got no case?"

"Mrs. Ortiz was arrested during the recent disturbance when she—"

"Disturbance?" Longo laughed. "Is that what they're calling it now?"

The man shrugged. "She was walking down the street, pushing a shopping cart. There were some items in the cart."

"Riot area?"

"Yes."

The prosecutor found the file, opened it, and began to read. "Yeah, quite a few items."

"Yes."

"Three dresses . . . box of candy . . . crate of dishes . . . electric toothbrush . . . steak knives . . . blender . . . electric drill . . . Quite a little shopper, your client."

"As I said—"

"She have a receipt for any of this?"

"Of course not."

"Uh-huh."

"But, then, Mr. Longo, she doesn't need to produce a receipt. I mean, she doesn't have to prove she *didn't* steal the goods, does she."

"No, I guess not."

"*You* have to prove that she *did*. And, frankly, I just don't see how you're going to do that, do you? I mean, what have you got? A woman pushing a shopping cart of goods down the street. That's it. That's your case."

"She just decided to go shopping, late at night, in the middle of a riot. And she gets stopped half a block from a looted department store. With one of their carts."

"I mean," the lawyer continued, "is there *any* evidence that these goods had been stolen? Is there any report anywhere listing serial numbers? Can anyone at this store identify any of these goods as theirs?"

Longo snorted.

"No," the man said.

"Bottom line, Counsel?"

The lawyer nodded. "Dismissal."

The prosecutor shook his head. "We'll take our chances in trial."

"No you won't."

Longo studied the man for a moment. "Petty theft, time served."

"Done."

Longo began to write the deal on the file jacket.

The lawyer turned to leave. "Oh," he said, stopping and looking back, "I heard about the Yamaguchi motion."

Longo's jaw clenched slightly as he continued writing.

"Tough break," the man said with the trace of a smile. Then he turned and walked away.

Yeah, Longo thought to himself. Tough break.

Soon after the verdict, Mike Yamaki had filed a motion with Judge Bascue to set aside the conviction and order a new trial. The lawyer alleged two grounds for vacating the guilty verdict. First, Longo had committed prosecutorial misconduct. In his closing argument, Yamaki claimed, the prosecutor had said, "Did you ever hear Mr. Yamaguchi explain why he had that gun in the car?" The lawyer argued that this statement violated the defendant's constitutional rights: The prosecution was prohibited from commenting upon the defendant's decision to exercise his Fifth Amendment right and not testify.

Second, Yamaki argued in his brief, a juror was improperly influenced to change her vote:

> The attached declaration of Eleanor Wong reveals that during the juror deliberations in this case, Ms. Wong, who was pregnant when the trial began, lost her baby during the course of the trial. As the declaration states, both the loss of her baby and the trial of this case were very emotionally disturbing to Ms. Wong. In an effort to minimize the emotional

drain on Ms. Wong, her boyfriend discussed the case with her and thereafter instructed her to change her vote from manslaughter to first-degree murder. Ms. Wong followed her boyfriend's instructions and resigned herself from the jury deliberation process. She states that although she wanted to vote for manslaughter, she wrongfully abided by the instructions of her boyfriend, who apparently plays a dominant role in their relationship.

Longo quickly responded to the allegations. In his summation to the jury, the prosecutor wrote in his reply brief, he had been referring to *Yamaki's* failure to explain the gun during the defense summation—not Yamaguchi's. It was possible he had mistakenly confused the names in the heat of argument; if so, the mistake would have been clear to the jury from the context. In any event, he doubted that the name switch had even taken place and demanded that the court reporter, Ginny Ishida, provide the court with an official transcription of her notes of his argument. Ishida had, apparently, provided Yamaki with an unofficial advance copy of the transcript, without providing either the judge or prosecutor with one.

Judge Bascue set a date for a hearing on the motion.

Longo immediately assigned a D.A. investigator to begin interviewing Wong, her boyfriend, and each of the other jurors. The prosecutor was suspicious about her story.

Meanwhile, however, because of the Rodney King riots Longo's investigator was unable to reach some of the jurors who lived in the affected areas. He managed to interview and obtain affidavits from five. Some of them indicated that, contrary to what she said in her affidavit for Yamaki, Wong had voted for first-degree murder on the initial ballot—*before* she was supposed to have been influenced by her boyfriend. And on their last day together as jurors, Wong had indicated that she was still pregnant.

The investigator continued trying to contact Wong to question her. But, he told Longo, the woman was hiding from him. However, he had located her brother. According to the brother, she had no boyfriend.

The courtroom was packed for the hearing. Wong nervously appeared in court, this time with an attorney of her own. The attorney asked for immunity for his client before she testified, but Longo refused. The attorney then asked that she be permitted to testify in the privacy of the judge's chambers. Judge Bascue agreed.

In chambers, Longo cross-examined Wong on the contents of her declaration, which claimed that she had an abortion during the trial. But during his questioning the juror broke down crying. Bascue ordered a recess. When they reconvened, the prosecutor asked her for the name of the boyfriend, as well as that of the doctor involved in the abortion. She refused to give the names, then refused to tell how she voted on the first ballot. When Longo asked Bascue to order her to give the information, he refused. As she began crying again, the judge brought a halt to the questioning; Longo would not be permitted to cross-examine her further.

Back in open court, Yamaki offered Wong's declaration. In reply, Longo called four of the jurors to testify. When they were finished refuting her affidavit, Judge Bascue announced his decision: He was granting Yamaki's motion.

Longo objected furiously. There was no official transcript of his argument yet, he said. And he had not been permitted to finish his cross-examination of Wong. But Bascue stuck to his ruling; the conviction was set aside and there would be a new trial.

The D.A.'s Office immediately appealed Judge Bascue's ruling. Meanwhile, Longo subpoenaed Ginny Ishida's original stenotyped notes of his argument, intending to have the ink analyzed to see if the name "Yamaguchi" in his summation had been substituted for "Yamaki." Ishida informed the prosecutor that the original notes were lost.

The deputy D.A. handling the appeal assured Longo that there were solid grounds for getting Judge Bascue's ruling reversed: The conviction would eventually stand.

A harsh voice cut into the prosecutor's thoughts.

"Faleen D'Jabouti,*" the next lawyer said, stifling a yawn.

"Faleen *what*?" Longo said, rifling through the stack of files again.

"D'Jabouti."

"Yeah, right, so what's his *real* name, Counsel?"

"Aka Jefferson Washington Parker."

The prosecutor shook his head. "So talk to me," he said.

"Mr. D'Jabouti was apprehended in the riot area. He was black. Ergo, he was arrested."

Longo pulled out a file, scanned the review sheet inside. "Uh-huh. And the can of kerosene he was carrying, what was that for, a little midnight barbecue?"

"I wasn't aware it was a crime to possess kerosene."

"It's not," the prosecutor said with a sigh. "Curfew? Time served?"

"Acceptable."

Longo scribbled the plea bargain on the outside of the file. "Next," he growled.

Epilogue

On June 7, 1994, the California Court of Appeals rendered a decision in the Yamaguchi case.

First, the justices addressed Longo's comment in his summation to the jury about the failure to explain Yamaguchi's possession of the gun as evidence of premeditation. Even if he was referring to *Yamaki's* lack of explanation in the defense summation, they wrote in their opinion, the jury could have interpreted it as referring to *Yamaguchi's* failure to explain it from the witness stand. And that was an impermissible comment upon Yamaguchi's Fifth Amendment privilege. "We cannot conclude that the jury would not have understood [Longo's summation] as constituting a reference to the defendant's failure to testify," the justices wrote.

The Court then turned to juror Eleanor Wong. They decided that her discussion of the case with her boyfriend after the claimed abortion resulted in denying Yamaguchi a fair trial. According to the justices, Wong "committed misconduct by succumbing to the demand of her apparently domineering boyfriend to vote for a first-degree murder verdict. . . . She followed her boyfriend's directive to avoid any more emotional strain on herself and changed her vote from manslaughter to first-degree murder, consistent with the views of her boyfriend and her fellow jurors."

The case was sent back to Department 127 for a new trial.

In the meantime, however, Larry Longo had requested and was

granted a transfer to the D.A.'s Beverly Hills office. His mother had finally passed away, and he now wanted to work where he could spend more time with his family in Malibu.

With Longo gone and a newly elected district attorney in the front office, Mike Yamaki approached Garcetti's chief deputy. The men quietly began negotiating the terms of a plea bargain.

On September 29, 1994, Yamaguchi entered a plea of guilty to the reduced charge of voluntary manslaughter. Judge Bascue sentenced him to eleven years in state prison, the highest term allowed by law. With credit for time served and good behavior, he is expected to be released in 1999.